THE
DEFINITIVE
DESERT
ISLAND
DISCS

THE DEFINITIVE DESERT ISLAND DISCS

IAN GITTINS

Foreword by Lauren Laverne

BBC
BOOKS

BBC Books, an imprint of Ebury Publishing
20 Vauxhall Bridge Road,
London SW1V 2SA

BBC Books is part of the Penguin Random House group of companies whose
addresses can be found at global.penguinrandomhouse.com

This book is published to accompany the radio programme entitled
Desert Island Discs, broadcast on BBC Radio 4.

Text © Ian Gittins 2022
Desert Island Discs is licensed by the BBC © BBC 2022
Text design © seagulls.net 2022

Ian Gittins has asserted his right to be identified as the author of this Work in
accordance with the Copyright, Designs and Patents Act 1988

First published by BBC Books in 2022

www.penguin.co.uk

A CIP catalogue record for this book is available from the British Library

ISBN 9781785947957

Typeset in 11/13.3 pt Baskerville MT Pro by Jouve (UK), Milton Keynes
Printed and bound in Great Britain by Clays Ltd, Elcograf S.p.A.

The authorised representative in the EEA is Penguin Random House
Ireland, Morrison Chambers, 32 Nassau Street, Dublin D02 YH68

Penguin Random House is committed to a sustainable future for
our business, our readers and our planet. This book is made from
Forest Stewardship Council® certified paper.

CONTENTS

FOREWORD

LAUREN LAVERNE

Long before I hosted *Desert Island Discs*, I was a devoted listener, first to the peerless Kirsty Young and then to her predecessors, whose buried audio treasure I unearthed in the BBC's extraordinary online archive. *Desert Island Discs* has been broadcasting for eighty years, and while (generally speaking) I keep my focus on the castaway at hand, every now and again I'll remember that in all that time only five of us have been entrusted with the task of marooning our guests on the island in their mind's eye, and my head will spin. As I write, *Desert Island Discs* has just celebrated its landmark anniversary and it remains one of BBC Radio 4's best-loved and most popular programmes, with an audience all over the world. For me, it is a dream job – literally and metaphorically: each week we invite someone with a fascinating life to dream for us, to lose themselves in their imagination and tell us what they find there.

If you could make a new world, what would it look like? The island a person creates says a lot. Radio is known as the 'theatre of the mind', and the *mise en scène* our castaways construct fascinates me. Is the island a prison to be endured or a paradise to be enjoyed? Is creating this new world a challenge to be relished, a grim grind or a game? There are no right or wrong ways to approach the programme, but I love it when a castaway has total commitment to their method.

Poet John Cooper Clarke told me he'd been working on his list of tracks for forty years. He took the idea of the island very literally and chose the things that he knew he could not live without – women's voices, a song by his old friend Nico and a luxury item that ... actually, I won't spoil it. Let's just say it's not for the fainthearted. Comic firebrand Alexei Sayle took the invitation as an opportunity to stage a revolution of his own devising, founding the 'Tropical Socialist Republic of Alexei Sayle' and choosing the Battle Hymn of the Soviet Air Force as its anthem. *Cloud Atlas* author David Mitchell meanwhile selected the programme's archive as his luxury item, saying, 'In the many years of its history *Desert Island Discs* has become this Library of Babel: of human stories, experience and language ... hunger for voices and company that isn't my own will be assuaged.' Speaking of hunger, Sophia Loren's luxury was a pizza oven, which – strictly speaking – is far too practical, but I allowed it on the basis that 1) a pizza made by Sophia Loren is technically a work of art rather than a foodstuff (she likened making a pizza to writing a poem) and 2) well, you try arguing with Sophia Loren and see how far you get.

What about the music? Castaways' choices have prompted plenty of kitchen dancing, joy, tears, rage and even academic enquiry over the years (for more on that last, try the thought-provoking *Defining the Discographic Self: Desert Island Discs in Context*, Oxford University Press, 2017). People tend to assume that my own preferences are important to me, but nothing could be further from the truth. In fact, some of my favourite episodes include discs that may not be my thing, but for that story are just *perfect*. One example from the archive is *Dragons' Den* star Hilary Devey, who sadly passed away at the age of 65 earlier this year. You'd be hard-pressed to find a more dramatic tale than this one from the tough-as-they-come entrepreneur whose hardscrabble success as a trucking magnate contrasts with dramatic family secrets, three marriages, one lover's secret family and coming back from the brink after serious illness. Only Celine Dion could soundtrack it, and she does. I'm also a sucker for discs that – as only music can – carry the atmosphere of the place and time to which a castaway's story takes us. Whether it's the Trinidadian calypso of Savile Row master tailor Andrew Ramroop's youth, the symphonic synths of screenwriter Jack Thorne's family holidays (like me, he often had to sit in the boot) soundtracked by Jean-Michel Jarre or Malala Yousafzai's unexpected decision to take 'Love Always Comes as a Surprise' from the animated film *Madagascar 3* to the island – to celebrate rediscovering her childlike, playful side after the attack that almost killed her.

One of the great pleasures of hosting *Desert Island Discs* is the meaningful impact it has – on listeners and on guests, too. The latter might not always be as visible, but since so many castaways have told me about it later I wanted to mention it here. There's nothing quite like witnessing an outpouring of love for someone who has been brave enough to tell their story, particularly when doing so is difficult, and it is often a profound experience for them. Ian Wright's emotional episode detailed the domestic violence he lived with as a child and his tribute to the teacher who gave him hope during that time. The day we recorded he apologised to listeners, worrying what they would think of him 'turning into this bumbling, crying guy', but Ian's programme went viral – thousands of people sent supportive messages and he went on to write a book and make a documentary about his experiences, continuing the conversation he started in the studio. Richard Osman, Joe Wicks and Stephen Graham were brave enough to be vulnerable, and it was wonderful to see that rewarded with waves of compassion from the public. Stephen revealed for the first time that he once attempted to take his own life, Richard talked about coping with food addiction and Joe was incredibly honest about the struggles he went through living with a mother suffering from mental health issues and a father with a drug addiction, which often made family life difficult. Samantha Morton reflected on growing up in and out of the care system and actor Wendell Pierce discussed the racism he experienced as a black child in the New Orleans of the 1960s. In each case, their honesty was motivated by the hope that their story might reach ears that really needed it, and every time it did.

It is the deepest honour to be the first listener to stories that bring a new perspective on someone we thought we already 'knew', but I reserve a special place in my heart for the stories that – were it not for *Desert Island Discs* – we might not otherwise hear. The firefighter and research psychologist Sabrina Cohen-Hatton, statistician Professor Sir David Spiegelhalter and shepherd, author and historian James Rebanks are three of my favourite examples. One minute you think, *How much do I really need to know about breeding Herdwick sheep in the Lake District?*, and the next you're having your mind blown by the tale of an angry boy-genius who ran away from his family farm to study history at Oxford, came back with a double first and set himself up with a plot of his own, as a leading voice in the fight for a more sustainable farming system and as an international troubleshooter for UNESCO. *Thank you, D.I.D.*

But don't take my word for it, read on. This book includes eighty of the most moving, entertaining and inspiring encounters from eight sparkling decades of this jewel in radio's crown, as well as interviews with castaways about making their programmes. I do hope you enjoy it.

INTRODUCTION

Like many great ideas, the concept was so simple that it bordered on genius. Cast a famous person or public figure away on a theoretical desert island, ask them which eight records they would like to take with them, and discuss how that music had impacted on, and reflected, their lives.

This particular brainwave came, in 1941, courtesy of a twenty-seven-year-old freelance actor and broadcaster named Roy Plomley. Plomley was in the regular habit of pitching format ideas for radio programmes to the BBC, and sent his latest inspiration to a commissioning editor at the corporation.

The rest is history – history that is still unfolding. Eighty years and well over 3,500 castaways later, *Desert Island Discs* is a British institution, with millions of listeners tuning in to Radio 4 – or listening online – every week to hear its shipwrecked souls. Only *The Shipping Forecast* and *The Daily Service* have lasted longer on the network.

It's not difficult to define *Desert Island Discs'* enduring appeal. Put at its simplest: all human life is there. Famous figures who might usually shun in-depth confessional interviews will open up on the island, seduced by the show's format, tradition and iconic status.

Kirsty Young, who presented the show from 2006 to 2018, gave a typically astute summary of its ethos ten years ago in her foreword to a previous commemorative book, *Desert Island Discs: 70 Years of Castaways*.

'It works best as a sort of triangulated conversation,' she wrote. 'It's castaway, host and listener sitting around the table, engaged in a no-hold-barred dialogue about how the guest of honour got to where they are, and what's it's like to live the life they have lived.'

It's hard to better this appraisal and yet maybe, just maybe, one of the castaways in this book has done so. Reflecting on his 2019 appearance on the island, the brilliant TV screenwriter and producer, Russell T Davies, links the show to advice he always gives to upcoming writers looking for tips.

'I tell them that *anyone* can write about chases, and explosions, and monsters, and detectives, and murders, and ghosts,' he says. 'But all you have to do, all you *must* do as a writer, is to understand the human soul.

'You have to understand psychology: why people do things, where they are from, what built them, what they're capable of. That's what *Desert Island Discs* does. It lays open a person's life. And there is nothing more dramatic, or interesting, or beautiful than that. It's the ultimate drama.'

The human soul. The ultimate drama. These are large claims and yet, week after week, *Desert Island Discs* justifies them. And this book ranges far and wide across eight decades of a truly unique programme to compile eighty of the most memorable guests from its illustrious history.

There was Arthur Askey, wisecracking his way through a visit in 1942; Sir Cliff Richard, first appearing as a callow youth in 1960 before returning, older and a great deal wiser, sixty years later; Joan Collins, airily explaining why Bob Hope really was *so* much nicer than Bing Crosby.

Victoria Wood described a tense, troubled childhood. George Michael, Martina Navratilova and Billie Jean King recalled the pain and stress of being outed. Malala Yousafzai described being shot in the head by the Taliban before making a new life as a global activist. And Bono from U2 told the world about a secret half-brother.

'I've always wanted to do this!' admitted Adele. 'I've been making my list of records for sixty years!' said John Cooper Clarke. 'And I'm not even joking!' While the poet Lemn Sissay confides, in this book, that he splits his life into *before* and *after* he appeared on *Desert Island Discs*.

This book revisits such landmark episodes from the show's eighty-year history. It also allows selected castaways to reminisce about their visit to the island, and how much they enjoyed it, in specially conducted new interviews titled 'Isle never forget ...'

What attracts so many venerable figures to the island, and makes them want to share such intimacies? Is it the sea air? The seagulls' caws? Does the prospect of soul-searching isolation lead castaways to open their hearts? Or does it come down to what Noël Coward famously called *the potency of cheap music*: long-loved tunes forever triggering memories and passions?

Maybe it's all of these. Or maybe, sometimes, it's best not to analyse those so-simple-it's-genius ideas too closely, but just to accept that they work, brilliantly – which *Desert Island Discs* certainly does. Here's to the next eighty years.

ROY PLOMLEY YEARS

1942–85

Despite being *Desert Island Discs'* ingenious progenitor, Roy Plomley did not initially intend to host the programme. His original proposal to the BBC was that he should be a background figure, identifying and contacting potential castaways and helping to put the show together.

The Beeb begged to differ, insisting instead that Plomley should be the show's presenter. This visionary figure's clipped tones were thus to be synonymous with the programme in the listeners' minds right from the off – and, indeed, for the following forty-three years.

Plomley provided the BBC with a first list of potential castaways. It consisted mostly of entertainers and playwrights. J.B. Priestley and Noël Coward were on there. So was Leslie Perowne, head of popular music programmes at the BBC, and thus the man that Plomley was pitching to! (He never actually appeared.)

Before the first broadcast, there were a few tweaks. Plomley's initial letter had suggested each castaway chose ten discs. The programme's producers whittled this down to eight, as a more natural fit for the show's thirty-minute length.

There was also the little matter of a theme tune. The BBC went with composer Eric Coates's 'By the Sleepy Lagoon', augmented with waves crashing on a shore and discreetly cawing seagulls. This gentle valse serenade has introduced every single episode from show one.

It seems a curious concept now, but initially the programmes were scripted. Roy Plomley would write both sides of each episode's dialogue in advance and the castaway would sit in the studio and read it with him. This practice was, understandably, dropped after a few years.

The first ever *Desert Island Discs* was broadcast on the BBC Forces Programme at 8pm on 29 January 1942. The castaway was an Austrian musician and comedian, Vic Oliver, a hugely popular figure who was then starring in a West End show, *Get a Load of This*.

The critic and essayist, James Agate, followed, then a naval officer and broadcaster, Captain A.B. Campbell. They set the tone for Plomley's early castaways, who were largely drawn from the worlds of theatre, film, radio and journalism, with the odd emissary from the military.

With his immaculate received pronunciation, and a background in light entertainment rather than journalism, Plomley was the archetype of a courteous BBC interviewer. While they can't help but sound dated to modern ears, his early shows were sharp, witty ... and very entertaining.

The host was not on a quest for deep psychological insights into his castaways' characters. His priority was that his guests should enjoy the show, the questioning should not cause them any discomfort – and the chat should make for pleasant listening. Which it invariably did.

To set the tone – and loosen their lips? – Plomley would usually take his guests for a slap-up lunch before the show, preferably at the nearby Garrick Club. Reminiscing in this book, Dame Judi Dench speaks fondly of those Plomley luncheons: 'It set you up for the afternoon!'

Desert Island Discs was not a weekly radio staple in its earliest years. Its first, fifteen-week series came to an end in May 1942, with Plomley himself in the castaway's chair. There were a further ten episodes at the end of the year, then only fourteen in the whole of 1943.

After a five-week series at the start of 1944, there was a gap of nearly a year-and-a-half before shows in the second half of 1945 that included appearances by Celia Johnson and Deborah Kerr. After a single episode at the start of 1946, the show then went off the air for five years.

Desert Island Discs returned in the first week of 1951 with, for the first time, not a limited run but an open-ended, indefinite commission. The security and permanence of this new arrangement allowed Plomley and his team to approach – and secure – some ambitious castaway targets.

The first part of this book draws on highlights from these Roy Plomley years. There was Petula Clark, an eighteen-year-old child prodigy when she washed up on the island in 1951. The 'Lancashire lass', Gracie Fields, was rather more established, a bona fide British superstar, when she dropped in later that year.

David Attenborough was but a tyro TV producer and presenter when, in 1957, he made the first of his four visits to the island. Joan Collins was younger still, just twenty-eight, when she was marooned in 1961, but had just returned from seven years of shooting major movies in Hollywood.

By then, a tweak to the programme's format let castaways pick a favourite book to take to the isle with them, alongside the Bible and *The Complete Works of Shakespeare*. They were also allowed a luxury item, and required to nominate one disc to save, were a tidal wave to sweep away the rest (in this book, these choices are shown in bold in each castaway's list of music).

Shipwrecked in 1964, Cilla Black was still coming to terms with fame after being whisked to pop stardom by Brian Epstein. At the opposite end of her career, Hollywood legend Tallulah Bankhead was struggling with alcoholism and horribly incoherent when she met Plomley.

Upcoming comedy titans Morecambe and Wise were in scintillating form on the island in 1966: it's genuinely impossible to read their exchanges without smiling. Pulp-fiction novelist Barbara Cartland also made for great radio as she detailed rejecting forty-nine marriage proposals.

James Stewart arrived on the island sounding remarkably humble for a true cinematic living legend. Les Dawson reminisced about moving to Paris to try to be a writer before reinventing himself as a wisecracking comedian and deadpan TV gameshow host.

A strength of *Desert Island Discs* is its variety. In 1979, Norman Mailer described longing to go to war in order to find the inspiration to pen a literary masterpiece. Trumpeter Dizzy Gillespie recalled growing up in the US Great Depression before running away from home at fourteen.

In 1983, Terry Wogan reminisced about being a bank clerk in Ireland before beginning his own illustrious BBC career. Two years on, Julie Walters explained how she first met Victoria Wood – an account that Ms Wood herself would soon corroborate on *Desert Island Discs*.

Without Roy Plomley, there would have been no *Desert Island Discs*. He invented the show and, despite his initial protestations, was to present it for forty-three years and 1,784 episodes. For millions of listeners throughout the decades, he will be forever synonymous with this much-loved show – and quite right, too.

1
CAPTAIN A.E. DINGLE

SAILOR, WRITER, REAL-LIFE CASTAWAY
12 March 1942

Three years into the Second World War, a guest washed up on Roy Plomley's imaginary shore who remains unique in *Desert Island Discs* history a full eighty years later. He was a genuine, real-life castaway.

Captain Aylward Edward 'A.E.' Dingle was a truly intrepid cove. Born in Oxford in 1874, he spent twenty-two years at sea, and was fond of boasting that he had been shipwrecked five times, which might arguably call into question his maritime navigational abilities.

Dingle's most notable shipwreck came in 1893 when he was half of a two-man crew on a schooner, the *Black Pearl*, that sailed from Mahé in the Seychelles to the Crozet Islands in the southern Indian Ocean. Their mission was to retrieve gold from an immigrant ship, the *Strathmore*, that had sunk there eighteen years earlier.

Dingle and his crewmate located the ship but were unable to remove the heavy strongbox while being buffeted by gales. On their way home, the *Black Pearl* was shipwrecked on the remote, volcanic St Paul Island. The two crewmates survived but the ship sank to a watery grave.

Capt. Dingle and his fellow castaway spent eleven weeks on the island, surviving on raw penguin and goat meat and rainwater. Remarkably, while stranded, they found treasure on an 1870 wreck half-buried in the sand, before being rescued by a passing French sailing vessel.

In his later life, Dingle moved to New York and churned out magazine articles and pulp-fiction pot-boilers with titles such as *The Pirate Woman*, *The Bomb Ship* and *The Corpse Came Back*. Unsurprisingly, however, it was his shipwreck stories that most intrigued Roy Plomley.

• • •

The palpably impressed Plomley opened the show marvelling that his guest, 'a real man of the sea', to whom he referred throughout by his nickname and sometime nom-de-plume, Sinbad, could draw from his real-life experience of having been a castaway.

'Yes, I have got the advantage of being able to tell you not just the music that I think I would like to take on a desert island, but the sort of music that I actually wanted to hear while I was there,' replied Dingle. 'Of course, there are many things I would choose to have before gramophone records!

'The real obvious trouble on a desert island, of course, is depression.

There were two of us on the bleak little volcanic island on which I spent eleven weary weeks, and we got so depressed and fed up that by the end of the first fortnight, we weren't on speaking terms with each other for days at a stretch.'

'I should think that's understandable,' sympathised Plomley. 'What sort of music did you want to hear under the palm trees on that desert island?' This triggered an amused reaction from Dingle.

'*What* palm trees? People seem to think that all desert islands are like picture postcards of Miami, with white sandy beaches and shady palms and running fresh water! The island we were on was craggy and bare, with no trees or vegetation at all except a few patches of coarse grass.'

'Just complete desolation?' asked Plomley.

'Absolutely!' agreed Dingle, before choosing Peter Dawson's 'The Floral Dance', a disc to remind him of 'England and home – smooth green lawns and clean clothes and shaves and pubs and a little comfort'.

'Sinbad, how did you get on for food?' wondered Plomley.

'There wasn't even a bit of wood to light a fire,' recalled Dingle. 'And we hadn't got a knife or anything like that; not even a rusty nail. We lived on penguin and wild-goat meat, eaten raw. We killed them with stones and dismembered them with our bare hands.'

'And water?' asked Plomley.

'Rainwater pools. The water was hot and stale and tasted as if old boots had been boiled in it.'

'That sounds a wicked diet!' exclaimed Plomley, bizarrely jumping sixty years into the future and twenty-first-century teenage slang.

Dingle turned to black humour, surmising that his mood on the island could have been lifted by listening to 'an absurd little nonsense tune about shipwrecks that always makes me chuckle and which I often find myself whistling.' It went by the catchy title of, 'He Played His Ukulele as the Ship Went Down'.

'I must say, I admire your sense of humour, Sinbad,' noted an approving Plomley. 'Let's hear some more about that desert island. How did you come to get there?'

'We were looking for treasure on one of the Crozet Islands in the Indian Ocean. Another man and myself had a small sailing sloop and a diving suit and we were trying to reach the wreck of the *Strathmore* that had gone down there thirty years before with quite a lot of money in the skipper's strongbox.

'But we were driven off our mooring by a storm. We rode the storm for the rest of the day and struck hard on a desert island called St Paul after dark. The sloop was smashed up completely and we didn't even find a single spar left. It was a miracle we got ashore. I can't swim.'

Dingle chose Paul Robeson's 'Old Man River' 'for no other reason than I like it'. Plomley commented that the tune is a 'treasure' that might have provided some consolation for not finding actual treasure on the voyage – at which point, Sinbad dropped a bombshell.

'We did find treasure! Incredible as it may sound, we found treasure on the island we were wrecked on. One day, about the seventh week we were there, my companion came across a broken old hulk of a ship half-buried in the sand. We were excited because it was firewood and we might have enough to make a raft. But the wood was rotten and crumbling.

'Anyway, we went on digging. We got enough nails and spikes to make fish hooks and spears and traps, and then one day we came across an iron strongbox.'

'How did you open it?' asked Plomley.

'By fire. And in it were two thousand golden Australian sovereigns.'

'Did you manage to get it away when you were rescued?'

'Yes, we bundled it up in goat-skin bags and tied it to our bodies.'

'Good work!' exclaimed Plomley, clearly captivated by this real-life *Boy's Own* adventure.

Dingle wrapped up his tale of derring-do by explaining to Plomley how he got rescued: 'We stuck a shirt up on a flagstaff that had been put up by French traders, years before. One day a little barque saw our signal and picked us up and landed us in Mauritius.'

'Thanks, Sinbad, for a very interesting story,' said Plomley at the end of the broadcast. 'That eleven weeks on that desert island must be something to look back on with real horror – in spite of finding the buried treasure!'

'Actually, I don't think the desert-island experience was my worst one,' mused Dingle. 'There was another time when I sailed alone 1,600 miles through a hurricane and went five days without water. But, as Kipling says, that's another story ...'

• • •

Captain A.E. Dingle returned from New York to Britain and died in the seafarers' county of Cornwall in 1947. He is likely forever to remain the sole true castaway to wash up on *Desert Island Discs*. Oliver Reed doesn't count.

DISCS CHOSEN
J.F. Wagner's 'Under the Double Eagle'
Band of HM Coldstream Guards

'The Floral Dance'
Peter Dawson

Fritz Kreisler's *Caprice Viennois*
Fritz Kreisler
'It would give a sort of contentment to the mind that might help induce a well-fed feeling'

'He Played His Ukulele as the Ship Went Down'
The Two Leslies

'Old Man River'
Paul Robeson
'That's a gem of a record'

'Bunger Up of Rat 'Oles'
Jack Warner
'I should want another bit of nonsense'

Beethoven's *Moonlight Sonata*
Wilhelm Backhaus
'It would dispel the mulligrubs and bring peace'

Overture to Offenbach's *Orpheus in the Underworld*
Bournemouth Municipal Orchestra

ARTHUR ASKEY

MUSIC HALL STAR, COMEDIAN, ACTOR
2 April 1942

Diminutive Liverpudlian comic 'Big-Hearted' Arthur Askey was already well on his way to national treasure status when he called in at *Desert Island Discs* in 1942. Forged in the music hall, his irrepressible, cheeky-chappie persona was poised to dominate both radio and television.

Having been one of the very first BBC TV performers in the early thirties, Askey then starred in the corporation's first radio comedy series, *Band Waggon*. Running from 1938 to 1940, it saw him work alongside the man who was to be his long-time comedic foil, Richard Murdoch.

Along with Vera Lynn, later a castaway herself, Askey then took it upon himself to help to lift the nation's wartime spirits. Having recently diversified into films, he had starred in Gainsborough Pictures comedies including *Charley's (Big-Hearted) Aunt* (1940) and *I Thank You* (1942).

Before your very ears, Askey now extended this remit of non-stop gag-cracking gaiety to the *Desert Island Discs* studio. Co-opting Roy Plomley as his gamely willing straight man, Askey turned his appearance into an entertaining radio comedy sketch which bears repeating.

• • •

Roy Plomley: 'Good evening, everyone. Tonight, we are privileged to have on our desert island a man whose tireless activities and brilliant work in the field of ...'

Arthur Askey: 'I still think we should have used the studio at Tottering Towers.'

Plomley: 'Don't keep harping on about that. Anyway, it was your fault. We came here on your bicycle and you were steering.'

Askey: 'I followed the wrong bus.'

Plomley: 'You should have turned off at Tottering Court Road.'

Askey: 'I couldn't turn the handlebars, what with you and all that baggage.'

Plomley: 'Yes, for Pete's sake. What is all that baggage?'

Askey: 'These are my records. You asked me to bring eight records, didn't you?'

Plomley: 'But eight flat discs don't take up all that space!'

Askey: 'They're not flat discs.'

Plomley: 'What are they, then?'

Askey: 'Cylinders.'

Plomley: 'Phonograph cylinders?'

Askey: 'Yes, I much prefer cylinders. We buy 'em wholesale – by the yard, like a roll of lino. Then we cut off a piece when we feel like it.'

Plomley: 'And what's in that basket?'

Askey: 'That's my gramophone!'

Plomley: 'But the BBC has plenty of gramophones!'

Askey: 'Not like *my* gramophone! Swapped it with Mrs Bagwash for a plush-bottomed tea cosy and Vic Oliver's autograph ...'

After Askey had supposedly demonstrated the unlistenable, strangled-cat strains of his rickety old gramophone, Plomley attempted to reassert some control over proceedings.

Plomley: 'Right-o. Formal introduction coming up. On your desert island tonight is Arthur Askey – castaway number ten.'

Askey: 'Do you mean to tell me this has been going on for ten weeks and you've only just asked me?'

Plomley: 'We've had a lot of very important people.'

Askey: 'You should have done them in alphabetical order!'

This rollicking badinage left Plomley and Askey little time to talk about anything except for the particular choices of music. However, Askey did venture a touching little tale when explaining his reasons for choosing 'To a Wild Rose', a piece by an American composer and pianist, Edward MacDowell.

Askey: 'It was soon after my wife and I had got engaged. I wasn't on the stage in those days.'

Plomley: 'What were you?'

Askey: 'I was a clerk in the Liverpool Education Office. I had been there for eight years, and it looked a nice steady job for life with a pension at the end of it, but I had been messing about in my spare time with odd local concerts and I was all for taking the plunge and going on the stage, full time.'

Plomley: 'And what did your fiancée think about it?'

Askey: 'She was absolutely grand about it! She believed in me and, although it meant us parting for quite a long time, she encouraged me to go.'

Plomley: 'Where does this orchestral piece you were talking about come into it?'

Askey: 'We used to do our courting in the local park. The local municipal orchestra seemed to have a very small repertoire, but they always played one lovely little melody we both adored. We sort of adopted it for a theme tune and when the band didn't play it off its own bat, which wasn't often, we used to send up a request for it. It was to the strains of this tune that I decided to go on the stage!'

It was a heart-warming tale – yet as soon as the strains of 'To a Wild Rose' had faded, Askey was straight back into joke-machine mode.

Askey: 'Is this the studio where you do all the other *Desert Island Discs* programmes?'
Plomley: 'Yes.'
Askey: 'I thought so. I've been sitting on a bit of ship's biscuit left by Commander Campbell.'
Plomley: 'Arthur, you promised me not to gag for half-an-hour!'
Askey: 'So I did, but it's very difficult. I want some Schubert next.'
Plomley: 'Sherbet?'
Askey: 'Now who's gagging? Come, come, comely – remember you're a Plomley ...'

The programme rolled along in this bantering vein. Askey divulged that he hated hearing his own singing voice on record, even on his signature tune 'The Bee's Song' ('I don't sound a bit like I think I do!'). He was far more admiring of the talents of Gracie Fields, with whom he had played wartime concerts to entertain British troops in France.

'She was simply grand!' he marvelled. 'She wasn't at all well but she worked like a Trojan. She kept at it all day long and, however tired she was, I never once saw her without a grin on her face.'

Askey's final choice of record was a recording of the opening of the last of his *Band Waggon* radio shows from two years earlier, which he still regarded as a career – and life – highlight. Then, naturally, he departed Plomley's studio with one last gag routine.

Askey: 'Now, I'd better get my bits and bobs together again and trundle off home. I've left Stafford on his own. It's my turn to mind him tonight.'
Plomley: 'You mean to say you've left that poor boy all alone?'
Askey: 'Oh, he'll be quite happy, I gave him a box of matches and some scissors to play with. Ta-ta, Roy. Thanks for having me.'
Plomley: 'Goodbye, Arthur. Can you manage?'
Askey: 'I think so. I hope the bassinette doesn't get stuck in the lift like it did on the way up. You might tuck this watering can under my chin, old boy?'
Plomley: 'Yes. I'll open the door for you.'
Askey: 'Ah' thang-yaw! Goodnight, playmates!'

• • •

Arthur Askey was the first castaway to make a repeat appearance on *Desert Island Discs*, on 21 April 1955. He was to appear four times in total, a record that he held in splendid isolation until it was equalled by Sir David Attenborough in 2012.

Askey's 1955 visit to the studio was less of a comedy routine and more of an actual conversation. He confessed to Plomley that his father had been livid when he left his job at the Liverpool Education Office to go on the stage, and divulged he was still trying to reclaim eight years of pension contributions from the local corporation.

Arthur was shipwrecked again on 20 December 1968 and, as usual, chose mainly classical music. Why? He confessed to Plomley that 'I hate pop groups ... they're a load of rubbish!' then made an exception for his fellow Scousers, the Beatles, and 'All My Loving': 'At this point, they were very civilised and nice young fellows.'

His final trip to the island came twelve years later to the day, on 20 December 1980, at the age of eighty. His longevity in showbusiness was reflected by an anecdote about working on the BBC's first ever television broadcasts, with a bossy John Logie Baird, in 1934: 'I thought, *This fellow's an idiot!* But I was getting a guinea-and-a-half ...'

• • •

Arthur Askey's phenomenal career in music hall, comedy, theatre, films, radio, television and pantomime made him one of the most famous all-round entertainers in Britain for nigh on five decades. He continued to work until just before he died in 1982, for which an appreciative nation could only reply: '*Ay*'*-thang-yaw!*'

DISCS CHOSEN (1942)

Coates's 'The Three Bears'
Jack Hylton and His Orchestra
'I like nearly everything of his – the melodies, the scoring, and the ideas behind them' (This was just as well, as Coates was also the composer of the *Desert Island Discs* theme tune.)

'Canoe Song'
Paul Robeson
'The greatest singer in the world'

'To a Wild Rose' from Edward MacDowell's *Ten Woodland Sketches*
Victor Olof Sextet

'Serenade' from Schubert's *Schwanengesang*
Webster Booth

'The Bees' Wedding' from Mendelssohn's *Songs without Words*
Sergei Rachmaninov
'That lovely, swirling, dizzy piece of music'

'Sing as We Go'
Gracie Fields
'A person I admire tremendously, both as an artist and a woman'

'Andante Cantabile' from Tchaikovsky's String Quartet No. 1
Budapest String Quartet
'I couldn't spell it and I'm not sure what it means'

Band Waggon
Final episode of Askey's 1938–40 BBC radio comedy show
'So much fun – I could almost live on the memory of it for the rest of my life'

3
PETER USTINOV

WRITER, ACTOR, WIT, RACONTEUR
7 March 1951

Noted polymath Peter Ustinov was an illustrious visitor to the desert island even in his relative youth. He had still to turn thirty in March 1951 and yet, as an impressed Roy Plomley marvelled, had already written several hit plays, starred in West End roles ranging from revues to Russian tragedies, and written, directed and appeared in many films.

A true citizen of the world, Ustinov was an endlessly fascinating figure – and, unlike many of Plomley's guests, a passionate and informed music lover, with a record collection stacked to the ceiling of his Chelsea flat. 'I've never considered gramophone records an extravagance, but a necessary decoration to life!' he declared as the broadcast began.

The ensuing conversation confirmed that dedication.

• • •

Plomley opened the interview by commenting on his guest's insatiable love for travel, which Ustinov attributed to his mother, Russian-born painter Nadia Benois, frequently taking him to exotic locales during his school holidays in search of subjects to paint.

'We got as far as Estonia once!' he recalled. 'I found it a little unsettling to return from more or less living a Gipsy life in some far-flung corner of Europe to a very conventional and tradition-loving public school where top hats were worn.'

Asked by Plomley why he had chosen the theatre as a career, Ustinov ascribed it to his fear of the School Certificate: the exam that was then taken by all sixteen-year-olds in mainstream British schools.

'I'd always been able to imitate my father's friends, much to his embarrassment, and I used that as a lever to get myself transferred to a drama school where they had never heard of the School Certificate,' he confessed.

'A smart move!' admired Plomley.

'One learns from experience, even early in life,' concurred Ustinov, before relating a curious story about having been at school with the son of Joachim von Ribbentrop, the foreign affairs minister of Nazi Germany.

'I wrote an uncomplimentary review of his activities in the school art competition for a London paper,' he recalled. 'To my delight, it was accepted, and I was offered seven and six. I forgot to answer the letter.

'They sent me a guinea, obviously thinking my feelings had been hurt by the paltry reward originally offered. I've never been in a hurry to answer a letter since. Nine or ten months is a fair average.'

Ustinov was famously a treasure trove of such charming, self-deprecating anecdotes. Yet the business of *Desert Island Discs* was music, and he was determined to focus his laser mind on what he found so attractive about his choices.

Selecting soprano Jennie Tourel singing a love song from an Offenbach operetta, Ustinov lauded it as epitomising 'the rich, untroubled world before 1914 ... *La Belle Époque*,' and contrasted it favourably with most contemporary music offerings.

'Modern light music is either too sentimental for my tastes or else its artificially inseminated, cannibal rhythm has me nodding off,' he said. 'But this ... it has no particular association for me, but I wish it had.'

Yet Ustinov was clearly dissatisfied with his own analysis, because as Tourel's dulcet tones faded away, he returned to the topic.

'A minute or two ago, I was mildly insulting to modern light music,' he said. 'I'd like to make it clear that that didn't apply to modern serious music as well. I like modern music. I believe it to be our duty to try to understand it.

'In these self-conscious times, the problems of the artist have a great deal in common. We have to create something out of a tired world, and that something must be beautiful, expressive, captivating or witty.'

Ustinov applying his singular intellect to the dissection of music was a joy. Rhapsodising the merits of Brazilian composer Heitor Villa-Lobos, he became carried away by his own erudition.

'The whole thing is so pure!' he told Plomley. 'The melody line is so exquisite! Do you mind putting it on, because I'm beginning to talk like a programme note?'

It's fair to say that Ustinov had given his record choices rather more thought than had Arthur Askey. Yet he was at pains to stress that, while his selections might be relatively obscure, he was no musical contrarian.

'In case it might be thought that my choice so far is eccentric, I do feel I must make it clear that I'd take most of Beethoven, Bach and Mozart with me if I had the chance,' he explained.

'But, you know, while recognising the greatness of the great, I have my particular favourites which are pets of mine, and which I would rather be with, under the desolate circumstances you have prescribed. I'm not possessive by nature but I am unreasonably, aggressively possessive about my *Desert Island Discs*!'

'And why not?' acquiesced Plomley.

The eclectic tone continued as Ustinov selected two works by Czech composer, Leoš Janáček, then rounded off the programme with a dash of Russian Orthodox Church music.

'It is the most elevated music I know: both sad and serene, anguished and uncomplaining,' he said. 'This is the record I shall save for when the water runs out on my island.'

'How poignant that is indeed,' agreed Plomley as the music faded away. 'It's been a most unusual and fascinating choice you've given us. After records from Sicily, France, Russia, Brazil, Austria and Czechoslovakia, perhaps you'd like to say "Goodnight" in English?'

'Goodnight, everyone,' said Peter Ustinov.

• • •

Ustinov was to be shipwrecked just once more, in November 1977. This was a less music-focused, more discursive appearance, and his razor-witted bon mots and anecdotes were, unsurprisingly, a delight.

Typical was his answer to being asked by Plomley what he would be happiest to be away from on the desert island. 'I said this year that my idea of paradise is a country without telephones,' he mused. 'And my idea of hell is a place where telephones don't work.'

Similarly enlightening was his response to Plomley's question, 'Were you bright at school?'

'No, I was a matt finish, on the whole,' said Ustinov. 'I once said that I thought that a British education was probably the best in the world, if you could survive it. And if you couldn't, there was nothing left for you but the diplomatic corps. I still feel that quite strongly, on occasion!'

Plomley chuckled appreciatively as his guest related tales of being turned down to be a British spy ('They said that my face would be very difficult to lose in a crowd') and of, extraordinarily, serving as David Niven's batman during his Second World War military service.

Yet Ustinov's genius as a raconteur was most evident in his account of the instructions that he was given during three singing lessons he took while filming *Quo Vadis* in 1951.

'I took three lessons at Rome Opera House,' he recalled, 'from a man who confided in me that he only did it because he needed the money, because "the grandmother is old and the children are young". I said, "Well, that consideration is not entirely absent from *my* thinking!"'

'He said, "In three lessons, to teach you to sing is impossible. Three years, perhaps. But I will try to squeeze a year a lesson." "Fine!" I said.

'He said, "The first thing to remember is to breathe with the forehead." I said, "What?" He said, "Try, you must always try to breathe with the forehead!" So, I wrinkled my brow and tried to give the impression that there was a small pulse in it.

'He said, "You are really very quick on the uptake! Good! Tomorrow, we will see how good your memory is. You will breathe with the ..." I said, "Forehead?" "Bravo, that's incredible! So quickly you learn!"'

'In the second lesson, he told me: "Not only breathe with the forehead, but think with the stomach." I said, "Oh, I see!" and I tried to wear a rather constricted look, as though I was thinking with my stomach – not forgetting to wrinkle my forehead, to demonstrate that the little pulse was at work there.

'On the third lesson, he said, "I will see how much you remember of the lesson so far." I said, "Yes." "I ask you to think with the ..." "Stomach." "Bravo! And to breathe with the ..." "Forehead." "It's incredible! I never heard a student so quick!"

'"And now, the last thing I must tell you, the third lesson – remember always, under any circumstances, to sing with the eye." And I'm afraid I may on occasion have forgotten to breathe with my forehead, or think with my stomach, but never *ever* did I forget to sing with my eye! I think that's probably the only part of me that *was* singing, at times ...'

The genius that was Peter Ustinov ended his second *Desert Island Discs* appearance by asking Roy Plomley for writing paper as his luxury item.

'I'll make my own books,' he explained. 'I hope there may be a few bottles around with something to drink. As I expend the bottles, I can fill them with writing and set them off on their road to oblivion by launching them in the sea ...'

• • •

After a life whose achievements included Academy Awards, Golden Globes, BAFTAs and a Grammy, becoming a goodwill ambassador for UNICEF and, in 1990, being knighted, Sir Peter Ustinov died in 2004 at the age of 82. There really wasn't a lot that he *hadn't* done by then. Including, obviously, singing with his eye.

DISCS CHOSEN (1951)
'A la Barcillunisa'
Giuseppe Di Stefano
'It has the exquisite feeling of maritime nostalgia'

'Ô mon cher amant' from Offenbach's *La Périchole*
Jennie Tourel
'Still nostalgic, but gayer – a love song, in fact'

Prokofiev's Violin Concerto No. 2 in G Minor
Jascha Heifetz
'An example of modern lyricism at its most poignant'

Villa-Lobos's *Bachianas Brasileiras* No. 5
Bidu Sayão

Schubert's String Quartet No. 13 in A Minor
Philharmonia String Quartet
'The superb resignation and fatalism and simplicity of Schubert'

'Odesli' from Janáček's *Jenůfa*
Štěpánka Jelínková

Janáček's Sinfonietta
Czech Philharmonic Orchestra
'Pulsating with joy and gaiety'

'Prière de Saint-Siméon'
Choir of the Russian Cathedral in Paris
'Of all church music I've heard, this is the most beautiful'

4
PETULA CLARK

SINGER, ACTOR
2 May 1951

Petula Clark was only eighteen when she fetched up on the desert island in May 1951 but she already had a considerable showbiz career behind her. A wartime BBC radio child entertainer, she had also toured Britain, as 'the Singing Sweetheart', with fellow tyro Julie Andrews.

Having had her first film role aged twelve, Clark had since then become a movie veteran, including starring with Anthony Newley in *Vice Versa*, directed by our previous castaway, Peter Ustinov. She had also hosted her own after-noon BBC TV programme and had recently launched her recording career.

Yet despite these laudable achievements, she was still a teenager, with little real-life experience or worldly sophistication to draw upon, as was evident from her *Desert Island Discs* interlocution.

• • •

With his avuncular yet patrician manner, Roy Plomley's interview with Petula Clark took a notably gallant tone. This courtesy was evident from the off, as he addressed his 'attractive' castaway as 'Pet', adding, 'I hate to think of you wasting your sweetness on a desert isle!'

'Records do mean a lot to me,' began Clark. 'I've collected them ever since I was a child ...'

'*All* those years?' teased Plomley.

'I like new things,' she persisted. 'This means that, with two or three excep-tions, the eight records I stagger up the beach with are my present favourites, and how long it would be before I tire of them and want new ones, I have no idea.'

Clark introduced her first record, 'Aba Daba Honeymoon' from the soundtrack of a movie called *Two Weeks with Love*, as 'a love song of two chim-panzees'. Plomley affected to be perplexed by this.

'It's recorded by two chimpanzees, is it?' he enquired.

'Do try to be serious about this!' admonished Clark.

'What does "aba daba" mean?'

'That's chimpanzee language.'

As the song finished, Clark hoped that its use of chimp-speak might be useful to coax monkeys on the island down from the trees to lend her some company.

'You may not have monkeys on the island,' warned Plomley.

'Surely *every* desert island has monkeys?' she asked.

'We had a castaway on this programme once who had actually been shipwrecked on a desert island, and the only inhabitants he found were penguins and wild goats!' exclaimed Plomley, clearly still not over the thrill of meeting Captain A.E. Dingle.

'I think I should get on well with penguins,' Clark speculated. 'I like comedians.'

Plomley widened the conversational remit to ask his guest how she would get on with making a fire and cooking on the island.

'I'd have a shot at cooking – I'll try anything once – but I wouldn't have a clue about making a fire,' she replied.

'Pity – because a fire does help when you're cooking ...' he pointed out, before returning to the topic of her extreme youth.

'Pet, we all know that you're just eighteen, but you seem to have been on the radio and in pictures for a few years now. At whatever age did you start?'

'I made up my mind I wanted to be an actress when I was six years old,' she explained. 'It was on top of a bus.'

'Why on top of a bus?'

'My father had just taken me to see my first play: Flora Robson in *Mary Tudor* at the Streatham Hill Theatre. I came out of the theatre in a bit of a daze and on the way home, I said, "I'm going to be an actress." I firmly made my mind up at that moment and I never changed it.'

'And did you start right away, at the age of six?' Plomley asked.

'No, I had to wait, because of LCC [*London County Council*] regulations, until I was twelve. I have to say, I waited *fuming* with impatience!'

The broadcast wended to its end with a little more desultory chit-chat about Clark's remaining record choices. As Plomley wound things up by saying, 'There you are, Pet, that's your eight!' he sounded as if he was patting her on the head as if she were, indeed, a pet.

'That's the eight I'd take this week but, as I warned you, my favourites change, and if I were to be cast away again in a month's time, I might have a quite different eight,' Clark replied.

'I might take you up on that,' said Plomley.

• • •

Yet it was actually thirty-one years before an older, far worldlier Petula Clark returned to Plomley's island in 1982. By then she was a huge recording star not just in Britain and America but across Europe, due to a canny habit of also recording in French, Italian, Spanish and German.

After recalling her early, adolescent shipwreck, the now-savvier Clark talked of having back then been the youngest artist signed to the Rank Organisation, and regretted how they had tried to artificially prolong her spell as a child star as it was coining them so much money.

'They kept you in ankle socks?' asked Plomley.

'And bound in my bosom,' sighed Clark.

'It was very mean of them!' sympathised Plomley.

'Yes, it was rather mean,' agreed Clark. 'I wasn't allowed to grow up. It was very difficult for me. I was not very happy during those years.'

The host and guest moved on to a happier topic, reminiscing about working together on a satirical BBC radio show written by Plomley, *The Rhubarb Room*, in 1949.

'Why *was* it called that?' wondered Clark, laughing.

'I don't know,' admitted Plomley. 'I wanted something ridiculous.'

Far more significant was Clark describing being asked to begin recording in French in 1957. Unable to speak the language, she demurred, but reluctantly agreed to play a one-off show at Paris's Olympia Theatre.

'I sang for about fifteen minutes and pulled the place down,' she told Plomley. 'I couldn't figure out why [*because*] I sang very badly! I had a very bad cold and looked dreadful.

'The next morning, the record chief was trying to talk me into recording in French. I was still saying no, blowing my nose and saying, "I want to go home!" Anyway, the lights went off in this record chief's office and he said something in French, which I obviously didn't understand.

'This boy came in, stood on the desk and changed the light bulb. The light went on and *there he was*. I said, "Who's *that?*" The boss said, "Oh, that is Claude Wolff, he's our promotions person. If you did make a record, he would be showing you around Paris ..." So, I said, "Oh well, all right, I'll have a go, then!"'

Clark did not speak French and Wolff had little English. ('The only English Claude knew was some rather nasty American jazz slang, which I found rather shocking!') Yet four years later, they were married. They were to have three children and remain married for fifty years.

• • •

Clark was to move to France to live with Claude Wolff once they were married. This upheaval also opened her eyes to different ways to sing and to be a popular entertainer, as she explained to Sue Lawley when she made her third visit to the desert island, on Christmas Eve 1995.

On this visit, Clark concurred with Lawley's suggestion that she had cut her showbiz teeth in the British music hall tradition of sequins and big ballads. On crossing *la Manche*, she realised that performing could be done with greater depth, nuance and subtlety.

'I remember going to the music hall for the first time in Paris,' she said. 'I saw Piaf and I thought, *Well, what's all this about?* This little lady comes out in this rather shabby little black dress and sings about death and madness and sex and all kinds of heavy stuff. It was, like, *but this isn't music hall!*

'I'd never seen anything like that before and, of course, she wasn't the only one. There was Aznavour, obviously, but also so many, many singers like that and it just taught me so much.'

Clark was far too modest to say so, but Lawley pointed out that, within two or three years, her guest had beaten Piaf to be regarded by the French as the very best *chanteuse* extant. 'You were the number-one female vocalist in France, weren't you?' she asked.

'Yes, and it was amazing, really!' marvelled Petula Clark. 'I never really understood how that happened ...'

• • •

One of the most talented and tenacious female stars in the history of British music, Petula Clark has sold nearly 70 million records worldwide and starred in numerous high-profile movies and stage musicals. In 2019, at the age of eighty-six, she returned to the West End stage to play the part of the Bird Woman in *Mary Poppins*. She splits her time between homes in Geneva, the French Alps and Chelsea, and continues to record and perform. That moment of inspiration on a Streatham omnibus really worked out rather well.

DISCS CHOSEN (1951)
'Aba Daba Honeymoon'
Debbie Reynolds and Carleton Carpenter

'The Story of the Stars'
Jack Pleis and His Piano
'This is one for the evening, sitting outside my little hut'

'Dear, dear, dear'
Champ Butler
'A piece of hot jazz. It starts in bop then just gets wild'

Ravel's *La Valse*
Paris Conservatoire Orchestra
'As close as I get to being classical'

'A Friend of Johnny's'
Jo Stafford with Paul Weston and His Orchestra

'Gipsy Fiddler'
Ray Martin and His Concert Orchestra
'Wild Gipsy music ... I like to fling myself about'

'Life's Desire'
Jimmy Young
'I'm afraid this one is sentimental'

'Temptation (Tim-Tayshun)'
Red Ingle and the Natural Seven
'This is a record that, in a way, debunks all the other records'

5
GRACIE FIELDS

SINGER, ACTOR
13 June 1951

There were few bigger stars in the British showbiz world in the thirties than Gracie Fields, 'the Lancashire lass'. As well as her vast repertoire of music hall songs such as 'Sally', she was also reputedly the highest-paid movie star in the world during the year of 1937.

Wartime, a cancer battle and a temporary move to America had reduced her ubiquity a little by the time of her first visit to *Desert Island Discs*, fourteen years later. Even so, such was her celebrity that Roy Plomley declared: 'I'm not going to *introduce* our castaway – all I have to do is to *announce* her.'

Famous for never losing her broad Rochdale accent, Fields's first words on the show were, 'This is a rum do I've got mixed up in! Eight records that would last the rest of my life, is that it?' It set the tone for a sweet and rather engaging exchange.

Also notable was Plomley's extreme respect for this particular castaway. Where Petula Clark had been 'Pet' to him, Gracie was 'Miss Fields' throughout.

• • •

Plomley opened by enquiring of his guest whether she had made use of the BBC Record Library while selecting her music.

'They were very helpful,' said Fields. 'They said, "We've got a quarter of a million records here and you can play them all, if you like."

'I asked, "How long is that going to take?" and they said, "If you keep at it, day and night, you can manage it in just under two years." I said, "I can't stop now – I'm late as it is!"'

She then enquired of Plomley exactly what conditions on the desert isle were like. 'It's quite deserted, nobody about, no warmth, no comfort,' he reported. 'That sounds like some of the places I used to play on tour, years ago ...' she deadpanned, no doubt following her host's script.

Moving beyond this initial joshing, Fields selected 'O Paradiso', from an opera named *L'Africaine*, by legendary tenor Enrico Caruso. 'You feel all the time that he's giving all he's got,' she commented. 'He did what I always try to do: give the lot or nothing at all.'

As the tune faded away, Fields divulged a further reason for her choice: 'If that desert island is as dreary as you make it out to be, it would take my mind off it by recalling for me the sunshine and the beautiful scenery of Italy.'

'You have a house in Capri, haven't you?' asked Plomley.

'That's right. That's my home, or, rather, one of my homes, because I think your real home must always be where you were brought up. And although I've got all my bits and pieces in that little house in Capri, the word "home" will always mean England to me.

'And my next record is, I think, the most English tune that I know. It's "Greensleeves". A wonderfully restful melody. It conjures up a picture of smooth, green lawns and shady trees and old houses. The picture you always have of England when you're away from it.'

Plomley moved on to enquire of 'Miss Fields' what made her go into the theatre. 'Were your family professionals?'

'No, I just liked singing, that was all. I went into the [*cotton*] mill when I was twelve years old as a half-timer: half my day at school, half at the mill. I used to sing while I worked. I jolly near got the sack for it, too!'

'For singing?' puzzled Plomley.

'I used to dance, as well, you see. Well, the idea of being paid for singing and dancing, for what I liked doing better than anything else in the world: I *had* to go on the stage!'

Plomley: 'Were you taking lessons?'

'I've never had a singing lesson in my life. We had them at school, but they wouldn't let me join in. They said my voice was too noisy.'

'How did you start in the business?'

'Singing at concerts, locally. Then I started in variety. I was doing a solo act when I was fifteen. Come on, let's have another record!'

Fields chose *Zigeunerweisen* by Spanish composer Pablo de Sarasate, played by Russian violinist Jascha Heifetz. 'There must be some Gipsy blood in me,' she mused. 'Every time I hear Gipsy tunes, I want to dance. You can imagine me leaping about on the sand. Well, I've got to keep me weight down somehow!'

Fields's refusal to take herself seriously was endearing. Yet her tone became notably more serious, even reverential, when she came to discuss 'Una voce poco fa' from Rossini's *The Barber of Seville*, sung by legendary Italian soprano Luisa Tetrazzini.

'We had a gramophone back home in Rochdale,' she recalled. 'One of the old sort, with a big horn that half-filled up the front room. We had a pile of records: Billy Williams, Gus Elen, Harry Lauder, Vesta Victoria. All the music hall stars of the day. That was what we used to like.

'But suddenly, among them turned up a record by Tetrazzini. *How* it got there, heaven only knows! It wasn't me. I'll swear it wasn't Dad or Mum – I can't think of anybody in the family bringing it home! But there it was. *Opera! Italian! Highbrow!*

'I used to play it and that was the first time – there was no wireless in those days – that I ever heard *proper singing*.'

Plomley: 'That record had an effect on you, did it?'

'It certainly did! I'm not putting myself in the same class as Tetrazzini, don't think that, but it did give me something to aim at. It showed me there was more to singing than I ever heard at the local music hall.

'I used to burlesque it. I was doing that one night when I was playing in *The Show's the Thing* at the Lyceum. I was doing a charwoman sketch: I was scrubbing the floor and singing the cadenza: a cod on the way that Tetrazzini did it.

'I got off, and had a big hand for it, and somebody on the side said, "Do you know who is in front?" I said, "No." He said, 'Tetrazzini." I nearly died! But she came round afterwards, and she was grand. A lovely person, she was.'

Bidding Miss Fields a courtly farewell at the end of the show, Plomley noted that he had omitted to ask her one of the programme's staple questions: how would she manage, alone on the island?

'I think I'd be all right, love. I'm quite a good housekeeper and not a bad cook, but I don't think I'd be as good as most other Englishwomen. I've been so busy, the past few years, I haven't had as much experience as other women have in making do and making not very much go round.

'The way the English housewife has been managing – bless her! She's a marvel! I think she'd take a desert island in her stride ...'

• • •

Gracie Fields returned to the desert island ten years later, on Christmas Day 1961. By then, she'd had success on US TV, being the first actress to play Miss Marple in Agatha Christie's *A Murder is Announced* and winning an Emmy nomination for her role in J.M. Barrie's *The Old Lady Shows Her Medals*.

Plomley found the pluck to address her as 'Gracie' and noted that she now had a lower profile in Britain: 'We don't see nearly enough of you these days ... it seems a shame to send you off to a desert island when you *do* get here!'

Fields explained that she spent eight months a year in Capri, splitting the rest of her time between England and the US. She admitted she had originally been driven to live on the Italian island by the pressure of her mega-fame in Britain.

'It was when I was being made such a fuss of,' she said. 'I never got the chance to even learn a new song! I was always opening a bazaar, or something. It used to be from eleven o'clock in the morning, they'd pick me up in any town I went to, and I never had any day to myself.

'I couldn't learn new programmes so I used to go to Capri. If it was only for a week, I'd have two days on the train, three days in Capri, and two days coming back again. I'd stick the songs under my arm and I could be there quietly without being disturbed, because it took two days to get a telegram to you and I wasn't on the phone.'

And yet, despite Gracie Fields's embrace of life in Italy and America, her musical selections still included the none-more-English 'Greensleeves'. The Lancashire lass was to continue to perform right up until she died, aged eighty-one, in 1979.

DISCS CHOSEN (1951)
'O Paradiso' from Meyerbeer's *L'Africaine*
Enrico Caruso
'There's no faking; no little tricks'

'Greensleeves'
Hallé Orchestra

'Old Sam (Sam, Pick Oop Tha' Musket)'
Stanley Holloway
'It's got the character of the North Country people'

Sarasate's *Zigeunerweisen*
Jascha Heifetz with the London Symphony Orchestra

Selection from *Show Boat*
Geraldo and His Romance in Rhythm Orchestra
'Theatre music: to make me imagine the curtain going up, and all the lights and colour and excitement'

Intermezzo and serenade from Delius's *Hassan*
Hallé Orchestra
'It's got a sort of Eastern fatalism, which would be appropriate for a desert island'

'Una voce poco fa' from Rossini's *The Barber of Seville*
Luisa Tetrazzini

Tchaikovsky's *Romeo and Juliet*
Vienna Philharmonic Orchestra
'Lots of romance, lots of violins, a lovely melody'

6
NORMAN WISDOM

COMEDIAN, ACTOR, SINGER
17 April 1953

Roy Plomley had invented *Desert Island Discs* and he had a determined vision of how the show should be. His interview encounters were invariably charming and easy on the ear. However, a polite reticence to probe meant that he rarely dived too deep beneath his castaways' surfaces.

Typical was his April 1953 encounter with Norman Wisdom, a man with an extraordinary backstory. Beaten by his father as a boy, he had run away to a children's home, slept rough, been a British Army flyweight boxing champion in India and connected Winston Churchill's phone calls during the Second World War before becoming an entertainer.

However, the reliably urbane Plomley eschewed these tantalising topics in favour of a characteristically entertaining humorous exchange. As both parties were very skilled in this particular discipline, it was still a highly enjoyable episode.

• • •

In fairness to Plomley, Wisdom was equally keen to turn his appearance on the island into an Arthur Askey-style comedy routine. The tone was set when he arrived in the studio apparently grunting and puffing.

'What are you doing, Norman?' asked Plomley.

'Getting packed.'

'Getting packed? But you're not allowed to take anything with you!'

'All right, well, I'll change here, then.'

'But you can't change! You must go as you are!'

'Go as I am? But I've got a smashing outfit ready! I've got a grass skirt and a beautiful double-breasted fig leaf ...'

Wisdom abruptly dismissed his host's suggestion that he should build a hut on the island, pointing instead to his time sleeping rough in London as a child: 'If you've done it in England, you can do it anywhere!'

'You had a pretty adventurous childhood, didn't you?' asked Plomley.

'I don't know about adventurous, but I had a pretty tough one.'

'You ran away from home when you were about eleven?'

'That's right.'

'What sort of jobs did you hold down?'

'Well, I didn't hold any of them down, but I had a lot of fun trying.'

'For instance?'

'Oh, pageboy, errand boy, cabin boy on a ship going to South America ... that was a nice safe job.'

'Safe?!' exclaimed Plomley.

'Yes, well, they can't very well sack you in the middle of the South Atlantic ...'

Wisdom was by now thirty-eight yet it was clear his nomadic days were not entirely over. Invited by Plomley to begin nominating his music choices, he commented that he was no expert, as he had only recently begun collecting records.

'I've only just got myself a house,' he admitted. 'I've been touring in a caravan until now, and there is no room to collect anything in a caravan. We were so short of space that where other fellows could take their wives home boxes of chocolates, I had to take my wife half-a-dozen hundreds and thousands!'

Miffed at having to miss the imminent coronation of Queen Elizabeth II while he was on the island, Wisdom chose a tune named 'Coronation Scot' to soften the blow. Then, before his next tune, 'Dummy Song', he directly addressed its performer, Max Bygraves.

'Are you listening, Max?' he wondered. 'Do you remember those not-so-far-off days, just after the war, when we were demobbed and we used to work those tiny little music halls, far from civilisation, with our names outside on the bills down in the right-hand corner, about the same size as the bloke who'd printed 'em?

'And do you remember we used to go on stage and flog ourselves to a standstill then come off and sit in the dressing room and say, "Wouldn't it be wonderful if we were stars?" Then we'd come down to earth and say, "Wouldn't it be wonderful if we were *working* next week?" Good luck, Max – I'd like to have your voice on my island ...'

Plomley turned the questioning to Wisdom's army career. His guest spoke of it fondly.

'I have a great deal to thank the army for,' he said. 'Firstly, and I'm not afraid to admit it, for a square meal and a bed when I needed it very badly. Plus, a smashing warm overcoat and that wonderful thing called companionship, which I think is more prevalent in the army than anywhere else. And, strangely enough, although I didn't get my career in the army, my career came *from* the army.'

Plomley: 'In what respect, Norman?'

'I joined the band and learned a lot about music. Have you ever listened to Harry James playing the trumpet, Roy? I'd take one of his records with me.'

'Any particular reason?'

'Well, when I was in India, all the chaps in the band, including myself, had to play a trumpet in order to carry out guard duties, you know: like

"Cookhouse", or "Reveille", or something like that. I used to go and struggle through various calls at about half-speed with a handful of wrong notes thrown in. It sounded as if I was blowing a trumpet while I was riding a bike on a rough road.

'Then I'd go back into the guard room, put on this record of Harry James playing "Flight of the Bumble Bee", and think to myself, *Cor, strike me lucky! How does he do it?* And if you know, you tell me!'

As the interview neared its end, Wisdom made a heartfelt plea for Plomley to bend *Desert Island Discs'* rules. He had recently become a father for the first time (his son, Nicholas, would in later years play first-class cricket for Sussex). Could he possibly take his small boy with him?

'How small?' asked Plomley.

'Six pounds seven ounces! Not very heavy. He wouldn't take up much room!'

'Not allowed, I'm afraid!'

'Oh, this is just the same as any other digs!' sighed Wisdom. 'No dogs or children – and no musical instruments after eleven, I suppose?'

'You've got to be fair to the seagulls!' cautioned Plomley.

'But he's quiet! He never cries!'

'What would you feed him on?'

'Coconut milk and seagull eggs.'

'Nourishing but monotonous,' decided Plomley. 'Anyway, he can't go, it's against the rules.'

There was just time left for Wisdom to choose a record by Gracie Fields: 'I look upon her as my good fairy because, when I started, she was very kind to me.' His episode had been fun, but it would have been nice to hear his experiences of homelessness, boxing and Winston Churchill.

• • •

When Norman Wisdom returned to the desert island in August 2000, at the age of eighty-five, he had just been knighted. He had not yet come to terms with the honour, as was evidenced by his reaction when the show's host, Sue Lawley, addressed him by his new title.

'I'm sorry, but I can't help laughing when you say "Sir Norman!"' he admitted. "Most people are still saying "Tich!"'

Despite this, he and Lawley appeared to have an instant rapport, and he was more than willing to fill her in on the details of his homelessness as a teenager.

'I was sleeping rough behind the Marshal Fox statue in Victoria station,' he recalled. 'I used to go over at about half past two in the morning to a coffee-stall attendant and look over the counter. And the bloke eventually said, "What's the matter with you?"'

'I told him the truth so he pushed me a hot pie and a cup of Bovril.

He did this for about seven or eight nights, then he said, "Why don't you join the army? You'll have somewhere to sleep!" I said, "I can't get in the army at my size!" I was four foot ten-and-a-half and I weighed five stone nine!'

Wisdom told Lawley that he nevertheless went to a recruiting centre, where a military band master took pity on him, enlisted him and turned his fortunes around.

'Two weeks later, I was on my way to India, having the time of my life! Wonderful weather, my own bed, wonderful food, football, cricket, swimming, and I was put on to clarinet and saxophone. Those six years I did in India were the happiest time of my life.'

Wisdom also opened up on his troubled family background, describing an abusive father who would bounce him off the sitting-room ceiling, and who beat his mother until she was forced to leave.

'He claimed custody of the children only because he didn't want her to have them,' he said. 'He was a chauffeur and he'd be away for weeks or, sometimes, months. It became a question of beg, steal or borrow. That's what we'd do: steal.'

After Wisdom's mother was driven out, he told Lawley, she vanished and he did not see her for decades – until they reunited in a most extraordinary manner.

'I was doing a show at the Cambridge Theatre in '51,' he recalled. 'We were on the stage for the applause. I was only on the second row because I wasn't the star. Suddenly there was this voice from up in the gods: "Norman Wisdom! Norman Wisdom! Well done, Norman Wisdom!"

'She kept on and on! The stage manager even took me by the arm and led me to the front. She shouted, "Congratulations, Norman Wisdom!" Then I was in the dressing room and the doorkeeper came and said, "Norman, a lady would like to see you." And it was my mother.'

Lawley: 'That would have been twenty-seven years since you'd seen her?'

Wisdom: 'That's right. And I kept her and I never let her go.'

Wisdom also recalled a brief period in his life when he had appeared likely to break America. In the late sixties, he had starred in a Broadway show, made a movie – *The Night They Raided Minsky's* (1968) – and worked with Audrey Hepburn, Charlie Chaplin and Laurel and Hardy.

Sue Lawley wondered why this had come to an end: 'You had a very firm foothold in the States, because you were on Broadway. Why didn't you go on and make it big there?' And Norman Wisdom explained: he had not wanted to repeat the mistake of his own parents and abandon his children.

'It's a bit sad, but I'll tell you,' he said. 'I was married at that time and I had two children, a son and a daughter, and my wife found someone tall and good-looking. And, so, I packed it all in to come back to look after my children.

'And I'm very pleased that I did, because they're a couple of crackers ...'

• • •

Sir Norman Wisdom had a decade to get accustomed to being a knight of the realm. He retired from acting on his ninetieth birthday, in February 2005, in order to spend more time with his family and on his adopted home of the Isle of Man. Sir Norman was to pass away in a care home on the island, on 4 October 2010, at the age of ninety-five.

DISCS CHOSEN (1953)
'Coronation Scot'
Sidney Torch and His Orchestra
'A beautiful descriptive piece'

'Dummy Song'
Max Bygraves

'The Three Trumpeters'
The Band of the Royal Military School of Music

'My Heart and I'
Richard Tauber and the Luton Girls' Choir

'Flight of the Bumble Bee'
Harry James and His Orchestra

Sibelius's *Valse triste*
Philharmonia Orchestra
'I'm not really a classical fan, but this is my favourite piece of music bar none'

'What Is a Boy?'
Jan Peerce

'Now Is the Hour'
Gracie Fields
'A very sweet lady, loved by everybody in showbusiness'

LUXURY ITEM
Motor car and petrol
'Just so I can park it anywhere I like – on the wrong side of the street, up one-way streets facing the wrong way ...'

7

LESLIE CARON

ACTOR, DANCER
2 July 1956

Norman Wisdom came close to breaking America yet was ultimately happy to settle for being a very British performer with little profile outside of his homeland (except, a tad perplexingly, for being huge in Albania). In 1956, by stark contrast, Roy Plomley welcomed to the island a twenty-five-year-old French starlet with the world at her feet.

Leslie Caron had begun her career as a ballerina in Paris before being discovered by Gene Kelly, who cast her opposite him as the female lead in the 1951 musical comedy movie *An American in Paris*. Her success in this debut film role landed her a move to Hollywood and a seven-year contract with MGM.

Ms Caron had since gone on to win an Academy Award Nomination for her lead role in musical movie *Lili* (strapline: 'You'll fall in love with Lili!'). She was well on her way to becoming one of the most recognisable and bankable faces of the golden age of Hollywood.

She was also to make her own little piece of *Desert Island Discs* history. In February 2022, at the age of ninety, Caron returned to the show to talk to Lauren Laverne, more than sixty-five years after her first visit. It is the longest-ever timespan between two appearances as a castaway: a record that is unlikely ever to be surpassed.

• • •

In the opening desert-island exchanges in July 1956, Leslie Caron told Plomley that it was ballet that had inculcated her strong love for music: 'I have quite a large collection: about two hundred LPs!' In return, the host wondered when she had first resolved to become a dancer.

'It's difficult to say,' Caron replied. 'I can't quite remember when I first wanted. I think I have always wanted to dance.'

Plomley: 'How old were you when you started to learn?'

'Well, I was actually quite old when I went to my first dancing lesson. I was nine, which is very old for ballet.'

'Did your parents encourage you in your ambition?' asked Plomley.

'My mother did! She was a ballet dancer!'

Caron talked of joining a prestigious French company, Ballet des Champs-Élysées, when she was seventeen and enjoying touring with them, especially to London. Plomley wondered why she had left, after just over two years, to move to Hollywood.

'I was getting very tired. It's a very strenuous life. I found that I couldn't keep up with the company any more, and so I accepted Gene Kelly's offer to do *An American in Paris* with him.'

'Did you find that more restful?'

'No! I think it was quite worse!'

Plomley wondered how his guest had first coped with the limitations of having to dance within tight chalk marks in front of a film camera, after being used to having the freedom of the stage for ballet performances.

'It's very difficult, because you have to repeat over and over again,' Caron agreed. 'As you say, the marvellous thing about ballet is freedom. You *do* have to confine yourself ... it's no use dancing outside the camera range!'

At the time, Caron was in London starring in the lead role in a stage production of *Gigi*, a role she was to reprise three years later in a film that was to win nine Academy Awards. Yet before turning his mind to this production, Plomley awarded his guest what he no doubt considered to be a major accolade.

'I would like to compliment you on your excellent English!' he declared. 'Despite the fact that you've spent the last four or five years in the United States, you speak English with an *English* accent and not an American one.'

'Oh, thank you very much!' said Caron. 'That's quite a compliment! Actually, I learned English from a New England lady. She had a sort of British accent and we read Shakespeare for hours.'

Plomley wondered whether Caron had still to put in many hours of daily dance training while appearing in *Gigi*.

'Well, I would if I were still training, but I am not! I have abandoned dancing now.'

'You've abandoned dancing?' repeated the horrified host. 'That's sad news! Is that a firm decision?'

'Well, one can say anything is firm, really ... I don't know. I might take it up again but I don't think I would go back on the stage again ...'

Having absorbed the news of his guest's planned change of career, Plomley wrapped up the show, as was his wont, by asking Caron if she would make a good castaway. Her reply was surprisingly chipper.

'Oh, I'm sure I could be quite happy! I've already done it, as a matter of fact. I'm quite trained for it.'

'What have you done? Been on a desert island?'

'Yes, for a whole month. A very exciting island in Brittany, that was taken over by some pirates in about 1500, and they built a beautiful tower on it. When I wanted to eat, I had to build my own fire, and fetch the wood and get water from a well.

'When I wanted to go to the village, I had to go at low tide, harness a horse and drive the horse carriage myself. It was all very romantic!'

Plomley: 'So you've been very well-trained for this! Except that, on our island, you won't have a village to go to ...'

'Then I'm afraid I would eat seaweed!'

'Do you fish?'

'No, not at all. I'm sure I couldn't. The fish wouldn't take to me.'

'Oh, I think you'd charm the fish out of the water ...' concluded a smitten Roy Plomley.

• • •

Leslie Caron had lived a long and eventful life by the time she washed up on the desert island again, aged ninety, early in 2022. She never did return to ballet, but had scooped countless awards and accolades during what had been a truly glittering movie and theatre career.

With the calm and wisdom of age, she was also far more willing to open up about her life to Lauren Laverne than she had been to Roy Plomley more than half a century earlier. It made for compulsive radio.

Laverne asked Caron about her mother, an American divorcee who had danced on Broadway and been previously married before meeting her father. She also appeared to have been entirely lacking in any kind of maternal instinct.

'My mother was very honest,' claimed Caron. 'She said to me: "Listen, I don't like children and I'm not going to take care of you when you're little, because I'm not interested. But when you're a star, I will be there!" So, I knew what I had to do! It was quite clear!'

Laverne: 'You must have been heartbroken?'

Caron laughed a very French laugh: 'No, no! I wasn't heartbroken! I knew my mother: that's just the way she was. She would just say it the way she felt it.'

Caron recalled being eight years old when the Second World War broke out in 1939. She told Laverne that her grandfather had cried as she sat on his knee: 'He said, "My poor child! War is declared! Don't talk about your mother being American. There are men with machine guns."'

'Paris changed so much. All bags of sand and German signs everywhere, written in Gothic black and white letters. You couldn't recognise where you were: it wasn't Paris any more. It destroys the soul ... the horror of it all. The greyness!'

Caron went on to describe beginning her dance career after the end of the war, then being spotted by Gene Kelly and whisked to Hollywood to star in *An American in Paris*. Laverne asked if it was true that she had been so shy she had initially tried to shoot scenes with her back to the camera.

'Yes!' she laughed. 'Gene would tell me, "Kiddo, turn your face towards the camera, or your grandmother won't know you were in the film!"'

Laverne: 'You were no pushover though, Leslie. You had idea of your own about how you wanted your character to look. You had strong thoughts on your hair?'

'Yes! I thought, *These people don't know what the latest Paris fashion is!* I kept telling them, "Shorter! Shorter! Shorter!" but they wouldn't do it. So, the night before, I took my little nail scissors and chopped it all. Chopped my hair like a boy. I arrived at make-up ... *disaster!*

'Everybody turned up: the producer, Vincent Minelli, Gene Kelly. I was with my shoulders against the brick wall and they were all facing me exactly like a firing squad.'

Laverne: 'They weren't too happy?'

'No! They shook their heads and said, "My God!" Gene took me aside and told me, "Honey, they fire girls for less than that!" They had to postpone shooting that day, and for two or three weeks. It was a disaster: "You can't do that!"'

Caron had also enjoyed a lively personal life. Married and divorced by the age of twenty-three, she had then married British theatre director Peter Hall and had two children. When that marriage was under strain at the start of the sixties, she began an affair with Warren Beatty.

'What distressed me was that Peter didn't want me to work and didn't want to work with me. I was to stay home,' she explained to Laverne. 'So, I walked out. Then Warren happened to be there.'

Laverne: 'What was life with him like?'

'Warren was real Hollywood. He understood the workings of Hollywood – to keep your status, you must always be in front of the press. For me, that was exhausting, and I didn't like it: I thought it was artificial. So, our affair lasted two years and that was it.'

Caron may have disdained those workings of Hollywood but she was a true survivor of its golden age and a fount of glorious anecdotes – one of which emerged when, second time around, she chose a cutlass as her luxury item for the desert island, in memory of a 1964 movie role.

'I happen to know that this takes you back to filming *Father Goose* in Jamaica with Cary Grant,' prompted Laverne. 'And you stayed in a house with your own butler?'

'We were each given a house. Cary had a house, I had a house and, every morning, my butler, who was dressed in black with a bow tie, would take off his shoes, take a cutlass between his teeth and climb up a coconut tree. And when he got to a coconut: *slash!* He would get me one or two coconuts for breakfast ...'

• • •

Like a true Old Hollywood star, Leslie Caron has never stopped acting. In 2006 she won an Emmy Award for her portrayal of a rape victim in US TV crime drama *Law & Order: Special Victims Unit*. In 2016, her life was drama-tised in a documentary, *Leslie Caron: The Reluctant Star*. She continues to make both movies and TV shows into her tenth decade.

DISCS CHOSEN (1956)
Vivaldi's Concerto for Strings in G Major, *Concerto alla rustica*
I Virtuosi di Roma Orchestra
'I think he's very gay and has very great elegance and style'

'Strawberry Woman's Call' from Gershwin's *Porgy and Bess*
Helen Dowdy
'It reminds me of the French street criers that we still have'

Stravinsky's *Petrushka*
Orchestra de la Suisse Romande
'It's very abstract music for most people'

'Bravo for the Clown'
Édith Piaf
'She represents Paris for me'

Saugnet's *Les Forains*
Orchestre des Concerts Lamoureux
'Quite sentimental and sweet'

Dutilleux's *Le Loup*
Orchestre du Théâtre des Champs-Elysées

'Écoutez Bien, Messieurs'
Sacha Guitry
'He talks about the theatre and women. It's very witty'

Bach's Passacaglia and Fugue in C Minor
Stokowski Symphony Orchestra
'My favourite composer'

LUXURY ITEM
Artists' materials
'That would be absolute heaven'

8
DAVID ATTENBOROUGH

BIOLOGIST, NATURALIST, BROADCASTER
6 May 1957

David Attenborough was only thirty and at the start of one of the most illustrious careers in British broadcasting when he swam ashore the desert island in 1957. He had joined the Beeb in 1952, after spells in the Royal Navy and working in publishing.

Attenborough began his BBC career as a producer on such programmes as the quiz show *Animal, Vegetable, Mineral?* He moved in front of the camera to present natural history series *Animal Patterns* and then, in 1954, began presenting a nature documentary series, *Zoo Quest*.

Attenborough was to go on to become the controller of BBC Two and BBC director of programmes, but was to be best known for making some of the most ambitious, spectacular nature programmes in global television history. These included *The Living Planet*, *Natural World*, *Planet Earth* and, in the twenty-first century, the superlative *The Blue Planet*.

Knighted in 1985, Sir David remains to date the second of only two four-time *Desert Island Discs* castaways. A big topic of conversation on his first visit was *Zoo Quest* – a show in which he accompanied London Zoo staff to exotic locales to see them capture creatures to take home to the zoo.

• • •

Introducing his guest as 'the *Zoo Quest* man', Roy Plomley opened, not unreasonably, by enquiring whether Attenborough had visited any real-life desert islands.

'The nearest qualifier was the island of Komodo,' said Attenborough. 'It's got everything I think a desert island should have. It's got waving palm trees, white beaches, coral reefs. It's also got people ...'

'No, I'm afraid that doesn't count. It has to be completely uninhabited,' interrupted Plomley. 'How big a part does music play in your life?'

'Oh, quite large! I play a piano and guitar at home and, on these sorts of trips, I've developed a fairly strong interest in folk music: Balinese and African music, and so on.'

Attenborough confided that in choosing his discs, he had taken note of his holiday reading habits: 'I take Dostoevsky or Tolstoy, and the only things I read are some detective novels that I've cadged from somebody else on the way! So, I've decided the thing to do is not only to take serious things but one or two light ones, too.'

Prompted by Plomley, he described how he had found his way to being a television naturalist and wildlife expert.

'I wanted to have something to do with animals and, on that basis, I did a degree in zoology. Then it dawned on me that the majority of the jobs in zoology involve cutting up dead rats, and I wasn't interested in that. I was interested in the live animals in the tropics.

'I applied for a job as a television producer and was lucky enough to get it. For the first year, I produced an extraordinary variety of programmes – teaching yourself to paint, and folk songs, and short stories. I even did some ballet, once.

'But, when I had been there a year, it suddenly occurred to me: *maybe here was a chance to get back to animals.* And I managed to persuade the BBC it would be a good idea if they sent me to West Africa.'

'How many trips have you done now?' asked Plomley.

'Well, I've done three. After West Africa, we went to British Guiana in South America, and then last year we were in Indonesia: in Java and in Bali and islands eastwards.'

'Which one did you find the most exciting?'

'I think this last one, when we finally got to Komodo and found our dragon. That was one of the most exciting things I've ever done.'

Plomley opined that Attenborough's job looked particularly dangerous: 'You know, when we see you going after a ten-foot python with a sack.' Which task had been the trickiest?

'I don't know about the trickiest, but one of the least pleasant was once when we were trying to film orangutans in Borneo,' remembered Attenborough. 'We had a report that one was nearby and dashed off through the forest with our equipment and a couple of Dayak guides.

'We had to cross a small creek and the only way to get across was on a log that spanned the thing. I dashed across and held on to a rotten branch, which collapsed. I fell, and on the way bust a couple of ribs.

'The nice thing about that experience was the Dayak. Just after that, I had a dose of malaria and they could not have been nicer or more charming in nursing me in their longhouse.'

'They are no longer head-hunters?' worried Plomley.

'No, they're not, really,' Attenborough reassured him. 'They've got a few skulls hanging around on the rafters, you know, but I didn't ever think they were going to knock my head off.'

'Not a pleasant thing to have hanging over you,' reflected Plomley.

The host then turned his mind to the possibility of new animal species being discovered in the future. What were Attenborough's chances of finding 'something really big, that nobody knows about? A real monster [*from*] a sort of science-fiction lost world?'

'I don't know about science fiction,' cautioned Attenborough, 'but I'm sure there must be lots of animals in this world we know nothing about. I jolly well hope so, anyway! I'm a sucker for believing in things like the Loch Ness Monster.'

Plomley: 'Or the Abominable Snowman?'

'Yes, I don't think anybody has really accounted for the signs and the tracks which they found in the Himalayas. I don't say it's another sort of Man, but I wouldn't be surprised if it was a new animal altogether.'

'Is it one of your ambitions to go and look for it?' asked Plomley.

'Oh, I'd love to, but I think it's a task which would probably take many years. I don't think the BBC are agreeable to sending me off for three or four years to find it.'

Asked how he'd cope on the island, Attenborough admitted that he was quite good at building animal traps in the wild but, once he'd caught them, 'I wouldn't have the heart to slit their throats and eat them – I'd just let them go again!'

Despite this, Plomley concluded his guest would be a very proficient castaway. This was just as well as David Attenborough was to capsize three more times.

• • •

The first of these return visits was in March 1979, by when Attenborough had finished his stints as a senior BBC executive. It had been a thrill, he told Plomley, to commission series such as *Civilisation* and *The Ascent of Man*, but he had hated the bureaucracy and 'twenty-two meetings a week'.

Having returned to programme-making, his huge televisual project in 1979 was *Life on Earth*, about which he waxed lyrical.

'The idea [was] that we should start with the very simplest animals and very simplest forms of life and work our way through as animal life developed,' he said.

'The whole story of evolution?' asked Plomley. 'It must have taken a huge amount of preparation!'

'Yes, because each programme was a mosaic. One programme on birds, one programme on amphibians, and so on.

'Obviously, if you're going to do a programme on birds, you need birds from the North Pole and South Pole; from Africa and South America. It was no good going to Australia to film bower birds, coming back and realising you should also have filmed frogs, or coral on the Barrier Reef!

'You had to have the whole series written before you started. So, I sat down and wrote a script a fortnight for six months.'

'How long altogether for the job?' wondered Plomley.

'Three years. It was almost exactly three years ago that we seriously started full-time.'

Forty years on, *Life on Earth* remains the game-changing colossus of nature documentaries. Nobody who has seen it would ever dispute that those were three years of Attenborough's life incredibly well spent.

• • •

The by-now-knighted Sir David Attenborough fetched up on the island for a third time on 27 December 1988, this time interrogated by Sue Lawley. She quickly elicited that her guest's fascination with the natural world was initially sparked, growing up in the East Midlands, by his parents interesting him in the fossils abundant in their local area.

Lawley was also eager to discuss one of the most famous episodes from Attenborough's illustrious career presenting television nature shows: the occasion in 1979 when he got up close and personal with mountain gorillas in Rwanda.

'Your head [*was*] popping up from beneath ten tonnes of mummy gorilla,' she recalled. 'Was that ecstasy or naked fear on your face?'

'Total ecstasy!' said Attenborough. 'To be accepted by this creature, which was much closer than I thought it was going to be. She just sort-of emerged out of giant nettles and put her hand on top of my head.

'She put the other hand under my chin, turned my head and looked me in the eyes. I did think, *This [his head] could come off if she turns it a little more!*'

'And her children were attacking your feet!' recalled Lawley.

'Well, she let me go and I was looking at this huge thing smelling rather nice, rather salty. Then I felt this weight on my feet and these two little things were undoing my shoelaces. I was just ravished: it was just marvellous.'

Lawley questioned whether such experiences over the decades, and being so close to the wonders of nature, had tempted Attenborough to abandon his Darwinist philosophy and believe in God.

'People do sometimes say, "When you see extraordinary natural beauty – a hummingbird, or a bird of paradise, or something – don't you feel that this is a demonstration of proof of the existence of the Almighty?"' acknowledged Attenborough.

'But you must not *only* think of hummingbirds. You've also got to think of a parasitic worm boring into the eye of a child living on the banks of an African river, for example. Presumably, that worm, too, is a product of the Almighty?

'So I don't think that the complexity of the natural world or its beauty, or its savagery, or whether in fact it evolves through Darwinism or not, is necessarily anything to do with religious conviction about a deity ...'

• • •

Sir David Attenborough emerged from the desert island's undergrowth for a fourth time on 3 February 2012 as a particularly illustrious guest to mark the show's seventieth anniversary. The interviewer's mantle had by now passed to Kirsty Young.

Young's awe of her venerable castaway was clear from her introduction: he had, she said simply, 'seen more of the world than any person who has ever lived'. She asked Sir David if he found this fact staggering.

'Well, I suppose so,' he replied. 'But on the other hand, it's salutary to remember that perhaps the greatest naturalist who ever lived, and had more effect on our thinking than anybody, Charles Darwin, spent four years travelling and the rest of the time thinking.'

Long spells away from home are hard for any parent. Young pointed out to Attenborough that, as the father of two boys, he would have been unable to pursue his stellar career without the ceaseless support of his wife, Jane, whom he had met at Cambridge University in 1945.

'Yes, if you go away for three or four months of the year, you can't just abandon children,' agreed Attenborough. 'So she looked after the children. And spent her life doing that.'

Young: 'She was untypically accommodating? You didn't just bring back film to make TV programmes. You brought live specimens!'

'Yes, she turned out to be a brilliant carer for live animals, particularly primates. I mean, we had little bush babies, you know. We had a whole room in which they lived and bred. We had twelve births and watching them breed, and so on, was beautiful.'

'How do they mark their territory, I'm wondering?' asked Young. Her guest laughed.

'You know perfectly well that they pee on their hands and run around plonking their urine all over the place! That's why they have to have a room of their own. But Jane really looked after them – and her skills were recognised at London Zoo.

'One day they rang up and said that they had a baby gorilla, imported illegally. It was dying of colic, and indigestion, and diarrhoea, and one thing and another. [*They said:*] "What it really needs is tender loving care. Could you take it?"

'And Jane brought this little creature in and it simply wanted to hang on to her. And she made a little sling for it. So he lived permanently on her, really, and used to talk to her. And, of course, gibbon language, it's sort of eructation ... [*Attenborough illustrated his point by making a noise that sounded like a very loud burp.*] She used to answer the phone and talk and Sammy would lean over and go *BURP!* And Jane never knew whether to say, "I beg your pardon!" or "I've got a gibbon on my shoulder!" Which sounds a bit boastful ...'

Later in the programme, the host asked Attenborough to recount one of his most memorable unexpected globetrotting encounters – with indigenous tribespeople on the island of New Guinea in Australasia.

'You opened your eyes one morning not to the canopies of the forest, or even to the clear blues skies, but to seven other pairs of eyes looking down on you,' she said. 'What happened?'

'We were with a patrol, crossing one of the last patches of unexplored territory in Central New Guinea,' he replied. 'It was thought there was a tribe of people living in the middle of it. From aerial photographs, they'd seen little pinpricks of clearings, so there must be people.

'So, we walked across this great expanse of forest ... and I woke up, as you say, and saw these extraordinary people. Feathers and quills in their nostrils, and huge headdresses. And they were just staring at me.

'I started trying to find out if we'd got any common words. But, of course, you don't need words – well, you *do* need them, but it's not necessary to have words to show that you are amiably inclined.'

Young: 'Didn't you use your eyebrows to communicate with them?'

'Well, yes. If you go into a crowded room, you may see someone you know across the other side, but there is so much talk going on that you can't communicate. But, if you catch their eye, you just lift your eyebrow.

'That just says, "Here I am. I know you. You know me. How are you? I will try to catch up with you." And I thought I would try this to see if it could actually transcend race.'

'[*Another time*] I was in Fiji and I said to the camera, "I will see if I can communicate to people coming into the market." But after a bit, I came to realise that I could get myself into very serious trouble and be carted off by the police! So, we had to pack that in ...'

Approaching the end of the show, Young marvelled at the extraordinary life that Sir David Attenborough had lived to date. She wondered, at the age of eighty-five, and many years after the death of his wife, how he managed to stay moved and motivated by the world.

'I'm very lucky that I'm able to go on working,' he replied. 'I hope I'm not slowing down. I don't think I am. I'm never short of anything to do and, for this, I'm very grateful.

'I mean, quite a lot of people, at my age, certainly are liable to be sitting in a chair and saying, "What do I do with the next hour?" And I, at the moment, have got more than I can probably deal with ...'

• • •

At the age of ninety-six, Sir David Attenborough continues to film and narrate nature documentaries and remains a passionate campaigner on global environmental issues. His innate positivity and optimism for the future of the planet and its inhabitants remain intact: at the 26th United Nations Climate Change Conference (COP26) in 2021, he declared: 'In my lifetime, I've witnessed a terrible decline. In yours, you could, and *should*, witness a wonderful recovery.' You can only hope that Sir David will be able to make a record-breaking fifth visit to the desert island in 2026, on the occasion of his hundredth birthday.

DISCS CHOSEN (1957)
'Trouble in Mind'
Ottilie Patterson and the Chris Barber Jazz Band
'A piece of jazz sung by a very wonderful English singer'

Prelude in E Major from Bach's Violin Sonata No. 6
Serge Koussevitzky and the Boston Symphony Orchestra
'It's the theme tune to Animal, Vegetable, Mineral?*'*

'Stars and Stripes Forever'
Boston Promenade Orchestra
'Something really brash to remind me of crowds and ceremonies'

Schubert's Quintet in C Major
Hollywood String Quartet
'A really serious record – the equivalent of War and Peace*'*

'Maladie d'Amour'
Henri Salvador
'The first record which my children got to know'

'Haste Thee, Nymph' from Handel's *L'Allegro, il Penseroso ed il Moderato*
Glasgow Orpheus Choir

Sibelius's *Tapiola*, Symphonic Poem for Orchestra
Concertgebouw Orchestra of Amsterdam
'I would yearn to get back to snow and tundras'

'The Old Hundredth' arranged by Vaughan Williams (for the coronation of Queen Elizabeth II)
'Something to remind me of London'

LUXURY ITEM
A large, very expensive grand piano
'I promise not to live under it'

9

JOAN COLLINS

ACTOR
27 November 1961

Bob Hope and Bing Crosby's usual leading lady in *The Road to ...* films was Dorothy Lamour. When it was decided, a tad ungallantly, that she was too long in the tooth (at forty-eight) to play the role in *The Road to Hong Kong*, they turned to a young British talent: Joan Collins.

Collins was just twenty-eight when she was shipwrecked in 1961 but she was already a movie veteran. She had broken through in Britain in the early fifties, playing a teenage rebel in *I Believe in You*, starring Celia Johnson, and starring opposite Kenneth More in *Our Girl Friday* before heading to Hollywood.

Signed to a seven-year deal by Twentieth Century Fox, in 1955 she was given equal billing with Bette Davis in *The Virgin Queen*, then took a role intended for Marilyn Monroe in *The Girl in the Red Velvet Swing*. Later movies saw her billed above both Richard Burton and Jayne Mansfield.

She was truly a star on the rise, yet the headstrong Collins had recently fallen out with the huge American studio over the roles she was being given and successfully negotiated to be released from her contract. When she met Roy Plomley, she had just returned to England.

• • •

Plomley opened his chat with 'a very well-known young film actress' by asking how she felt about being marooned on a desert island.

'Terrified!' trilled Collins. 'I don't think I'd be able to make it, really. The thought of being there by myself for years and years is too spooky.'

'Have you ever experienced loneliness?'

'Yes. I've tried to get away from it as much as possible because I can't bear it. The loneliest I've ever been was when I first went to America and I was there without knowing a soul, other than businesspeople, for about three weeks.

'I was completely alone, completely cut-off, in a strange country. Terribly sad! I cried myself to sleep every night.'

Plomley: 'Are you anything of a musician?'

'Not really. I love music. The gramophone plays from dawn to dusk whenever I'm around. I love to dance. I play an occasional drum.'

'Do you? Where?'

'Well, if I find one lying around somewhere, I'll beat on it for a bit!'

After Collins had chosen her first two records, her host commented that she was originally a Londoner and from a theatrical family.

'Yes. My father's an agent, my grandfather was an agent, and my aunts were one of the first sister acts ever to be in variety.'

'And how early in life did you decide that this was the life for you?'

'Very early. About three-and-a-half, I would say.'

Collins described attending the Royal Academy of Dramatic Art, then going into repertory theatre when she was sixteen. 'I was the assistant stage manager at Maidstone Rep and I played maids and various odd characters like that.'

'Were you an efficient ASM?' asked Plomley.

'No, I was always losing the props.'

'And then?'

'And then I went back to dramatic school, and started in-between times to do a little photographic modelling for magazines. I was discovered by an agent who wanted to know if I wanted to be a film star. I said, "No – definitely not!" I thought it was terribly degrading, the whole idea.'

'You wanted to stay with the theatre?'

'Oh yes, definitely. Still, he talked me into it, and I made a test for a film which I didn't get, but I played a small part in it. And that was how it started.'

'What was the film?' enquired Plomley.

'It was called *Lady Godiva Rides Again*. About beauty-contest winners.'

'And you were one of the winners?'

'I was one of the runners-up.'

'What happened after that?'

'I did many film tests and then I played the part of a juvenile delinquent in a film, and it started me on a long career of juvenile delinquent-ing.'

'You were rather typed for a long time, weren't you?' nodded Plomley.

'Oh, yes! Years! I did nothing but wear a split skirt and platform shoes and stand in Piccadilly!'

Collins recalled signing to J. Arthur Rank and touring Britain in plays ('none of which got to see the lights of the West End'). 'Then, Warner Brothers in America wanted me to play the wicked Egyptian queen in a film called *Land of the Pharaohs*, which was being made in Rome.'

Plomley: 'A sort of *Egyptian* delinquent?'

'Yes. Except that this time I wore nice dresses. And while I was in Rome, I was approached by Twentieth Century Fox. They wanted to buy me from Rank, which was done. I was sold. And off I went to Hollywood.'

Collins explained that she had come to enjoy her time in LA making 'some films I liked and some I loathed'. *The Girl on the Red Velvet Swing* and *Seven Thieves* belonged in the former camp. A 1958 Western, *The Bravados*, fell very much into the latter.

'One of the great disasters of the age!' she declared. '*Me! On a horse!* I was roped onto a horse with Gregory Peck and ... I don't like horses. And, it's a terrible thing to say, they don't like me. Every time I went near the horse, it looked like it was going to kick me.'

'Joan, we were always reading in the papers that you'd been suspended by the studio for one reason or another,' regretted Plomley. 'Were you unhappy there?'

'I was just going from one rather dreary part to another, and I wasn't terribly happy with any of the films that I'd been in. Plus, I wanted to do more comedy and all the comedy parts were going to other people. I was ... choked.'

Collins told Plomley delightedly that she had extricated herself from Twentieth Century Fox and was now 'free for the first time in my life, practically'. She looked forward to doing more plays, radio and TV: 'I find that new vistas have opened up.'

Breaking off for a music choice, Collins chose Anthony Newley's 'I Was Never Kissed Before'. 'I like all of Mr Newley's recordings,' she added. She evidently liked rather *more* than that: two years later, he was to become the second of her five husbands.

As the lively conversation wended to a close, Plomley noted that his guest had appeared in not one but two castaway movies: *Sea Wife* and *Our Girl Friday*. Had they given her any clues how to cope on a desert island?

'Yes. Have a couple of men to help me!'

• • •

Joan Collins was to waft onto the desert island again nearly thirty years later, on 22 July 1990. Sue Lawley, a somewhat more forensic interviewer than the genteel Mr Plomley, got her guest to open up rather more on her fabulous life when she first moved to America.

'I have to admit that, going to Hollywood at that particular time, it was the last days of true glamour,' said Collins. 'Of wonderful restaurants, amazing nightclubs, glorious premieres, and a time when the press still had a certain respect for stars and celebrities.

'Within the first week I was there, I met Gene Kelly, Judy Garland, Humphrey Bogart, Frank Sinatra, Marilyn Monroe. You'd see Gary Cooper, Merle Oberon and Errol Flynn, and these people looked just as good as they did on the screen.

'Of course, I was terribly young, I was just twenty, and it was quite astonishing. I used to just sit with my mouth open in awe.'

Despite her reverence for these old Hollywood stars, Collins was not averse, fifty years on, to dishing the dirt on them. Sue Lawley asked her how she had got on with Bette Davis when they filmed *The Virgin Queen*.

'Well, Ms Davis was not a great admirer of young, attractive actresses,

I have to admit. She was quite intimidating. She's quite an ogre: one of those people who came from the school of hard knocks. She always had to fight. But I think it probably didn't make her as nice a person as she should be.'

'You didn't take too kindly to Bing Crosby, either, did you?' prompted Lawley.

'No, he's not *nearly* as nice as Bob Hope. Bob Hope is adorable and sweet and funny and the crew love him. You can always tell about an actor or actress by the crew, and far be it from me to speak ill of the dead, but the crew did *not* like Bing Crosby on *The Road to Hong Kong*.

'They all loved Bob Hope and I agreed with them. I just think that some people care about other people and some people don't, and the crew can very, very shortly tell who's nice and who isn't.'

Throughout the eighties, Collins had once again enjoyed a stratospheric public profile, on both sides of the Atlantic, due to playing the ruthless, scheming Alexis Carrington in uber-glamorous US soap *Dynasty*. It was, she told Lawley, a role she had taken to with relish.

'I had been watching *Dallas* previously,' she explained. 'And I had told my agent: "I really would quite like to be in one of those soaps. I think I could probably do something with one of those roles."

'When it came along, I thought it was a part that should be played with a certain tongue-in-cheek, rather grand, glamorous, woman-of-the-world quality. They bought me, first of all, these funny little suits. And I said, "I'm not going to wear *those*! I want furs, gloves, hats, veils ..."'

Glamour had always been central to Joan Collins's world. Sue Lawley was moved to ask her why, relatively recently, she had posed for the centre-fold of *Playboy* at the age of fifty. Was it because she was proud of how she looked?

'Yes,' agreed Collins. 'I think I was saying that, OK, perhaps not every woman of that age can do that, but it is not only a girl of twenty-three who can look good. I think there's far too much emphasis on the physical nowadays.

'By the same token, it was a sort of statement. In a way, it was saying to women: "Look, *maybe you can't look exactly like this*, but you should be able to know that you can look pretty good ..."'

• • •

At the age of eighty-nine, Joan Collins is still looking more than pretty good. Having been made a dame in 2015 and won countless acting awards, including a Golden Globe, she continues to make movie and TV appearances and tour deeply entertaining one-woman shows with titles such as *One Night with Joan, Joan Collins Unscripted* and *Joan Collins Is Unapologetic*. Do not rule out future soap superstardoms, magazine centrefolds or *Desert Island Discs* reappearances.

DISCS CHOSEN (1961)
'Come Fly with Me'
Frank Sinatra
'I love to travel – it's my favourite thing'

'Lover'
Peggy Lee
'I love everything she's done'

'Hava Nageela'
Harry Belafonte
'Terribly stirring and a very moving record'

'Serenata'
Sarah Vaughan
'I could listen to it millions of times'

'I Was Never Kissed Before'
Anthony Newley

'Mambo Inn'
René Touzet and His Orchestra
'I'd like to practise my cha-cha and mambo on the beach'

❤ **'My Ship'**
Toni Harper
'A record that always makes me cry'

'Milord'
Édith Piaf
'I think her voice is just the end'

BOOK
A large volume of all the major foreign languages of the world
'So when I was finally rescued, I'd be able to converse fluently with them'

LUXURY ITEM
A television set that runs on batteries
'I can't be cut off from the rest of the world that much'

'ISLE NEVER FORGET ...'

'I'd just come back from America to England when I first went on *Desert Island Discs* in 1961. It was an honour to be asked. There wasn't much television in those days but radio was very big – oh, what was it that Gloria Swanson said? "It's the pictures that got small!"

'They always treat you very nicely at the BBC. They give you a cup of tea and a biscuit and they talk to you like you would to the lady next door. Did Roy Plomley take me for lunch? I can't remember now, but, if he did, I'm *sure* that I adored it.

'My music choices were very different each time [*Dame Joan's choices in 1990: Sinatra, Pavarotti, two Puccini works, Vera Lynn, Elvis Presley, Cliff Richard & Sarah Brightman and Lionel Richie*]. Well, one's tastes *do* change between your twenties and your fifties. You're not the same person.

'On my first visit, I chose Anthony Newley out of loyalty. I was engaged to him. Although I *did* always admire his talent. The next time, I called Bette Davis an ogre? Did I *really*? Well, she *was*! Everyone said that, not just me! And Bob Hope *was* much nicer than Bing Crosby.

'*Desert Island Discs* is something one thinks of incredibly fondly. It's been there from one's childhood right until now. It's a quintessentially British pro-gramme, which I, being patriotic, love. Long may it go on!'

10
BOB HOPE

COMEDIAN, ACTOR
18 December 1961

The growing profile and reputation of *Desert Island Discs* was making it increasingly able to attract the biggest showbiz names not only in Britain but also from across the Atlantic. And few stars shone brighter in America's light entertainment firmament at the start of the sixties than the apparently-nicer-than-Bing-Crosby Bob Hope.

Hope was born in Eltham, south-east London, in 1903, but emigrated to the States with his family aged just four. Starting out in vaudeville in his twenties, as a comedian and dancer, he had moved through Broadway productions to dominate American cinema, radio and television.

A radio star in his early thirties, Hope was also a marquee name on US TV, where he fronted countless programmes and Christmas specials. The wisecracking star regularly hosted the Academy Awards and, by the time of his 1961 encounter with Roy Plomley, had made fifty movies.

Foremost among these were *The Road to* ... films with Crosby. Like Joan Collins, that pair were shooting *The Road to Hong Kong* in England in December 1961 when Hope made a detour to the *Desert Island Discs* studio.

• • •

The somewhat staccato opening to this episode betrayed the fact that these were still the days when Mr Plomley's castaways read their lines from his pre-prepared script.

'Cast away this week is an international star who really must have expected to be shipwrecked,' began Plomley. 'Because, through the years, he's taken the road to various places, such as Singapore and Rio, with some fairly unreliable company. It's Bob Hope!'

'Thank you, Roy!' began Hope. 'Here at Shep ...'

'You're reading my line!' a laughing Plomley pointed out. 'Here at Shepperton Studios, you're making another *Road* picture?'

'That's right. We're doing *The Road to Hong Kong*.'

The host got straight down to business: 'Now we're marooning you, all alone, on this desert island, is there any one thing you'd be glad at having got away from?'

'I think it's work,' decided Hope. 'You know, the way I've been running around and everything. That's what I'd like to get away from.'

'Do you think you're the kind of man who could endure solitude?'

'I think I could stand it for about three or four hours, then I'd start getting up into a high coconut tree and screaming.'

'What's the first record you've chosen?'

'Judy Garland's beautiful "Over the Rainbow". Of course, it's a very sentimental record with me, because Judy started on my Pepsodent show – oh, we can't say "Pepsodent"?' [The Pepsodent Show Starring Bob Hope *ran for ten years on NBC Radio in the US from 1938.*]

'On your *toothpaste* show,' corrected Plomley.

'On my *toothpaste* show, years ago when she was sixteen or seventeen. I used to hear her just kill audiences with this wonderful song.'

A man normally of famously reactionary tastes, Hope next went against type and chose Elvis Presley's 'Jailhouse Rock', calling it 'a novelty record'.

'I never thought of you as a rock and roll man?' marvelled Plomley.

'Well, I don't knock it. You never know when we're going to get our hips lubricated and walk right into that business. I figured this'd be a good record to take to the island in case I'm invaded by seagulls. I could just put this record on and clean out the island in tempo.'

Hope told Plomley that he had moved from England to Cleveland aged just four ('I was marked for export from an early age'). His host asked if there was any other theatrical talent in his family.

'I think my father did a little comedy work. I've seen his pictures: I'm sure he didn't drink *that* much. My mother was Welsh and did as much singing as the Welsh people do. She could sing it up pretty good.'

'Was the theatre your first job when you left school?'

'Oh, no, no! I worked in a butcher's shop. I sold shoes. I worked in a motor company during the war, a nightshift, trying to help a little bit, because I was too weak and small to carry a gun. We won't say *which* war – we'll just move it along, Roy ...'

'What brought you into the theatre?' wondered his host.

'Money! No, I started to sing quite a bit, then I started to dance, then I found you could make a living at it without getting up real early in the morning. Then, unluckily, I got into pictures. Now I get up *real* early in the morning.'

Plomley: 'At that time, Bing Crosby was also working in vaudeville. Did you ever meet him?'

'Yes, that's where I met Bing the first time. In 1932, we played Capitol Theatre, New York, together. We did some ad-libbing and we started working together ...'

'And you've been doing it ever since.'

'Yes. That's true.'

Plomley touched briefly on Hope's Broadway career before homing in on his move to Hollywood.

'Had you ever thought of yourself as a screen actor?'

'*I* had but *they* didn't! I made a test for MGM way back in 1931 and my nose came on the screen ten minutes ahead of the rest of my body. I found out later that the cameraman was a drinker! I was pretty mad at that whole business, until they made me a good offer and I finally went out there in '37.'

Staying with showbusiness, Hope noted that his next choice of record, Ella's Fitzgerald singing 'It's Only a Paper Moon', came with romantic strings attached.

'It was a number that my wife, Mrs Hope, was singing when I met her,' he said. 'She was working in a club in New York and this is the number she was singing. I went back too many times, to hear it, and wound up as her partner. I was hooked for life, and still am.'

A touching tale, this was somewhat at odds with Hope's reputation as a notorious womaniser. Eschewing this observation, Plomley instead asked him if it was true that he had a 'platoon' of gag writers thinking up jokes for him.

Hope confirmed that it was: 'At one time, Roy, when I was with *The Pepsodent Show*, I had thirteen writers writing for me. My show went from nothing to the number-one show in America. We stayed on top of the heap for five years.'

'With your quickfire gag routines, you must use up jokes tremendously,' said Plomley. 'How many would you use in a five-minute spot?'

'Oh, in my show, in a five-minute spot, I would use about fifty jokes.'

Asked to name his own favourite comics, Hope nominated Billy Higgins and 'a sick comic', Lenny Bruce. Plomley moved on to Hope's well-documented love for golf. Did he ever play against his pal, Bing Crosby? Who usually won?

'Well, if I can get enough shots out of him, I might steal a little of his loot, which is very hard to get without an attorney,' Hope quipped. He then chose to take one of Crosby's songs to his island: the somewhat seasonal 'White Christmas'.

'Mr B. Crosby is the father of our country!' he declared. 'In view of the fact that he's just had another child, making his seventh. But I think this record is a beautiful record. Bing's performance is almost as good as Perry Como's.'

Bob Hope rounded off his musical selections with one of his own songs: his signature tune, 'Thanks for the Memory', sung with Shirley Ross.

'It's a little selfish, but it brings back all the memories of my career,' he said. 'If I'm out there alone, I've got to have these kinds of memories. It's been a pretty tough fight, you know, all the way through, and it'll sort of unfold all these marvellous memories.

'While this is playing, it'll all kind of flash through my mind. All of the experiences in my showbusiness career, all my family, and *the whole thing*.'

• • •

Having been born at the onset of the twentieth century, Bob Hope was to make it through to the twenty-first. The all-American entertainer from south London died at his Los Angeles home on 27 July 2003. He was one hundred years old.

DISCS CHOSEN
'Over the Rainbow'
Judy Garland

'Jailhouse Rock'
Elvis Presley

♥ **'It's Only a Paper Moon'**
Ella Fitzgerald

'Smoke Gets in Your Eyes'
Andre Kostelanetz and His Orchestra
'A number that has been very involved in my career'

'Thank Heaven for Little Girls'
Maurice Chevalier
'On a desert island, it would be nice to be reminded that there are little girls ... who could grow up'

'White Christmas'
Bing Crosby

Debussy's 'Clair de Lune'
Stokowski Symphony Orchestra
'For a change of pace – it's a beautiful record'

'Thanks for the Memory'
Bob Hope and Shirley Ross

BOOK
Gone with the Wind – Margaret Mitchell

LUXURY ITEM
A little money
'I'd put some money in a bottle and ship it out with a note'

11
CILLA BLACK

SINGER, TELEVISION PRESENTER
24 August 1964

Joan Collins and Bob Hope were established stars when they waltzed onto Roy Plomley's desert island. In stark contrast, Cilla Black was very much still a wide-eyed ingénue, despite having fairly recently rocketed to overnight success.

Just two years earlier, the Liverpudlian Black had still been a teenage typist and struggling club singer, then performing under her real name of Cilla White. Friendly with the Beatles, she was introduced by John Lennon to their manager, Brian Epstein, who took her under his wing and became her manager. Chart success followed in short order.

Black's second single, a version of Dionne Warwick's 'Anyone Who Had a Heart', raced to number one in Britain in 1963, closely followed to the top of the chart by its follow-up, 'You're My World'. Roy Plomley thus met a precocious young star getting used very quickly to being famous.

• • •

After some initial chit-chat about Black's fear of spiders, which she felt could be an issue on an island where there were 'bananas, and things', and a couple of records, Plomley turned the conversation to her roots.

'You're from Liverpool, Cilla. Which part of Liverpool?'

'Scotland Road. It's very famous for its pubs because it's got one on every corner.'

'Near the river?'

'Oh, yes! I've rowed on it or been on a boat across it many a time.'

'Do you come from a big family?'

'Well, today people would say it's a big family, but I don't think it's a big family at all. I've got three brothers.'

'Did you have any particular ambition as a schoolgirl?'

'Yes, I wanted to be a film star, like every schoolgirl. Up to the age of fourteen, I really believed I was going to be the Shirley Temple of the north. It was a terrible thing to find out that I wasn't.'

After absorbing this blow, Black told Plomley, she had worked as a clerk typist in a cable-manufacturing company for four years. 'And when did you first sing in public?' he wondered.

'When I was sixteen. I used to go around with a lot of girlfriends. We'd go to all these clubs and we got friendly with the boys [*in bands*]. And one night, one member of a group came down from the stage and passed me a hand mic to sing, just for a giggle.

'He didn't know that I sang, so I said, "All right, mate, I'll show you!" I just continued from where he left off and it all happened from there. I joined another group.'

Plomley: 'Which groups did you sing with?'

'The Big Three, and a group called Kingsize Taylor and the Dominos. But I had to leave them because those groups were going to Hamburg: that was very popular at the time. My parents wouldn't let me go because I was too young.'

Plomley: 'Were you paid, or was it just for fun?'

'Well, at first it was just for fun, then I got paid very handsomely: thirty bob a night! I sang with the Beatles [*but*] I wasn't their permanent girl singer. I did a lot of singing with the Beatles, Gerry and the Pacemakers, the Four-most and many of the Liverpool groups who are famous today.'

'A girl singer is quite a rarity with a Merseyside group?' asked Plomley.

'Yes, it was a novelty, really. I was very popular with all the girl fans of the groups, because they used to come up to me and ask me little secrets, like, "What's so-and-so like?"'

Plomley: 'What was the big thing that happened that enabled you to stop being a typist and become a full-time singer?'

'One night, I went to the Blue Angel club in Liverpool. A modern jazz group asked me to get up and sing. When I came back to my seat, who should be there but Brian Epstein! He had already got the Beatles on the map by this time, and he said, "Cilla, I have an idea ..." From then on, I knew everything was going to happen.'

'He put you under contract,' clarified Plomley. 'Cilla Black isn't your real name, is it? Did he change it?'

'No, no, it was a misprint in a newspaper! It was a very bad mistake, really, because I'd have liked to have been Cilla White. But it couldn't be helped. Now everyone knew me as Cilla Black and that was that.'

'Was your first record [*'Love of the Loved', written for her by John Lennon and Paul McCartney*] a success?'

'It was a big success to me, but not to other people! It went to number twenty-five in the charts and then dropped.'

'But big enough for you to be able to go out on the road?'

'Yes, I did my first tour with Gerry and the Pacemakers. I widened my geography knowledge. I'd thought that Carlisle was in the Chester area and I found out it was on the way to Scotland!'

Cilla then talked about her two 1964 number ones: 'Anyone Who Had a Heart' and 'You're My World'. At the time of this *Desert Island Discs* appearance, she was performing at the London Palladium.

'Were you schooled intensively for this great big event?' asked Plomley.

'No, I taught myself, really. I watched really professional artists work. I went to the Palladium before I played it. I was sitting in the audience and I was terrified because I thought, *If I've got to go on stage here, I'm just going to die.*'

Black selected Frankie Vaughan's 'Priscilla'. Plomley lightly teased her by asking if it was dedicated to her.

'At the time [*when she was fourteen*] I thought it was, because I was crackers on Frankie Vaughan! I was in his fan club and everything. I'd like to take this record on the island because, at the moment, I'm appearing with Frankie Vaughan. You've no idea what a thrill it is to be actually appearing with one of your idols ...'

Asked by Roy Plomley, at the end of the broadcast, which record she would take to the island if only permitted one, Black chose her own.

'I suppose this sounds very big-headed,' she conceded. 'But my record on the island would be a treasure to me. Because I've got eight records, by seven marvellous artists, and then *I, myself, a mere Cilla Black*, is on record as well. And that's a thrill to me.'

• • •

An older, and far worldlier, Cilla Black returned to the island to meet Sue Lawley in October 1988. At this point, her singing had largely taken a back-seat to her second career as a presenter of hugely popular, and populist, TV shows such as *Blind Date* and *Surprise Surprise*.

On her second visit, Cilla spoke freely of her nose job in her twenties, her sorrow at the death of a two-hours-old daughter in her thirties, and her wish both to have another number-one single ('Please write one for me, Paul McCartney!') and ... to be regarded as a sex symbol.

'When I enter a room, I would love all men to fall at my feet, rather than slap me on the back and say, "Hi, Cilla!" or 'Surprise surprise!'" she confessed. 'I admire sex symbols like Joan Collins, I really do.'

'Maybe you can't be a sex symbol if you've got a sense of humour?' wondered Lawley.

'Oh, I think you can!' Black disagreed. 'I know Joan – she's a Gemini, the same as me, and a very funny lady. Look at Marilyn Monroe! Do me a favour! She had the greatest sense of humour and it hit you right across that screen.'

Lawley moved on to her guest's burgeoning television career and gently teased her that *Blind Date* had not yet match-made so successfully that any contestants had ended up getting married.

'I don't think people actually come on *Blind Date* looking for a wife or a husband,' explained Black. 'I think they want fun, and the thrill of being on the telly, and maybe going somewhere special on the date if they're picked.'

Lawley: 'Do you ever wonder about encouraging people to make fools of themselves?'

'Oh, I don't like that! It's a strange thing: a lot of people on *Blind Date* remind me – I hate to say this – of myself, when I was their age. They're dead flash. I mean, they've got some front, to go on that show!

'They've never been on a television show before, they don't see the studio until the actual day, they have very little rehearsal, then they're sent away to the dressing room and at seven-thirty that red light goes on and they're on. So they've got to be quite flash, very like myself.'

'Did you ever go on a blind date?' wondered Lawley.

'I didn't have the bottle, no! I remember one day, when I was working in the office just around the Cavern as a clerk typist, I had to relieve Jean, the telephonist, in her lunch hour. I had to man the phones.

'This fellow got chatting to me and, yes, we made a date. But I bottled out because I thought, you know, *Gosh, I could turn up and he might look like Quasimodo!* And I wasn't ready for that.'

Lawley turned the conversation to the love of Cilla Black's life: her husband, Bobby, whom she had met aged just sixteen while working as a waitress in a Liverpool bar. Having married in 1969, they had raised three children, and Bobby was also his wife's manager.

'Bobby is hovering over this programme,' teased Lawley. 'You mention him every three minutes.'

'I know, yes! It was [*initially*] very much a teenaged kind of relationship. It was like everything you see in those Frankie Avalon films and it was really nice. I always think about Bobby ...'

Lawley: 'He's your manager, he's your mentor, he's your friend, he's your husband, he's your lover, he's your everything' (the presenter arguably missed a trick by not concluding 'he's your world').

'Yes – he's a right clever dick, actually!' laughed Cilla Black.

• • •

Cilla Black never did have a Paul McCartney-penned number-one comeback single, and she lost her beloved Bobby to cancer in 1999. However, she was to present both *Surprise Surprise* and *Blind Date* into the new millennium and remained a constant TV presence thereafter. Black died in August 2015, at the age of seventy-two, after a fall in her home in Spain. A statue of her now stands outside the Cavern Club in Liverpool, where it all began.

DISCS CHOSEN (1964)
'My Yiddishe Momme'
Sophie Tucker
'I always remember my mother singing it'

'America' from *West Side Story*
Cast recording
'It's so real and so truthful'

'Love Me Do'
The Beatles
'I really owe my success to Brian Epstein and the Beatles. Without the Beatles, I don't think Cilla Black would have existed'

❤ **'Anyone Who Had a Heart'**
Cilla Black
'I'd like to remember, on my island, the very big thrill of getting to number one'

'Moon River'
Henry Mancini and His Orchestra

'Priscilla'
Frankie Vaughan

Bach's Fugue in D Minor
The Swingle Singers
'I never realised it was classical music'

'September in the Rain'
Dinah Washington
'It wasn't until she died that I thought, Oh my goodness, I really admired her*'*

BOOK
Alice in Wonderland – Lewis Carroll
'It's the most fantastic story and I could go on reading it and reading it'

LUXURY ITEM
The *Mona Lisa*
'Is she smiling because she's happy, or is she smiling that sort of sad, pathetic smile, or is it a cunning sort of smile?'

12
TALLULAH BANKHEAD

ACTOR, ACTIVIST
14 December 1964

Every now and then, genuine A-list American theatrical royalty visited the BBC's desert island. This was never truer than in December 1964, when the legendary Tallulah Bankhead washed up on its shores for a somewhat memorable encounter.

Or maybe we should say she *sloshed* up. Bankhead was both a hugely gifted stage actor and a noted social activist, lobbying passionately for the US civil rights movement. In her private life, however, alcoholism and drug addiction had taken an increasingly heavy toll.

Roy Plomley was later to admit that, as he greeted his guest outside the BBC, 'I was shocked to see how old and ill she looked as I helped her out of a taxi. She had come from her hotel in a mink coat slung over a pair of lounging pyjamas, and leaned heavily on my arm as I supported her to the lift.'

Bankhead seemed to have arrived at the studio somewhat ... *refreshed*. In addition, her emphysema, caused by smoking a reputed four packs of cigarettes a day, meant that she coughed her way through the show, breathed heavily and had some difficulty speaking.

The *Desert Island Discs* producers salvaged a broadcast-able show from the encounter and yet the following entry, drawn from the original transcript of the studio interview, demonstrates how hard Roy Plomley and his team had to work to do so. Ms Bankhead was rambling and incoherent throughout and, as well as frequently asking the host to repeat his questions, was in the unfortunate habit of calling him 'Ron'.

Roy Plomley's patience and understanding saved the day, yet while this transcript of his conversation with the illustrious Tallulah Bankhead at times makes for comic reading, it also has an inescapable underlying note of sickness, sadness and tragedy.

• • •

'On one of her rare visits to London is Tallulah Bankhead!' opened Plomley. 'Now, Miss Bankhead, the first question I want to ...'

'Ah, ah, before we went on air, we had an agreement that you would call me Tallulah!' interrupted Bankhead. 'Otherwise, you don't like me.'

'I'm sorry, I *do* like you, Tallulah,' the host assured her. 'My first question: could you endure loneliness for a long time?'

The producers gallantly cut from the broadcast his baffled-sounding guest asking him to repeat the question: 'Could I *what*, darling?'

'Could you endure loneliness?'

'Well, if I could have so many more records, and so many more books, and food and drink from time to time... but no, I don't think I could, because I love bridge and poker games too much...'

'No poker games, no,' regretted Plomley. 'As some slight consolation, what would you be happiest to have got away from?'

'I haven't thought of such a thing!' she exclaimed. 'Oh, I know. Mice!' A rattling smoker's cackle followed. 'Mice!'

Plomley related that Bankhead was born in the American South. The *Desert Island Discs* listeners heard her concur: 'I was born in Hunsford, Alabama.' However, the answer she gave in the studio was rather more spectacularly discursive.

'I was born in Huntsville, Alabama, where, on my birthday, you know the trouble we had after Sputnik ... the first, er, explorer went up and I went down as a guest of the government to open Bankhead Halls myself and met Doctor von Brunn, and the president was there. I wouldn't get on the platform with him although I worshipped him, and my fingers were practically empty ...'

Plomley wisely shifted to a fresh conversational tack. 'What inspired you to become an actress?' he asked, again being obliged to repeat the question.

'Well, *inspired* is hardly the right word. I am so lazy I should never have gone on the stage. But I can't make a living any other way.'

'Did you see a lot of theatre when you were a child?'

'No, because I lived in a small town' was Bankhead's answer on air. Her un-broadcast reply in the studio was, again, somewhat more freeform.

'My family wasn't... I didn't see many things ... we would go to the State Fair, little fairs that come to town. My sister would get me in this Ferris wheel and, at the top, would start rocking it ... and my, not claustrophobia, agoraphobia ... but, no, I didn't see many plays...'

Plomley coaxed out of Bankhead the story that her first break came at the age of fifteen, when she sent a photo to a competition in *Picture Play* magazine. She won the prize of a trip to New York and a minor part in a movie.

However, the host's subsequent attempts to steer Bankhead through the highlights of her life and career were largely met with a welter of slurred, unhelpful non-sequiturs. He reminded her of moving to London in 1923, aged twenty-one, to star in West End plays.

'The impact you made was roughly akin to the impact the Beatles made last year!' he marvelled. 'You had girls queuing up to mob you outside the theatre ...'

'Yes, I know, darling! But I think they annoyed people, because they were screaming, you know, "Tallulah – you're wonderful!" before I had even done anything ...'

'You were in London for eight years. How many plays did you do during that time?'

Bankhead appeared stymied by this question. 'Oh! I did *The Green Hat* with Michael Arlen. *Her Cardboard Lover* with Leslie Howard ... er ...'

'Noël Coward's *Fallen Angel*?' prompted Plomley.

'*Fallen Angel*, of course, and, er ...'

'*The Gold Diggers*?'

'Yes. You *know* these, so why ask me?' she chided. 'I don't remember the things I've done ... I've done so many.'

While primarily a stage actor, Bankhead spent two years in Hollywood in the early 1930s, making half-a-dozen movies including *The Devil and the Deep* with Charles Laughton. Plomley wondered if she had enjoyed this experience.

'No.'

'You didn't like the movies?'

'No. I cannot stand semi-tropical weather!' came the puzzling reply.

'So, you said goodbye to Hollywood,' said Plomley, prudently abandoning that line of questioning, 'and went and tackled the Broadway theatre. How did you do?'

The *Desert Island Discs* listeners were spared Bankhead's answer: 'Well, I just went back because they wanted to keep me on there. But I just couldn't take the heat... nothing was ever alive... flowers not ever quite fresh and they were never quite dead, you know...'

Plomley gallantly reminded his guest that she had enjoyed a great deal of success on Broadway in the early forties, including picking up many critics' awards. 'I wish I knew as much about my career as *you* do,' she sighed, clearly humorously aware of her glaring memory lapses.

'Tallulah, in your autobiography, you wrote that you hated acting,' noted Plomley. 'Is this true?'

'Well, I shouldn't say that ... I like ... I don't like crowds but I love them in the theatre, you know. No, I'm lazy, darling, you know, I don't like doing anything. I'm the type ... you know, I never stand up if I can sit down, I never sit down if I can lie down, you know ...'

'What is the next job when you get home?' asked Plomley. 'How about coming back here to do a play?'

After once again requiring her put-upon host to repeat the question, Bankhead proved distinctly un-tempted by his proposition.

'Well, darling, I don't want to be vulgar or sordid but I couldn't afford to do a play here, with my upkeep!' she declared. 'You see, you poor British ... you lose so much with exchange where we gain ... I'd be losing money.'

'Have you a big ambition left professionally? A part you'd like to play?'

'No. Just to retire.'

After Bankhead had nodded towards her activist, anti-racist roots by selecting Billie Holiday's 'Strange Fruit', Plomley asked if she would be able to look after herself on a desert island. Her reply was vehement.

'I couldn't! I can't even put a key in a door, darling. I can't do a thing for myself.'

If she found a raft, would she try to escape or sit it out on the island?

'I'd sit anything out… I could just float… I had a swimming pool once like an Olympic pool, but I don't think I ever got to the end of it… I'm too lazy to try to swim.'

'You'd have a raft,' persisted Plomley.

'Oh, I'd have a raft? But I wouldn't know how to work it. I can't even row a boat. I mean, how can I? I don't … I've no … I could just float away …'

'I think we'd better stick to music,' resolved Plomley. At the end of a decidedly taxing interview, he enquired of his guest which record she would take to the island if she were only permitted to choose one. This question was not to Ms Bankhead's liking.

'I would take all eight, and a thousand more, and that's all you're going to get out of me about that!' she scolded him. 'How can I pick, out of these divine people, my favourite?

'I had a gardener once, and I asked him, "What is your favourite flower, Louis?" He said, "I don't have any favourites. If I had a favourite, the others wouldn't come up for me!"'

The producers cut from the broadcast Plomley's wry reply of 'No comment!' It seems reasonable to speculate that, by now, even this legendarily courteous interviewer was a man very near the end of his tether.

The interview ended as it had begun. Nearly sixty years on, yellowing programme notes show that Plomley bade thank you and farewell to Tallulah Bankhead, only for her to tick him off again: 'Thank you *Tallulah*, you should say!'

Plomley humoured her by doing so on a retake. Presumably to preserve their erratic guest's dignity, the producers did not air her reply.

'Well, thank you, Ron, you have been a darling!' Tallulah Bankhead slurred. 'And bless you all, dear listeners!'

'You've called me Ron again,' sighed Plomley. 'Let's do it again…'

• • •

She was one of the greatest acting talents of her generation, yet her continued heavy drinking, smoking, drug abuse and addiction to sleeping pills meant that Tallulah Bankhead's health soon declined to the point that she was no longer able to work. Four years after washing up on the desert island, this gifted yet tragic soul died in New York from double pneumonia at the age of sixty-six.

DISCS CHOSEN
'On the Sunny Side of the Street'
Louis Armstrong
'Whenever I come into a nightclub where he is playing, he stops whatever he is playing and plays this song for me'

'Vesti la giubba' from Leoncavallo's *Pagliacci*
Enrico Caruso
'He has that sob without losing a pure note'

'My Funny Valentine'
Frank Sinatra

'September Song'
Walter Huston

'Strange Fruit'
Billie Holiday
'A great negro singer ... about a lynching, really, pretty frightening!'

'Love for Sale'
Ella Fitzgerald
'Anything of Ella Fitzgerald is OK with me'

'Liebestod' from Wagner's *Tristan and Isolde*
Kirsten Flagstad
'The greatest voice of that type in the world'

'The Lord's Prayer'
Perry Como and the male voices of the Robert Shaw Chorale
'I think it's very beautiful'

BOOK
The Human Situation – William Macneile Dixon
'I have it in front of me here and I certainly haven't got the time to read it!'

LUXURY ITEM
Painting of herself by Augustus John
'[A friend] said to me, "Tallulah, I always knew you had a soul, but it took Augustus John to let the world know it."'

13

ERIC MORECAMBE
AND ERNIE WISE

COMEDY DOUBLE ACT
29 August 1966

Tallulah Bankhead's sojourn on Roy Plomley's desert island was marked by its unintentional comedy. Thankfully, when Eric Morecambe and Ernie Wise dropped in two years later, the humour was entirely deliberate.

The wisecracking comedy duo were not yet the national treasures that they were to become in Britain throughout the seventies and early eighties. Nevertheless, by 1966 they already had their own ITV comedy show, *Two of a Kind*, and had made two feature films.

Roy Plomley had by now dropped the practice of writing the scripts for his guests, but even if it still survived, it would have stood no chance against Eric Morecambe's non-stop ad-libbing. The episode was a classic of the kind of rapid-fire repartee that the comic pair had made their hallmark.

And who would want it any other way?

• • •

Plomley opened the show, as was his wont, by asking his two castaways what they would be keenest to get away from on the island.

Eric: 'Income tax.'
Ernie: 'The noise and bustle. I'd like to go somewhere very quiet.'
Eric: 'So he can count his money.'

The duo were allowed to choose four records each. Plomley enquired whether they had similar musical tastes or would be forced to play their selections on opposite sides of the island.

Ernie: 'No, I think I like some of the music that Eric likes.'
Eric: 'But I don't like any of the four that he's chosen.'

Having won a coin toss to go first, Eric nominated Count Basie's 'The Kid from Red Bank'. His host asked him why.

Eric: 'I feel, getting up in the morning, I'd need something to cheer me up, and this would cheer me up.'

Ernie: 'It would depress me.'

Eric: 'Well, get up before me, then!'

'Eric, are you anything of a musician?' asked Plomley, as Basie's strains faded away.

Eric: 'I was taught to play the piano, clarinet, trumpet, the euphonium, the trombone and the piano accordion. And I can't play a note.'

Ernie: 'I tinkle with the piano.'

Eric: 'He can't reach the notes, though. That's his trouble.'

After Ernie had chosen his first tune, Dave Brubeck's 'Summer Song', Plomley attempted to fill in some biographical detail on the duo: 'Eric, where were you born?'

Eric: 'In Morecambe.'

Plomley: 'So one may guess that Morecambe isn't your real name?'

Eric: 'No, Blackpool's my real name. But I never tell anyone.'

Eric took a short break from the one-liners to explain that he had taken dancing lessons as a boy before joining a touring theatrical troupe in 1940 when he was thirteen. Plomley asked what his act was like.

Eric: 'Terrible.'

Ernie had joined the same revue shortly afterwards and the pair had quickly decided to become a double act ('on a train between Coventry and Birmingham,' recalled Ernie). They now had to settle on a name.

Plomley: 'Did you call yourselves Morecambe and Wise straightaway?'

Eric: 'No. I was only kidding about Blackpool. My real name is Bartholomew.'

Plomley: 'So it was Bartholomew and Wise?'

Eric: 'Bartholomew and Wiseman [*Wise's real surname*]. But it looked too big on the bill, so we cut it down – Morecambe and Wise.'

The pair recounted how they had tried to get into variety when they were sixteen but found it difficult. The war interceded: Ernie joined the Royal Navy and Eric became a Bevin Boy and went down the mines.

Once peace had broken out and they resumed their career, explained Eric, they joined a novel venture: a travelling variety show under canvas named Lord John Sanger's Circus.

Eric: 'It was a new idea. It wasn't a round tent – it was square, with a stage at one end. Many was the time when we put the tent up, and put all the chairs in, and not a soul arrived. You just had to take it all down again.'

'Heart-breaking!' sympathised Plomley.

Having run away from this ill-fated circus, the pair continued to work in variety theatre but, said Ernie, always found it difficult to get work in London. Or in the south as a whole, added Eric.

Ernie: 'It was always "No" to a northern comic.'

Plomley suggested that this prejudice was now being broken down.

Eric: 'I'm very glad to say.'
Ernie: 'People like Ken Dodd have done that. And ourselves, of course.'
Plomley: 'Was there any particular opportunity that got you out of the rut?'
Eric: 'Television, I'd say.'
Ernie: 'Yes. We did a television series for the BBC [*Running Wild*, 1954]. Although it wasn't a success – we got slammed, absolutely – it brought us to the eye of the public, and ...'
Eric: '... they didn't like us.'

After another break for music, the pair discussed their current ITV show and having done a little American TV with Ed Sullivan. 'You must use a tremendous amount of material,' said Plomley. 'Who writes it for you?'

Eric: 'Dick Hills and Sid Green since 1961.'
Plomley: 'Before that, did you write it all yourselves?'
Eric: 'Yes, that's why we never got anywhere.'
Plomley: 'Do either of you want to play *Hamlet*? Do straight acting?'
Ernie: 'No.'
Eric: 'I've seen him doing it, once. It makes you laugh.'

Eric chose 'Yesterday' by the Beatles before Plomley commented that his guests were a very successful work partnership. Did they, he asked, also socialise together?

Eric: 'No, not a lot.'
Plomley: 'Do you live near each other?'
Eric: 'No, I live in Harpenden ... where do you live?'
Ernie: 'Peterborough.'
Eric: 'Do you really? How nice!'

As the broadcast began to head towards its close, Plomley pulled out a reliable interview chestnut. How would they build a hut on the island?

Eric: 'I'd be the foreman. Ernie would build the hut.'

Ernie: 'Yes, I'd build the hut and I could do the cooking. I'd start a fire by taking Eric's glasses and holding them in the sun.'

Plomley: 'Ernie, you've been in the Merchant Navy. Could you build a boat?'

Ernie: 'I think I could build a raft, yes. I'd pull the trees down and tie them together.'

Eric: 'You must have very strong hands!'

Ernie: 'But where could we go?'

Eric: 'Around the island.'

Plomley: 'Very pleasant. How's your navigation?'

Eric: 'It's fine if he keeps to the left.'

Roy Plomley wrapped up the pleasantries by thanking Eric Morecambe and Ernie Wise for letting people hear their *Desert Island Discs*.

Eric: 'It's a pleasure, believe me. If you're ever on the island, come and listen to them.'

Plomley: 'I will, indeed. Goodbye, everyone.'

[Pause]

Eric: 'What a charming man!'

Ernie: 'He *was* charming, wasn't he?'

• • •

Morecambe and Wise were to bestride the BBC's seventies and early eighties TV schedules like light-entertainment colossi. Their self-titled comedy shows routinely topped viewing charts, with some Christmas specials attracting more than 20 million viewers.

Eric Morecambe died on stage in Tewkesbury, Gloucestershire, in May 1984, shortly after making his sixth curtain call for an appreciative audience. Ernie Wise died of heart failure in March 1999. Both were awarded posthumous BAFTA lifetime achievement awards in 1999.

DISCS CHOSEN

Eric Morecambe:

'The Kid from Red Bank'

Count Basie Orchestra

'My Future Just Passed'

Carmen McRae

'It's a lovely song and she sings it beautifully'

'Yesterday'
The Beatles
'They knock me out! I think they're fabulous'

❤ **'I Wish You Love'**
Jack Jones
'Because it would remind me of my wife'

Ernie Wise:
'Summer Song'
Dave Brubeck Quartet
'I'm very fond of the piano'

'Begin the Beguine'
Artie Shaw and His Orchestra

❤ **'Pennsylvania Six-Five Thousand'**
Glenn Miller and His Orchestra
Ernie: 'It's the first record I ever bought'
Eric: 'I'm sure he's got a girl at that number'

'Mister Snow'
Barbara Ruick

BOOK
Eric: *Encyclopædia Britannica*
'With all the pictures. Ernie can read me to sleep with it at nights'
Ernie: *A History of the English-Speaking Peoples* – Winston Churchill

LUXURY ITEM
Eric: A deckchair
Ernie: 'One of those little machines that go "Ting!", so I can charge him sixpence every time he sits in the deckchair.'

14
BARBARA CARTLAND

NOVELIST, CAMPAIGNER
11 July 1970

From the outset, *Desert Island Discs* had an admirably open-minded booking policy. It regularly hosted composers, classical musicians and Shakespearean thespians, yet was equally welcoming to emissaries from what might politely be called more lowbrow culture.

And no British novelist was more populist than Barbara Cartland. An indefatigable author of Mills & Boon-style romantic fiction and love stories, she had penned no less than 122 such potboilers when she wafted on to Roy Plomley's island, aged sixty-nine, in 1970.

In her trademark pink chiffon, blonde wig and dramatic make-up, Ms Cartland was famously, and fabulously, as melodramatic in person as were her books. Had she concocted herself as a fictional character, she would certainly have been way too far-fetched to believe.

As a castaway, though, she was tremendous fun.

• • •

After their opening exchanges, Plomley noted that Cartland's general public image was of success and wealth. 'Were you brought up to the life of a rich young woman?'

'No, no!' stressed Cartland. 'My grandfather, who was a very important financier, went bust in 1902. My mother and father were left with very little money and then my father was killed in 1918, in Flanders.

'My mother said to me, "You must get a job!" Well, everybody who'd been in the war was unemployed. They were wandering the streets, playing instruments, trying to get jobs. In those days, *we ladies didn't work*! But I wrote a book and it was a huge success.'

'And you wrote a play very early?' prompted Plomley.

'I wrote two rather bad plays in my life.'

Plomley: 'You were, in fact, one of the bright young people?'

'We were all pretty gay! I don't think anybody today realises the gaiety of the twenties, and all the fun we had. The men were so grateful to be alive, having come from the trenches, and we were all so young, and it was all so new and exciting.

'We'd come out of a schoolroom where you never saw a man, weren't allowed to go dancing – weren't allowed to do *anything*! And, suddenly, you were thrown into a wonderful world where you could enjoy yourself.'

Plomley: 'Yes. You kept a record of the number of marriage proposals which you refused?'

'Forty-nine,' his guest confirmed.

Cartland talked breezily of her early years as a socialite and newspaper columnist, side careers designing greetings cards and running a hat shop, and travelling the world with her two sons. Then Plomley turned the chat to her romantic fiction.

'Why do you think there is a continuing market for the light, escapist novel?' he wondered.

'Well, in the last year, I sold a million-and-a-half paperbacks all over the world. I was talking the other day to my agent and he was saying that I have sold *enormously* in the Middle East. Now, I think that's because the Middle East has always appreciated romance.

'They like chaste, romantic women. They like women who are women, and the man runs after them – *not* them running after the man! And I've always written about very tender heroines because I think it's more romantic to be pure.

'I've had rather gay, dashing heroes. I think that women, particularly, are sick to death of kitchen-sink [*drama*] and the frightful promiscuous society where everybody's naked, rolling around on beds! I don't think they want that. They want everything veiled, and beautiful, and mystic, and going back to being a feminine woman.'

'Have you never wanted to write a *serious* novel?' asked Plomley, a tad ill-advisedly.

'Oh, I'm not going to allow you *that*!' scolded Cartland. 'A romantic novel isn't a serious novel? *Of course* it is! As a matter of fact, I *have* written what you'd call a serious novel: *Sleeping Swords*. It's the only novel that's ever been accepted by the House of Commons library.'

Plomley: 'Are you a disciplined writer? Do you write for so many hours a day?'

'Yes. [*Novelist*] Ian Hay taught me that many years ago. He said, "Never wait for the muse – it never turns up! If you're going to write, get down and write!"'

'How *do* you write? By hand? Typewriter?'

'Oh, no! I dictate my novels to a secretary. I tell a lovely, lovely story. I tell it to myself beforehand and then a secretary takes it down. I sit after lunch for two hours and I've done six thousand words.'

'That is pretty good going!' admired Plomley.

'Yes, frightfully quick. When I was young, I used to do ten thousand words every day because I had to have money. *That* was very hard work.'

Despite her frivolous image, Cartland was a doughty campaigner with, as Plomley noted, 'a great social conscience'. Her fourth record, 'I'm in Love', was self-written and sung by her daughter, Raine (then known as Mrs Gerald Legge but later to remarry and, famously, become Princess Diana's stepmother).

'We wrote it when we wanted to make some money for one of my campaigns, which was for old people,' explained Cartland. 'Out of the proceeds, we bought five buses, which we gave to the local authorities for old people to go on outings.'

Not all of her missions were so universally popular. She recounted how she had been horrified to learn that Gipsy children did not go to school, and had started a campaign to establish Gipsy camps so that they could be educated in local schools.

'For three years, people really spat at me!' she told Plomley. 'They were so rude, and said that I was encouraging Gipsies [*and that*] they were awful people.

'We had this terrible, terrible, terrible battle, and suddenly the councils realised we were on the right thing. The minister of housing said that local authorities had to provide camps for the local Gipsies, on top of which we managed to get our own camps started.

'I have a camp called Barbaraville, you'll be surprised to hear!' Cartland added, triumphantly. '[*It was called that*] by the Gipsies themselves!'

Prompted by Plomley, the novelist also discussed in depth her further campaigns against the addition of fluoride to water and as president of the National Association for Health: 'We're against chemicals ... we are trying to get food with no chemicals in it into the health food shops.'

After choosing the standard 'Keep Young and Beautiful', Cartland divulged that she would transfer her quest for natural food onto her desert island.

'I should keep myself extremely well by finding some wild honey,' she resolved. 'You can live on honey. It's a wholefood with all the values and vitamins and minerals you need. Not only would you look very beautiful but you'd be beautifully slim, because honey makes you thin.

'So I should come back – if I ever got back – looking very elegant! I'd certainly try to keep myself looking as beautiful as possible, in case a lovely ship came along with a beautiful sailor.'

Barbara Cartland rounded off a thoroughly entertaining half an hour by using her final disc choice, Harry Secombe's 'If I Ruled the World', as a springboard to share her philosophy on life. It was not a worldview with which Germaine Greer, say, would have been greatly enamoured.

'I'd like to have something to show what I would do if I got the chance of being – no, not prime minister of England, *because I don't think women would be very good at that*,' she declared. 'But I'd like women to influence the men more than they are at the moment.

'The world has always been ruled, from the pillow, by women – the petticoat government behind the government. I think women today have ceased to be feminine: they're too busy trying to be pseudo-men and to have equality, which is ridiculous!

'You can always rule things *far* better by being a superior and very, very elusive and attractive sex. I think women bring happiness. Women are the flowers in life and that's what they should aim at: to leave the world a lovelier place because they've been in it.'

• • •

It is believed that at least 750 million copies of Barbara Cartland's novels have been sold worldwide. And there may even have been something in her preference for a life of unbridled romance and wild honey: the novelist died peacefully in her sleep, in May 2000, aged ninety-eight.

DISCS CHOSEN
❤ **'April in Paris'**
Frank Sinatra
'My husband and I had our honeymoon in Paris, and every year – except in wartime – we went back and had another honeymoon'

'Say a Prayer for Me Tonight'
Leslie Caron
'For my mother – a wonderful person. Whenever we're in trouble, we ring her and say, "Mummy, will you pray for us?"'

'40 Years On' (Harrow School song)
West End cast of *40 Years On*
'For eight years, I used to go to Harrow every weekend to see my sons'

'I'm in Love'
Mrs Gerald Legge

'Climb Every Mountain'
Sammy Davis Jr
'It typifies what one has to go through to get something one really wants in the world'

'Keep Young and Beautiful'
Roy Fox and His Orchestra

'If You Are but a Dream'
Frank Sinatra
'I hope all the women listening feel really feminine when they listen to this'

'If I Ruled the World'
Harry Secombe

BOOK

The Knave of Hearts – Louise Saunders (a pseudonym for, er, Barbara Cartland)

LUXURY ITEM

Make-up
'Make-up is tremendously psychologically important to women'

15
JUDI DENCH

ACTOR
17 June 1972

One of Britain's first ladies of stage and cinema, Dame Judi Dench has, to date, made three appearances on *Desert Island Discs*. Her first came in 1972 when, at the age of thirty-seven, she was already possessed of a formidable reputation and a hugely impressive thespian CV.

Dench recalled to Roy Plomley her remarkable big break when she was selected to play Ophelia in an Old Vic production of *Hamlet* while still a mere stripling of a drama student. The awed reviews she received for this extraordinarily high-profile 1957 debut had launched her into the acting stratosphere.

Dame Judi's star had risen inexorably higher by the time she returned to the island to encounter Sue Lawley in 1988, and she had been at the top of her game for nigh on sixty years when she met Kirsty Young in 2015. Yet even the mightiest of mortals can be prone to self-doubt and lapses in confidence.

Dench lost faith in her list of music and changed her choices constantly during her last visit to the island. 'I was a nightmare!' she tells us now, awarding herself a rare bad review. 'When I heard the show broadcast, I sent [Kirsty] a note: "Silk purse out of sow's ear!"'

An old-school trouper, Dame Judi nevertheless carried off all three of her performances ... and there were no such dramatic meltdowns when she sat down on the shore with Roy Plomley in 1972.

• • •

After his guest's first two musical choices, Plomley ascertained that she had been born in York, where she had attended boarding school, and had an older brother, Geoffrey, who went to drama school. Had acting always been her ambition?

'No. I trained after school to be a theatre designer. I never quite know why I changed, but I think I caught the fever and enthusiasm of acting from my brother.'

Dench described attending the Central School of Speech and Drama in London, where she received an extraordinary career break.

'We were doing audition speeches in our final year at Central, at the Criterion Theatre. There was no audience, just a few people invited, and a representative from the [*Old*] Vic [*Company*] was there. A few days later, our director of drama said the Vic wanted to see me.

'I went up to see [*Vic director*] Michael Benthall. I thought it was time to [*audition for*] walk-on [*parts*] and got wildly excited. Then he said, "Look, Judi, will you come back tomorrow and do a bit of Ophelia?" And I still didn't know they were going to do *Hamlet*.

'I mean, it's like a dream ... I didn't even consider it ... and at the end of it, he said, "I'm going to take an enormous risk. I'm going to ask you to play Ophelia. If, after two weeks, we think it's not working out, you must stand down and we'll recast it."

'I remember crying at that moment. He also asked me not to tell anyone. So, I didn't, for months. I don't know how the strain didn't kill me!'

Dench's high-profile 1957 debut in the Old Vic's *Hamlet* was deemed a huge triumph and led to other major roles. Plomley sped her through them: *Romeo and Juliet*, *She Stoops to Conquer*, *The Importance of Being Earnest*, plus tours of Europe, the US and Canada.

'Well, this was a wonderful beginning, wasn't it?' the host twinkled, before detailing Dench's move in 1961 from the Old Vic to the Royal Shakespeare Company: 'So now you were working for the opposition?'

'I suppose I was,' Dench laughed. 'It worried me a lot at the time!'

The interview continued in this affable vein as Plomley turned his attention to a very unexpected career left turn for his guest: playing the lead role of Sally Bowles in West End musical *Cabaret* in 1968.

'Actually, when I was asked, I thought it was a joke,' she confessed. 'I said to my agent, "This has to be somebody winding me up." But it wasn't, and I had a very, very happy time. I enjoyed every moment.'

'How long did *Cabaret* run?'

'Nine months.'

'Do you like long runs?'

'No, I find them taxing and difficult to sustain the same standard every night. I like the repertoire system where one is given a chance of doing a play on a Monday night, another on a Tuesday and something else on a Wednesday. It is more difficult to do a long run of the same play.'

Plomley concluded his summary of Dench's career by noting that she was currently appearing in a London play with her husband, Michael Williams, and her brother. 'Judi, have you planned your career?' he wondered.

'No, I haven't. I can't plan *anything*, Roy. I'm very bad at that. Every time I imagine something will happen, or I try to plan it, there's a man with the bucket of ice-cold water right around the corner.'

An interview that was essentially a scrupulously polite dinner-party conversation meandered to its close with Dench fancifully imagining herself, on the desert island, 'gloriously brown, and covered in flowers'. It was a pleasant mental image to close a gentle encounter.

● ● ●

Dench met with a doughtier interrogator in Sue Lawley when she was back on the island in April 1998. Lawley asked her guest why she took on roles for which she might be thought unsuitable, reminding Dench that, asked to play Cleopatra in *Antony and Cleopatra* at the National Theatre opposite Anthony Hopkins in 1987, she had initially replied: 'You don't want *me* – I'm a menopausal dwarf!'

'Well, having committed myself to something like Lady Bracknell or Cleopatra, I had a whole host of people openly laughing in my face!' recalled Dench. 'I mean, people saying, "You're not *really*, are you? You have to admit you're not the right casting, or build, or *anything* for Cleopatra!" And then there is something in me that sees purple, and I think, *Whatever happens, I'm going to do that!*'

This same topic of proving doubters wrong came up again later when Dench recounted attending a film audition early in her career and being informed that 'every single thing is wrong with your face'.

'Soul-destroying stuff?' wondered Lawley.

'I just thought, *Oh well*. I didn't mind – except, of course, that I have remembered it, haven't I? What a giveaway!

'It made me unsure of myself in films, which I *am*, but it has also made me so much stronger in my belief that you can get away with so much more in the theatre. So many people have said to me, when they've come round to meet me afterwards: "Gosh, you've no height at all!"

'But I know that I can give the illusion of being much taller and I can be that tall, willowy blonde on the stage. Whereas I can't be that in a film.'

Lawley: 'And you're five foot one?'

Dench: 'One-and-three-quarters.'

Despite her misgivings about her screen image, Dench had recently been nominated for an Oscar for her lead role as Queen Victoria in *Mrs Brown*, co-starring Billy Connolly as the monarch's equerry and rumoured lover. Lawley surmised that working with Connolly must have been a laugh: 'I gather you nearly drowned together, at one point?'

'We were in an old Victorian boat and it just filled and filled and filled with water – not *dangerously*, but uncomfortably. We were out on the loch for about four hours and it seeped up through boots and corsets and everything. The cold water was right up to our waists and we still laughed.'

Lawley: 'And you were heavily upstaged by the horses, I understand?'

'Yes, we had a tricky time with my pony, Blue. He farted all the time, in every single scene. I don't know whether it was the weight of me on him? They had to get library steps to put me on. I mean, me getting on is OK, but me getting on with all those clothes, and the corsets, and the boots ... he just used to go *oh!* every morning. Poor chap!'

Lawley: 'Billy Connolly and a farting horse together must have been impossible?'

'Billy was terrible! We both thought it was each other [*farting*] ...'

• • •

Kirsty Young had taken over the interviewer's chair by the time Judi Dench made a third visit to the island in September 2015. The good dame's all-conquering status in the acting world by then was reflected in the host's introduction.

'She has been acting for fifty-eight years and counting,' she noted. 'Her work ranges across theatre, television and film. If you're buying a birthday gift, don't make it a doorstop: she has eleven BAFTAs, seven Oliviers, a Tony, two Golden Globes and an Oscar. And street slang now has a "Dench" to describe something that's particularly cool.'

Young wondered why, having played so many major theatrical roles from Shaw to Ibsen to Chekhov, Dench had never performed a one-woman show. Her guest reacted with horror.

'No, no! That's something I couldn't *possibly* do! I couldn't do it because so much a part of being in the theatre is being part of a company, being part of a kind of jigsaw, and being able to present this finished picture to the audience.

'I wouldn't even know who to rely on if I was on my own, and I wouldn't even know who to get ready for. You'd have none of those wonderful larks that go on sometimes in the dressing room or in a company of people.

'Michael [*Williams, her late husband*] used to say: "It's because you're so nosy, you have to know about everybody and what they're doing and if it's their grandmother's birthday." I don't think it's *that*: it's just being part of something. It's the same as being on my own. I don't like it.'

Young asked whether, now Dench was such an illustrious figure, young actors came to her wanting advice and guidance.

'They ask, "How do I get the next job?"' or, "How do I get an agent?"' related Dench. 'I love answering questions from actors if it's a two-way conversation. But I can't stand there and *spout about acting*. I think acting shouldn't be talked about, it should be done, and it should either be a success or not a success. *Just get on and tell the story*.

'I always say to students: "If you want to be an actor, *do* watch other actors and make your mind up about whether you like that or whether it conveys the story to you. Because only *that* way can you learn."'

One amusing sub-thread of Dench's third appearance was the castaway worrying that her musical choices were too melancholy and downbeat. 'You're worried about your list – what's wrong with it?' Young enquired after playing Billie Holiday's 'Strange Fruit'.

'I *am* rather, now I hear it all together,' admitted Dench. 'It's going to make us all drop off, isn't it?' Indeed, the sole exception to the discs' lugubrious tone was Frank Sinatra's 'I've Got You Under My Skin'.

The upbeat quotient was scarcely improved by Dame Judi going on to nominate a reading from the shipping forecast and Miles Davis's plangently melancholic 'Blue in Green'. Pressed by Young to choose her favourite tune to take to the island, she struggled to do so.

'I would take ... I'm so sorry, I don't want *any* of these,' she laughed. 'I don't want to go to the island. I don't want any of those records with me. What do I take? I'll take Sinatra ...'

'Dame Judi Dench, thank you very much for letting us hear your *Desert Island Discs*,' said Kirsty Young.

'Thank you, Kirsty. What a nightmare!'

• • •

Now nearing her eighty-eighth birthday, Dame Judi Dench remains one of the most acclaimed actors in British stage and screen history and her indefatigable work ethic has hardly dimmed. At the time of writing, she is filming *Allelujah*, a film adaptation of Alan Bennett's original stage play, alongside Jennifer Saunders, David Bradley and Derek Jacobi. In July 2022, an interviewer inquired of her whether she intended to retire. 'How dare you!' she replied.

DISCS CHOSEN (1972)

Bach's *St Matthew Passion*
William Parsons with the Jacques Orchestra
'It's a huge aria'

'The Lark in the Clear Air'
Dara Carroll
'It comes straight to my mind if I'm out walking in the open air'

Deposition speech from Shakespeare's *King Richard II*
Sir John Gielgud
'I don't think I would be happy on my desert island if I didn't take a record of Sir John Gielgud's'

'The Bonnie Lass o' Fyvie'
John Mearns

'Pirate Jenny' from Brecht's *The Threepenny Opera*
Lotte Lenya

❤ **Elgar's Cello Concerto in E Minor**
Jacqueline du Pré with the London Symphony Orchestra

'The Way You Look Tonight'
Edward Woodward
'Teddy is a very good friend. We've played opposite each other in rep'

Purcell's *Music for the Funeral of Queen Mary*
Geraint Jones Orchestra
'So stirring!'

BOOK
The Book of Kells
'It's so exquisitely beautiful'

LUXURY ITEM
Basil Brush films and projector
'I'm his greatest fan'

'ISLE NEVER FORGET ...'

'*Desert Island Discs* is terrific! I've always found it irresistible. You listen to the conversation and learn about someone, and then along comes a piece of music that tells you even more about them. It's a brilliant idea – who first thought of it? Roy Plomley? *That* doesn't surprise me.

'When I was first asked to go on, in 1972, it was very exciting. I loved being taken for lunch by Roy before the recording. It set you up for the afternoon! There again, I heard that first appearance again, recently. My God – what was my voice doing *up there*?

'When I first went on, I chose all classical music. But then I discovered jazz when I went to America with the Vic. I met Miles Davis, and I saw Billie Holiday for three nights. *Wow!* I will never forget it. When I went back on, I *had* to include them.

'When I was on with Kirsty, I was *so* undecided about my music. I kept changing my mind: saying, "Oh, no, I don't want to hear *this*, after all! I want to hear *that*!" And they had to keep roaring back to where all the records were kept!

'I was a nightmare but Kirsty was *immensely* patient. When I heard the show broadcast, I sent her a note: "Silk purse out of sow's ear!" I hope she didn't think it was any reflection on her! It was entirely me saying how they had managed my ineptitude brilliantly.

'I have been on *Desert Island Discs* three times, but I understand David Attenborough and Arthur Askey have both been on four times. Would I like to join that elite club? *You bet!*'

16
JAMES STEWART

ACTOR
25 May 1974

Roy Plomley's introduction of his 1974 guest James Stewart as 'one of the Hollywood greats' was, if anything, an understatement. During his forty-year career, the talismanic star had transcended mere cinema and seemingly come to embody the very ideal of American manhood.

Having worked with Frank Capra and then won an Academy Award in 1941, Stewart became a decorated fighter pilot in the war, including two years stationed in England. He then took the lead role in Capra's classic 1946 Christmas movie *It's a Wonderful Life* before moving into horror movies with Alfred Hitchcock and Westerns with John Ford.

Despite these remarkable achievements, Stewart proved to be a studio guest every inch as humble and self-effacing as his 'aw shucks!' silver-screen persona implied. In a rapidly changing world, this old-school star carried himself like the golden age of Hollywood incarnate.

• • •

Plomley's world-famous guest began by identifying himself as a big music lover. The host asked if he'd ever learned to play an instrument.

'No, and that's one thing I regret in my life,' drawled Stewart. 'My mother, bless her heart, tried to get me to take music lessons. She played the piano beautifully – played the organ in church – and I wish I'd learned some of the fundamentals of it.

'My mother taught me a few chords in the key of C and I guess, through her, I was blessed with a sort of ear for music. So, I've used those chords in C all through the years and I can play a few tunes that I enjoy myself. I can't get too much of an audience, though ...'

Two records in, Plomley asked his castaway: 'Jimmy, what part of the States do you come from?'

'I was born and raised in Indiana, Pennsylvania. It's a small town right in the middle of the soft-coal area, sixty miles from Pittsburgh.'

'Yes. As a youngster, what did you want to be?'

'A railroad engineer.'

'At Princeton, you read architecture?'

'Yes. I was going to be an architect.'

Stewart described appearing in plays at university purely as a hobby. On his graduation, two fellow students invited him to join their new theatre company in Massachusetts – but not as an actor.

'I played the accordion at Princeton, or thought I did. So I was to play the accordion in a tearoom connected with the theatre.'

'Just a few chords in C?' joshed Plomley.

'Just a few chords in C. My first night was a near disaster but they all attributed it to first-night nerves, and so did I. I thought, *It can't be that bad.* The second night, the boom fell, because people said my playing spoiled their appetites. That was the end of my accordion playing.

'Then they gave me odd jobs in the property department. I painted scenery, and then the small parts started to come. So getting into acting after Princeton was almost by accident.'

In Stewart's amused telling, his early years in theatre were an uphill struggle. Moving to New York, he was given a role that required an Austrian accent.

'I remember going to a woman called Frances Robinson Duff, who taught diction and voice. A lot of actors and actresses went to her, and she took me on. After three lessons, she called me into her office.

'She told me, "I'm going to have to let you go. There's no way I can do *anything* to give you a suggestion of an Austrian accent! But in case you ever want to learn to speak English correctly, come back and see me. I may be able to help."'

Despite this unpromising beginning, Stewart was then spotted by a talent scout and summoned from New York to California to make his movie debut.

Plomley: 'What was the name of your part in that first film you did in Hollywood?'

Stewart: 'It was a movie called *Murder Man* and I was a newspaper reporter named Shorty.'

Plomley: 'So, they shipped a man of six-foot-three a thousand miles to play a man called Shorty?'

Once in Hollywood, Stewart became a contract artist for MGM. 'That meant hard work, didn't it, more or less every day?' asked his host.

'Yes. In those days, when you were under contract to a studio, as a contract player, you came to work every day. It wasn't just when you were doing a picture.

'The big studios weren't only producing pictures. They trained personnel, including actors and writers and directors and everything. You learned your craft, and in the best way I know of learning to act, which is by acting.'

Plomley: 'From the pre-war days, which films do you remember with particular pleasure?'

'Well, I remember *Mr Smith Goes to Washington*, a Capra picture. I remember *The Philadelphia Story*. I remember ...'

Plomley: '*The Philadelphia Story* got you an Oscar, didn't it?'

'Uh-huh,' came the downbeat, gentle reply.

Plomley skipped over the wartime service that saw Stewart fly twenty combat missions over Germany and get promoted to brigadier-general. Instead, he asked his guest why, on his post-war return to Hollywood, he had switched from starring in romantic comedies to Westerns.

'I just found, after the war, I was falling back on light comedy and it didn't work,' he recalled. 'People weren't accepting that kind of thing. They wanted a very different, dramatic, serious type of thing.

'So, the Westerns came pretty much as a desperation move on my part. Fortunately, my father always had a horse around, and he'd taught me to ride when I was very young. So I had that in my favour.'

Plomley commented that he had read that his guest liked to wear the same cowboy hat and chaps in every film. 'Are you superstitious?'

'Oh, terribly, terribly! I wore the same hat in the Westerns. It was a very good hat to start with and it disintegrated. But I pasted it together with Scotch tape and everything and I wore it for years.'

Stewart discussed having recently moved into working on made-for-TV movies. He sounded perfectly happy with this transition, yet Plomley wondered if this true Hollywood A-lister ever found it depressing that 'the great days have gone'.

'Well, I for one miss them, yes. It's not *depressing*, actually, but it was ... people do say it was the golden era, or whatever you want to call it. It was a very exciting, glamorous, golden time.

'But I don't think that it necessarily has to return. You know, eras have a tendency not to return ...'

• • •

James Stewart starred in eighty movies before, with his hearing failing, he semi-retired in the mid-eighties and was awarded America's highest civilian award, the Presidential Medal of Freedom. The great Hollywood icon died, at the age of eighty-nine, in 1997.

DISCS CHOSEN

'On the Road to Mandalay'
Kenneth McKellar
'My father used to sing it. He was a big man and he held pitch very well, but he didn't pay too much attention to the words ...'

'Bye Bye Blues'
Bert Lown and His Orchestra
'A tune that reminds me of college'

'I've Got a Crush on You'
Betty Grable

'I Hadn't Anyone till You'
Ray Noble
This reminds me of Marlene Dietrich, when we did a picture together called Destry
Rides Again *just before the war*'

'There, I've Said It Again'
Vaughn Monroe and His Orchestra
I connect this very closely with England and the war'

'Don't Cry, Joe'
Gordon Jenkins Orchestra

'Moonlight Serenade'
Glenn Miller Orchestra
I made the picture about Glenn Miller's life [The Glenn Miller Story, 1954] *and it
was quite the experience*'

♥ **'Dream'**
The Pied Pipers

BOOK
A book of Dave Brubeck musical arrangements
And instructions on how to change them, if they're in the key of F, to the key of C'

LUXURY ITEM
A piano

17

BILLY CONNOLLY

COMEDIAN, MUSICIAN, ACTOR
30 July 1977

Billy Connolly regularly tops polls to find Britain's favourite stand-up comedian. However, when he first visited the BBC's desert island in summer 1977, he had only five years earlier completely transitioned from his previous career as a folk musician into being a full-time comic.

Previous to that, Connolly had famously worked in his native Glasgow's shipyards. The star used his encounter with Roy Plomley to talk *Desert Island Discs* listeners through this singular and distinctly unorthodox career path.

Plomley may feasibly have felt a tad wary about hosting the profane and freewheeling Connolly, but Scotland's funniest man was on his best behaviour between the palm trees as he described a showbiz career that was initially inspired by, of all things, *The Beverly Hillbillies*.

• • •

After Connolly got the ball rolling with a record by a fellow Glaswegian, Frankie Miller, Plomley commented that his guest was 'a Glasgow lad with an Irish name'. Did he have Irish roots?

'It's west-coast Ireland and west-coast Scotland,' explained Connolly. 'My grandfather came from Galway; my maternal grandfather from Mull, on the west coast of Scotland. Identical types of community – fishing people.'

Plomley: 'You were brought up by your father?'

'That's right – my father and some aunts.'

'What was your first job, Billy?'

'I was a message boy in a bookshop in Glasgow. I was fired. It was Christmas, stealing was rife in the despatch department, and I'm afraid the buck stopped at me. Somebody had stolen a Christmas book and I got the blame.'

'What happened after that?'

'After that I became a van boy, delivering bread in and around Glasgow. Then, when I was sixteen, I became an apprentice welder on the Clyde.'

Plomley: 'You had quite a long time in the shipyards?'

'Aye, I was there for seven or eight years.'

'When did you discover music, and get interested in the guitar and the banjo?'

'It was strange, really. I didn't start playing until I was twenty-one or twenty-two. It was late by anybody's standards. The introduction music to *The Beverly Hillbillies* had a banjo. I thought, *Oh, I'd like to play that*, so I went and bought a banjo for £2 in a market place called the Barrows in Glasgow.'

Plomley: 'And a shilling for the instruction book?'

'You didn't get instruction books in the Barrows!' laughed Connolly. 'You just got the banjo and got on with it!'

Connolly described taking banjo lessons and making his live debut, for 6s 8d, with a musician called Matt McGinn at a folk club in Glasgow in the early sixties. 'It was folk music [*for you*] from the start?' asked Plomley.

'Oh, aye!' his guest confirmed. 'I used to play Real Folk Music and introduce it very seriously.'

Connolly recalled spending his days in the shipyards and his nights in the folk clubs for more than two years. Plomley wondered whether it had been a big step to quit the yards and become a full-time musician.

'Well, it became rather obvious that was what I should be doing, because I was playing at night and working in the day and I was fading away. One had to go – and there was no way I wanted to be a welder!'

Newly professional, Connolly initially played in folk groups. He gave Plomley a potted history of this hit-and-miss time of his life.

'I was in a really strange band called the Craig Dhu. Craig Dhu is a mountain in Scotland and they were very much mountaineering types: bearded guys with black polo-necked pullovers. They were all a great deal older than me.

'They used to sing folk songs [*that were*] a very manly stamp on the floor and shouting words about battles. I didn't really like it much. I was the banjo player and I wouldn't wear the polo-neck outfit so they threw me out. I was a bit flash and it didn't suit their image.

'Then I joined a bunch of lunatic guys called the Acme Brush Company. We'd go by public transport to the gigs and we had "Acme Brush Company" written on the guitar cases. People must have thought, *What an unusual way to carry brushes!*

'You had some pretty rough times on the road?' wondered Plomley.

'Yes! I know my way around a Bedford van! I slept in many vans and on people's kitchen floors! They have this thing in folk-music contracts: "Fee plus accommodation". It must be the biggest joke I've ever heard! There was always the committee running away at the end of the show, and me [*shouting after them:*] "What about the accommodation?!"'

Touching very briefly on Connolly's time in the Humblebums with Gerry Rafferty, Plomley moved the conversation forward to 1971, when his guest went solo. The Big Yin told him that this provided an opportunity to radically rethink his act.

'I realised I was just another of the "sing-a-song, tell-a-joke" brigade. I wanted to be slightly different, so I rearranged all my songs to give the act a beginning, a middle and an end. The motto for Glasgow is "Let Glasgow Flourish" so I called it "Billy Connolly's Glasgow Flourish".

'It was a success, and I went from there to write "The Great Northern Welly Boot Show" with an Edinburgh poet called Tom Buchan. It was terrible in Glasgow, but [by the time] we did the Edinburgh Festival, it was a bit special. I don't think the festival has quite recovered!'

Connolly confessed that the fame this breakthrough had brought him had led him to move from Glasgow to a village near Loch Lomond.

'It was getting really silly in Glasgow,' he said. 'People were outside my house like it was Buckingham Palace. When I passed the dining-room window, a wee cheer would go up in the street!'

His consequent success had enabled Connolly to broaden his horizons considerably. 'You've done a lot of travelling about, haven't you?' asked Plomley.

'I have indeed and I enjoy it immensely. I even enjoy Australia! I had a riot there last year, in Brisbane!'

'How was that?'

'Oh, some Scottish guys in the audience went crazy and started to shout and bawl. I think that they expected one of those sort of kilted Scotsmen, with a velvet jacket and square buttons and all that. When I turned up in tights and banana boots, they couldn't handle it!

'You see, *the exiled Scot is a strange beast in many ways*. They have this weird idea of what Scotland is like. They like songs about little cottages in the heather, and I don't. And when they don't get [*them*], in massive doses, they tend to riot!'

• • •

The Big Yin returned to the desert island on 19 July 2002 to find that Sue Lawley was far more intent on probing him about what she called his 'deprived, often brutal' Glasgow childhood. It was a line of questioning that he handled well.

'My mother left when I was four,' he said. 'It was the middle of the war and I've never held it against her. I can see it: I think I might have done the same. She was a teenager, the Germans were bombing the town, my father was in India [*in the army*] and we lived in a slum place.'

After his mother vanished one day, Connolly was raised by his father's sister, Auntie Mona. It was a far from happy process.

'There was something wrong with my aunt. She was eventually found to be schizophrenic and stuff. She loved to humiliate me. Every day, she would tell me that I was stupid and worthless. She would do it in front of people.'

Shortly before Connolly capsized near the desert isle for the second time, his wife, Pamela Stephenson, had written a biography of her husband, *Billy*. This book detailed how, after his father had returned from the war, he had regularly sexually abused his son.

Lawley asked the comedian how he had coped with the awfulness of his childhood.

'My sister, Flo, was a guardian. She looked after me all my life. She used to hit people for me. Bullies and stuff. Big girls who were picking on me – she'd belt them around.

'I told my sister about the sexual abuse right after my father died. I told Pamela as well and I had told a couple of people, very secretively, as I grew up. The trouble was that I'd never confronted my father. I learned later that very, very few people do.

'Flo is more hurt by what happened to me than I am. She's much more wounded than me because she thinks she should have protected me from that. And she wasn't there.'

Lawley asked whether finally talking about what he had concealed for years had made Connolly feel worse or better. '*Much* better,' he said.

'You're carrying it around like a rucksack full of bricks for your whole life. And the more you do it, the more you feel you've got something to hide. You've got a big boil on the back of your neck but you wear this big scarf all the time.'

Lawley: 'How has it changed you? You've dumped the rucksack? You've lanced the boil?'

'It isn't so long since I dumped it, but I feel as if I'm out of jail. It's a lovely feeling. There was a kind of film over me, and it's gone.'

The host also touched on another affliction that had blighted Connolly's life: alcoholism. 'I come from a long line of drunk people, and it's good fun,' he replied, adding that he'd now been sober for seventeen years.

'Not touched a drop?' wondered Lawley.

'Not a sausage. No, I did once: somebody gave me vodka instead of water as a joke. He didn't know, you know, that I was off the booze.

'Another time, a woman gave me whisky in my porridge on the Isle of Arran. I asked for porridge and she said, "How about porridge royale?" I said, "What the hell is that?" but I had just had a big mouthful and it had whisky in it.

'The funniest thing happens. It's like alarm bells go off: your body says, *Now you're talking! That's the one! Come on, let's go!* and my fingers tingle. My stomach goes all butterflies and it lasts all day: *Yippee!*

Lawley asked how he found the willpower to resist this pull.

'You have to be really strong. You have to have a picture in your mind of what it did to you before.'

'What's the picture you have?'

'It was an evening I spent in an undertaker's place. I met him in a pub and I was blitzed. He said, "I'm an undertaker," and I said, "Oh, wow! I've never touched a dead person since I was a little boy. *How do dead people feel?*"

'So, we ended up down there, opening coffins and touching the dead to see how they felt. [*And I thought:*] *Oh, my God! I've got to change!* You let yourself go. Your standards plummet. Your taste in women doesn't half change ...'

• • •

Alongside his sell-out comedy tours, Billy Connolly was later to develop a parallel career as an actor, including a BAFTA nomination for his superb performance opposite Judi Dench in *Mrs Brown*. He was diagnosed with Parkinson's disease in 2013 and, having been knighted in 2017, was forced to retire from live comedy the following year. The Big Yin wrote his autobiography, *Windswept & Interesting*, in 2021, and, nearing eighty, has developed a successful late-life career as a painter as well as continuing to host TV travelogue shows.

DISCS CHOSEN (1977)

'Bridgeton'
Frankie Miller
'If I was going to write a song about Glasgow, I'd want to say these things. But it's too late now, Frankie's done it!'

'Save the Last Dance for Me'
The Drifters
'It reminds me of my youth – the dance hall era'

'Imagine'
John Lennon
'If I have a favourite performer, it's John Lennon'

'Across the Universe'
The Beatles
'To remind me of that lovely sixties era that the Beatles almost single-handedly created'

'The Postman's Knock'
The Albion Band

'You Are My Flower'
Nitty Gritty Dirt Band
'When I first met my wife, Iris, I invited her up to my flat: come and see my etchings! She assumed that I'd have Frank Sinatra smoothie records. When she discovered my records were like this, she was happy!'

'Sorry Seems to Be the Hardest Word'
Elton John
'I was his support in America. I learned humility'

❤ 'At the Ball, That's All'
Laurel and Hardy
'Sitting on my island, I think it would make me smile'

BOOK
Catch 22 – Joseph Heller
'I've read it ten or eleven times, and it's a different book every time I read it'

LUXURY ITEM
An electrical device to heat shaving foam
'The most absurd luxury I've ever seen in my life. I saw it in America. It would remind me of what nice beasts the human race are'

18
LES DAWSON

COMEDIAN, TELEVISION PRESENTER
8 April 1978

Just under a year after Billy Connolly was cast away, another much-loved working-class British comedian was marooned on Roy Plomley's island. Yet the longer-in-the-tooth Les Dawson's appearance was very different in its tone.

Where's Connolly's forte was expansive observational humour, Dawson was more of an old-fashioned gag merchant. With a wit honed by years working the nation's pubs and clubs, the veteran comic responded to Plomley's gentle probing with a trademark string of droll one-liners.

Yet with his love of poetry and music, Dawson was no one-trick pony, either as an entertainer or as a person. As the broadcast made clear, his deadpan, gruff stage persona veiled an individual of far greater richness and complexity.

• • •

Asked whether he would be lonely on the desert island, Dawson shot back that 'to be a comedian is lonely'. Plomley then reflected that his guest had grown up in a 'rundown' part of Manchester. Had he known hardship as a boy?

'We lived in a road called Miracle Road and if the houses stood, it was a miracle,' joked Dawson. 'Up to the age of fifteen, I thought knives and forks were jewellery.

'There were times my mother took the bones from her corset to give me something nourishing. Life wasn't easy. My father was superstitious. He wouldn't work if there was a Friday in the week ...'

Plomley: 'Were you a comic at that age? The school jester?'

'Yes, because I was fat. The thing is when you're fat, you can't run and you can't fight, so you have to be merry with people, and pleasant.'

Plomley asked Dawson how he learned to play the piano.

'It's a long story. I played the piano as a child and the neighbours loved it. They used to break the windows to hear me better. My father used to help me to keep time by banging the lid up and down on my fingers.'

'What was your first job when you left school?'

'Apprentice electrician.'

'What did you want to do?'

'Anything except apprentice electrician.'

'You were pretty good at boxing?'

'Well, I was the only boxer ever to be carried *into* the ring as well as out. I was carried out the ring so often that I had handles sewn on my shorts.'

Prompted by Plomley, Dawson talked about his wartime service in the army tank corps, where he played piano at regimental concerts. After his peacetime discharge, his life took a very different turn.

'I'd always had this bee in my bonnet to be a writer,' he recalled. 'So I went to Paris, which I thought was Valhalla for the arts in those days. And I played the piano.'

'Where?'

'In a brothel.'

'Successfully?'

'The brothel was successful – I wasn't! I didn't know [*when hired*] that the place *was* a brothel. I was engaged to play the piano from three in the morning until six.'

After a year, Dawson returned to England ('Why? Starvation. I was so thin they were using me as a hat rack'). While working in London as a babysitter and washing dishes in a Lyons café ('because I could get three meals a day'), he also began playing piano and performing comedy in clubs.

'What sort of material did you use?' wondered Plomley.

'It wasn't doleful. It was sort of, "Hi, there! I love you people!" like the Americans, because I thought you had to be like that and say wonderful funny stories. It died very successfully.'

Dawson told his host that he spent many months pursuing this failed comedic strategy: 'I was going through a sticky period. I was signing on the dole so often that they asked me to MC the staff dances.' Then he had an epiphany during a week-long club booking in Hull.

'It was a sort of Belsen with lights. I was paid £18 for the week. And I didn't just die – I was resurrected nightly! People used to throw tape measures: I think they were undertakers. I died the death of deaths.

'By the Thursday night, I had had sufficient, so I got completely and utterly incapable through drink. I went back to this club and when the makeshift, faded old curtains opened, I was slumped on the piano. I couldn't rise: I was incapable of it.

'I said the first thing which came into my mind: "It's a great pleasure to be in this reconverted kipper depot!" And instead of being hooted off, as I had in the past, they started to laugh. And I began to realise what I had done was to actually be myself. Not be a phoney.'

Plomley: 'You began to sort things out from there?'

Dawson: 'Yeah. I'm still a flop, but I'm making more money!'

Having seen his fortunes transformed by being true to his character on stage, Dawson's big break came with a successful appearance on a BBC

Blackpool Big Night Out TV show in 1964. He'd since done many radio and TV shows – yet still didn't see himself as a traditional comedian.

'If people listen to what I do,' he advised Plomley, 'it isn't really stand-up comedy, as such. It is a situation with one man. That's the basis of the act.'

This yearning to step outside of his stereotype was clear as Dawson told his host he had written TV plays and would love to act in Shakespeare productions. He added that he had also written three novels, with the first, *Card for the Clubs*, drawing on his early performing years.

'I just thought that nobody has ever written about the lowest aspects of showbusiness. The basics of clubs in the north of England. I mean, some of those clubs were pretty grim! If they liked you, they didn't clap you: they *let you live.*'

Having shown listeners that he had a broader cultural hinterland than they might have imagined, Dawson happily reverted to comedic type when Plomley enquired how he might fare on the desert island. Was he a keen gardener?

'Unfortunately, I've got a very bad garden. I've got a greenhouse to grow weeds. It's very hard land where I live. I drill, and put plants down with a rawl plug.'

Plomley: 'Have you done any fishing?'

'Yes, my father used to send me shark fishing. He always seemed to get annoyed when I fell off the hook ...'

Selecting his final record, Chopin's Étude in C Minor, Dawson lauded it as a tune that gave him strength to carry on in adversity. 'Every time I have a row with the wife, I play this! Last week, I played it sixteen times ...'

• • •

Les Dawson achieved his childhood desire of being a writer, penning many fiction and non-fiction books in-between his countless lugubrious TV and radio turns hosting variety and game shows. He died in 1993, aged sixty-two, from a heart attack during a medical check-up in a Manchester hospital. You suspect he would have appreciated the irony.

DISCS CHOSEN
❤ Ravel's *Pavane pour une infante défunte*
Suisse Romande Orchestra
'The ultimate in beauty'

'Matchstick Men and Matchstick Cats and Dogs'
Brian and Michael
'It reminds me so much of Lancashire life – the seediness of Salford, mist from the canals ...'

'Non, je ne regrette rien'
Édith Piaf
'A remembrance of Paris'

'Passing Strangers'
Billy Eckstine and Sarah Vaughan

'You Make Me Feel Brand New'
The Stylistics
'A great orchestral feel'

'The Day I Drank a Glass of Water'
W.C. Fields
'On his deathbed, he had a Bible in one hand and a glass of Martini in the other. He said, "I'm looking for loopholes"'

'Don't Cry for Me Argentina'
Julie Covington

Chopin's Étude in C Minor
Sviatoslav Richter

BOOK
Trustee from the Toolroom – Nevil Shute
'It summarises one small man's fight, which he wins'

LUXURY ITEM
Any piece of Georgian furniture
'I think that when the Georgian period ended, civilisation ended'

19
NORMAN MAILER

NOVELIST, JOURNALIST
15 December 1979

There was no more significant, provocative or controversial figure in American literature than Norman Mailer when the novelist, journalist and playwright fetched up on the desert island in the dog days of the seventies.

A great American man of letters, Mailer wrote a string of bestselling novels including the ground-breaking *The Naked and the Dead* (1948) and was an acclaimed political and counter-cultural journalist. When he met Roy Plomley, he had just published *The Executioner's Song*, which was to win him his second Pulitzer Prize.

A far from bookish figure, Mailer was also renowned for his machismo, fascination with violence and extreme behaviour, and volatile personal life. His encounter with Plomley was uncharacteristically decorous.

• • •

Mailer opened the show by admitting to a general ignorance of music, and explained one of the criteria behind his selections: 'I've been married a number of times. [*A lot of*] these records reminded me of different women I've been in love with and ... what have you.'

Plomley commented that Mailer had studied aeronautical engineering at Harvard yet also enrolled for a writing course there. Why did he do this?

'It was compulsory, because I didn't do well enough in my entrance exam in English,' explained Mailer. 'But they let us write a little fiction – and I was off to the races! I had discovered the joy of writing.'

Mailer recalled writing two 'very bad' novels as a teenager before being drafted to fight in the war. Plomley said he understood that Mailer had wanted to enlist to get great background material for his next book.

'Yes! I went to the army with the idea that I was going to write the great American war novel. I almost wept the day the invasion started. I didn't cry because young men were being killed on the beaches. I came near to weeping because I wasn't there, and thereby I was losing a great novel.'

Mailer recounted writing long letters to his first wife from his postings in the Philippines and the Pacific. These letters, and his experiences, fed into his first published novel, *The Naked and the Dead*, which was to be widely lauded as one of the greatest war novels in literary history.

As the book spent a year on the *New York Times* bestseller list, Mailer, like

Les Dawson, had a sojourn in Paris ('as all young writers should!' approved Plomley). Then he went to Hollywood. This move was not a success.

'I should have gotten the best agent in Hollywood and had him call up a couple of studios and say, "*Mr* Norman Mailer is in town and will consider movie offers for one week." But I didn't. I was out there for a year and I got no work at all.'

Back in New York, Mailer wrote a less successful second novel, *Barbary Shore* (1951), and entered what Plomley described as 'a sort of personal wilderness': 'You went to live down in [Greenwich] Village, as one of the hip generation ... it was an unsettled time for you?'

'I broke up with my first wife and was married again,' said Mailer. 'A number of these records come from the fact that I became very interested in jazz in this period. American jazz: the jazz of the fifties.

'I used to hang out at a place called the Five Spot. And we used to hear Thelonious Monk there; once in a while, Miles Davis or Sonny Rollins. I've chosen records by Sonny Stitt and Sonny Rollins and Miles Davis because it brings back that very rich period to me. A period where everything started in America.'

After playing that jazz triptych, Plomley moved on to Mailer's infamous reputation: 'You used to be a violent man. The columnists delighted in detailing your fisticuffs at parties. Are you through that?'

Mailer: 'Well, you know, I was never in *that* much. It takes very little to build a legend for yourself these days. I keep thinking of eighteenth-century London, and how many fights a man had to get into before he could build a reputation for himself!

'In New York, all you have to do is get into three or four fights in the course of a few years. If you have a name, it gets to the point where you come through the door at a party and the host or hostess says, "Please don't punch me if I say the wrong thing!" It's ridiculous!'

Plomley noted that despite Mailer's fame being as a novelist, only five or six of his twenty-five published books were actually novels. ('Well, novels are hard to write!' interjected Mailer.) Most had been journalistic books.

'Some of them, frankly,' suggested Plomley, rather boldly given his guest's pugnacious reputation, 'were potboilers.'

This did not play well with Mailer: 'Roy! Excuse me, Roy, but I've *never* written a potboiler!

'Picasso was famous for making little squiggles,' he elucidated. 'A friend would ask him for the equivalent of a hundred dollars. Picasso would do a squiggle on a piece of paper, sign it and hand it over. You know, authority printed upon emptiness is money.

'Someone said to him, talking about one of his works, "It's not really a very good Picasso." And he shook his head and said, "There's no such thing as a *bad* Picasso. There are some Picassos that are better than others, but there is no such thing as a *bad* Picasso."

'I've *never* written a potboiler. I've written any number of books for money. But my idea of a potboiler is a book that you write with a certain cynicism.'

'I accept the distinction,' said Plomley, wisely, before turning to his guest's most recent work; *The Executioner's Song*, a 'true-life novel'. Mailer described it as 'an extended biographical essay about Gary Gilmore', and then explained its subject.

'He was the ex-convict who killed two people in Utah. He was sentenced to death, and then said to the authorities in Utah: "All right, you have sentenced me to death. Now execute me!"

'They naturally began to go through the various appeals processes, but he said to them: "You're silly. You people are not serious, you're cowards. You're afraid to execute me." Eventually, after many a legal process, he was executed some months later.'

'He was also very much in love with a girl named Nicole Barrett. Before it was all over, he and Nicole Barrett entered into a suicide pact. Each tried to commit suicide. They both failed and she was committed to a mental hospital.

'There were bizarre headlines at the time: GILMORE REMOVED FROM HOSPITAL TO DEATH ROW. And funny comments by the doctors, unwittingly: "If we can save Gilmore's life, we'll be ready to send him back to death row." It all became a media circus.

'I thought there were any number of novels to it. And the more I began to work on it, the more I realised that there was an extraordinary social panorama in the book. People from all walks of life and all branches of society.

'It's never enough, you know, to write a large social novel with a great many people in it. You've got to have a story that will hold it all together. And here I had this incredible operatic story to tell, with a truly touching and powerful love story at the centre of it.

'This girl was absolutely poor and uneducated and had had a horrible life. And Gilmore was a very bad man and a very unpleasant man but with a streak of humanity running right through the middle of him. It gave an edge of dignity to an awfully sordid life.

'And, well, those are the sort of things you go looking for when you are looking for truly interesting material ...'

• • •

Norman Mailer was to write twelve novels and countless biographies, essays and collections of political journalism, and become a true icon of American literature before his death, aged eighty-four, in November 2007. He married six times and fathered nine children. He was, arguably, the textbook definition of a man who lives life well but not always wisely.

DISCS CHOSEN

Elgar's *Pomp and Circumstance* March No. 1 in D Major: 'Land of Hope and Glory'
London Symphony Orchestra
'It reminds me of moments of great pleasure, in my childhood, seeing movies like Gunga Din*'*

''Arf a Pint of Ale'
Gus Elen
'My first wife used to sing little parodies of music hall songs'

'Nice Work if You Can Get It'
Sonny Stitt
'He plays a wonderfully, beautifully lyrical saxophone'

'The Way You Look Tonight'
Sonny Rollins

''Round Midnight'
Miles Davis Quintet
'My fourth wife was emotionally involved with him for years before I met her. I loved his music so much despite the fact he was a great pain in the neck to me'

'Lili Marlene'
Lale Andersen
'It brings back the Second World War for me'

❤ **'Imagination'**
Carmen McRae

Beethoven's Symphony No. 3 in E Flat Major: *Eroica*
'Perhaps, someday, I'll be able to do something like this in literature'
Chicago Symphony Orchestra

BOOK

Labyrinths – Jorge Luis Borges
'Probably the greatest living writer that we have in all languages'

LUXURY ITEM

A stick of the very best marijuana
Plomley: 'This is illegal talk, Mr Mailer.'
Mailer: 'Well, here we are, in trouble again.'

20

DIZZY GILLESPIE

VIRTUOSO JAZZ TRUMPETER
19 January 1980

Roy Plomley ushered in the eighties on *Desert Island Discs* by welcoming a castaway who had revolutionised one key area of music a full four decades earlier. Dizzy Gillespie was a true original and one of the founding spirits and progenitors of be-bop and modern jazz.

Alongside Charlie Parker, Gillespie was one of the most influential musicians in the jazz canon. His trumpet playing manifested a complexity and degree of improvisation that was simply breath-taking. His influence over Miles Davis, for one, has never been in question.

Gillespie's musical accomplishments were staggering and had led him to rub shoulders, during a forty-year career, with pretty much every figure from the world of jazz. His encounter with Roy Plomley yielded something close to a personalised potted history of the genre.

• • •

Plomley began by establishing that, despite his stellar career, Gillespie had come from humble stock: born and christened John Gillespie, he was the youngest of nine children in a family in a small, agricultural town named Cheraw in South Carolina. Was his early life pretty hard?

'Oh, I came up during the Depression,' confirmed Gillespie. 'It was horrible.'

'Were you bright at school?'

'Yeah, I was bright. I caught up to my brother, who was two-and-a-half years older. I could've passed him but I didn't want to embarrass him!'

'How did music come into your life?'

'Well, my school came into possession of some instruments from the state, somehow. All of us waited around to get an instrument. I got a trombone. I was about the age of eleven.'

Plomley: 'Why did you switch from the trombone to the trumpet?'

'The fellow next door had a trumpet and he let me practise on it. I liked the sound of it.'

'Were there many places to play outside of the school?'

'Yes, we played for the other school, too. The white school. There was a black school and a white school.'

Gillespie recalled studying agriculture in his teens: 'That was the easiest subject for me.' Plomley asked if it was true that he had picked cotton during the Depression.

'Well, I never did pick too well, because I was too small ... that was when Roosevelt came in, in 1932.'

Saved from a life of farming when his family moved to Philadelphia in 1935, when he was seventeen, Gillespie developed a fervent love for jazz inspired by hearing Roy Eldridge on the radio.

'He meant more to you than Louis Armstrong?' wondered Plomley.

'Roy Eldridge was the epitome of trumpet players to countless young trumpet players. Every age has its own idols. The age before us idolised Louis Armstrong. Our age idolised Roy, the age after idolised me, and the age after me, it was Miles and Fats [*Navarro*] and Clifford Brown.'

Moving from Philadelphia to New York aged nineteen, the gifted Gillespie joined bandleader Teddy Hill's big band, where he gained the nickname Dizzy because he was 'always clowning'. This didn't prevent him moving on to the legendary Cab Calloway's orchestra.

Plomley: 'You were already developing an experimental style? You were inclined to play what Cab Calloway called "Chinese music"?'

'Oh, he didn't know *anything* about music!' laughed Gillespie. 'He was a performer and a singer. There was very little he knew about what was going on. He'd rely on other people to tell him how good a guy was.'

Plomley: 'You and Calloway didn't get on awfully well? There were fisticuffs, I believe, when you left? You had a bit of a scrap.'

'Let's call it an *altercation*.'

'Yes,' agreed Plomley. 'That's a tactful way of putting it. After that, you worked with Ella Fitzgerald for a while?' At this point, his guest voiced concern at the turn the questioning was taking.

'You are making me divulge my whole book here!' Gillespie scolded. 'You know my book is coming out in February? Are you copying from my book?'

Plomley assured him he had not seen his imminent memoir [*To Be or Not to Bop*] and his mollified guest confirmed that, yes, he had played in Ella's band 'for a hot moment'. Plomley asked him why he had diversified his career and started writing musical arrangements.

'Well, it became important to livelihood! When things got rough of playing, you could sell arrangements to the bands. All the bands wanted some be-bop.'

Plomley: 'You had become progressive? Some of it was pretty far out!'

'Music evolves. Music is the same as life – in a constant state of flux. So, if you are one of those people with the foresight to see a little into the future, you are one of the fortunate ones!'

Gillespie refuted Plomley's suggestion that the modern jazz he helped to invent was a 'revolt' against swing-era trad jazz. Yet, asked to define what 'be-bop' meant, his answer was itself pretty freeform.

'There is no actual explanation for the word "be-bop" except that *the music sounds a little like that*. Be-bop is the *phrasing* of the music, not the music in itself.

You can [*even*] phrase that way playing "God Save the King" – or Queen ... whoever they save over here at the minute ...'

Plomley: 'Technically, it was more demanding than swing?'

'Every age is more demanding on everything! In religion, everything is demanding!'

Plomley turned to Gillespie's close association with Charlie Parker. Had he seen his kindred spirit's tragic end coming?

'No. No one thinks of death when you are alive, except the one that is getting ready to die. But I had no information at all that Charlie Parker was going to split.'

Gillespie notably closed that line of questioning down fairly quickly. However, he soon returned to the subject of Parker, 'the biggest influence on my life', when selecting one of his tunes, 'Parker's Mood'.

'He is the guy who I think is mainly responsible for the changing of American music in the forties,' he reflected. 'He was the main source of inspiration for countless thousands. He brought joy into the lives of so many people.

'It's such a strange thing that he had to die when he brought so much joy into the world. But his advent into the world will be remembered for a long, long, long time ...'

Plomley pointed out that Gillespie had not chosen any of his own discs to take to the island. 'I don't like many of my records!' he concurred. He was notably happier talking about his final musical selection.

'My last record is by Ella Fitzgerald, who I have been closely related to for many years,' he declared. 'As a matter of fact, one of her husbands came out of my band!'

'I hope it was a good one?' chirped Plomley.

'Ray Brown. Course, they're not together now ...'

• • •

Dizzy Gillespie was to lead the United Nations Orchestra in the eighties, and continued his formidable, fifty-six-year touring career until diagnosed with pancreatic cancer in 1992. He died at the age of seventy-five in January 1993 and was buried in New York City.

DISCS CHOSEN
'Rockin' Chair'
Roy Eldridge with the Gene Krupa Band
'Roy was my first inspiration – the catalyst among trumpet players'

'Body and Soul'
Art Tatum
'There are just no words to describe the dexterity and the creativity'

'Lament'
Miles Davis with the Gil Evans Orchestra
'I am to him what Roy Eldridge is to me'

'Deep Purple'
Sarah Vaughan with the Robert Farnon Orchestra
'The divine one'

'Dashoud'
Clifford Brown
'He had a very short but brilliant life'

'You Don't Know What Love Is'
Billy Eckstine
'My favourite male vocalist'

❤ **'Parker's Mood'**
Charlie Parker

'Passion Flower'
Ella Fitzgerald with the Duke Ellington Orchestra

BOOK
A Bahá'í prayer book

LUXURY ITEM
His trumpet
'My horn. That's it, and I would be satisfied with that'

21

HELEN MIRREN

ACTOR
27 November 1982

Not yet a dame, Helen Mirren was nevertheless already a prodigious force of nature in British theatre and engaged in a precipitous ascent to its upper reaches when she turned up on Roy Plomley's desert island in November 1982.

Born Ilyena Lydia Mironoff in London in 1935, to an exiled Russian aristocrat father and a working-class cockney mother, Mirren excelled as an actor after joining the National Youth Theatre in her teens and playing Cleopatra in the West End, aged twenty, to adulatory reviews.

Yet for all her rarefied acting accomplishments, Mirren was nobody's idea of an earnest theatrical luvvie. Indeed, her responses to Plomley's respectful interrogation revealed her as a decided wild card with a subversive sense of fun and endearing utter lack of self-importance.

This was exemplified when her favourite record to take to the island, from the millions of hours of recorded music available to her, was 'Pass the Dutchie', a novelty pop-reggae hit by Musical Youth that had hit number one in the UK earlier that year. Who'd have thought it?

• • •

Plomley began his enquiries, understandably, with Mirren's exotic parentage: 'Your father was Russian, wasn't he?'

'Yes,' confirmed Mirren. 'He was born in Russia. We changed our name when I was about thirteen or so. It was not easy to be an immigrant in England in those days – I'm sure it still isn't – especially with a "funny accent". I think he wanted to become as English as possible.'

Mirren recounted being born in Chiswick in west London ('A record birth – I came out in twenty minutes!') then growing up in Leigh-on-Sea in Essex, where she attended a convent school. 'What were your main interests in school?' asked Plomley.

'Dreaming. I was a great dreamer and fantasist. I liked drama and sort of hooked on to that from an early age.'

Plomley: 'You were very bright at school? Seven O levels and two A levels?'

'Well, *that's* not very bright, is it?' his guest corrected him. 'One of my A levels was Art, so you can't really count that. Another was English: you can't count that either. And it took me three goes to pass my Maths O level.'

'When you left school, what did you set about doing?'

'I made the great mistake of going to a teacher training college.'

'What did you want to teach?'

'I didn't want to teach anything! I hated school even worse as a teacher than as a pupil. It was just something my school and my parents both thought I ought to do. I wanted to be an actress, but they – parents *and* school – thought that was impossible and ridiculous.'

Mirren's escape from blackboard hell was to apply to the National Youth Theatre 'secretly'. ('I didn't tell my parents. Not because I thought they'd disapprove, but because I'd be so embarrassed if I didn't get in!') Accepted, she was quickly given a prime series of leading roles.

Having shone for the NYT as Helena in *A Midsummer Night's Dream* and, to rave reviews, Cleopatra in *Antony and Cleopatra* at the Old Vic, Mirren turned professional at twenty-one. Her first professional engagement, she told Plomley, was somewhat less stellar.

'I did a play called *Little Malcolm and His Struggle against the Eunuchs* at the Alhambra Theatre [*actually the Empire*] in Sunderland. It's a huge theatre, vast, one of those real barns, and I should think we had about fifty people a night.

'One of my lines in the play was: "Would you shaft me?" At this point, of those fifty people, at least twenty-five would get up and leave. And they had those seats that went *Bang! Bang! Bang!*'

'Sounded like a round of applause?' hoped Plomley.

'A rather distant round of applause! So, we used to regularly lose half of our audience of fifty.'

Mirren described going on to do six months in repertory theatre at the Royal Exchange in Manchester before being invited to join the Royal Shakespeare Company. This pleased her greatly.

'Yes, I did very much want to be a classical actress,' she recalled. 'The area of acting I'd always found the most magical was not films or television. It was going to early Royal Shakespeare and early National Theatre productions.'

At this point, Plomley delicately noted that the press coverage that had greeted Mirren's elevation to the upper echelons of the theatre world had been less than high-minded.

'Despite the fact that you were playing serious parts in classical plays,' he said, 'you were described in the press as "Stratford's Sex Queen" and "a magnificent animal". This wasn't the usual way to greet a new recruit to the serious theatre?'

Mirren: 'No, I suppose that's why they did it, probably. They liked the contrast, or the contradiction. It's a contradiction that I've not exactly encouraged, but I ... *haven't not enjoyed*.'

'Well, you did rather clinch matters by going off to play in a couple of films in which you had to take all your clothes off ...' murmured Plomley.

'Yes, but *everyone* has to do that nowadays.'

'But I assume the producers were cashing in on your sexy publicity?'

'I don't think that occurred to them. I don't think they probably even read newspapers in that way,' said Mirren, possibly a tad optimistically.

Mirren described wanting a break from the RSC after four years: 'It was a wonderful experience but I felt I was in a kind of culture factory ... just churning out good, laudable productions with an awful regularity.' So, she took a leap leftfield into improvisational theatre.

Joining an experimental group run by renowned director Peter Brook, she spent time with them in Paris then went on tour in Africa.

'We didn't really do productions, we did improvisations in villages,' she recalled. 'Audiences varied between literally three women and six goats – that was one of our crowds – to two thousand tribesmen at a festival. Very varying!'

'Did you learn a lot?' asked Plomley.

'I did! It seemed so very alien from the sort of work I'd done before. But in retrospect, actually, I learned an enormous amount from it.'

Plomley picked over Mirren's major roles since returning to UK theatre, including a Ben Travers farce, *The Bed Before Yesterday*, and *Teeth and Smiles*, a David Hare drama about the music industry. 'I played a sleazy rock and roll singer,' explained his guest.

'So you did some singing?'

'I did! It was a nightmare, because I can't sing! But I got through it. It was rather like when Dame Edith Evans played one of those Restoration comedies where everyone talks about how beautiful she is all the time.

'Dame Edith's not the prettiest of women,' added Mirren, in somewhat unsisterly manner. 'But she looked in her mirror every night saying, "I am beautiful! I am beautiful!" Then she walked on the stage with such a conviction of beauty that the audience found her beautiful.

'Well, I did the same with my singing. I made the audience believe I could sing by the sheer force of my mental power over them!'

As the encounter neared its end, Plomley turned the conversation to politics, informing Mirren that she was 'a political person'.

She demurred: 'I used to be *sort-of political*. Now I'm not political at all, actually.'

Plomley reminded her that she had once stood for election to Equity's council as a member of the Workers' Revolutionary Party. 'Are you still a revolutionary worker?'

'No. I wasn't a member then: I have never been a member. But I agreed with what they wanted to happen in Equity.

'It was a slightly rogue-elephant thing to do. Any mention of the WRP and my friends used to go into a complete fit. It was like I was talking about joining the Moonies or becoming a fascist! They were excessive in their reactions and it bought out the devil in me.'

'Well, the party was advocating a communist state!' cautioned Plomley. 'It was a very extreme party!'

'Oh, absolutely! Totally! I *agree* with the extremes. I think they're very necessary. There used to be a party in Italy – which I would have joined – called the Radical Party. It said it was the pepper in the ass of all the other parties. Just something to get everyone galvanised and angry.'

Plomley: 'So this [*standing for election for the WRP*] really was a sense of mischief? To be outrageous?'

'Yes,' chuckled Helen Mirren. 'I'm afraid it was, really.'

• • •

Since her forty-years-old *Desert Island Discs* appearance, Helen Mirren has ascended into the acting stratosphere. Back then, she was a *force majeure* in the theatre world: today, the grand dame's dominance also effortlessly encompasses cinema and television.

In recent years alone, Mirren has received an Oscar and a BAFTA Award for playing Queen Elizabeth II in *The Queen*, as well as BAFTAs and four US Emmy Awards for her lead role as Detective Chief Inspector (and later Superintendent) Jane Tennison in TV crime drama *Prime Suspect*. Made a dame in 2003, she is also the recipient of a star on the Hollywood Walk of Fame.

The venerable Dame Helen must surely be overdue a return visit to the island, and – who knows? – maybe, second time around, her favourite song of all time *won't* be Musical Youth's 'Pass the Dutchie'...

DISCS CHOSEN

Bruch's Violin Concerto No. 1 in G Minor
Kyung Wha Chung with the Royal Philharmonic Orchestra
'It will remind me of my dear father, who died just a year ago'

❤ **'Pass the Dutchie'**
Musical Youth
'This is just to dance around to'

Albinoni and Giazotto's Adagio in G Minor for Strings and Organ
Maria Teresa Garatti with I Musici Orchestra
'It makes me cry every time I hear it. It's wonderful'

'Doctor Brownie's Famous Cure'
Sonny Terry and Brownie McGhee

Lyubimov's 'Beatus Vir'
Male Chamber Choir
'This appeals to my Russian side – a Russian liturgical choir singing a beautiful chant'

Mad scene from Donizetti's *Lucia di Lammermoor*
Joan Sutherland with the Paris Conservatoire Orchestra

'Raga Bhairavi'
Suryanarayana
'I know very little about Indian classical music except that I love it every time I hear it'

'Falling in Love Again'
Billie Holiday
'Falling in love again has been the main guiding force in my life to this point, I would say'

BOOK
The Bhagavad Vita
'An ancient Indian book of knowledge. I keep trying to read it. I can't understand a word'

LUXURY ITEM
Silk underwear
'The best! The most expensive!'

22

TERRY WOGAN

BROADCASTER
21 May 1983

By 1983, Roy Plomley had moved into his fifth decade of presenting *Desert Island Discs* and had long since become a BBC institution. In May of that year, however, he entertained a castaway who was well on his path to becoming even more of a goliath of British broadcasting.

Having worked as a Dublin bank teller after leaving school, Terry Wogan had then joined Ireland's national broadcaster, Raidió Teilifís Éireann (RTÉ), as a newsreader, DJ and game-show host. In the mid-sixties he began broadcasting for the BBC, initially on the Light Programme and then, from 1967, on the newly launched Radio 1.

The genial presenter had taken over the breakfast show on Radio 2 in 1972. Over the following decade, his singular brand of gentle whimsy had first earned him a cult following and then turned him into one of the most loved and ubiquitous figures in British showbusiness.

By the time Wogan dropped in on Plomley, he was attracting close on 8 million listeners a day to his Radio 2 breakfast show plus hosting a Saturday night BBC One chat show and the *Blankety Blank* game show – and, infamously, providing an annual scabrous commentary for the UK's coverage of the Eurovision Song Contest.

There was a lot to talk about, and so Terry and Roy did exactly that.

• • •

The opening exchanges saw Wogan slightly chide Plomley for asking him whether he liked music: 'I love it! Obviously, you couldn't do what I do for a living and *not* like it!' The host moved on to ask his guest about his roots.

'I come from Limerick, a place which many other people in Ireland regard as being far from the Athens of the south,' explained Wogan. 'It's a strange and, in a sense, lovable little place.'

'Did you go to school there?'

'I did. I went under the aegis of the Jesuits, who beat me into shape.'

'What were you good at, at school?'

'I wasn't bad at sports. I wasn't a bad student. But I had no application. I still haven't. I know people find that hard to believe, because I appear to be working a great deal, but I have what Shaw called "the constant application of the congenitally lazy".'

'What did you want to be?'

'Nothing. I could never actually define *what* I wanted to be. I think I wanted to be a writer, or a journalist. I think I still want to be a writer.'

Wogan breezily recounted joining a debating society in school ('perhaps where I gained whatever confidence I have in addressing a microphone or a group of people') and appearing in stage musicals, both in Limerick and after his family moved to Dublin when he was fifteen. Two years later, he left school and got a job in a bank.

'Did you work on the counter?' enquired Plomley.

'I did. I was a very kindly teller and it was a jolly bank. We used to spend many a happy hour. We had a martinet of a manager who used to wear children's sandals and an ill-fitting hopsack suit.

'Whenever a pretty girl came in with a lodgement, you could always rely on one of the other tellers sneaking up behind you with a broom handle and letting you have it in the behind, so that you would spring out over the counter at this rather frightened girl! I had a lot of fun in the bank. I wouldn't have regretted it if I'd stayed there.'

Nevertheless, after a year or so Wogan answered a press advert for an 'announcer/newsreader' at the Irish national broadcasting service, RTÉ. There were 5,000 rival applicants.

'This was the beginning of the sixties in Ireland, everybody wanted to get into television and radio, and Ireland was just coming out of a depression,' he told Plomley. 'To my astonishment, I was offered a job.

'I resigned from the bank and joined RTÉ as an announcer for the princely sum of £1,500 per year. This was a king's ransom in 1961: I was only earning £5 a week in the bank at the time.'

Plomley asked his guest how his career had progressed at the Irish broadcaster, and how he came to approach the BBC.

'Well, I had done five or six years at RTÉ. Television had started and I became a newsreader and then I moved on to quiz shows. I suppose I was one of the most popular people there [*because*] they had never had any home-grown stars in Ireland.

'Then I thought, *I'm a big fish in a small pond*. I thought there were things I could do in Britain that I couldn't see myself doing in Ireland. I could see that there was going to be more freedom for me in the BBC than at Irish radio and television. And so it's proved.'

Wogan recalled sending the BBC a tape of one of his Irish radio shows, which he had forgotten to rewind to the start: 'They had to respool it! To their eternal credit – thank God! – they did!' The BBC offered him a weekly show on the newly launched Radio 1, and he resigned from RTÉ.

'And moved over here?' assumed Plomley.

'No, I worked for two years as a freelance in Ireland, flying over every week at a cost of about £40 by the time I'd paid for my hotel and the flight.

The BBC generously paid me £35 a programme. So, I actually lost money every week working for the BBC!'

'It can be done, Terry!' Plomley assured him.

Wogan recounted how he came to present an afternoon show that was broadcast on both Radio 1 and Radio 2 before, in April 1972, being asked to host the newly launched breakfast show on the latter station. This transition, he said, was not without its teething problems.

'It was a bit of a challenge and a change. For the first six months of that programme, I got a great deal of abuse. There was resentment among some people who had been listening to John Dunn and Ray Moore beforehand and [*liked*] a certain style of presentation.

'I was perhaps a little too abrasive, a little too fast, a little too talkative for them. I remember the *Sunday Express* taking grave exception to me! But I never had any lack of self-confidence. I never felt that I was going to fail.

'I had the experience of working in Ireland. I knew how to communicate with a radio audience. Radio has always been my medium rather than television. I'm much more at home with it, being self-conscious. Talking to a microphone, for me, is the easiest thing in the world.'

The subsequent eleven years had seen Wogan effortlessly overcome all doubters to become the don of British breakfast radio. Plomley worried that, living thirty miles out of London, he must have to get up at 5am every day to get to work. His guest put him straight.

'No, I come in like a bat out of hell! Luckily, when I'm coming in in the mornings, the police are on their teabreak. This was explained to me by the chief constable of Thames Valley. I've never seen a police car on the M4.

'I get up at the last possible moment. It means that they [*his colleagues*] don't panic if they don't see me until twenty-five past seven. I get up at six in the morning. If I'm doing television, I wash my hair. I have a little fresh fruit and a cup of coffee and I drive into London.

'It's no trouble at that hour of the morning. I get in in thirty-five minutes. I get into my studio, put the first two records on, put the cassettes on, take out the mail and start the programme.'

'Have a quick doze while the records are playing?' suggested Plomley.

'That's right. Naturally, I have to identify with the listeners, and they're all half-asleep anyway.

'I don't find it a great strain because, don't forget, *what I'm doing is not earth-shattering*. I'm communicating on a very everyday and ordinary basis. I rely a great deal on the listeners' letters.

'The great thing about a listener writing in is that unlike a scriptwriter, who has to be funny all the time, a listener only has to be funny once. When you get a really good listener's letter, no scriptwriter could be funnier.'

Plomley moved on to quiz his guest about his successful TV chat show, commenting that, as far as he knew, Wogan was the only interviewer at such a rarefied level not to use a clipboard of pre-prepared questions.

'The reason that I don't is that I like to maintain eye contact. I want to keep in touch with the person I'm interviewing. I don't want him to feel he's lost my attention while making an answer. The best interview is where the interviewee does all the talking. Your questions are brief, and his, or her, answers are long.'

At this point, Plomley turned his attention to the spangly, gaudy, tinsel-covered elephant in the room: the Eurovision Song Contest. Wogan at once declared his huge affection for this ridiculous beast.

'I love doing it! I take it with a pinch of salt. The Eurovision Song Contest is a monument to banality and mediocrity and everyone knows that. I give the viewer and the listener credit and so I don't take it seriously. I send it up.

'Occasionally, viewers write to *Points of View* giving off because I'm talking too much or I'm interrupting. But, you see, I don't believe it's a piece of Wagner. I don't believe it's a piece of art. I believe it's a piece of rubbish.'

'Yes, we agree about that!' concurred a laughing Plomley.

The host wondered what the future might hold for his guest. Would he carry on doing what he was doing for the next thirty years?

'No, not at all. Over the last couple of years, the exposure that I've been getting is so intense, and – for want of a better word, and in all modesty – the popularity level that I have reached is such that it cannot be sustained.'

Plomley: 'And you write books – or, rather, you publish books. You make them up from your listeners' mail.'

'Well, Bob Monkhouse says I've got it sewn up. My radio programme is based on the scripts provided by my listeners – the unpaid scriptwriters. Then I take those unpaid scripts which they write to me, put them into a book and sell them back to them.'

And Terry Wogan laughed. 'I suppose it's true ...'

• • •

Terry Wogan made a return visit to the desert island with Sue Lawley on October 9, 1988, and a third trip on New Year's Day 2012. Sir Terry, as he was by then, had acquired British citizenship in 2005, promptly been knighted, and quit his beloved Radio 2 breakfast show, switching instead to a less onerous Sunday morning slot on the same network.

On this last occasion, Kirsty Young heralded her guest as a man who had made a career for forty years out of 'just chatting' and 'putting the wit into wittering', an introduction with which Wogan seemed highly delighted. She began by referencing his huge celebrity in Britain.

'Have you a carapace to deal with it?' she asked. 'To always have to have a kind word, to be nice to a taxi driver, to talk to the woman in the newsagents?'

'It shouldn't feel like a carapace,' replied Wogan. 'It should be within your heart to be nice to people if they're being nice to you. If they're being rude to you, it's a different thing and you don't give them the time of day.

'I remember, early in my career, walking down Carnaby Street. A voice said, "You! Hello?" So, I turned around, and he said, "Sign this, will you? It's for my wife. I can't bear you, myself!" It's important to remember that the more people like you, the more others will despise you.'

Having lived in England for forty years by now, Wogan talked to Young about his sporadic sentimental returns to Ireland and the fact that he found people he'd known his whole life essentially unchanged.

'I go back to reunions in Belvedere, my school in Dublin, and nobody has changed, except on the outside,' he mused. 'The people who were comedians are still comedians. The eejits are still eejits. I think that when you're seventeen you're fully formed: the person you're going to be.'

Young pointed out that, unusually for an Irish person of his vintage, Wogan had no interest in the Church. 'Was there a specific point at which you lost your religion?' she asked.

'Well, I was brought up by Jesuits, who were very clever men. So, my mother always said it was the Jesuits' fault that I didn't believe because they made me think! I personally believe in people.'

Yet Young pointed out that Wogan's public identity had always been wrapped up in his Irishness: 'It's important to remember that you were doing the Radio 2 breakfast show, the most prominent show on the station, throughout the years when the IRA's bombing campaign was at its height. Did you feel your Irishness more keenly than ever?'

'Yes,' said Wogan. 'I never, obviously, denied my nationality. I never apologised for it, certainly. Why would I? What was being done was not being done in my name.

'It was very difficult. I was very conscious, for instance, you'd come up with a cheery morning voice after some horrific bomb incident. Being in the privileged position I was, I never came across any antipathy, and years later, Irish people living in Britain came up to me and said they were grateful for my being an Irish voice without apology.'

The host asked if it was true that Wogan had a parcel bomb sent to him at Broadcasting House in 1994.

'It was. My producer carried this parcel to the post room and he was roundly castigated by the BBC. He nearly lost his job for trying to blow himself up. And whoever sent in the bomb with my name on it can't have been much of a fan, because I was on holiday ...'

Young turned the chat to cheerier matters – the TOGGs: Terry's Old

Geezers and Gals, as the DJ affectionately regularly referred on the air to his Radio 2 listeners. 'How do you know if you're a TOGG?' she asked. Wogan happily filled her in on a few criteria.

'You're asleep, but others worry that you're dead. You're proud of your lawnmower. The end of your tie doesn't come anywhere near the top of your pants. You see *Time Team* on the television and get drawn in. You can live without sex but not without your glasses ...'

'And there are TOGG conventions?' asked Young.

'There are! I go to them and we all meet. They dance and they behave disgracefully and so do I. They're the people who keep me going – the people with the wit and wisdom and the ability to take things laterally rather than vertically: that strange sense of humour.'

Young wondered what the future held for Wogan. He was, she said, a 'mere stripling' compared to Sir Bruce Forsyth, who was then still going strong in his mid-eighties.

'But look at him!' said Wogan. 'Dainty on the feet, fit as a flea – he'll go on forever. *I* won't go on forever. I'll fold my tent and silently steal away one of these days ...'

• • •

Sir Terry Wogan continued to host his weekend Radio 2 show and the annual BBC TV Children in Need charity fundraiser until he was forced by illness to fold up his tent, silently steal away, and retire in 2015. He died of cancer at his home in Berkshire on 31 January 2016 at the age of seventy-seven. A public memorial service at Westminster Abbey the following September was broadcast live on Radio 2 and, shortly afterwards, the BBC renamed the building that housed the station Wogan House. This felt a fitting and entirely correct tribute.

DISCS CHOSEN (1983)

'Stardust'
Nat King Cole
'The greatest romantic singer in the world, and I'm a rapidly ageing romantic myself'

❤ **Rimsky-Korsakov's** *Scheherazade*
London Philharmonic Orchestra
'Everything is lovely. There isn't a weak spot in the whole work'

'Carrickfergus'
The Chieftains
'One of the loveliest Irish airs'

'The Cobbler's Song'
Paul Robeson
'My father loved Paul Robeson and so do I'

'Heartbreak Hotel'
Elvis Presley
'I knew that music would never be the same again'

'The Easter Hymn' from Mascagni's *Cavalleria Rusticana*
Gabriele Santini with Rome Opera House Orchestra

'My Funny Valentine'
Frank Sinatra
'Frank Sinatra is the greatest song stylist ever, and Rodgers and Hammerstein are legitimate genii of popular music'

'You'll Never Walk Alone'
Shirley Jones
'This would inspire me to keep going when all appeared to be lost'

BOOK
At Swim-Two-Birds – Flann O'Brien
'The funniest book ever written'

AND

The Collected Works of P.G. Wodehouse
'I don't want Shakespeare. Wonderful when performed, terminally boring when read!'

LUXURY ITEM
A couple of cases of vodka
'I feel there are oranges on this island so at least I'd be able to have a vodka and orange. Smash a few down at six o'clock'

23
PRINCESS MICHAEL OF KENT

ARISTOCRAT
28 January 1984

Princess Michael of Kent was not the first royal personage to grace the desert island. HRH Princess Margaret, the Queen's sister, had capsized in 1981, railing against 'aggravating' media coverage of her private life and confiding that 'one was brought up to be able to talk to anybody'.

A highly glamorous royal emissary also washed up later that same year: Princess Grace of Monaco, who talked of her previous incarnation as Hollywood star Grace Kelly before retiring at the age of twenty-six to marry Prince Rainier. Tragically, the princess was to die in a car accident the year after the broadcast.

Despite these precursors, the appearance of Princess Michael of Kent at the start of 1984 was still a major event. Born in Sudetenland [*now the Czech Republic*] in 1945, Baroness Marie-Christine Anna Agnes Hedwig Ida von Reibnitz was of royal blood even before she married Prince Michael of Kent, a first cousin to the Queen, in 1978.

The princess was a contentious addition to the British royal family, as both a Roman Catholic and a divorcee. She had also been subjected to negative press coverage due to her father's history as a German officer in the First World War and a Nazi party member in the Second.

Roy Plomley gave most of these potentially troublesome conversational topics an extremely wide berth, but the princess had plenty of other topics from a fascinating life to talk about.

• • •

'We're very glad to welcome you to our island, ma'am,' said Plomley, although his guest's reply gave the distinct impression that it had not been a foregone conclusion that she would be allowed to attend.

'You originally asked me about four years ago to do this show,' she said, briskly. 'At the time it was thought, perhaps, that as no one had done it in the family, *it might not be quite the moment.* So, ever since then, I've been making lists [*of records*].'

Plomley reminded his listeners that the princess had been born in what was by 1984 Czechoslovakia and asked her about her father, the late Baron von Reibnitz, who had been fifty when she was born.

'He was from Silesia and he was so old that, as far as he was concerned, he was from a previous incarnation when Silesia was still part of the Austro-Hungarian Empire,' she said. 'It's now Poland. These borders change rather rapidly, so one has to try to keep up with that. He wasn't around a terribly long time. I was brought up by my mother's family.'

'She's a Hungarian countess?'

'Yes.'

Plomley: 'When your parents split, you stayed with your mother and went to Australia. Why Australia?'

'Well, my mother was not only a historian by training but she was also a great skier, and she skied in the 1936 Olympics. At the time, the only other people who appeared to be skiing were British, so she had a lot of English friends.

'After the war, they told her, "You know, Austria's such a mess, why don't you come out to Australia and bring your children for a few years until Europe settles down a bit?" They assured her there was very good skiing in Australia, so off we went.'

Plomley asked how she had coped at school in Sydney. Could she even understand English?

'Yes, because I had an English governess. I was a little bit, "*The vall is vite, the grrass is grreen*," but I was trying. I wanted to do everything that I did as well as I possibly could. I think I wanted to be a historian, like my mother.'

'When you left school, you went to Europe. Was that to stay with your father?'

'No,' answered the princess. 'My father had a farm in Africa and I went there. I was a little bit too young for university and I thought, *Well, it's time to go and meet the father who I haven't met before.* It was a terrible shock to meet a very much older person, who could have been my grandfather.

'But it was also an introduction to Africa, and Africa became a great love of my life. I loved going on safari. I hated killing the animals: never shot at them and did everything I could, like playing loud music, to stop them being shot at. But I loved being in the jungle in Africa.'

Plomley: 'And from Africa, you went back to Austria?'

'Yes, to meet all the cousins about whom I knew every little detail. That was the role of a central European: to know everything about one another's relatives. Unlike *here*, where you don't even know your first cousins, sometimes!'

'That is sadly true,' regretted Plomley.

'But I discovered after a while that I did not want to settle in Austria but to learn interior design. I came to England, because there wasn't such a study in Austria. It was thought if your house had been good enough for your grandmother to live in, it was good enough for *you* to live in. Why should you wish to do anything so *nouveau riche* as do it up in a new, modern way?

'My mama had great English friends from her skiing days. One of them was a very excellent interior designer who decided, out of her great generosity, to take me on as an apprentice.'

The princess described her apprenticeship as teaching her 'everything that an interior designer should know in order to correct her workmen and her builders'. She then did a short spell in an advertising agency where she 'learned enough to know how to tell others to work for me'.

Princess Michael next set up an interior design company. How did it go? wondered Plomley. 'I did very well and made lots of money. I was very successful!'

Plomley went on to touch delicately on his guest's entrance into the British royal family. 'You were a Roman Catholic and a divorcee – a church wedding at that time wasn't possible?'

'It certainly would have been possible in the Catholic church because, after all, my first marriage had been annulled by Pope Paul VI!' noted the princess. 'The problem arose that Prince Michael could not have Catholic children.' The issue, she explained, had been resolved: 'Our children are very much remaining Anglican, and I very much wish to remain, and *shall* remain, a Catholic.'

Plomley turned his mind to the royal couple's sporting interests. Prince Michael, he noted, was a former British bobsleigh champion, as well as being a rally driver and a horseman. Did any of these pursuits interest his wife?

'You could offer me any money and I would not go down a bobsleigh! I think he feels a little bit the same about hunting, but he does it out of love for me.'

Plomley: 'But you like horses, and riding?'

'I like horses but I'm not very expert. I sort of believe in having a good horse and heading for the highest fence because that's the biggest thrill. But I also have the biggest spills as a result!'

Prince and Princess Michael, the host observed, were very diligent in discharging their royal duties. Was it true that they attended around three hundred official functions per year?

'News to me!' the princess replied. 'I've never counted them up. But if you say so, I believe you.'

Plomley: 'All at your own expense, I believe?' His guest's response was utterly formal and yet spoke volumes.

'Well, my husband was brought up to believe that you cannot have the privilege without the obligation,' she declared. 'Therefore, he fulfils what he sees as his obligation. And I, as his wife, follow him.'

As a rare glimpse behind the curtain at life in the royal family wended to its close, Plomley regretted that his guest was occasionally vulnerable to 'silly stunts'. At a recent public event, she had been attacked by a man dressed as a wolf 'to get newspaper publicity'.

'Yes, but the letters that one gets [*afterwards*] are so delicious that they make it all right!' the princess said, chortling. 'A lovely lady wrote to me, saying, "Quite honestly I wouldn't be upset, if I were you, because for a married woman of your age to still be attractive to wolves is quite something in itself!"'

'Oh, that's charming!' murmured Roy Plomley.

'Yes! It cheered me up no end ...'

• • •

Since washing up on the island, Princess Michael of Kent has written two books about royalty. She has served on the board of the Victoria and Albert Museum, where she once studied interior design, and supports a large number of national and international charities, including in Africa. At the age of seventy-seven, she continues to accompany her husband as he fulfils his royal duties from which they are both about to retire.

DISCS CHOSEN
Dvořák's Cello Concerto in B Minor
Mstislav Rostropovich with the Berlin Philharmonic Orchestra
'It reminds me of my grandmother – my model in all things and a very beautiful and grand princess'

Strauss's *Die Fledermaus*
Vienna Symphony Orchestra
'In honour of my mama – not that she needs to be remembered'

The opening of Dylan Thomas's *Under Milk Wood*
Dylan Thomas
'The beginning of my love of English literature'

Beethoven's Symphony No. 5 in C Minor
Vienna Philharmonic Orchestra
'I played it in the jungle and my father screamed that it would frighten away the buffalo and the elephants. I didn't care, and it did'

Lehár's *Gold and Silver* waltz
Johann Strauss Orchestra of Vienna
'With which we opened our wedding ball in Vienna'

Act 3 from Puccini's *Tosca*
Giuseppe Stefano with the Orchestra of La Scala, Milan
'As a typical central European, I like a good tragedy'

Mahler's Symphony No. 5 in C Sharp Minor
Chicago Symphony Orchestra

❤ **Mozart's Violin Concerto No. 3 in G Major**
Anne-Sophie Mutter with the Berlin Philharmonic Orchestra

BOOK
The Histories – Herodotus
'*I can read him again and again*'

LUXURY ITEM
A pregnant oriental cat
Plomley: 'No, I will give you anything you want, except a cat. It must be something inanimate'
Princess Michael: 'I'm having a cat!'

24
JULIE WALTERS

ACTOR, COMEDIAN
2 February 1985

Roy Plomley welcomed hugely popular British actor Julie Walters to his desert island two years after she had made her big movie breakthrough in *Educating Rita* as a working-class girl craving more from her life but unsure where to begin looking for it.

It was difficult not to think that there were parallels to Walters's own life as she described her early years in Birmingham working as a nurse, and then casting around despairingly for an entry into acting before finally, fortuitously, locating a way in.

In addition to her film and theatre roles, by 1985 Walters was also well-known for her burgeoning television comedy partnership with Victoria Wood, and these topics all featured in an enjoyable conversation in what will be Mr Plomley's final hosting appearance in this volume.

• • •

Plomley opened the discourse by establishing that his guest was from Birmingham, and enquired whether she was bright in school.

'Well, *I* thought I was,' replied Walters. 'The fact that the teachers didn't is another matter! What did *they* know? But, no, I wasn't really academic. In fact, I was asked to leave.'

'You *weren't?*' asked the horrified host.

'Yes – please don't be shocked, Roy! I was never there: I suppose that was the main problem. There was a cake shop that sold tea and coffee in the local high street. I was usually in there with my friend.'

Having been defenestrated from the education system with very few qualifications, explained Walters, she had trained as a nurse without being entirely sure why.

'I did it first of all because my mother wanted me to, and secondly just because I'd been accepted,' she said. 'That's why I ended up in nursing. I was there by mistake, really.'

Plomley: 'Did you find it rewarding?'

'Yes, I did. I loved all the eating of grapes and the chit-chatting with the patients, and the washing, and I liked all the junior nursing activities.'

'But you didn't finish the course?'

'No, because it wasn't really what I wanted to do. I was doing it for the wrong reasons and I thought, *I've got to do what I want to do now.*'

Having resolved that she wanted to get into acting, Walters confessed to Plomley that she was initially at such a loss about how to do so that all she could think of was contacting her (infamous) local TV soap opera.

'I wrote to *Crossroads* and asked them if I could come down there and show them how to do a Birmingham accent! This was 1966. They wrote back saying it's a difficult accent, but they were full up and didn't need anybody.'

This may feasibly have been a lucky escape. Plomley commented that he had read that Walters had always been good at impersonations.

'Yes. I always thought that other people could handle situations better than me, and they had the key to how you coped with life that I didn't have. So I was watching them, and how they did things, and I suddenly realised I could impersonate people.

'My brothers would say, "Go on, do Aunty Kathleen!" "Do Mrs O'Neill from school!" I thought, *Oh, I like this!* Then I became more interested in what people were *thinking* in different situations, even if they were just buying a cup of tea. From that, I became interested in acting.'

Plomley: 'Did your parents encourage this?'

'No, my mother went completely bananas when I told her what I was going to be! I had to get my brothers to protect me from her: "Oh, may the great God look to me now, what have we reared?!"'

Plomley: 'Your mother's Irish?"

'Yes!' Walters laughed. 'I'm glad you spotted the accent!'

Walters described 'looking up drama in the telephone directory' and phoning 'something called the British Drama League'. 'A very worthy institution!' opined Plomley. 'Huh! They were very snooty to me, I'm here to tell you, Roy!' his guest replied.

A more productive opening offered itself via a boyfriend at Manchester Polytechnic who suggested she enrol in their drama course. Walters did so. 'Did you enjoy it?' asked Plomley.

'Oh, I loved it! I loved it because it was like getting into the right gear. Do you know, I felt as though I'd been driving a car in the wrong gear, uphill, all my life until I started doing that ...'

Post-polytechnic, she told Plomley, when she began the traditionally laborious process of looking for auditions and acting work, she got a lucky break straightaway.

'I wrote about two letters, and one was to the Everyman Theatre in Liverpool. I was called immediately because somebody had had to come out of something, and I went along and did auditions, most of which I had written.

'They were sort of set audition pieces but I'd changed them to suit me, thinking, naively, that the person interviewing me – the actor Jonathan

Pryce – would not have seen the plays. Of course, he *had* but, luckily, he had a sense of humour, so I got in.'

Walters described an initiative whereby the Everyman did free shows in local Liverpool pubs. 'They weren't exactly easy pubs – bottles were flying! You'd go in and do your party piece and add anything you liked. I used to do Shirley Bassey impersonations.'

Plomley: 'You were learning the hard way?'

'To survive, yes!'

Plomley led Walters through her first London stage appearances: with Richard Beckinsale in *Funny Peculiar*, and in Willy Russell's *Breezeblock Park*. She then met Victoria Wood when they were both doing a revue, at the Bush Theatre in Shepherd's Bush, called *In at the Death*. 'It was appropriately named,' she noted.

'No good?'

'It wasn't an enormous success, no! But she wrote a sketch for me and we got on terribly well. Then one day we were out having lunch and she said to me, "I've met you before, you know." I said, "No, I'd remember you!" and she said, "Did you go to Manchester Polytechnic?"'

'And then I remembered her! In my first year, I was there ushering in new auditionees and she was one of them. I remember this small girl being sick everywhere. It was Victoria. She didn't get in.'

After Walters described moving into TV work with Wood, Plomley was keen to talk about her film break in *Educating Rita*. The director, Lewis Gilbert, had offered her the role after seeing her play the same part on the London stage – but this was no guarantee that she would get it.

'No – he said that it was likely that the people putting the money up would want a star to play it. He was right: when he went to America, they wanted Dolly Parton. Well, I'm sorry, Roy, but I couldn't possibly compete! But could *she* do a Liverpool accent?!'

Gilbert managed to raise the finance himself and Walters played the film role opposite Michael Caine. ('Good box office insurance!' declared Plomley.) It was to win her an Oscar nomination – and a Golden Globe. 'What's a Golden Globe?' wondered Plomley.

'Well, actually, as we're in England, I can tell you – it's a rather ugly-looking thing which is marvellous for keeping windows open when the sashcord's broken!'

As Plomley guided this deeply entertaining encounter to its close, he noted that the Oscar nomination had opened new career doors to Walters, but she had chosen not to go through all of them: 'You turned down a big-budget Burt Reynolds film!'

'Yes, I did,' she confirmed. 'I was in New York for the beginning of a tour selling *Educating Rita* and there was a script from Burt Reynolds. I thought,

Here we go, everybody! I'm in New York, a script from Burt Reynolds – this is wonderful! And then I read it, and it spoilt everything.

'It was Burt, rushing out beating everybody up and having very quick affairs with lots of women, of which I was to be one. The story was not interesting. And they'd asked me to play – you'll never believe this! – this upmarket American, very classy, stock-market whizz-kid.

'I met him, and I said, "Burt, this is a Candice Bergen part." Which it *is*. It's that sort of woman. And he said, "Well, you know, what we want is a bit of cross-casting, or something." Because the script was so boring that they thought it would be interesting to have someone completely wrong for the part, and that might gyp the script up a bit!

'And I thought, *Why don't you just get a good script?*'

• • •

Since turning down Burt Reynolds and encountering Roy Plomley, Julie Walters has starred in numerous box-office smashes including *Personal Services*, *Billy Elliot*, the Harry Potter series, *Calendar Girls*, *Mamma Mia!* and *Paddington*. She has also become a beloved staple of British television, winning a record-breaking four BAFTAs for best actress. In 2017, she was made a dame for services to drama. Bad call, *Crossroads*!

DISCS CHOSEN
'It's Raining Men'
The Weather Girls
'I think it's really funny – the thought of hundreds of men raining through the air! Imagine the mess they'd make ...'

'Harlem Shuffle'
Bob & Earl
'It takes me back to 1966, to the Locarno in Birmingham'

'New York City Serenade'
Bruce Springsteen
'It reminds me of my Everyman [Theatre] *days – it was a wonderful time and nothing's ever been like that since, really'*

'After Midnight'
J.J. Cale
'I like it because he's just so completely laidback'

'Not a Day Goes By'
Carly Simon
'It's so heart-rending – I love a good weep'

'I Can't Stand the Rain'
Ann Peebles
'I always loved it as a teenager and then I heard that it was John Lennon's favourite record, so I always pop it in'

❤ **'I Get Along Without You Very Well'**
Carly Simon
'I think it's very appropriate on a desert island, don't you?'

'T'Aint Nobody's Biz-ness If I Do'
Billie Holiday

BOOK
The Magus – John Fowles

LUXURY ITEM
A telephone system
'I'd have to talk to people! All my relationships are conducted on the phone!'

MICHAEL PARKINSON YEARS

1986–88

Roy Plomley had been quietly ill for a while. The *Desert Island Discs* progenitor and host had been diagnosed with lung cancer but kept the news to himself. This meant that his death from a heart attack linked to pleurisy, on 28 May 1985 at the age of seventy-one, was a complete shock.

It also raised an existential question over the show's future. It had been inextricably linked to the presenter since its inception: would it be able to continue without him? Nor did the BBC even hold the rights to the format. These now passed to Plomley's widow, Diana Wong.

The BBC gave serious thought to laying *Desert Island Discs* to rest with its creator – but then decided against it, as Radio 4 controller David Hatch was to explain at the start of November 1985.

'We wondered whether *Desert Island Discs* should continue after Roy's death,' he admitted. 'But hundreds of devotees of the programme wrote asking us to bring it back. And Mrs Plomley is happy, as Roy's name will be perpetuated.'

The show was to return the following January – but who would be the host? Various names were in the frame. Mrs Plomley's preference was reportedly for barrister John Mortimer. Newsreader Richard Baker was mentioned, as was *Ask the Family* host Robert Robinson.

Instead, on 11 November 1985, the BBC turned to another of its star presenters – who was already the most famous interviewer in the land.

Michael Parkinson's *Parkinson* chat show had routinely attracted 6 or 7 million TV viewers to BBC One every Saturday evening from 1971 to 1982. The biggest names in British showbiz, sport and current affairs had beaten a path to his door, along with visiting Hollywood superstars.

Parkinson was reportedly wary about taking on the *Desert Island Discs* mantle. He had been a castaway himself in 1972 but later complained in his autobiography, *Parky*, of finding the experience underwhelming and 'dispiriting'.

His prime complaint was that the producers had not played his musical choices in the studio during the interview, preferring to edit them in later. He made two requests: to be able to choose his own castaways, and to play them their discs as they talked. Both were granted.

As Parkinson was to explain: 'If Roy Plomley had seen the show as a chat with music, I very much saw it as a chance to explore exactly what music meant and what part it played in the castaway's experience – to analyse the soundtrack of their lives.'

Desert Island Discs returned from its short hiatus on 5 January 1986 and Parkinson's first guest was film director Alan Parker, who laid into the UK film industry. The next month, Parky asked dress designer Bruce Oldfield whether designing frocks was 'a proper job for a man'.

The new host appeared minded to import a newfound abrasiveness or edge into the show. This was never going to happen without hitches. The BBC Review Board admonished him for his provocative question to Oldfield, which it felt was 'too obtrusive'.

Barnsley's Parky was also flummoxed when this same overview body accused him of turning *Desert Island Discs* into an outlet for the 'Yorkshire mafia', claiming that his first six guests had all been born in the county! He was to point out that this was true of only one of those castaways: Maureen Lipman, who opens this section.

After these initial ructions, the experienced Parkinson settled into the job and became a very solid *Desert Island Discs* host. His rapport with his castaways was doubtless helped by the fact that he had previously encountered many of them on Saturday-night TV.

Joanna Lumley was reliably enchanting as she described her childhood in Malaya and travails as Purdey in *The New Avengers*. Victoria Wood surmised that she would probably love the desert island: 'I like being on my own better than with other people.'

A particularly remarkable episode saw Parkinson meet Maya Angelou, the prodigiously gifted American writer and activist who talked of Deep South racism, being raped as a child, and seeing two close friends and colleagues, Malcolm X and Martin Luther King, assassinated. Here was an extraordinary life, beautifully told.

Michael Parkinson proved that *Desert Island Discs* could survive the loss of Roy Plomley but his own tenure on the show was relatively short. He left the desert island in March 1988, later commenting, in *Parky*, that 'I didn't want to spend the rest of my life hosting a parlour game.'

It was to be all change on the island again.

25
MAUREEN LIPMAN

ACTOR, WRITER, COMEDIAN
19 January 1986

Of a similar vintage to Julie Walters yet blessed with a mother far more encouraging of a career in showbusiness, Maureen Lipman proved a highly diverting castaway when she showed up on the desert island in the early days of Michael Parkinson's tenure.

Parkinson expressed the view that, growing up in a Jewish family in Yorkshire, his guest was a rather unlikely candidate to succeed in light entertainment. However, Lipman gave the distinct impression that, alongside the necessary talent, she had made it through sheer willpower.

In his introduction, Parkinson reflected that Lipman had been described as both 'a female Woody Allen' and 'the Lucille Ball of Muswell Hill'. Both comparisons had a certain merit, but the conversation that followed demonstrated that her waspish wit was entirely her own.

• • •

Greeting his guest, Parkinson wondered whether music had been a big part of her life as she grew up in Hull, where her father had worked as a tailor.

'We didn't have what you'd call a music house,' reflected Lipman. 'We had some of those old seventy-eights but we used to melt them down to make fruit bowls out of them, and then it's difficult to get the right sound, isn't it?

'Then I heard the records of Alma Cogan, which had an incredible effect on me – this girl with the laugh in her voice. She was a nice Jewish girl, and she was big in our house. I heard her singing "Dreamboat" when I was four or five and began doing impersonations of her, heavily encouraged by my mother.

'My mother would stand me on the sideboard and say, "Do your Alma Cogan impersonation for our visitors!" And she would sit in the wings saying, "Roll your eyes, Maureen! Sing out! Don't forget the laugh in your voice!" And years later, I thought, *God, that's just the sort of thing I'd hate as a grown-up, to see a performing midget like that ...*'

Lipman's Jewishness had obviously been a major part of her upbringing, commented Parkinson. Was she still religious?

'I suppose I'm an Orthodox hypocrite, really. I do the best I can, under the circumstances. It's very hard for me to say to the West End management, "I'm not coming in on Friday night because, you know, I'm cooking the chicken." You just can't do it.

'But all the stage things about being Jewish are part of my life. I mean, I love all the Yiddish words and I love the food. I love the warmth and the feeling of belonging, even if it's not number-one priority in my life.'

Parkinson wondered when his guest had realised that the theatre was her calling. 'Was there one moment, a school play or whatever, when you thought, *This is for me?*'

'I think I always knew. I've said that I started acting as the placenta hit the pedal bin and it feels as if that was true. But I was a bit of a rebel and a bit naughty at school, and more concerned with making the class laugh than with actually learning anything.

'The school play one year was *Dr Faustus* and it was an all-girl school, so I was playing Dr Faustus. It got a big laugh when I kissed Helen of Troy, but then it would. I got a very good review in the *Hull Daily Mail*, and I think even by then I was certain there was nothing else I would do.

'When the careers officer came round, I said, "I'm going to be an actress." They looked a bit askance, because I didn't look like one, and said, "You must have something to fall back on." I said, "I'm going to fall back on the casting couch." And I've been waiting to do it ever since ...'

Lipman described applying to drama schools and being accepted by the London Academy of Music and Dramatic Art (LAMDA). Parkinson was concerned with how her mum would have taken this news.

'A typical Jewish mother, as you say,' he mused. 'She must have been absolutely distraught and distressed – her daughter, seventeen or eighteen, down in London by herself ...'

'Yes, that was difficult,' agreed Lipman. 'But she found me nice Jewish digs in Barons Court and I was totally looked after. I had no idea of what you do on your own.

'When I went in a phone box in Earl's Court and it rang, I thought that was just what happened in London. I got propositioned over the phone from three boxes along and ran like a snake all the way back to LAMDA. I was totally innocent.

'I dressed like I was forty-five in those days. I wore everything matching – beige boots, beige dress, beige coat – I went about looking like a buff-coloured envelope. It took me a very long time to actually achieve any level of maturity and learn how to cope on my own. I'm still not terribly good at it, which is why this island is worrying me a bit.'

Parkinson produced a hoary old chestnut by way of an enquiry: is it harder for a woman to be funny than a man? 'A man can go on stage and crack jokes,' he said. 'If a woman does it, it's more of a problem, isn't it?'

'It *was*,' corrected Lipman. 'I do think it's getting better. I think, with the women's movement having made the steps they've made, this is becoming a thing of the past. It's to do with losing your femininity.

'If you listen to Sophie Tucker and Mae West, you realise they were saying the most extraordinary lewd jokes and getting away with it by being cod-sexy, in a funny sort of way. But you can't be "feminine" in inverted commas and funny: it doesn't work. You have to do what Joan Rivers does, and I do, and put yourself down all the time. I don't know why that should be.'

Parkinson recalled that his guest's big TV break had been starring in a hit sitcom, *Agony*, in which she played the lead role as an agony aunt. 'Did this change your life tremendously?'

'Not really, no. I didn't go out and get mobbed, let's put it that way. What it did do was enable me to open bazaars, and that always gives you a lot of material.

'I went once to open a fete, made a speech for ten minutes and then walked around buying cakes. I came to a stall and one of the ladies serving said to me, "Ooh, I know your face!" The other one said to her: "Have you gone mad? She just opened the fete! This is Miriam Karlin!"'

Lipman's breezy self-deprecation was enjoyable, but the interview hit a more serious strain when Parkinson quoted one of her own lines back at her, from her autobiography: that 'behind every success story, there is a guilt complex'.

'Well, I don't know what drives *you*, Michael, but I wish I knew what drives me to do the amount of things I do,' she replied. 'I don't believe you can be all things to all persons, but it is the current trend to try.

'People are always saying to me, "How do you manage to be a wife, a mother, a writer, an actress?" And I literally have to say, "Because I do them all less than the standards to which I strive."

'We are living in an age in which, particularly for women, we've got to prove that we can go out to work and still get the casserole in the oven and still be there in the black negligee at night. And it's just out of the question.

'All these magazines are telling us that other people do it. Well, *I* don't believe it. People like me are running around, chasing our tails and trying to prove that we can be everything. And it's absolutely exhausting.'

Nevertheless, for all of her characteristic anxious self-flagellation, Maureen Lipman was clearly making a very good job of juggling life and career. She was never too distracted to spot a good gag, as evidenced when Parkinson asked her to supply an epitaph in case she were to perish on the desert island.

'She was only a tailor's daughter,' proclaimed his guest, 'but she had them all in stitches!'

• • •

In the near-forty years since that tailor's daughter fetched up on the desert island, Maureen Lipman has become woven into the very fabric of British light entertainment through numerous theatre productions, television roles in everything from *Smiley's People* to *Coronation Street* and *Doctor Who*, countless quiz and game shows and her timeless turn in the late eighties as Jewish grandmother Beattie in TV ads for BT: 'Oh, now he's got an *ology*!' In 2020, she was made a dame for services to charity, entertainment and the arts.

DISCS CHOSEN
'Dreamboat'
Alma Cogan

'True Love Ways'
Buddy Holly
'He was my brother's favourite singer'

'Imagine'
John Lennon
'I discovered what life was all about by listening to Beatles records – John Lennon in particular'

'First Flight'
Joyce Grenfell
'She is my heroine ... Insidiously funny without ever being cruel'

'Lady with the Braid'
Dory Previn

'L'amour est un oiseau rebelle' from Bizet's *Carmen*
Maria Callas with the Paris Opera Orchestra
'It went through me like a wire'

❤ **Beethoven's Triple Concerto in C Major**
Berlin Philharmonic Orchestra
'I have quite a strong melancholy streak. I think all comics have'

'The Bell Song' from Delibes's *Lakme*
Mady Mesplé
'This beautiful, tinkling song might get me in communication with the birds on the island'

BOOK
Complete works of Jane Austen
'Insidious wit and extraordinary delineation of character'

LUXURY ITEM
A parking meter and a caravan
'With a wooden floor to tap my days away until I'm rescued'

26
VICTORIA WOOD

COMEDIAN, ACTOR, WRITER
8 February 1987

Victoria Wood was a genius at finding comedy in the mundane. Her forte was locating humour in routine, everyday transactions and places: before her, nobody even *knew* that reciting the words 'Cheadle Hulme' in a droll, dead-pan manner was intrinsically hilarious.

By 1987, Wood was already a big enough star for her February *Desert Island Discs* appearance to be repeated later that year in the prestigious Christ-mas Day slot – yet you wouldn't have thought so from listening to the programme. Every self-effacing answer that she gave to Michael Parkinson's enquiries appeared intended to convey her resolute ordinariness.

She was fooling nobody. A natural comedian, Wood's dry, irrepressible wit infused every moment of the conversational exchange. Broadcast at breakfast time, the repeated episode made an excellent backdrop to opening Christmas presents up and down the land, not to mention a fine precursor to the Queen's Speech.

• • •

The reliably perceptive Parkinson opened the show by observing that Wood was 'a very funny woman' and asked whether she might enjoy the experience of being marooned on a desert island. 'Yes,' she replied, simply. 'I like being on my own better than with other people.'

Wood grew up in Bury, Lancashire. Parkinson asked about her family background: 'What did your parents do?'

'My father is that very northern occupation – an insurance underwriter. We were just sort of ordinary middle class. No clogs, I'm afraid! No mines!'

'And was it a happy childhood?'

'It was just very ordinary, really. I was a very boring child. Youngest of four. Occupations: playing the piano, eating and watching television. Which is all I do now.'

'What ambitions did you have as a child?'

'I wanted to be a boxer first of all, then I wanted to be famous.'

Parkinson hit his guest with the theory that, for comedians, being funny is a vocation. She was dubious: 'I think it's more just a love for it than an actual vocation.' The host asked her when she had realised that she was funny.

'About fifteen. I joined Rochdale Youth Theatre and started to get parts in the plays and they were always the funny parts. And that was when I thought, *Oh, I can do this!* Because I hadn't been able to do anything before that.'

'Did your parents support you?'

'Yes. I think they were just glad I'd found something I could do.'

Before continuing her account of her life's progression, Wood digressed to tell Parkinson that, despite her childhood ambition to be famous, she actually found fame not all that it was cracked up to be.

'It's useful for selling tickets but it's a nuisance,' she admitted. 'When you want to go and buy your knickers and things, it's an irritation when people come up and *poke* you.'

'Do they actually *poke* you?'

'They do! They come up and want to know if you are who they think you are. This covers a range of people, from the woman who does the lipreading on Sunday mornings to Angela Rippon. They know you're somebody that they've seen on television.

'It's part of the job, but what I mean is, it's not what you imagine. It's not swanning about in a fur coat. It's people saying, "Oh, my wife's seen *all* of your programmes, and she hasn't liked *any* of them yet."'

Parkinson returned to his guest's life story and asked her about reading drama at Birmingham University. 'It was the only place I could get in, because I only had two O levels,' she admitted. 'It was the only place that was barmy enough to take me on.

'I never got to do any acting – it was all done by these very tall, blonde girls. They got all the parts and I never got anything. So, I just used to do the stage management and sweep the stage.'

'I auditioned for Joe Orton's *Loot* and didn't get it. They said, "Well, you can play the piano at the end while people are walking out." I did, but as they were all leaving, I stood up, said, "Don't go!" and sang a song about how I should have had the part. I got my own back on them.'

Asked how she had first met Julie Walters, Wood confirmed the story told by her comedy partner to Roy Plomley two years earlier.

'I auditioned for Manchester Polytechnic and she was one of the people showing people around. I was ill with nerves the whole day. Then I felt better and suddenly noticed this strange woman, with the smallest eyes I'd ever seen, talking nineteen-to-the-dozen, doing an impression of a nurse wheeling a commode down a ward. I thought, *This is odd! Funny!*

'I didn't get in so I never saw her again for years. Then, in 1978, I met her in Shepherd's Bush at the Bush Theatre and did a double-take: *Oh, that's that woman!* And she said, "Oh, you were the one that kept throwing up."'

Parkinson wondered why Wood's early auditions were so unsuccessful. What kind of material was she performing?

'We used to do pieces of Shakespeare, so I did Juliet's death scene. So stupid! I did it with glasses on and a Lancashire accent and a midi-skirt. It was ludicrous: terrible. I'm not surprised that I never got in!'

Parkinson: 'And after you left university, what did you do to earn a living?'

'I went in for the Pub Entertainer of the Year competition. I don't know why, because I never went in pubs and it wasn't entertaining. There were five acts: I came third. The piano was bolted to the floor and I had to play with my back to the audience. Probably a blessing in disguise.

'The act that won was three enormous girls in enormous hotpants. The second prize was a man dressed as a skeleton, who climbed out of a coffin and sang, "T'aint no sin to take off your skin/And show 'em your bones!" I came third to them and thought, *I'm not going to get on!*

Wood related that her career took a turn for the better when she won a heat of TV talent show *New Faces* in 1974. However, even this was to prove a false start.

'The whole series was won by Marti Caine, Lenny Henry came a close second or third, and we were all given a most appalling television show together called *The Summer Show*. I've never met anybody who's seen it, or who admits to having seen it.

'It was one of those really bad variety shows where they've got the scripts out of other people's dustbins. I remember Marti Caine saying to me, "Eh, the money's rubbish, innit?" It was £125 per week, which I thought was marvellous. I hadn't earned that much in years.'

Wood's next big break was performing comedic songs on BBC light entertainment and consumer affairs show *That's Life!* on Sunday nights. Even this, she sighed, was not without its drawbacks.

'A producer told me every song had to last two minutes ten seconds. It was to fit some stupid format of his own. For years after that, all of my songs were two minutes ten seconds. I used to stop in the middle!'

Parkinson: 'But *That's Life!* brought you to the notice of the public?'

'It brought me to their notice but they didn't like me. They used to say, "You're Pam Ayres!" They got me mixed up with everybody else.'

Post-*That's Life!*, Wood described a career hiatus of being 'sat around feeling miserable for ages' until a change of direction saw her write a play, *Talent*, which won her an award for Most Promising Young Writer in 1978.

Parkinson: 'Did you think, *That's my career ahead of me now*?'

'No, I've only written one play since! It must have put me off. I keep meaning to write another one ...'

Wood explained how the stage production of *Talent* was seen by a Granada TV producer, Peter Eckersley. 'He said he couldn't really make head nor tail of it!' Despite this, he commissioned a TV version starring Wood and Walters – and then made Wood an offer.

'He said, "Do you want your own show?" And I said, "No, I don't. I want my friend with me." So, we did *Wood and Walters*. We did the pilot: we were about to do the series when Peter went into hospital and died.'

Parkinson noted that Wood had since dedicated a published collection of her scripts, titled *It's Up to You, Porky*, to the late Eckersley: 'He obviously had a very deep influence on your life?'

'He did. He was one of the funniest and cleverest people, and just the perfect person for me to meet at that time. You could bring a script to him that you thought was quite good, and he'd tear half the pages out and hand it back, and you'd think, *Oh, that's MUCH better!*

'He wouldn't do it in a nasty way. He was just fantastic. And I was so knocked back when he died. I'd only known him for four years and I was looking forward to knowing him for about another forty-eight.'

Parkinson: 'Why the title: *It's Up to You, Porky*?'

'Oh, it's a line from a sketch set in a boutique. A normal-sized woman goes in and the assistant is bone-thin. The woman says, "Have you got these trousers in a size fourteen?" and is told "Yes." Then she asks, "Can I try them on?" And the assistant says, "It's up to you, Porky ..."'

Since *Wood and Walters*, Wood had played successful live tours and, in 1984, transferred to the BBC to film TV series such as *Victoria Wood: As Seen on TV*, featuring the inimitable mock-soap opera *Acorn Antiques*. Her recent career had largely been a tale of uninterrupted success.

Yet this didn't stop Victoria Wood, as was her wont, from dwelling on bathetic previous points in her life when things had been rather less triumphant. When Parkinson asked her what was the smallest audience she had ever played to, she was quick to reply.

'It was seven people and a man on a portable life-support system, just outside Birmingham. I very nearly said: "What *is* that dreadful noise? Will somebody please switch the fans off?" And: "No – it's his life-support system. You'll kill him if you switch it off ..."'

• • •

It was Christmas again when Victoria Wood returned to the desert isle to talk to Kirsty Young in 2007. In the intervening twenty years, she had enjoyed continuing comedy success writing and starring in series such as *dinnerladies* and also moved into serious drama: her 2006 ITV film, *Housewife, 49*, was to win her a BAFTA.

Wood had characterised her upbringing to Michael Parkinson as merely 'ordinary'. Discussing it with Young, it became clear that it had actually been far more eccentric, traumatic ... and unhappy.

'There were four of us children, all in separate rooms, and [*my family*] never sat around a table,' she said. 'I had a room with a piano in there, and a television, and books, which was really all I needed. And I used to bring food in and we were all on our own.'

Young: '*Bring food in*? Was food not made?

'No, food wasn't made. I used to make all my own food and just take things in – I ate all the time because I had a huge eating problem. I used to eat from the minute I got out of school until I went to bed.'

'Did you have friends around to your house?'

'No, no! We never, never ever had any visitors at all.'

'At best, it sounds like an eccentric set-up,' commented Young. 'At worst, it sounds miserable.'

'It was quite isolated and it didn't help me learn to get on with people. My mother was very depressed and didn't really want to talk. My father loved working – when he wasn't working, he was in the house, writing. Their interest was not in their children, really.'

'Did your mother ever talk to you about your eating?'

'No! We never talked about *anything*! No, no, no, no! But she had an eating problem as well, I'm quite sure. She was always on a diet all the time or overeating. One of the two.'

Young switched her attention to her guest's educational performance: 'You were a smart little girl? You got on well in primary school?'

'Yeah, I was always top of the class then,' recalled Wood. 'But when I went to grammar school, I couldn't deal with [*the fact that*] everybody was just as clever. I couldn't deal with it and I really, really just went under and didn't do any work.

'I didn't have clean clothes. I didn't wash. I was supposed to make my own packed lunches. I didn't make them. I couldn't do my homework. If I hadn't done it, I'd steal somebody else's. If I didn't have any money, I'd steal money from people. It was just a mess. A big mess.

Young: 'You weren't the class clown?'

'No, I wasn't, at all. I didn't even have any friends, let alone try and be funny. Sometimes I would write things and read them out – that was all. I was a bit of a misfit, really.'

'Did you watch the class clown and think, *I could be funnier than that*?'

'No, I didn't think that. I was envious of all the people that were *in a group*. There was a horsey group, and the girls that went out with boys, and there were the clever ones. And I did a lot of observing. The good thing about being isolated is you get a really good look at what goes on.'

Young asked how her guest felt, in middle age, looking back at her childhood self.

'I feel really sorry for her: that's all. I don't want to make it sound like I had an absolutely terrible childhood. I absolutely didn't, and I'm fine. But I think she was neglected, really, looking back at her.'

Later in the interview, Young returned to the topic of Wood being an outsider having 'a really good look at what goes on'. At the root of all of her comedy, she suggested, was 'acutely observed human behaviour'.

'I suppose so, yeah,' half-agreed Wood. 'But, you know, I can't help that. I don't do it deliberately. I don't go around looking, with a notebook.'

'Do you not?'

'No, I don't.'

'Some people do, though, don't they?' persisted Young. And Victoria Wood's non-answer gave the best window possible into her humour:

'Yeah, they do. I have *got* a notebook, but there's nothing in it, really, except a shopping list ...'

• • •

Victoria Wood was to scoop countless comedy awards and win four BAFTAs for her work both as a writer and an actor. Arguably the most talented female comedian in the history of British entertainment, she was just sixty-two when she died from cancer of the oesophagus at her north London home in April 2016. The BBC broadcast a seven-part tribute to her life and genius the following year. In May 2019, a statue of Wood was unveiled in her home town of Bury. Characteristically, the bronze version of her appears to be grinning at the whole daft palaver.

DISCS CHOSEN (1987)

Coates's 'Saxo-Rhapsody'
Jack Brymer with the Royal Liverpool Philharmonic Orchestra

Third movement from Prokofiev's Symphony No. 7 in C Sharp Minor
London Symphony Orchestra
'My husband once spilled black shoe dye on a pale green carpet while this record was playing. We nearly got divorced after that'

❤ **'African Ripples'**
Fats Waller
'I can play this with one hand at a time, but not both'

'Inbetweenies'
Ian Dury and the Blockheads
'Ian Dury's and Noël Coward's are the only people's lyrics that I listen to'

Gershwin's Piano Concerto in F Major
London Symphony Orchestra

'Let's Do It'
Noël Coward
'It's him in Las Vegas, making a killing and a few bob for his old age'

'In a Mist'
Bunny Berigan
'I used to play this every morning writing my TV series'

'Lock Me Up'
The Weather Girls
'I'm a mad walker and this is my favourite thing for walking to'

BOOK
The Collected Works of Arthur Marshall
'He's the only person that makes me laugh out loud when I'm on my own'

LUXURY ITEM
A cinema organ: a mighty Wurlitzer
'They probably take ages to learn to play, what with all those bits and bobs and knobs and stops and things'

27
MAYA ANGELOU

WRITER, POET, ACTIVIST
2 August 1987

Victoria Wood was a prime example of a castaway who painted her life and personal history as relatively mundane. Other visitors to the island, by contrast, had led lives so multifaceted and extraordinary that it was difficult to absorb that so many things had happened to one person.

Maya Angelou was a tremendous case in point. Born into impoverished circumstances in the American Deep South in 1928, she had suffered a terrible assault and trauma as a child before becoming a professional dancer and singer and then an international civil rights activist.

Shocked into depression by the assassination of her close friend and associate Martin Luther King on her fortieth birthday in 1968, Angelou had then been coaxed into writing an autobiography, *I Know Why the Caged Bird Sings*. This coruscating account of life as a woman of colour in modern America spent two years on the *New York Times* bestseller list.

When she met Michael Parkinson in 1988, Angelou had just completed her fifth volume of autobiography and become the first black woman to write both the screenplay and music for a major movie. An inspirational figure, she did not lack for things to talk about.

• • •

'Autobiography can be stranger than fiction,' remarked Parkinson at the start of the show, informing the listeners that his illustrious guest had been 'a writer, a stripper, a political activist, waitress, editor, singer, actress, dancer and a few more things beside'. It's a sign of the richness of Angelou's life that many of those topics remained untouched as there simply wasn't time to talk about them.

Instead, Parkinson prompted Angelou to talk about her early childhood, when, after her parents had broken up when she was three and her brother four, they were sent to live with her grandmother in Arkansas during the Great Depression. 'What do you remember?' he asked.

'My grandmother had the only black-owned store in town. She was a typical West African market woman. The people had no money but the poorer people would get the handouts. Powdered eggs. Powder milk. Lard. They'd bring it to the store and swap with grandmother. She'd give them tins of mackerel for buckets of powdered egg.'

Parkinson asked whether Arkansas in the thirties was rigidly racially segregated and received a terse affirmation from his guest. 'When did you first come across, directly, racial prejudice?' he enquired.

'I guess I was about eight. My brother and I went to the movies. There was a white girl in the box office who would take the dimes of all the white kids by hand. When my brother put our dimes up, she had a cigar box and told him, "Rake them into the box." And she was from a family so poor, they lived on my grandmother's land! I couldn't believe this meanness!

'All the white kids would go right in through the front door and the black kids would have to go up a very rickety outdoor staircase. It was very danger-ous: so shaky. Then we'd crawl into a roof that hadn't been swept since the place had been built: peanut shells and paper and all stuff on the floor.

'It was pitched at such an angle, that balcony they called the Buzzard's Roost, that you had the feeling you might topple down on top of all those white folk. It was just terrible. And I cried – I was such a nice girl, and being forced to live like that!'

Parkinson moved on to the awful shaping event of Angelou's childhood. 'You were mute. What were the circumstances of that?'

'Pretty dreadful. When I was seven-and-a-half, I was raped by my moth-er's boyfriend and the rapist was killed. The policeman told my grandmother that the man had been kicked to death, they thought, and I heard that.

'Somehow, with my seven-and-a-half-year-old logic, I decided that my voice had killed him: because I told who did it, my voice was the culprit. I decided that I had better not talk because anybody whose name I called, or who heard me, might die. So, I stopped.'

Parkinson: 'How long did that last?'

'About five years.'

'And what rescued you from that silence?'

'Poetry. A black lady in my town started me, at about eight, reading the books in the library. I'd write on a tablet whenever anybody asked me any-thing. My grandmother owned most of the land so people couldn't be too unkind to me. But, out of her hearing, they'd say, "Mm. Mm. It's a shame Sister Henderson's granddaughter done gone mental!" They were brutes.

'Finally, Mrs Flowers, this lovely lady, had me over to her house. I was almost twelve. She'd ask me about things I'd read, what I liked, and I'd write. Then she said: "You think you like poetry? You *don't* like poetry!"

'I couldn't believe that! She *knew* I loved poetry! I was writing furiously, "I love it!" and she said, "You'll never like it until you feel it come across your tongue, through your teeth and over your lips."

'I ran out of her house. I ran to the store. She came to the store and pointed her finger at me: a very serious thing for black Americans. We have a saying that goes from Jesse Jackson to the wino on the street corner: "Don't put your finger in my face!" She did it to shock me, and she said, "You don't like poetry!"

'Well, she continued harassing me for months until finally I went under the house and I tried to speak poetry, and I had a voice. And so, Mrs Flowers and poetry returned my voice to me.'

As Parkinson probed deeper into Angelou's background, it became clear that she had inherited much of her singular, defiant spirit from her mother.

'I called her in 1959,' she recalled. 'She said, "Oh baby!" – she's five-foot-three-and-a-half, five-foot-four, and I'm six feet tall, but that's how she talks to me. She said, "Oh baby, I'm going to sea. I'm going to become a seaman." And [*I was like*] "*Why*, Mom?!"'

'I mean, she owned hotels; she was a surgical nurse and a real-estate broker. *Go to sea?!* She said, "Yes, because they told me they wouldn't let black women in their union. Baby, I told them: "*You wanna bet?* I'll put my foot in that door up to my hip till every woman of colour can walk over my foot, get in that union, get aboard a ship and go to sea!"

'And when my mother retired, in 1980, the black, white, Hispanic and Asian women shipped out of San Francisco and gave a party for her. It was wonderful, Michael. They called this little, bitty woman "Mother of the Sea".'

Parkinson marvelled that his guest had so far turned her remarkable life into five volumes of autobiography. Would there be more to come?

'I suppose there will be a sixth and final book, which will lead up to me writing *Caged Bird*. I will hesitate some time before attempting to write it, because it has to begin with the assassination of Malcolm X, who was a friend and brother to me, and then of Martin King, who was a friend and leader for me. It's a very hard book.'

Parkinson: 'Will the end of the book be optimistic?'

'Yes, indeed. I would be just about to write *I Know Why the Caged Bird Sings* and why I thought it was important to write of one's life using the first-person singular but meaning the third-person plural. Trying to write it so well that a middle-aged, middle-class white woman in Dorset can read it and say: "That's the truth. That is a human truth."

'The last book in the series will have to be hopeful, which is what I am. I'm an incurable – *I hope, incurable* – optimist, otherwise I wouldn't get up in the morning. I really believe that we are meant to be better ...'

• • •

The extraordinary thing was that Maya Angelou's life was still only just getting going. In addition to writing songs for Roberta Flack and being a mentor to a young Oprah Winfrey, she was to go to the South to be a university professor, direct a feature film, write a further *two* volumes of autobiography, and read one of her own poems, 'On the Pulse of Morning', at the 1993 inauguration of US president Bill Clinton. She was working on a book focusing on her interactions with world political leaders throughout her life when she died, in May 2014, at the age of eighty-six. Her legend and legacy live on.

DISCS CHOSEN
❤ **'How Great Thou Art'**
Mahalia Jackson
'My grandmother had a wonderful voice: like melting gold. The only similar voice is Mahalia Jackson's'

'A Quiet Place'
Max Roach

'Killing Me Softly'
Roberta Flack

'I Just Called to Say I Love You'
Stevie Wonder

'East of the Sun'
Sarah Vaughan

'One for My Baby (And One More for the Road)'
Frank Sinatra

'Summertime'
Leontyne Price

'Georgia'
Ray Charles
'I have moved back to the South and I do believe – once a Southerner, always a Southerner'

BOOK
The Negro Caravan – compiled by Sterling Brown and Ulysses Lee
'It has black American poetry from the eighteenth, nineteenth and twentieth centuries'

LUXURY ITEM
Kumasi Market by John Biggers
'It's a huge painting in oil, about two thousand figures. All the beautiful shades of black people: I could spend years trying to see what the people are doing'

28
JOANNA LUMLEY

ACTOR, MODEL
13 September 1987

Joanna Lumley swam ashore Michael Parkinson's desert island in September 1987 with quite a story to tell. After an early childhood in India and Malaya, thanks to her military father, she had been a convent schoolgirl and a successful model before turning to acting.

Lumley's big break came in 1976 when she secured the part of high-kicking, all-action, frequently leather-clad secret agent Purdey in hit ITV drama series *The New Avengers*. She then went on to star on the same channel in the bizarre, slightly camp sci-fi series *Sapphire & Steel*.

Her public profile was already high, but it had become stratospheric by the time she returned to the island in 2007, thanks to her magnificent portrayal of hard-drinking, drug-taking, promiscuous fashion-magazine editor Patsy Stone in Jennifer Saunders's *Absolutely Fabulous*. And both times she capsized, as you would expect, she was charm incarnate.

• • •

In a well-intentioned but now somewhat dated-sounding attempt at gallantry, Michael Parkinson opened by describing his guest as both a 'sex symbol' and an 'exotic bird'. 'Do you think of yourself that way?' he asked.

'I think I've probably had quite an unusual life,' Lumley conceded. 'I feel perfectly normal in the middle of it, but when I look back over some of the things I've done, they *do* seem quite exotic.'

This was certainly true of being born, in 1946, in Kashmir, where her father was stationed in the army: 'We left a year after I was born, so I can't remember it at all. I've been back and find it quite spectacularly beautiful and strangely familiar, although of course, it can't *really* be.'

Lumley did, however, hold strong memories of Malaya, where she had lived for three years from the age of five: 'Terribly hot! Being tropical, it rained every day, it seemed. I *loved* it there. I can just remember the noises and the smells. Everything was very vivid and immediate!'

Parkinson asked her about moving to a boarding school in England, aged eight. 'Yes, I loved that! And then I moved to an Anglican convent near Hastings, which I simply adored. I was a boarder and, being baddish by nature, I found it very pleasant to be sent off to a place where I could be bad solidly for three months at a time.'

'Were you a rebellious child?'

'*Faintly* rebellious, not horribly rebellious. I would never have set fire to the chapel, or anything like that.'

'And what did you look like in those days?'

'The most unattractive child you could imagine! I grew very fast, so I had very long legs and a body like a bit of dough: a sort of wodge. My hair became incredibly frizzly and crispy and a mass of spots came out. I suffered terribly from turning into this sort of Incredible Hulk.'

Parkinson: 'What did you want to be?'

'Although I was lazy at biology, I wanted to be a surgeon. I wanted very much to be prime minister, but that was because I was so bossy, I couldn't see why I shouldn't rule the country.'

Her Incredible Hulk days, presumably, behind her, Lumley described leaving school and enrolling at the Lucie Clayton school of modelling. 'Of course, I went well over the top! I stuck on false eyelashes and fingernails and made black lines everywhere.

'That's where I got the penchant for painting my face like the Whore of Babylon. Which I still do, because I love it. And we learned to get in and out of an E-type Jaguar with our knees together!'

'Were you a successful model?'

'Yes, after a bit. I was never a top, top model like Jean Shrimpton or Twiggy, but I worked all the time and was called one of the top-ten models. It was good magazines – even as grand as *Vogue* or *Harpers & Queen*, sometimes.'

Despite this success, Lumley explained, she felt the need to act. Turned down by RADA ('Which was a frightful shock!'), she instead gained her Equity card by 'weaselling her way into' a one-line role in a film, then three lines in a Bond movie: 1969's *On Her Majesty's Secret Service*.

Parkinson: 'How much of a struggle was it [*getting parts*]?'

'It was odd. I did several films, then starred in a film and had my name above the title (*Games That Lovers Play*, 1971). But then there was a dearth. I was doing very small parts, being paid perhaps £60, then another three weeks, or months, without work.

'This was the time they'd started to advertise for *The [New] Avengers*. I put my name forward and they wouldn't see me: "*No! Frightful! Don't darken our doors!*" And I got quite desperate – bloody knuckles beating on the door!

'Eventually, I went down and got into a queue at Pinewood, like people waiting for the dentist. They were so astonished and amazed that they promised to test me. I had to test and test again. It wasn't a piece of cake. It was quite a struggle. Thank goodness I got it.'

Lumley explained how relieved she was that *The New Avengers* had led to her having 'permanent employment' even though 'we were actually paid peanuts'. However, she had a 'terrific tussle' with the producers over Purdey's clothes.

'They said, "Joanna Lumley will be a stockings-and-suspenders girl." And

I went, "No, hang on, I'll be a gym-shoes-and-tracksuits girl!" But they absolutely pushed that aside.

'My great argument was that, if she was a good spy, she'd wear dark clothes and creep around in the bushes. Instead, I was stuck in these high heels with very flimsy dresses, always shinning up trees!'

Parkinson turned the conversation to his guest's private life. She had been a single mother by the age of twenty-one. 'How much has that been a problem to you, in your career?'

'It's always the practical problems – you have to work, but you've also got to be a parent. You've got to be shopping and cleaning and working and collecting the child from school. You find, perhaps, you're doing pantomime over Christmas. Heart-breaking!'

She had, however, recently married for the second time – to conductor Stephen Barlow. 'How much has that changed your life?' the host enquired.

'Fantastically! In every way! It's just been terrific. I wake up grinning in the morning and I'm happy as a bee. Truly, I believe in magic now.'

As Parkinson brought the chat to a close, he asked a standard *Desert Island Discs* question about how Lumley would manage on the deserted isle: 'Would you be able to cope?' His guest had clearly given the topic far more thought than most castaways did.

'I think so, yes!' she replied, briskly. 'I'd create some make-up out of twigs and squeezed berries. I'd get some sort of papyrus and make a kind of ink and write a few notes. Or a book. And I'd construct a house! I'd do everything, yeah!'

Who would have thought that these bold claims would later be tested in real life?

• • •

By the time Joanna Lumley returned to the show and met Kirsty Young in 2007, she had done two things of great note. One was that she had spent fifteen years playing the glamorous, wanton monster Patsy in *Absolutely Fabulous*. The other was that, for the purposes of a TV show, she had spent a short spell as an actual desert-island castaway.

Unsurprisingly, Young wanted to start with the *Ab Fab* hell-bitch. 'What did you think when you first saw the character on paper?'

'Well, she didn't really emerge until episode two or three. And [*initially*] Edina wasn't as wild. They both grew like ghastly sort of septic funguses in the corner. They just got worse and worse.

'Patsy's hair got taller and taller, and the smoking became more and more obsessive until they were on about a hundred and twenty a day. Their language got fouler, their behaviour got worse ... but it just grew out of performance, really.'

Lumley confessed that on first reading for the part, she 'couldn't get the handle of it' and found it hard to talk to the shy, retiring Saunders. Certain that she was 'not the right person', she asked her agent to extricate her from the role. 'But they said, "Oh, look, it's only a pilot! *Just do it!*" So, I did.'

Young: 'How did you find the key, then? Because watching, as a viewer, you seemed to know *exactly* who Patsy was.'

'I don't know. I just tried to make Jennifer laugh – that's the truth of it! That's all I ever tried to do.'

'Had you known that you could play comedy as well as you did?'

'I never really thought I *couldn't* do anything. That's not being vain. I mean, comedy was so much ... laughing hysterically was so much part of one's life!'

Young: 'People were shocked, though, that *Joanna Lumley* was doing this. You did a lot of things that people had never done before on screen. You got viciously drunk, you took a lot of drugs, you swore, there was a lot of sex ... it was meaty stuff.'

'But this is Jennifer, you see!' Lumley protested. '*She* wrote it all! I just did it! Some of the things, I used to go: "We can't do *that*!" As a prim convent girl! But, of course, we *could*.'

'Like what?'

'Some of the remarks they'd make. The cruelty to Saffy was incredible, you know. That Patsy hates a child so much she would've aborted it is strong stuff, and it had never been done in a comedy before.'

Young: '[*Patsy*] actually said that in one episode, didn't she?'

'Yes – "I'd have done a knitting needle! I'd have got rid of you!" You know, this is dark stuff!'

'And Patsy's job, in so far as she ever made it to the office, was being a fashion editor on a glossy magazine. Have you encountered people like Patsy in real life?'

'Yes, I'm afraid I have! And they are terribly funny. I mean, they laugh at themselves, but *there's an awful lot of wiffle-waffle* ... and the fashion world adored it because it was *just dead right*, you know.'

Young also asked her guest about her attempt to mirror Captain A.E. Dingle by becoming a real-life castaway. In 1994, she had filmed *Girl Friday*, a one-off TV show in which she had spent nine days alone on an uninhabited island off Madagascar. How had this come about?

'Well, it was bizarre. The BBC said to me, "What about putting Patsy on a desert island, with no vodka?" And I said, "It might not last a whole programme because it'd be funny for about five minutes. But what about *me* going on a desert island and really trying to tough it out?"

'And they gave me terribly little. I was trained for a bit with the Irish Guards and I was given a sort of SAS handbook on how to extract water from socks, or something. And I was sent off to this desert island.

'There was a tiny, skeleton crew, about five people, who lived on a diving boat, which would arrive every morning at about seven o'clock. They would film me every day, and then go away again in the evening.

'They miscalculated the food. They gave me a pound of uncooked rice in a bag and that was it. They said, "Oh, the island will be dripping with fruit!" but there'd been a late monsoon, all the mangos had dropped to the floor and rotted. So, there was nothing to eat except my rice.

'I had to purify the water on fires, which I had to light with a flint, and because the wood was wet, it took forever. I wasn't allowed a spoon, or a fork, or a dish. I had to eat out of shells, *with* shells. I didn't have soap or a comb or mirror; nothing to read, nothing to listen to, so I lived like an animal on the island. Really fantastic!'

Young: 'How were you with the physical hardships?'

'Very good,' declared Lumley. 'I'm an old toughie at heart so I don't mind roughing it. I slept in a cave. I didn't mind not wearing make-up. I liked not having to change my clothes, or care about things like that.

'The thing I missed the *least* was newspapers, and news. Not hearing bad news every day was incredible. You start finding everything good in the world. You'd listen for birdsong; you'd sit and appreciate things. But I worked jolly hard because a lot of the day was spent just surviving ...'

• • •

Since her second *Desert Island Discs* appearance, Joanna Lumley has appeared in films including *The Wolf of Wall Street* and *Absolutely Fabulous: The Movie*. She has also hosted a number of TV travelogue shows that have taken her up the River Nile, across Asia on the Trans-Siberian Express, along the Silk Road and to Iran, India and Japan, and has been a vocal activist for the Gurkhas (with whom her father served) and the exiled Tibetan government, among other causes. In 2022, she was made a dame for services to drama, entertainment and charity. She remains, in Parky's immortal words, an 'exotic bird' indeed.

DISCS CHOSEN (1987)
'Mary Had a Baby, Yes Lord'
Paul Robeson

Overture from Rossini's *Semiramide*
NBC Symphony Orchestra
'I love Rossini because he's so good-natured and happy'

Chopin's Nocturne in E Minor, Op. 72, No. 1
Tamás Vásáry

'Cry My Heart'
Eddie Calvert
'I remember this from Malaya. My mother didn't care for it much and Daddy used to play it, rather defiantly'

Mozart's Symphony No. 39 in E Flat Major
Berlin Philharmonic Orchestra
'A piece that charms me enormously'

Extract from Act 2 of Donizetti's *Lucia di Lammermoor*
Maria Callas

Bruch's Violin Concerto No. 1
London Symphony Orchestra

❤ **Beethoven's Symphony No. 3 in E Flat Major:** *Eroica*
BBC Symphony Orchestra
'My great, great hero – he stands like a giant above everybody'

BOOK
A Dance to the Music of Time – Anthony Powell
'This just encompasses English life and it's very, very long'

LUXURY ITEM
A painting (to be commissioned) by Royal Academician painter John Ward of all her family and friends
'I shall look at them all and think of them all and wait for them to come and get me, as I'm sure they will'

'ISLE NEVER FORGET ...'
'I remember *Desert Island Discs* right back from when I was a child in Malaya. My father would be away in the jungle with the Gurkhas and my mother and I would sit, at night-time, listening to the BBC World Service.

'My sister and I would be in bed, under our mosquito nets. We would hear the strains of the programme's theme music, unchanged through the decades, as my mother sat at her Singer sewing machine, sewing our school dresses. I've literally known the show all of my life.

'When I first got asked to be on, the weeks leading up to it were agony. All I could do was bore people to bits with my lists of music. *How do I whittle it down to eight?* Afterwards, someone asked me, "How could you *not* have had the Beatles?" But I just didn't have room for them.

'I'm quite a muscular, tent-erecting, river-wading kind of character, so I loved it when Roy Plomley used to ask the castaways how they would cope: "Could you run up a shelter of some kind?" Now, the focus on that practical side of things has gone. I think that's a bit of a shame.

'Today, the show is more about people's lives and their feelings. It's all about the woes that have afflicted people rather than how they'd try to cope with jolly little. Whereas I took the "desert island" concept very literally. I was a complete bore about it!

'The first time I went on, I hadn't been on a desert island. The second time, I *had*. So, I knew that you *can't* build a boat. You *can't* swim to another island. And, if I am honest, the *last* thing you want to do is to listen to music or read a book!

'Desert islands are pretty scabby places. You get bitten to ribbons; you get foot rot; you get torn to shreds. You're in and out of the sea all the time to avoid getting burned by the sun. You have nothing to wash with and so you scratch like a dog.

'The second time I went on, I chose completely different records from the first because, having been on an island, I knew that *you bury your treasures*. I dug a deep hole and buried my things in the sand. So, I knew my original records would still be there and I'd actually have sixteen ...'

SUE LAWLEY YEARS
1988–2006

Michael Parkinson had helpfully announced his resignation from *Desert Island Discs* six months before his departure. It meant that, in contrast to the uncertainly that followed the death of Roy Plomley, the BBC had ample time to select a successor and plan the show's next move.

It was to be a slightly unexpected one. *Desert Island Discs* was about to get its first female presenter – an assiduous journalist who came from a decidedly hard-news background.

Sue Lawley had made her name as a reporter on early-evening BBC TV news show *Nationwide*, then as a presenter on *Tonight*, a precursor to today's *Newsnight*. She had also been the first woman both to host *Question Time* and to be part of the Beeb's general election night team.

In more recent years, Lawley had been a newsreader, initially on the *Nine O'Clock News* and then the early-evening six o'clock bulletin. Her celebrity-interviewing experience was largely limited to occasionally filling in for Terry Wogan on his prime-time chat show, *Wogan*.

Lawley's appointment could thus have theoretically been viewed as a gamble. In fact, she was immediately to win rave reviews – largely for a journalistic thoroughness that saw her prepare for her castaways as assiduously as if she were grilling a government minister on *Tonight*.

In her later book, *Desert Island Discussions*, Lawley was to chronicle the painstaking steps she took to ready herself for each episode. 'The only way to do an extensive interview with someone is to read about them until you have soaked them up,' she wrote.

'When you have read about their lives, from cuttings or newspaper interviews, and then read, watched or listened to their work, you spot recurring themes and begin to create a sense of who it is that you are about to meet.'

In marked contrast to Roy Plomley's convivial pre-broadcast lunches at the Garrick Club, Lawley also explained that she disliked meeting her guests in advance because she was 'worried that it will spoil the spontaneity of our exchange'. Their first hellos would be in the studio.

Lawley's first castaway, on 27 March 1988, was Quintin Hogg, aka Lord Hailsham, the former lord chancellor under Edward Heath and Margaret Thatcher. He was followed into the studio over the next two weeks by first the actor Jane Asher, then the miners' union leader, Arthur Scargill.

'Lord Hailsham is eminent and distinguished, Jane Asher intelligent, attractive and popular, Arthur Scargill important and controversial,' said Lawley in *Desert Island Discussions*. 'For me, these descriptions span the areas that *Desert Island Discs* can, and should, cover.'

A news journalist at heart, Lawley adopted a far more interrogatory and demanding tone towards her castaways than had her predecessors. She was not afraid to ask the hard questions, and was sharp-witted and dogged enough to ensure that they yielded revealing answers.

Given the gravitas that she imparted to the programme, it's thus ironic that the first castaway encounter we reproduce here is a summer 1988 meeting with Australian comedian Barry Humphries's infamous alter ego, the always-fabulous housewife superstar, Dame Edna Everage.

'I knew that when Dame Nature stooped over my bassinette when I was a bubba, that she'd planted a very special thing in me, a little talent,' Dame Edna assured her host. 'She'd given me a gift – as she's given you, *in a small way*, Sue, a gift.'

Lawley was in her element in November 1992 interrogating formidable US four-star General H. Norman Schwarzkopf Jr. He had masterminded the international coalition's victory over Saddam Hussein in the first Gulf War, yet admitted to feelings of self-doubt and vulnerability.

'How many times have you been married?' Sue asked venerable blues man John Lee Hooker. 'Three times too many!' he replied. Lawley also coaxed from redoubtable Hollywood star Kathleen Turner the heart-rending tale of how crippling rheumatoid arthritis had almost ended her career.

At the end of 2005, shortly before she was to quit *Desert Island Discs*, Lawley had a rambunctious encounter with a then-journalist and Tory backbench MP, Boris Johnson. She held his feet to the fire of what she termed 'his misdemeanours' so fiercely that he was forced to plead for clemency.

'Sue! You're a *brilliant* interviewer,' acknowledged the flailing Johnson, before humorously begging her for mercy, 'but, in the immortal words of Sue Lawley, "More music, please ..."'

You can't help suspecting that, at the end of that episode, Sue Lawley packed away her copious notes with a particularly happy smile on her face and gleam in her eye. Boris, possibly, not so much ...

29

DAME EDNA EVERAGE

HOUSEWIFE SUPERSTAR
17 July 1988

When Australian comedian Barry Humphries launched his Edna Everage alter ego in 1955, she was not an immediate success. A parody of a dull Melbourne housewife, Mrs Norm Everage (as she was then known) did not fly with his audience and he put the character on the back burner.

Humphries reinvigorated his creation in the seventies – *and how*! Now an exuberant, larger-than-life, beautiful monster, Dame Edna grew wings via a hit West End show, *Edna Everage: Housewife Superstar*, and gained the celebrity and notoriety she was fully aware she deserved.

By the time she flounced on to Sue Lawley's desert island in 1988, Dame Edna's wisteria perm and flamboyant specs were fixtures on British TV. She had hosted two BBC TV specials, no fewer than *three* ITV *An Audience with …* shows and a chat show, *The Dame Edna Experience*, in which she skewered such Hollywood A-listers as Sean Connery and Mel Gibson.

Faced with this Antipodean amazon's self-proclaimed fabulousness, *possums*, Lawley had little option but to play the straight woman and offer up a stream of hymns of praise to her guest's untrammelled magnificence. So, you know what? That's exactly what she did!

• • •

Dame Edna opened the show in, for her, pensive mode, pondering whether the isolation of a desert island would evoke in her 'the inner loneliness of the megastar'. Luckily, she had one major factor in her favour: 'I was born on a desert island – Australia!'

'We hear so much about your fame and superstardom,' noted Sue Lawley. 'But what were you like as a little girl?'

'I was a very shy child, Sue. As a kiddie, I used to learn little poems and songs at school and I was too shy to sing them to my aunties. I had to hide behind the curtains in our lounge and pretend to be the wireless!'

'Did you know even then, Dame Edna, that there was something special about you?'

'I felt different. *Apart.* I knew that when Dame Nature stooped over my bassinette when I was a bubba, that she'd planted a very special thing in me, a little talent. She'd given me a gift – as she's given you, *in a small way*, Sue, a gift.

'I was born a star! Isn't it funny? I think when she was, my mother, in the maternity ward, just getting her feet out, she said to the nurse, "What is it?" And they said, "I think it's a megastar."'

Lawley: 'But who discovered you?'

'Well, I was in a lot of little plays in kindergarten and school – and in church, too, because I'm a deeply religious person. Mother Teresa isn't a personal friend for nothing! I was spotted in a Passion Play, playing the part of Mary Magdalene. I was cast against type, there.

'There was a talent-spotter in the audience who snapped me up, and I started appearing in semi-professional shows in Australia with Barry Humphries – an unknown, and still comparatively unknown, Australian performer. And, of course, I stole the show every time.'

'Yours is a phenomenal success, there is no doubt about it!' confirmed an admiring Lawley. 'But I want to ask you what I think is a slightly difficult question.'

'Ask, ask, darling!'

'You're not always terribly *nice* to people, are you? You tick off your audiences for not listening. You criticise their clothes, or their husbands. You dropped Larry Hagman through a floor, didn't you?'

'Darling, that's called *tough love*,' said Dame Edna. 'Was your mother, Susan – be honest here – always adoring to you, or did she sometimes give you a little smack on your botty?'

Lawley: 'She did, yes.'

'Well, it was her way of loving you. A little tough love never did a kiddie any harm and it can never hurt an audience. If people think they can misbehave in my shows – eat choccies, take flashlight photographs, let their attention wander for a second – I'm sorry, I will not tolerate it!'

'You've had your problems, haven't you, in your family life?' asked Lawley. 'Not least a very sick husband to cope with.'

'Well, a man who's been clinically dead now six times – that's sick, I suppose,' admitted Dame Edna, before bridling: 'Is this an interrogation or something, Sue? I was told this would be an *enjoyable* experience!'

Lawley: 'No, no, I just ...'

'Probing and digging away! Well, I have coped, helped immeasurably by the public, who adore me. The letters have flooded in!'

The host wisely changed tack: 'I wonder how great a part fashion and grooming have played in your success?'

'I'm a very physical woman. My legs are my greatest asset – I have beautiful legs, the envy of so many members of my audience. I never thought of them, of course. I'd never realised, Susan, that I was, in fact, a great beauty!'

Lawley: 'And you radiate good health!'

'I do. People want to touch me. They say, "What beautiful skin you've got!" And I *have*. Feel it – feel this!'

'It is lovely. Beautiful!'

'Isn't it soft? It's gorgeous.'

'What's remarkable is ...'

'No, that'll do! You've felt it enough! You've felt it enough, Sue!'

'You've acquired a great personal fortune, Dame Edna,' noted Lawley. 'What gives you the greatest pleasure to spend your money on?'

'Well ... myself,' replied the great woman. 'I think of myself so *rarely*, Sue Lawley, that every now and then I think what a novelty it would be to lavish a little bit of TLC – not to mention pounds, shillings and pence – on me! And I try to make a point of doing that every day of my life.'

Lawley: 'You have houses around the world, don't you? London, Melbourne, Malibu, Cloisters. Which one's your favourite?'

'My home in Australia. Well, it's not my home any more, it's the Royal Edna Museum. It's the home where Norm and I spent our early married life; where he had his very earliest urological twinges.

'In the afternoon, after school, a lot of little local kiddies used to come in. They'd sit around the table, eating the lovely sandwiches I'd made them. Little Clive James was a bit of a handful. Germaine, of course, Olivia Newton-John and the Bee Gees. All to find fame later, and write me such touching letters of gratitude!'

As Sue Lawley's audience with greatness headed towards its close, the host wondered how her guest had managed to retain, among all her success, the common touch?

'Well, because I *am* common!' declared Dame Edna. 'I come, after all, from Australia, and we're all a little bit C, O, double-M, O, N, as my mother used to spell it. Not to mention O, R, D, I, N, A, R, Y. We can't help it. And there's nothing wrong with being a little bit earthy.'

Lawley: 'So your instincts are still very much those of the suburban housewife?'

'They are!' replied a delighted Dame Edna Everage. 'I am still, metaphorically, up to my wrists in washing-up water! I still wear spiritual Marigolds! It's something I came from! It's my roots!

'Whatever glamorous clothes I wear, however I might be photographed with the Larry Hagmans and the royal families of this world, I am, fundamentally, a Melbourne housewife who's struck it very, very lucky. And, of course, been prodigiously endowed by Dame Nature ...

• • •

Dame Edna rarely returns to the scene of a crime but Barry Humphries was back on the island in May 2009 for an audience with Kirsty Young. It was an encounter that allowed the host to probe beneath her guest's surfaces in a way that the irascible Edna would never have allowed.

Young opened by complimenting her guest on his cultural hinterland – a respected painter, he also owned more than 50,000 rare books – and asked him a suitably highbrow question: what did he think was the function of an artist?

'Well, *my* kind of art, if you could call it that, is cheering people up. To be in the cheering-up business is very gratifying!' said Humphries. 'I love the work of comedians.

'I was first exposed to them, as a child, during the Second World War. We had radio programmes where old British comedians did their acts. They were played in far-off Melbourne and listened to, avidly, by little Barry crouching beside his parents' radio.'

'Little Sunny Sam?'

'Little Sunny Sam, as my parents called me because of my perpetually, irritatingly sunny disposition.'

Young: 'You have described yourself as an only child with three siblings – a wonderful description. You were indulged? Spoiled?'

'*Very* spoiled. I just had to *look* at something and my parents would buy it for me. I don't think it was good for me that every request was granted. It made me seek, in later life, instant gratification – and *that* did me no good at all.'

Young: 'You have said: "My relationship with my mother left me feeling very cautious and circumspect over any relationship with a woman." Why was that?'

'My mother was an intelligent woman, wasted really because she lived in a Melbourne suburb in a big house with plenty of domestic help. So, her sense of humour was rather a cynical one. I think she had a sad and unfulfilled life – she had four children with whom she didn't properly connect.'

'What did she want for you, do you think?'

'The word "disappointment" was used a lot: "We're disappointed in you." I realised she was impossible to please. So, for some time, I would project this on to the women in my life: *This is another one of those unpleasable beings.*'

Humphries was married by twenty-one, 'which I think was totally stupid, but it seemed to be the only way I could get out of living at home.' He moved to Sydney and, he recalled, dipped a toe into performance art.

'These stunts usually took place on trains: a captive audience in the compartment, and a strange man sitting in the corner eating breakfast. The train would stop at a station, the window would open and an accomplice of mine would hand me grapefruit.

'At the next station, the toast, then the eggs, then finally coffee before we got into town. There would be no explanation: people were stunned at this little gesture of mine.'

Abandoning surrealist locomotive pranks, Humphries moved to London in 1959. He met and became friends with Peter Cook, who invited him to perform at his hip comedy and satire club, the Establishment. He died the death. Even an early version of Dame Edna went down badly.

'I thought, *That's it, my London career is over*. Then Joan Littlewood, a famous theatre director, invited me to Stratford East to her theatre and Spike [*Milligan*] asked me to join his company. I had two young children and a new, lovely wife and all looked very rosy.'

Appearances can be deceptive. Young asked Humphries to talk about 'your bleak years – the drinking years'.

'Yes, I was addicted to alcohol for about fifteen years,' he recalled. 'I think alcoholism is a disorder of the memory. You wake up groaning, saying, "Never again!" And by lunchtime you're on to your second Beaujolais or whisky.'

Young: 'You were a high-functioning addict? You kept the work going through it?'

'I did ... but at the end of the sixties, I realised there was no future in it for me. I had done everything I could with alcohol except die. And after that, things took off in a wonderful way. It was like I'd been driving in a car with the handbrake on for years.'

The host moved on to the topic of Dame Edna. ('A very shy, rather shrill and dowdy woman!' reflected Humphries.) He had taken the character to the US in the seventies but the shows had flopped: 'I didn't take it to heart. I just thought, *I'll never perform in America ever!*

'I waited nearly twenty-five years before I went back and I booked a theatre in San Francisco for two weeks. The season went for four months. I went to Broadway, I won a Tony Award, and now I have this strange experience of being popular in America.'

'Is popularity important to you?' wondered Young.

'Well, it is when you're earning a living from the sale of tickets! I don't have to, as I did in the old days, look through a moth hole in the curtain to see if there are enough people sitting there to start the show!'

As Young's encounter with the enormously popular Barry Humphries came to an end, she wondered if he was still Little Sunny Sam: 'I would tend to think that somebody who's been married four times must be a very optimistic soul?'

'Well, they say it's a sign of insanity if you do the same thing and expect different results. And, of course, I *am* slightly insane, but I'm very, very happy with my present situation ...'

• • •

Barry Humphries announced Dame Edna's retirement in 2012, saying (s)he was 'beginning to feel a bit senior', but the great lady, typically, appears to be having none of it. Since then, she has toured both the UK and US, made numerous television and radio appearances and, in 2019's one-off BBC special *Dame Edna Rules the Waves*, attempted to dispose of the ashes of her late sidekick, Madge, through a porthole on her luxury yacht. You just can't keep a good woman down, possums!

DISCS CHOSEN (1988)
'Home Sweet Home'
Nellie Melba
'One of the first great Australian dames in a tradition crowned by me'

'If I Had a Talking Picture of You'
Joan Sutherland
'Another wonderful Australian dame and a personal friend'

❤ **'I Feel Pretty' from** ***West Side Story***
Kiri Te Kanawa
'Another dame, whose damehood I recommended to the Queen'

'Sex Appeal'
Margot Lion
'A very spooky record – rather raunchy, too!'

'Wish Me Luck'
Gracie Fields
'One of the few songs that helped England win the war'

'A Little King Without a Crown'
Vera Lynn

'It's Raining Sunbeams'
Deanna Durbin
'Deanna Durbin – who remembers her? Rhymes with suburban'

'My Bridesmaid and I'
Dame Edna and Madge Allsop
'The most famous dame in the history of the twentieth century – myself!'

BOOK
Her Filofax
'Crammed with the ex-directory telephone numbers of famous people'

LUXURY ITEM

Her bridesmaid, Madge Allsop

Sue Lawley: 'You can't take a human being. It has to be an inanimate object.'

Dame Edna: 'I can assure you Madge is an inanimate object.'

Sue: 'You promise?'

Dame Edna: 'When I saw her last, she was pretty much comatose.'

30

A.S. BYATT

NOVELIST, POET, BIOGRAPHER
16 June 1991

A formidable woman of letters, the renowned novelist A.S. Byatt had recently been awarded the 1990 Booker Prize for her fifth novel, *Possession*, when she swam ashore Sue Lawley's desert island in 1991.

Possession was a complex and multilayered work. It told the story of two scholars researching a love affair between two fictional Victorian poets (reportedly loosely based on Alfred, Lord Tennyson and Christina Rossetti). Its labyrinthine text featured diary entries, letters and poems supposedly composed by those secret lovers.

Byatt's personal life was also the stuff of literary fiction. Raised by a brilliant but dominating mother frustrated at being unable to pursue an academic career, she was also the sister of novelist Margaret Drabble, with whom she endured a high-profile sibling rivalry.

Byatt's life had also been marked by tragedy when an eleven-year-old son from her first marriage had been killed in a car accident. It made for a sometimes difficult, deeply involving, desert-island encounter.

• • •

Sue Lawley described her guest as 'brought up in a family in Sheffield so clever, her mother and father thought nothing of reciting Wordsworth as they served the Sunday lunch'. 'Was this a typical scene?' she asked.

'Not typical,' answered Byatt. 'There was a lot of grumbling and irritability, but every now and then it all came together. We weren't always that happy and we didn't always have that sense of family occasion.'

Lawley: 'Is that something you've continued with your own family? Do you make literary allusions as you go about your domestic business?'

'I do, and it annoys almost all of them. One of my daughters, at a party, opened the door to guests and said, "I am the youngest daughter of this house. I do *not* read books and there are *too many* books in this house. Excuse me, I'll take your coat!"'

Lawley returned to her guest's childhood. Was it true that her mother was 'bitter' at having to give up her academic career to raise a family?

'Yes. I could see that not using her mind was torturing her. She told me, very late in life, that in her day, the state prevented you from teaching the moment you got married. It was a flat choice between husband and children or work.'

Lawley: 'But she took that out on you?'

'She *did*. She was very, very angry and all of her daughters learned the lesson that if you need to think, you had better make provision for working and having a life of your own.'

Lawley: 'You've talked over the years about her making you feel utterly inadequate and horrible. How did she do that?'

'Really, with noise. She had a capacity for making a loud, complaining noise. Anything that wasn't just as she had somehow envisioned it was going to be made her feel very nervous and hysterical. When you came downstairs, she would have found something you hadn't done that she didn't even really *want* you to do, but she would start to shout about it.

'That isn't *all* that she was. She gave us a great many books and there was a warmth in her as well. I talk about this because, of course, you can't talk about it when people are alive.'

Lawley: 'Can you remember how you felt when you heard that she'd died, eight or nine years ago?'

'I felt an immense space. I felt a huge amount of brilliantly coloured air coming in through the window, if I'm going to be truthful. And I also felt that she could stop hurting herself.

'After that, I started thinking about her as a young woman and I started mourning ... not for my mother but for the girl who'd gone to Cambridge and been so brilliant. I began imagining what she was like when she read Keats to herself. I grieve a lot for *that* woman. I miss her.'

Asked about her school life, Byatt described hating boarding school: 'I really do need to be alone for long patches. I'm not good at group life.' Lawley asked how her peers would have described her. 'Arrogant.'

'Why arrogant?'

'I used to say what I thought in class but I never spoke outside of class. I was extremely lonely. I had no social graces and no capacity to make friends.'

Byatt described having a happier time at Cambridge, where she wrote her first novel, 1964's *Shadow of the Sun*. She was followed to the university, three years later, by her younger sister, Margaret Drabble.

Lawley: 'She infuriated you, didn't she, because everything *you* did, *she* did one better?'

'Yes, she did,' agreed her castaway. 'She wished to, which was natural, because she's a very powerful and clever and brilliant person ... but, from my point of view, it was simply very frightening.'

'You suffered a lot from all that?'

'I was afraid. I suffered in the abstract and applied it to a person who was actually rather nice who was just fiercely coming along behind.'

Lawley persisted: 'You got a first, then she came along and got a starred first?'

'Yes, that was what did happen.'

'And did you feel that your mother was on her side?'

'Yes, very strongly! To whose advantage this *was* is another matter. I don't think my sister would claim it was awfully good for her that my mother was on her side.'

Lawley: 'Is there still friction between you, or is it overstated by gossip columnists?'

'It's *terribly* overstated by gossip columnists. I think we like each other and we have always liked each other, on the bottom line. If I meet my sister at a party, she's the one person who will know what I am talking about, if I explain some literary point. And we will smile at each other.

'But what I do *not* like is being interviewed by some journalist who says, "What's it like to be Margaret Drabble's sister?" That's what I am frightened of: of *not being anything*. Of being simply my position in the family, not a person.'

'Isn't that an advantage of having won the Booker? That you are now, absolutely, no longer "Margaret Drabble's sister"?'

'Yes, it is! It has given me that. I feel I should have had that anyway, but now it's fine.'

Lawley turned her thoughts to that Booker-winning novel, *Possession*: 'It's a romance but it's also a detective story, isn't it? Some thought went into the formula behind this prize-winning novel?'

'Yes. It wasn't designed to win a prize – it was designed to bring my life together. It was designed to bring together everything that I really care about and have fun along the way. And I think it worked.'

After more music, Lawley moved gently on to the topic of Byatt's own family. As well as three daughters, she had a son who was killed in the week of his eleventh birthday, in 1973, in a road accident: 'I presume that's a tragedy that a parent simply never gets over?'

'No, you don't get over it, and you suffer greatly from people supposing you will. You suffer from people not understanding the pace of grief. Most days, I think about him. I think if a child is killed at that sort of age, the actual symbiotic bond is still not broken.'

Lawley: 'What effect did his death have on your writing?'

'Writing has a large element of being done for pleasure. I lost that for a very long time.'

'Did you ever write about him?'

'I wrote a ghost story, once. And, last week, the first poem I've ever written under my own name was in the *TLS* [*Times Literary Supplement*] and that was about him.'

Lawley: 'In writing the short story, you must have been worried in case you were, in a sense, using his death? Using your grief?'

'Yes, I was. I wrote the story really partly to stop living only in that. It's an account of a woman grieving for her lost son, and her lodger can see the ghost and she can't. The writing of it was actually rather brutal.'

'Why can't the mother see him?'

'Because she's too realistic. She knows that he isn't there. I know a lot of women whose children have died who do really believe that their children speak to them in some ways, but I, myself, feel that the dead are gone, and that this is a lesson one has to learn.

'There was a sentence the woman in this book speaks: "There is no boy." The man in the story sees the boy all over – a very beautiful boy, the most brightly coloured thing in the story. But it was something I used to say to myself, waking up in the morning: "There is no boy."

'But you learn it very, very slowly. It takes you years and years not to wait for them to come around corners, and look down the street and see a child – a small, blond boy – dancing. It's not a good thing, really ...'

• • •

Like her sister and fellow (double) castaway, Margaret Drabble, A.S. Byatt has written prolifically throughout her later life – novels, short stories, critical essays and biographies – as well as editing literary texts. Made a dame for services to literature in 1999, she now lives between London and France and, aged eighty-six, continues to write.

DISCS CHOSEN

'He Shall Feed His Flock' from Handel's *Messiah*
Hanna Schwarz with the Bavarian Radio Symphony Orchestra

Mozart's Clarinet Concerto in A Minor
Reginald Kell with the Zimbler Sinfonietta Orchestra
'Tears always come to my eyes when I hear these notes'

Campion's 'Care-Charming Sleep'
Alfred Deller
'A haunting, uncanny sound'

'The Idea of Order at Key West'
Wallace Stevens
'A poem about what art does to the world'

'Dies irae' from Verdi's *Requiem*
Philharmonia Chorus and Orchestra

'*An apocalyptic vision of terror in medieval rhyming Latin*'

'When that I was and a little tiny boy' from Shakespeare's *Twelfth Night*
Cleo Laine
'Twelfth Night *was my A-level Shakespeare and Cleo Laine sings it with bounce*'

❤ **'Jetzt fand Ich's' from Wagner's *Das Rheingold***
Set Svanholm with the Vienna Philharmonic Orchestra
'*This one moves me terribly because it's something that's lost and always there*'

'Zweilicht' from Schumann's *Liederkreis*, Op. 39
Dietrich Fischer-Dieskau
'*The last line is so sinister: "Look after yourself, be careful and wary ..."*'

BOOK
À la recherche du temps perdu – Marcel Proust
'*I could use it to translate Shakespeare into French ...*'

LUXURY ITEM
Large filing cabinet full of A4 paper and pens
'*It has to be totally weatherproofed*'

31
VIVIENNE WESTWOOD

FASHION DESIGNER, ACTIVIST
28 June 1992

Vivienne Westwood had just been named Designer of the Year for the second year in succession when she strutted down the catwalk to Sue Lawley's desert island in 1992. However, her route to the apex of the fashion world had been idiosyncratic and highly unorthodox.

A war baby in a working-class Cheshire family, Westwood had moved to Harrow, married and had a son by the age of twenty-two. She was working as a primary-school teacher and selling self-designed jewellery from a market stall in London in 1965 when she met a soulmate: Malcolm McLaren.

McLaren and Westwood became a couple and launched a boutique on the King's Road in Chelsea, initially called Let It Rock, then Too Fast to Live, Too Young to Die, and then simply Sex. Selling Westwood's ground-breaking designs, it became a crucible – and the fashion/design wing – of the seventies punk-rock movement.

Westwood's outrageous and outlandish styles had since permeated from the cultural fringes into mainstream society and high-street retail. Fashion's *enfant terrible* had become its *grand dame*, and she told Sue Lawley exactly how this had happened.

(Oh, and interestingly for a woman who will be forever linked in the public memory with the Sex Pistols, every single piece of music that she chose was classical.)

• • •

Lawley began the programme wondering why it had taken so long for Westwood's influence to be formally recognised by the fashion world: 'So many of your ideas have actually, to put it crudely, been nicked by other fashion houses, haven't they?'

Westwood agreed: 'One of the explanations [*given*] for this is that my designs aren't commercial and therefore have to be watered down by other people later on. But it's *not* that they're not commercial: it's that they're new, so it takes a little longer for people to get used to them.'

'But that means somebody else will take the credit,' persisted Lawley. 'Your Mini-Crini, the short crinoline, became the puffball, which everybody else took credit for and made a commercial success of?'

'Well, there are many [*similar*] things I've done. Even something like a simple jersey skirt that you just pull up, which I called a tube skirt. It's really odd to think that nobody made a knitted, or sweatshirt, or jersey sort of skirt before I did it. It just seemed so obvious!'

Lawley turned quickly to punk rock, 'which you and Malcolm McLaren invented together. The hallmarks were anarchy and destruction. How did you arrive at that invention?'

'Punk rock was essentially an exercise about rock and roll. Malcolm said that rock and roll is the jungle beat that threatens white civilisation and it is, essentially, the idea that youth wishes to attack authority. I think that punk rock was a really fantastic and heroic attempt to understand whether there was such a thing as an establishment door that you could kick and have some effect on.'

Lawley: 'So you began to *dress* those ideas. What would you say were the hallmarks of punk fashion?'

'It was built up from all the motifs we'd been exploring in terms of what this youth rebellion would be. The first thing was Teddy boys but we got bored with them and more interested in rockers. And we started to get T-shirts with chains on and all these black things.

'Then we got arrested for doing this T-shirt, which was supposed to be pornographic, of two naked cowboys. The police saw a man wearing it and arrested him and we got done for it.'

'Because the cowboy's penises were hanging out?' asked Lawley.

'Yeah! I remember the judge said it was pornographic because their penises were too close together – and they were too large. Also, one of them was tying the other's necktie. *That* was the clincher!'

'And from there came the whole fashion of bondage and straps?'

'Yeah, we just decided to go all out. We called the shop "Sex" and we started to sell more pornographic T-shirts and put rubberwear in there. Our first shop walls had been covered with pictures from fifties pin-up magazines, with girls in torn clothing, so we started to rip clothes in that way. And we made this cult of our own: this punk rock.'

After punk's founding queen had chosen Stravinsky's *Petrushka*, Sue Lawley asked her if she had always been unconventional. Westwood replied by recalling receiving an OBE from the Queen, earlier that year, while apparently wearing a see-through dress.

'In fact, the dress wasn't see-through, and it was only when the [*press photographers'*] flashlights got on it that all was revealed!' she claimed.

Lawley: 'It was revealed that you had no underwear on?'

'I didn't have *much* on, let's just say that! And it really is typical of me. I think it comes from a kind of *joie de vivre*.'

Westwood recalled being a teenager in the fifties and delighting in the thrill of fashion. 'To put a pencil skirt on, a symbol of sexuality, was just great. The headmistress told my friend off because her petticoat was showing, and she said, "Oh, we've got to show a bit of lace!"'

Lawley took her guest back to her early adulthood, as a primary-school teacher with a young family. She reminded Westwood that McLaren had said that, when he first met her, she was 'desperately looking for something to do – she wanted an escape'.

'I agree,' said Westwood. 'I wouldn't call it an *escape*. I desperately wanted to get into a world where there would be some ideas. I needed brain stimulation and I didn't know how to find it.'

Lawley: 'Malcolm was living in the back of your brother's car when you met him, wasn't he? He had sort of set up home, and he says you used to walk past pushing the pram?'

'Yeah, that's true.'

'He said that you would follow any whim that he had: you seemed to fundamentally believe in him. Did you feel you'd arrived at something you'd been looking for?'

'I *was* very keen to listen to Malcolm. At first, he was almost like a god. He really did have the pot of gold at the end of the rainbow as far as I was concerned. He knew so many things that I wanted to know – but I certainly didn't do everything he wanted me to!

'One thing I remember he asked me to do that I certainly didn't do, he wanted me to go – *he* wouldn't do these things – to Madame Tussauds and set fire to the Beatles' waxworks! I had at the back of my mind that somebody might get killed and it was too dangerous. But I approved of the idea!'

After another classical choice in Tchaikovsky, Lawley asked Westwood if ridicule was something to be scared of: 'From time to time, the public have laughed at your creations. Does that hurt? Do you resent it?' Her guest referenced the most infamous time that had occurred.

'When you were standing in for Terry Wogan [*on his TV chat show*] and the audience laughed at my fashion show, I learned something from that. There is a wider audience out there. I've got to remember that some people might actually think the clothes are wonderful.'

Lawley: 'Did it only ever happen there, or has it happened before or since?'

'People used to laugh at me! Of course! I mean, I had terrible things shouted after me when I was a punk! Sometimes lovely things but, a lot of the time, not very flattering things: I won't tell you what. But I always feel quite heroic in my own clothes ...'

As the interview wound towards its close, Westwood mused that she would one day like to set up an intellectual salon for people to meet to discuss ideas and art: 'I really do feel that our age is a stagnant one, and that stagnation is directly related to the isolation of intellectuals.'

Lawley: 'Are you seriously saying you would be prepared to sacrifice some of your fashion career, if not all of it, for the creation of this cultural salon?'

'Yes. I shouldn't perhaps say this, because I don't want people to think that things are easy, but it's reasonably easy for me to do fashion. And perhaps people set more store by the thing that's more difficult for them to do. Perhaps there's something in that?

'I'm so sure that the genius of the human race is to use their conscious intelligence that I would feel that, unless I have contributed to that, personally, I wouldn't have done anything. If I were to die only having done my fashion career, I wouldn't feel that I've achieved all that I want to do ...'

• • •

The late Malcolm McLaren has long been supplanted in Vivienne Westwood's affections by Andreas Kronthaler, whom she met in 1989 and who was to become her husband and long-term design and business partner. Westwood wore non-see-through clothing and, it is believed, underwear when her OBE was upgraded to a damehood in 2006. In the twenty-first century, while running her fashion empire, she has been a vociferous activist for causes such as the British civil rights movement, CND, PETA and, primarily, the climate crisis. In July 2020, she protested outside the Old Bailey against Julian Assange's proposed extradition to the United States by donning a bright yellow trouser suit, suspending herself in a huge birdcage and proclaiming herself 'the canary in the coal mine'. Punk's original protest spirit looks to be very much alive.

DISCS CHOSEN

Milhaud's *Le boeuf sur le toit*
Czech Philharmonic Orchestra
'It's full of irony, and I use that a lot in my fashion shows'

'The Shrovetide Fair' from Stravinsky's *Petrushka*
Philip Moll with the Berlin Philharmonic Orchestra
'The first time I got excited by classical music'

Prelude to Debussy's *L'après-midi d'un faune*
Berlin Philharmonic Orchestra
'A very, very sexual piece of music'

♥ **'Panorama' from Tchaikovsky's *Sleeping Beauty***
Mincho Minchev with the National Philharmonic Orchestra
'The most perfect ballet ever done'

'Ondine' from Ravel's *Gaspard da la Nuit*
Louis Lortie

Mozart's Piano Concerto No. 21 in C Major
Ilana Vered with the Royal Philharmonic Orchestra

Chopin's Scherzo in B Flat Minor, Op. 31
Vladimir Ashkenazy
'Another piece of perfection'

Prokofiev's *Sarcasms*, Op. 17
Barbara Nissman

BOOK
À la recherche du temps perdu – Marcel Proust
'They say it's the greatest novel that was ever written'

LUXURY ITEM
A multilingual dictionary
Sue Lawley: 'I'm not sure one exists but we'll see if we can find one'

32

GENERAL H. NORMAN SCHWARZKOPF JR

UNITED STATES ARMY GENERAL
1 November 1992

'My castaway this week is a soldier,' said Sue Lawley, simply, but this introduction somewhat understated the distinction of the guest sitting opposite
her. At that point in time, United States Army four-star general H. Norman
Schwarzkopf Jr was the best-known and most significant military figure in
the world.

In August 1990, Iraq president Saddam Hussein's army invaded, and
annexed, the neighbouring nation of Kuwait. The following January, a thirty-
five-nation military coalition under Schwarzkopf's command launched a
devastating counter-offensive known as Operation Desert Storm.

With an aggressiveness and efficiency that earned him the tabloid-press
sobriquet 'Stormin' Norman', Schwarzkopf masterminded a Gulf War campaign that saw the Iraqi forces routed and Kuwait liberated within six weeks.
He also did so with remarkably few losses of coalition lives.

Throughout the conflict, Schwarzkopf naturally appeared a redoubtable
and intimidating figure, yet his desert-island visit revealed a character possessed of a ferocious sense of duty yet also far more depth, humour and
humanity than might have been anticipated. He certainly blew up a compelling Desert Island Storm.

• • •

Sue Lawley opened the broadcast marvelling that her guest had taken
successful command of 'the biggest military operation since the Second
World War'. She then cut straight to the chase: 'Why the nickname "Stormin'
Norman"? One reads it is because you are fearless in battle and storm
forwards, *and* because you have a terrible temper.'

'I think it's probably a little bit of both,' admitted Schwarzkopf. 'Really,
my nickname among the troops for many years was "The Bear" because of
my size. But I'm afraid "Stormin' Norman" has now hung around my neck
for perpetuity, so that's it, now.'

Schwarzkopf acknowledged that his opening record choice, Bob Dylan's
'The Times They Are a-Changin'', was likely to surprise many people ('I
don't consider it purely a hippy song'). As Dylan's whine faded away, Lawley
naturally turned the conversation straight to Desert Storm.

Pointing out that Schwarzkopf's command bunker had been in Riyadh, Saudi Arabia, she asked how frustrating it had been to be so far from battle and the 'thousands of troops and howitzers crossing the lines?'

'It *is* terribly frustrating, particularly when you've been there before, yourself. You want to be there again, somehow helping and assisting and influencing the situation,' he replied.

'At the same time, you realise that nothing would be more disruptive to the fellows out there, really having to do the job, than having this four-star general stomping around in their backyard. They'd be constantly looking over their shoulder at me.'

Lawley: 'But deeper than that frustration must be the anxiety of being in command?'

'Absolutely,' agreed Schwarzkopf. 'The waiting is terrible. All during the planning process, you agonise that you're dealing with hundreds of thousands of lives. And you want to have the plan *right*.'

'Do you pray?'

'Definitely. I am a religious man and I believe very strongly. There's an old saying: "There are no atheists in foxholes." Let me assure you, there are no atheists in generals' command bunkers, either.'

Lawley: 'But at the same time, you have to turn yourself into a fighting machine. You've said you had to talk yourself into a state of ferocity to brief your commanders. You told them: "I want you to go out there and *destroy* Saddam Hussein's Republican Guard. I don't want you to attack, or damage, or surround them – I want you to *destroy* them!"'

'Well, the unfortunate thing about battle is reluctant warriors generally get themselves killed, and a lot of *other* people killed,' Schwarzkopf replied. 'Go back through history, and you see they suffer incredible losses because of their lack of aggressiveness and offensive spirit.'

Lawley: 'You said, during the Gulf War: "You've got to forget the defensive bullshit."'

'That's it! Once committed, you're committed. If you want to know the difference between being involved and being committed, think of a bacon-and-egg breakfast. The chicken is involved: the pig is *committed*!'

Lawley stepped away from the battlefield briefly to touch upon the general's upbringing. His father had been a US Army major-general who served in Iran and Germany. His mother had issues: 'You had a pretty chaotic early childhood? Your father was away at war, and life at home was difficult because your mother had a drink problem?'

'Yeah,' concurred Schwarzkopf. 'My dad left when I'd just turned eight and was gone for four years. He came back only twice during that time, and then for very brief visits. The pressures on my mother were very great and she became an alcoholic.

'I didn't spend a lot of time at home because the evenings around the house were not a lot of fun. So, I was always out with my buddies, one place or another. Got in trouble a lot for staying out too late. But it was escapism as well.'

After leaving school, Schwarzkopf enlisted in West Point, the United States Military Academy. He rhapsodised about this stint to Lawley.

'My mother was a wonderful person and [*she and*] my father had both given me a moral, ethical code to live my life by,' he reflected. 'But West Point focused it all. It brought it into very sharp focus. It gave me a credo of duty, honour, country that I have lived my life by ever since.'

Lawley turned her attention to her guest's first, formative experience of combat – in Vietnam. '*That* really got you where it means something?'

'Yeah. I'm a child of World War II: Johnny came marching home again, to parades and streamers and flags. That, to me, was my childhood dream of what's supposed to happen to soldiers that go off to war for their country.

'In Vietnam, something entirely different happened. I went to war the first time, came back and nobody cared. Worse yet, I went to war the second time, and came back, and everybody was blaming it on me!'

Lawley: 'You did, though, save many lives out there, and won three silver stars for bravery in Vietnam. One was for rescuing some young soldiers who were trapped in a minefield. I don't want to embarrass you, but can you give me a brief description of what happened?'

Schwarzkopf's detailed reply was truly compelling.

'Let me just say – bravery is like beauty: it's in the eye of the beholder. Nobody on the battlefield ever says: "Well, I think I'm about to do a very heroic act." You're doing your job, and somebody else happens to see you and thinks it's an act of bravery so they recommend you for an award. But the idea of *being a hero* just isn't there.

'In this case, a company wandered into a mined area. A person was hurt. I flew in, in my helicopter, turned my helicopter over to them. They flew out with the casualty and I was on the ground there.

'All of a sudden, we found out that we were still in a minefield. A young man ended up stepping on a mine. He had a very bad fracture of his leg and he was flailing around and screaming. The other troops were about to panic – the *worst* thing that can happen in a minefield.

'Believe it or not, through my mind flashed the sign on Harry Truman's desk: THE BUCK STOPS HERE. I was the senior man there, and I felt it was my responsibility to go over to that young man and take care of him.

'I will tell you: I was *not* being brave. I was frightened to death. It's the only time in my life that my legs were trembling. My knees were knocking, literally. Every time I put my foot down, I was afraid I was going to step on a mine.

'I had to reach down with both hands to hold my knee, it was shaking so much as I walked through to get to this young man. And then, another mine went off, right where I had been standing before I went over to take care of the soldier.'

Lawley: 'And you were hit by the shrapnel?'

'Yeah, I was hit by the shrapnel. But I tell you, if I hadn't gone over and taken care of that young man, I would have been much more seriously injured or, perhaps, killed. So, fate just had a hand in it.'

After this extraordinary tale, Lawley returned to the Gulf War with a comment that nearly triggered Stormin' Norman's infamous temper. 'When it was all over, you hadn't achieved your final objective,' she opined. 'You had *not* destroyed the Republican Guard. They got away with a lot of their equipment intact, and ...'

'Now, let's *talk* about that!' interrupted Schwarzkopf. 'After every war, there are these people who come in and invent myths! And that's one of the myths that's been invented in this war!

'Let me give you some numbers. Eighty-five per cent of all the tanks brought into the Kuwait theatre were destroyed or captured. Ninety per cent of all artillery brought into the Kuwait theatre was destroyed or captured. Fifty per cent of all the other armoured vehicles that came into Kuwait were destroyed or captured ...'

Lawley: 'But does it sicken you that Saddam Hussein is still alive, and issuing threats?'

'No, it doesn't sicken me. I'll confess that, like many people, I would like to see Saddam Hussein meet his demise in one way or another. But if Saddam meets his demise, somebody equally bad, or worse, is going to take over. We've personalised the war too much.'

Schwarzkopf had retired from the military after the Gulf War. Lawley pointed out that he had a fifteen-year-old son, Christian: would he like him to follow in his footsteps to West Point?

'No, I don't think so at all. Once, in school, they had to draw a picture of what they wanted to be when they grew up. He drew himself standing in front of a jeep, said "General in the US Army" and brought it home. Of course, I was ecstatic! He was five at the time.

'Since that time, he's not indicated any interest and, frankly, I'm happy with that. One of the things I resented most about Saddam was, when I left home, Christian was in that wonderful period between being a little boy and a young man. One night, he'd climb up into your lap: the next, he'd shake hands with you and not even want you to give him a hug.

'I was really looking forward to spending the year watching him emerge into manhood. I was jerked out of my house. I came back nine months later and this young man was standing at the bottom of the steps. He'd grown six inches; his voice had dropped two octaves; he had discovered girls ...'

And General Schwarzkopf sighed.

'I missed the whole thing, and I really resent that ...'

• • •

After leaving the army, General H. Norman Schwarzkopf Jr moved to Florida to enjoy a low-profile retirement but, inevitably, remained an international figure of note. Resisting encouragements from various quarters to run for US president, he saw his 1992 autobiography, *It Doesn't Take a Hero*, become a *New York Times* bestseller and, the following year, survived prostate cancer. Initially supportive of the Second Gulf War in 2003, he then cautioned against it, and criticised it, after no weapons of mass destruction were found in Iraq. When he died, in December 2012, at the age of seventy-eight, US President Barack Obama said: 'General Schwarzkopf stood tall for the country and Army he loved.'

DISCS CHOSEN

'The Times They Are a-Changin''
Bob Dylan
'I like it because it portrays a very simple truth – nothing ever stays the same'

'Nessun dorma' from Puccini's *Turandot*
Luciano Pavarotti
'A song I listened to over and over again in the Gulf'

'I Dreamed a Dream' from *Les Misérables*
Patti Lupone
'Someone sent me a Les Misérables *tape to Riyadh. It was very special to me over there'*

❤ **'Battle Hymn of the Republic'**
Robert Shaw Chorale Orchestra
'I'm a spiritual person and this is a relationship between God, Man and battle'

'The Impossible Dream'
Peter O'Toole

Brahms's *Academic Festival Overture, Op 80*
Royal Philharmonic Orchestra
'I love heroic music and this piece is heroic'

'Piano Man'
Billy Joel
'The ultimate people-watching song'

Copland's *Lincoln Portrait*
Norman Schwarzkopf with the Saint Louis Symphony Orchestra
'I think the greatest president we ever had was Abraham Lincoln. I was given a chance to recite his words in this very American piece of music'

BOOK
The Prophet – Kahlil Gibran
'It talks about love, it talks about death, it talks about business, it talks about marriage. It puts it all together just right'

LUXURY ITEM
My dog
'He is usually inanimate and has no socially redeeming graces'

33
HUGH GRANT

ACTOR
16 April 1995

Sometimes, *Desert Island Discs* is a beautiful snapshot in time. When Hugh Grant sauntered on to Sue Lawley's island in 1995, he had just enjoyed huge success in *Four Weddings and a Funeral* but was not yet the all-conquering box-office goliath that he was to become.

'His career, as he admits himself, has had its ups and downs, and by no means everything he's done has been of the highest quality,' advised Lawley in her intro, and it is fascinating now to hear Grant's comedic take on his uneven first few years in showbusiness.

The actor's accounts of those early attempts to establish himself were reliably droll and self-effacing and it made for entertaining listening as Lawley delved beneath Grant's legendary surface charm, only to find ... more charm.

• • •

The host began by observing that Grant was widely seen as 'a cinematic symbol of a certain type of Englishman, a curious cross between Tigger and Lord Byron ... a kind of English Cary Grant.' Did he agree?

'Well, there are a few things there!' he laughed. 'Cary Grant, Tigger and Byron. Tigger, certainly! The "quintessential Englishman" thing is slightly annoying because I like to think that my range is *sensationally* wide and I'm *extraordinarily* versatile!'

Lawley wondered what influence the vast success of *Four Weddings and a Funeral* had had on the parts he was being offered.

'Well, for a time it was awful wedding-y scripts. Now, it's just about anything. I get scripts where the leading part is an elderly Jewish lady, and I say, "Why have you sent me this?" "We can fix it, Hugh!" The other day, someone pitched me the part of an Abominable Snowman.'

'And can you now name your price?'

'Certainly, it's gone up. My very terrifying Hollywood agents are very good at making me almost giggle when they mention figures now.'

After a break for a reading from Beatrix Potter's *The Tale of the Flopsy Bunnies*, Lawley talked her guest through his junior-school acting roles: the White Rabbit in *Alice in Wonderland* and a von Trapp sister in *The Sound of Music*.

'Animals and girls were my favourite parts, but they're hard to come by now,' he affirmed. 'I had an extraordinarily high opinion of my acting abilities at school – not really shared by others ...'

Grant's father was a retired executive in the carpet industry and his mother a teacher. The latter, he admitted, did not initially share his enthusiasm for going on the stage.

'She was wary. She used to say to me, "It's a little bit of a *prostitution*, isn't it, darling?" But I think she's come round to it a bit, since it started to, sort of, go right for me.'

Lawley turned to Grant's time at Oxford University, reading English at New College. 'What kind of figure did you cut?'

'I got very into the thirties poets: Auden and Isherwood and Spender and those people. I'm afraid I used to do my top button up and wear lots of V-neck sweaters and smoke cigarettes, even though they made me feel sick.'

'You also acted at Oxford. You made a film, didn't you?'

'Yes. We did a film called *Privileged*. I don't think the director [*Michael Hoffman*] would mind me saying it was one of the most pretentious films ever made. Especially as I've made another film with him, called *Restoration*, this year. He's a big Hollywood director now. *Privileged* was pretty awful but got an extraordinary amount of attention.'

This attention included agents telling Grant, 'Hey, we can make you a star!' at a time when he was poised to begin a PhD in the history of art at the Courtauld Institute in London. He was, he told Lawley, mildly intrigued by their approaches.

'I suddenly thought, *Well, maybe at least I can do this for a year, while I make up my mind what I REALLY want to do*. I assumed that I'd be a star overnight and it would be a cool thing to say at dinner parties ...'

Instead, he winced, he had ended up doing six months in repertory in Nottingham, playing 'very, very small parts – a tree in wind, a shouting peasant, a footman.' After which, said Lawley, he had 'become an alternative comedian'?

'No, we weren't at all alternative! That was the point of us, in a way. We used to do sketches about alternative comedians in a revue called *The Jockeys of Norfolk*. We did it in Nottingham, London and at the Edinburgh Festival.

'We wrote it and performed it and it got bigger and bigger and it was a success. But we went on TV and we didn't get it quite right, so say the least.'

Lawley: 'You died?'

'Yes.'

Grant had drifted into writing radio commercials for products such as Brylcreem and Red Stripe, which he said he had enjoyed. Then, at twenty-six, came a movie break – a major part in a Merchant Ivory film, *Maurice*.

Lawley: 'It's the story of E.M. Forster's early homosexual experiences. It must have been exciting? It's a beautiful film.'

'Yes, you're right, and I'm very proud of it now. But I was heavily into writing at the time. I remember my agent called up and said, "Go and meet James Ivory" and I said, "I don't think so. I'm a bit bored of acting now."

'He said, "No, go on!" So, I went and I got this part that put me on the cinema track. It's a strange system. Once you've done one film, you're apparently qualified to do others.'

Lawley wondered if Grant had, at this point, become typecast playing charming, well-heeled characters. 'Where does the acting end and reality begin? *Are* you those people, or is part of you those people?'

'That's rather a difficult question,' demurred her guest, pointing out he had played many characters who were not 'upper class or particularly charming'. He claimed also to have a 'darker, perhaps kind of colder side'.

Lawley: 'What form does this darker side take?'

'I'm pretty irritable and, if I think people are being dim, I'm quite ready to put them down.'

Lawley wondered if, despite his recent success, her guest would still be happier as a writer.

'Maybe, baby! Maybe. I'm not sure. I think I have to certainly cash in now, while things are going well for me as an actor. It's interesting to be in a situation where I can more or less do what I like. But I think I would be quite happy if I ended up just writing.'

After 'The Laughing Policeman' by Charles Penrose, Lawley turned her gaze to Grant's private life. He had by now been dating Elizabeth Hurley for eight years. The host wondered how they first met.

'We met doing a film in Spain called *Remando al viento – Rowing with the Wind*. It was the first of my Euro-puddings: directed by a Spaniard, starring Spanish, Italian and English actors, written in Spanish and then translated incredibly badly into English.'

'What was this film like?'

'It was heaven, really! I was playing Lord Byron and Elizabeth was Claire Clairmont. When she undressed me, she got to my boots and I had to say a great line: "Not my boots, ever!" Because I had a club foot. In fact, I had two, because the director thought that was more interesting.'

Lawley: 'She only fancied you because of your costume, apparently. She fancied Lord Byron, not Hugh Grant.'

'Absolutely right! And still does to this day.'

Hurley had recently become the public face of Estée Lauder. Lawley wondered if the couple found it hard 'living in a goldfish bowl'.

'It's quite tiring, to tell the truth. I'm relatively all right. I'm the one who gets shouldered aside so they can get pictures of Elizabeth. I think it's a bit miserable for her. But, to be honest, it's quite titillating as well, because I've never had any kind of recognition before.

'Sometimes I think, *Well, it would be nice if the tabloids didn't dig up every skeleton and lie and smear*. But, on the other hand, when they lie and smear and poke fun at other celebrities, it gives me *enormous* delight! So, I can't be too hypocritical.'

Lawley: 'You aren't married – like Charles in *Four Weddings*. He was wary of commitment. Is there an overlap there between reality and fiction?'

'I don't know,' hedged Grant. 'I suppose it is a fear of commitment – or it just seems *very grown-up*, really. It's something we never talk about – either Elizabeth or me.'

'Part of your act is very boyish – is that really you?'

'Yes, I think it might be. I mean, look at my record collection, for God's sake – *Flopsy Bunnies* and "The Laughing Policeman"!'

As the show neared its conclusion, Sue Lawley reminded her guest of an 'enigmatic' comment that he had recently made: 'I have a few more cards to play than people think.' 'What did you mean by that?' she asked.

'I don't know,' mused Hugh Grant. 'I think, perhaps, sometimes I feel a little patronised when people think I'm just, sort of, fluffy, charming, floppy-haired Hugh. I like to think there's a bit more to me than that ...'

• • •

After starring in box-office smash romantic comedies including *Notting Hill* (1999), *Bridget Jones's Diary* (2001), *About a Boy* (2002) and *Love Actually* (2003), Hugh Grant stole the show as a conceited fading actor in *Paddington 2* (2017) and won acclaim and BAFTA and Emmy nominations for his role as former Liberal Party leader Jeremy Thorpe in the BBC mini-series *A Very English Scandal* (2018). He also became hugely involved in the anti-phone-hacking campaign in Britain, donating a six-figure sum he was awarded in a High Court action against Mirror Group Newspapers in 2018 to protest group Hacked Off. Grant married Swedish television producer Anna Eberstein in 2018, and has five children.

DISCS CHOSEN
'We Don't Care' from Beatrix Potter's *The Tale of the Flopsy Bunnies*
Vivien Leigh
'We're going to play it at the right speed but it's better at 33rpm ...'

'The Reel of the 51st Highland Division'
Jimmy Shand and His Band
'This reel was invented by my grandfather and his fellow officers in a POW camp in Germany'

'The Curse of the Hebrew Slaves' from Verdi's *Nabucco*
Vienna Opera Orchestra

'Wake Me Up Before You Go-Go'
Wham!
'The Jockeys of Norfolk used to play it before we went on stage, to get some energy together'

'The Laughing Policeman'
Charles Penrose
'It was always the favourite record on Housewives' Choice*'*

❤ **'Somethin' Stupid'**
Frank and Nancy Sinatra
'It's Elizabeth's and my theme song'

'We're Called Gondolieri' from Gilbert and Sullivan's *The Gondoliers*
Richard Lewis and John Cameron

'Viva el Fulham'
Tony Rees and the Cottagers
'Is this the worst record ever to be on Desert Island Discs*?'*

BOOK
The Adventures of Tintin: King Ottokar's Sceptre – Hergé
'My favourite Tintin book'

LUXURY ITEM
A hankie
'I have a terrible nose-blowing problem'

34
MARIANNE FAITHFULL

SINGER, ACTOR, SIREN
28 May 1995

Marianne Faithfull was the poster girl for the swinging sixties who fell from grace. A natural beauty who, for a while, seemed to epitomise the permissive society, she had it all until she lost it all in a spectacular, arbitrary and horrible manner.

Faithfull was an upper-class schoolgirl when she met the Rolling Stones' manager, Andrew Loog Oldham, at a party in 1964 and he launched her into a recording career. The teenage ingénue had hit singles and began a high-profile, four-year relationship with Mick Jagger.

Faithfull's downfall began with a 1967 drugs raid at Keith Richards's mansion, where the tabloids salaciously claimed the police had found her naked and making a rather unorthodox use of a Mars bar. After she and Jagger split, three years later, she somehow became a homeless heroin addict.

Her terrible tale seemed destined for a tragic ending yet, in May 1995, Sue Lawley found Marianne Faithfull defiant, sober, once more a respected recording artist, and sharing far more stories of sex, drugs and rock and roll than the desert island was accustomed to hearing ...

• • •

Sue Lawley did not hold back in an introduction that detailed Faithfull's 'life of promiscuity and drug addiction', which had 'seen her survive two suicide attempts and three marriages'. Her guest's first musical choice was Jimi Hendrix's 'Hey Joe'.

'Jimi Hendrix, who you knew,' said Lawley as the song faded out. 'But he never seduced you, and you never seduced him – is that right?'

'He *tried*, and I wish I'd gone!' Faithfull replied. 'It's one of my only regrets in my life!'

'What about Bob Dylan? I thought you resisted him, too?'

'I did, yes. I don't quite regret that as much as not being seduced by Jimi Hendrix.'

Lawley: 'Gene Pitney, you *were* seduced by?'

'Oh, yes!'

'You had an affair with him and plenty of others, including three of the Rolling Stones. Does it all seem crazy now, or do you know even now how you fell into it all?'

'Well,' pondered Faithfull, 'I *fell into it all* because I was incredibly beautiful, I think!'

'Did you *know* you were incredibly beautiful?'

'Not really, no. Only now, with long distance and perspective.'

'It was to do with looking like you were supposed to look then?' speculated Lawley. 'Long legs, blonde hair, blue eyes, pouty lips ... it was exactly how the face of the sixties was supposed to be, and you had it.'

'It was the dream. I'm glad! I mean, it got me into a lot of trouble, but I wouldn't exchange a lot of it if I could. The only bit I would leave out, if I could, was the drugs.'

Faithfull described being a seventeen-year-old schoolgirl when she went to the fateful music-biz party. ('Literally, I walked into the room, everybody stopped talking and I was discovered!') Loog Oldham arranged for her to record a single, 'As Tears Go By', written by Jagger and Richards.

'I recorded it, it came out, and nothing happened,' she recalled. 'And I remember feeling, sort of, intense relief, because I had a vague idea that if this was a hit, all hell would break loose.

'This all went on in my summer holidays, so I was just thinking I'd got away with it and I would go back to school in September and get on with my A levels. Then in October it took off and that was that.'

Faithfull described herself as 'a nice little middle-class girl', which led Lawley to point out that her mother was an Austrian baroness: 'Did she bring you up to expect to be treated like a princess?'

'Yes, she did! And, actually, I don't think it was such a bad thing.'

Faithfull met and married an artist, John Dunbar. By the time she was nineteen they had a son, Nicholas. But she was about to be swept off her feet.

Lawley: 'Do you recall the first time you met Mick Jagger?'

'Yes, at the party where I was discovered. I guess all the Stones were there. I remember seeing Mick having a row with Chrissie Shrimpton.'

'You decided he was a cheeky little yob?'

'Yes. He wasn't my type.'

'How did he *become* your type, then?'

'With time, and I obviously fell in love with him.'

Lawley: 'Keith Richards was more your type, yes?'

'I don't know. I like very serious, clever ... Keith Richards probably *was* more my type, yes.'

'Is Mick Jagger clever?'

'Oh, terribly clever! As I got to know him, I discovered he wasn't at all what he seemed. He was much more interesting.'

'He saved your life once, didn't he? He got you to the hospital in time when you'd OD'd.'

'Yes. If he hadn't been there, I wouldn't have made it.'

Lawley turned the talk to 'the day your reputation was made – or, I suppose, destroyed': the February 1967 police drugs raid on Redlands, Keith Richards's country house in Sussex. 'You were dressed in nothing but a fur rug, and Mick and Keith ended up spending time in jail.'

Faithfull described what had happened that day. She recalled that she, Jagger, Richards and friends had got stoned and gone to the beach: 'We had a wonderful time, running around the beach like children!

'We got back to Redlands very tired and dirty and covered in twigs and moss and bits of sand and shells and pebbles. So, I went and had a bath. Everyone else was changing into fabulous costumes, that's what it was like in those times, but I had forgotten to bring a costume.

'On the bed was a huge, vast fur rug. As Keith said in the trial, it could have covered ten women. I put it on and it looked wonderful: I really did look like Venus in Furs. I went downstairs, we were just chilling out, as they say, and twenty-four West Wittering Constabulary walked in.'

'The stories that followed ... were very lurid and explicit,' noted Lawley.

'Well, you're alluding to the Mars bar story, which is not true, which has always upset me and angered me. That story took away my good name as a woman. Mick and Keith came out of this even more glamorous and wonderful and, sort of, outlawed. I was *destroyed* by it.'

The public vilification that followed the drug bust was one reason why, when Faithfull finished with Jagger in 1970, she lost custody of the then-four-year-old Nicholas to her ex-husband.

'That was all connected with leaving Mick. While I was with Mick, I had protection. The minute I walked out of that protection I was completely vulnerable.'

Lawley: 'Was that why you ended up on the streets in Soho?'

'I lost hope, yes. There didn't seem to be much point in *anything* once that was done ...'

'Did nobody come to find you?'

'I didn't *want* anybody to come and find me. It took a particular kind of respect for me to be able to let me be. I didn't do it to get attention. I literally didn't want anyone to know where I was. I wanted to be left alone.

'I believe there's something that looks after fools like me in that kind of situation, really. I was very lucky. People were very kind to me. That impressed me, because they didn't know me, didn't know my name, didn't know anything about me. For two years, I found out about ... the basic goodness of human beings.'

After Faithfull had chosen the Rolling Stones' 'Gimme Shelter', Lawley asked if she still ever saw the band.

'Not very often. I'm very fond of Keith. I'm very fond of Ronnie. I adore Charlie. The only one I have a problem with, and it's obvious when we meet, is Mick. There's a lot of blood under the bridge, and it's awkward and difficult. But Jerry [*Hall*] is always very nice and helps a lot.'

Faithfull had turned her life around. She made an acclaimed album, *Broken English*, in 1979, and had been free from drugs since 1985. By the time she hit the desert island in 1995 she was living in Ireland, a successful singer and actor ... and, celebrated Sue Lawley, a granny!

'All of a sudden, Marianne Faithfull is part of a family!' she marvelled.

'I'm part of the whole thing,' agreed her guest. 'And that's what I never used to feel. I'm part of my family, and I feel like I'm part of the human race ...'

• • •

Marianne Faithfull remains part of the human race. Over the last two decades, this perennially chic, increasingly iconic figure has released well-received albums and worked with a host of innovative musical stars including Nick Cave, P.J. Harvey, Jarvis Cocker, Damon Albarn, Beck and, of all people, Metallica. She's suffered health afflictions – breast cancer in 2006, hepatitis C, a broken hip, COVID, pneumonia – but, in characteristic style, she has survived them all. The sixties poster girl is still swinging.

DISCS CHOSEN

'Hey Joe'
Jimi Hendrix
'He was a wonderful man – I want this on my island so I can think about him'

Kurt Weill's 'Berlin im Licht'
Ensemble Modern
'The first time I recorded a Weill song, it felt like I'd come home'

'The Night They Invented Champagne' from *Gigi*
Amanda Waring, Beryl Reid and Geoffrey Burridge
'For years, I used Gigi as my life role model'

'Highway 61 Revisited'
Bob Dylan
'I couldn't live without it'

'Dear Mr Fantasy'
Traffic
'I play this very loud at four in the morning. I have great speakers'

'Gimme Shelter'
Rolling Stones

❤ **'Small Axe'**
Bob Marley and the Wailers
'A great spiritual charge'

Monteverdi's *L'Orfeo*
The Monteverdi Choir

BOOK
Robinson Crusoe – Daniel Defoe
'For inspiration, for tips, for philosophical wellbeing'

LUXURY ITEM
Pen and paper
'A special pen you can get at Asprey which has a magnifying glass on the end'

'ISLE NEVER FORGET ...'
'I was surprised to be asked to go on *Desert Island Discs*. It wasn't a show that . I often listened to but obviously I knew what it was. So, I was very pleased to accept and go on.

'The questions that I was asked quite offended me. I was very upset. But at that time in my life, people treated me like that. It's changed now, I'm glad to say. They have more respect and they understand me better.

'Back then, there were loads of people going around saying that I was – what was it? – "promiscuous" and "a drug addict". Well, I wasn't *always* a drug addict, and I wasn't even all that promiscuous! That all just got laid on me. It was really unfair.

'I found the questions upsetting but I'm very good at hiding my feelings. I didn't enjoy recording it, but I *did* enjoy hearing it back. I knew that I had done a good show, despite what I was being asked. I was pleased with it.

'I look at the list of records I chose and I still think it's quite good. They all meant something to me and I stand by them. I said on the show that I "couldn't live without" Bob Dylan – I don't feel quite like *that* now! But I do still love him. *And* Bob Marley.

'I still hear *Desert Island Discs* occasionally. Not often. I know as you get old, you're supposed to listen to the radio – that's what my mother did! But I'm not that kind of old person ...'

35
JOHN LEE HOOKER

BLUES SINGER, GUITARIST, LEGEND
11 June 1995

John Lee Hooker had recorded more than a hundred blues albums by the time he rocked up on Sue Lawley's desert island in 1995. Calling him 'the oldest star in rock music', Lawley stated that he was seventy-four but, in all honesty, she was guessing: his true year of birth was a mystery.

Hooker himself claimed to have been born in 1917 but census evidence hinted that 1912 was likelier. What was certain was that he had been the youngest of eleven children born to a Mississippi sharecropper, and had run away from home when he was just fourteen.

Discovered playing blues guitar in a Detroit club in 1948, he had gone on to become not just blues royalty but the blues incarnate: venerated by his peers *and* by rock superstars such as Eric Clapton and the Rolling Stones, he was one of the most influential musicians in rock and roll history. As it quickly became clear, he was highly aware.

Hooker had quite an ego and quite a story to tell, yet he was a man of few words. These words were growled in a gravelly basso profundo that sounded as if it was emanating from the centre of the earth and passing up through his legs to his larynx. It all made for most engaging listening.

• • •

Lawley opened the interview by positing a classic theory of the origins of the blues: 'In order to sing the blues, you've got to have suffered?'

In a voice that would make even Orson Welles sound as if he were on helium, Hooker corrected her: '*I* didn't have to suffer to sing the blues! God gave me the great talent!'

'But was it born in you because you're born of an American black family who had, generations before, known suffering?' wondered Lawley. 'Is it *in you*?'

'It's wasn't *black*. It wasn't *white*. It's just that I automatically was born a blues singer. The blues hasn't got any colour. So many white singers can sing the blues. Joe Cocker is a born blues singer. Eric Clapton.'

That point established, Lawley remarked that Hooker had not made a record for six years before returning with a huge global hit album, *The Healer*, in 1989. 'Had fashion come around to you again?'

'I wasn't doing anything different. It must have been my time.'

'The blues don't change, do they?' mused a philosophical Lawley.

'Never change. Old Man River just keeps on rolling. It rolls fast, but it keeps on rolling. It will never die.'

After a musical interlude, Lawley invited Hooker to talk about his family background. It had one very notable theme: 'If I've got this right, you're the son of a preacher, the brother of a preacher, and the father of a preacher?'

'My brother is a preacher,' confirmed Hooker. 'My father was a minister. I've got a son, Robert Jr, who is a preacher. I come from the church. I was taught to be loyal to the church. I'm still a Christian. I'm a Jehovah's Witness.'

'But your father didn't like you singing at home?'

'Not the blues. He called it devil music. But it's no devil music.'

Lawley: 'Your family were share croppers. What did that mean?'

'They had a whole lot of land. They rented all that land. They had their own land: raised their own fruit, own pigs, own cows, own cotton.'

'How did you and your family live?'

'We lived *good*. The South was bad back then but we were fortunate. I never went hungry a day in my life. My dad was a big minister. He was loved by everybody, so we didn't see a hard time.'

After Hooker's parents split when he was young, his stepfather taught him to play guitar, initially with 'a tyre attached to a barn door'. At fourteen, he ran away from home. Why? asked Lawley.

'Well, I was kind of different from my other family. I felt like I was going to really do things. I never doubted myself. When you're twelve, thirteen, fourteen, you got nerves like a piece of steel. You ain't scared of nothing.'

'I left there one night, with my guitar. I stepped out of my mom's house – I wanted to be in the limelight. I had $2 in my pocket that my stepdaddy gave me two weeks before. You could hitchhike then, and I got a ride all the way to Memphis.

'Then I got a little job at the New Daisy Picture Show. You come in, I show you your seat: "Follow me, please!" Red suit, red jacket, real neat and cute. I did that for a long time.'

Lawley: 'How many years was it before you saw your mother again?'

'I saw her once more, in my twenties. And then I didn't see her again, because she passed.'

Hooker moved to Detroit to work making cars during the Second World War. When peace broke out, he was spotted by a record-label owner playing guitar in a club. His first single, 1948's 'Boogie Chillen', was a huge hit.

'They gave me a contract: $2,000! I had never had that much money! I thought I was rich! I kept that cheque for two weeks. I showed it to everybody: "Look here, I got $2,000!" Then my landlady said, "Put it in the bank, boy!"'

As Hooker's status and fame grew, Lawley prompted him, he came to live in London in the sixties.

'Yes, for 'bout a year and a half. I lived in Oxford Street, upstairs over a clothing store. That was the place to be. When I came over, it was just like the president coming to town!

'Me and Eric Burdon used to run around. We used to go to parties all night. I was there when one of the Stones got drowned in the pool.'

Lawley: 'Brian Jones?'

'Yeah. I was there.'

'You also knew Bob Dylan, didn't you?'

'Oh yeah. Dylan wasn't doing anything: just hanging around in my apartment. One night I put him on the bandstand [*Dylan supported Hooker in New York in 1961*] and he got signed up.'

After a burst of Stevie Ray Vaughan, Sue Lawley wondered if her guest had a head start when it came to making music. Was Hooker so skilled on the guitar due to his double-jointed fingers? 'Can you play chords other guitarists can't?'

'I can do anything I want!'

'You can't read a lot of writing? [*Hooker was thought to be illiterate.*] All your songs are in your head?'

'Nobody gives *me* a song. I do it myself. I'm a genius: nobody can write for John Lee Hooker. I've got a good memory, like the elephant.'

With Hooker's musical magnificence firmly established, Lawley turned to his private life. 'Women played an important role in your life, John Lee Hooker. How many times have you been married?'

'Three times too many!'

'What happened? They all wanted you to stop playing?'

'Yeah. You're on the road all the time, it jumps in a woman's mind that you're doing it with other women. They read about how musicians play around. And I wasn't no angel. I loved my wives but they wanted me to quit playing music and get a regular job.

'Well, I said, "No way, José! I will *not* do that." And so, they split, and they did me a big favour when they did.'

'You've got no wife now – are you happier without one?'

'Oh, yes! Yes!'

'You said that with enthusiasm.'

'Yes!'

'You're seventy-five this year, aren't you?' speculated Lawley, hopefully. 'What's your idea of fun?'

'I'm a baseball nut, and I love buying cars. And women!'

'As long as they're not wives?'

'Right, right, yes!' chuckled John Lee Hooker.

• • •

After the large success of *The Healer* and subsequent albums, John Lee Hooker stayed single and lived out the end of his life with great wealth, accumulating no fewer than five homes in California. He died in his sleep in one of those homes on 21 June 2001. Nobody knew how old he was because he took the secret of precisely when he was born to the grave.

DISCS CHOSEN
'Got My Mojo Working'
Muddy Waters
'He was a great fan of mine and a great friend'

'Nothing But a Woman'
Robert Cray
'That's all I need – nothing but a woman!'

'Howlin' for My Baby'
Howlin' Wolf
'The mighty Wolf! A voice like an angel'

'You Shook Me'
B.B. King

'Flood Down in Texas'
Stevie Ray Vaughan
'He didn't sound like anybody'

'Layla'
Derek and the Dominos
'Eric Clapton – he's a big fan of mine ...'

'Crosscut Saw'
Albert King

❤ **'Going Down Slow'**
Bobby Bland
'Everything that man does chills me – he's got that voice ...'

BOOK
'One with a lot of pictures of pretty women in it'

LUXURY ITEM
His guitar
Sue Lawley: 'Of course. What else?'

36

KATHLEEN TURNER

ACTOR
14 May 2000

Just into the new millennium, a major Hollywood star with a fascinating and troubled recent history wandered on to Sue Lawley's desert island. She had built an A-list Hollywood career and then seen illness nearly take it all away from her.

The redoubtable Kathleen Turner had been working on Broadway and in a dire US TV soap opera when she was invited to audition for *Body Heat*. This 1981 dark, erotic thriller was a critical and box-office hit, establishing its female lead as one of Hollywood's most sensual and bankable stars.

Further successes followed in *Romancing the Stone* (1984), *Peggy Sue Got Married* (1986) – for which she was nominated for an Academy Award – and *The War of the Roses* (1989). However, she was then stricken by chronic rheumatoid arthritis, which threatened to end her acting career.

She had been through a bleak time, but Kathleen Turner arrived on the island with her disease in remission and her career back on the up. She brought along her reputation for being direct and forthright, which the following interview, happily, proved to be entirely merited.

• • •

Turner was in London to appear as Mrs Robinson in a theatre version of the movie *The Graduate* and Lawley began by applauding her bravery in getting naked on stage in her mid-forties. Was she doing it 'without a qualm'?

'That sounds much braver than I am!' her guest replied. 'The director and writer, Terry Johnson, left it to me, and I just gritted my teeth and thought, *OK, I can do this*.

'The funny thing is, in the beginning, Terry said to me, "There's an extra beat. You come out with a towel, you close the bedroom door, you turn and there's this extra beat I don't quite understand before you drop the towel. Is it a choice?" I said, "No, no! I'm just trying to drop the towel!"'

'Does it go on being that difficult, or has it got easier?' asked Lawley.

'It's gotten a little easier, although I still love to hear the gasps and stuff – especially at matinees!'

Turner wasn't new to performative nudity. Lawley reflected that she had emerged in the highly sexual *Body Heat* alongside William Hurt. Was it true that she had cried in her dressing room before filming the most explicit scenes?

'Oh, I did, I did! We started filming with the most revealing scene in the whole film. I was shaking like a leaf and Bill just marched me straight to his dressing room, opened a bottle of wine and said, "You're going to drink that!" I said, "No, I'm *not!*" He said, "Yes, you *are!*"'

Lawley: '*Body Heat* was your big break. How did they find you?'

'I was on Broadway and doing a soap for NBC. My character was just so incredibly stupid, I finally told the writers, "Make her a drunk! I can't possibly justify these words and actions unless the woman is blind drunk!"'

Having talked her way out of the soap opera, Turner was asked to audition for *Body Heat*: 'They'd seen five hundred women and hadn't cast the role.' The director was enamoured of both her performance and her deep, distinctive voice.

'Has it always been like that?' wondered Lawley.

'Yes.'

'It's not ten years of nicotine?'

'No. They put me in a boys' choir at church. I wasn't allowed to sing with the girls because my voice was too low.'

After *Body Heat*, recalled Lawley, Turner had made *Romancing the Stone* with Michael Douglas. Its sequel, *Jewel of the Nile*, had hit a few problems.

'Yes, well, they sued me for $25 million!' said Turner. 'I refused to do the script they gave me. I said, I had agreed to do a sequel but not to lower my standards. The script was nowhere near the quality of the first film.'

Lawley: 'You're obviously your own woman. Stubborn? Pig-headed?'

'Pig-headed? Yes, but usually right!'

After a burst of Billy Joel, Turner told Lawley that her father had been a diplomat and she had consequently spent her late teens, in the early seventies, in London. That was where she had first resolved to act.

Lawley: 'Your father was set against it. Did you have arguments?'

'Oh, yes! It was terribly sad because we had one huge argument and I stormed off to Stratford – the only time I ever ran away from home. And I came home and he had died.'

The seventeen-year-old Turner, her mother and sister then returned to the US and moved to the Midwest, which she hated. A spell in an all-girls dorm at Southwest Missouri State University was not a success.

'They had this lovely little custom where they had boards, to write on, left on the doors,' she told Lawley. 'Somebody would come by and leave you a message or a Bible passage. A big favourite was TODAY IS THE FIRST DAY OF THE REST OF YOUR LIFE.

'I got so fed up that I wrote on the door IT IS BETTER TO REIGN IN HELL THAN TO SERVE IN HEAVEN and I went off to the theatre. I got back that night and all the girls said, "You must erase that blasphemous message from our hallways!" And I said, "Well, that's it! I'm out of here!"'

Turner found her way to New York where, she claimed, having by now been married for seventeen years, she and property-developer husband Jay Wise were jokingly known as 'the Last Couple in Manhattan'. Lawley asked how they had met.

'I'd just come back from *Romancing the Stone* and realised I was living as I had as a student and it was time I actually spent some of the money and got a nice place to live. A friend who knew Jay asked if he would help me find a nice place.

'He said, "I don't rent apartments." She said, "It's for Kathleen Turner" and he said, "Oh!" He gave her a list of buildings, I went and looked at them and I didn't like *any* of them, so I became a personal challenge. He took me personally to look at the next batch of apartments.

'He picked me up in his car and this song, "Avalon" by Roxy Music, was on the radio. I said, "Oh, you know 'Avalon'?" And he said, "*You* know it?" Anyway, we met at one o'clock and he left at four-thirty that morning.'

At this point, Lawley turned sombrely to a less happy event in Turner's life – the moment when she had realised she was seriously ill.

'Well, I was shooting [*1994 comedy movie*] *Serial Mom* and I seemed to be swelling and I didn't know why. Suddenly, my shoes – size seven-and-a-half, lovely and petite for my height, I was very vain about it – were completely impossible.'

Turner described seeing a range of specialists unable to diagnose her condition, which worsened until she could not move one arm or turn her head. It took her own doctor to identify the malaise as rheumatoid arthritis.

'I went to my GP and said, "Don't tell Jay, but I really think I'm dying. You've got to find out what it is." He took blood, and most people have a rheumatoid factor up to about sixty. Mine was six hundred.'

Lawley: 'Rheumatoid arthritis is terribly painful, isn't it?'

'Chronic, endless pain. And you can't get away from it by sitting down, or putting your feet up, or lying down, because it's inside your joints.'

'How did you cope? With a little daughter, too?'

'I could not move, literally could not *walk*, without steroids. But they do damage to your body and appearance and your mind. They create great rage and great depression at the same time.'

'They blew you up, didn't they? And press photographs appeared of you.'

'Oh yes. There was great speculation that I had become a drunk, or something like that. And, of course, *I was just trying to walk*.'

Lawley: 'Why didn't you tell them the truth?'

'Because you won't be hired if you're sick! They will hire you if you're a drunk – look at the history of actors and Hollywood! They will hire you again and again. But if you're sick? I don't think so.'

It took her daughter's school parents' evening and a chance encounter with a friend, Sale Johnson, of the family who founded the Johnson & Johnson pharmaceutical company, for Kathleen Turner to find relief.

'I had to get up three steps to the school and I just couldn't do it. I was hanging on the railing, with tears running down my face, and Sale said, "What in the world is wrong with you?" I said, "I have rheumatoid arthritis and I cannot get up these stairs."

'She said, "Well, our child has juvenile rheumatoid arthritis, we have funded a research programme and you are going there tomorrow!" And she got me into a doctor who started me on some drugs that worked. And the pain has almost gone. There will always be *some* pain, but it's nothing compared to what it was.'

Lawley: 'It truly tested your stubbornness? Your determination?'

'Oh, they told me five years ago that I could not act any more. That I'd be in a wheelchair for the rest of my life. And I just said, "*You're wrong*. I have no other alternative. I will not do that."'

It was a hideous episode that had dented one of Kathleen Turner's best features: her sense of humour. This quality had since returned with a vengeance, as was illustrated by one exchange late in the interview.

Lawley noted that Turner's co-star in *Romancing the Stone*, Michael Douglas, was now dating Catherine Zeta-Jones. Was there any truth in the rumours that the couple might film a sequel to the movie?

'No, I can happily say that that was a complete fabrication by the British press!' clarified Kathleen Turner. 'I saw Michael for dinner last week. And I told him, frankly, that if he did *Romancing the Stone* again, with the same characters, Catherine would have to play our daughter.

'He did not think that was so funny. But I did ...'

• • •

After *The Graduate*, Kathleen Turner put on a one-woman stage show, *Tallulah*, about the 'self-destructive' life of one of *Desert Island Discs'* most infamous castaways, Tallulah Bankhead. Although she still makes movies, she has increasingly worked in theatre and on TV, including turns as Chandler Bing's cross-dressing father in *Friends* and as an oversexed boss in *Californication*. The Last Couple in Manhattan divorced in 2007 and Turner, as is entirely appropriate, now lives in an apartment on Broadway.

DISCS CHOSEN
'Gulf Coast Highway'
Nanci Griffith with James Hooker
'It's very American'

'Say Goodbye to Hollywood'
Billy Joel
'... which is very much how I feel about it'

♥ **Tchaikovsky's Piano Concerto No. 1 in B Flat Minor**
Vladimir Ashkenazy with the London Symphony Orchestra
'I would need the spine-stiffening that it would give me'

'Avalon'
Roxy Music

'I'll Find My Way Home'
Jon and Vangelis
'This was from my wedding'

'As Cool as I Am'
Dar Williams
'She's sassy and she's smart'

'Kathy's Song'
Simon & Garfunkel
Lawley: 'Does anybody ever call you Kathy?'
Turner: 'Not more than once.'

'Stay Strong'
The Suits
'My husband's band. I'm singing in the background'

BOOK
Emma – Jane Austen
'Austen's wit pleases me'

LUXURY ITEM
Roses
'My dresser suggested that if I chose a luxury on this show, I might get it in my dressing room as well as on the desert island. So, I'll say roses ...'

'ISLE NEVER FORGET ...'
'I knew *Desert Island Discs* because I used to tune in as a girl when I was at high school at the American School in St John's Wood. I listened to it religiously,

in fact. So, when they asked me if I wanted to do the show – *Yeah!* Absolutely I did!

'I don't remember taking a long time to choose my records. The choice I remember best is Dar Williams, "As Cool as I Am", which has this great chorus: "I will not be afraid of women!" And I'm proud to say that I have always felt that way.

'Looking at my choices ... I would still take Roxy Music. And Billy Joel. I'd just go with Paul Simon instead of Simon & Garfunkel: his music is *much* more interesting. Oh, and I think I'd lose my ex-husband's band! You can take *that* one off, thank you!

'I didn't listen to my episode back when it was broadcast. I don't really do that. It's like reading your own interviews: OK, you might be pleased with what you've said, but it's just not what I do. I don't look back.

'I haven't been to the UK for two years because there's been no travel and nobody going anywhere. But I'm coming over again in 2022. Will I tune in to *Desert Island Discs*? Yeah, probably ...'

37
BORIS JOHNSON

JOURNALIST, POLITICIAN, PRIME MINISTER-IN-WAITING
30 October 2005

Boris Johnson was still a mere backbench Conservative MP, broadsheet journalist, magazine editor and rising media star, possessed of a self-deprecating, comic persona and a lively and idiosyncratic turn of phrase, when he chanced upon Sue Lawley's desert island in November 2005.

Lawley introduced him as a 'Wodehousian' figure prone to 'getting into scrapes', and her guest had already weathered a few, from being fired from the opposition frontbench for lying about an affair, to grievously offending the entire city of Liverpool via an article in the *Spectator*.

Yet he had also lifted that political magazine to new circulation heights and his effortlessly entertaining, knowingly self-mocking turn on the desert island illustrated exactly why so many employers, colleagues, conquests and, ultimately, electors were to fall for his roguish charms.

In her last appearance in this book, Sue Lawley shrewdly observed that Johnson's 'self-deprecating humour and often-shambolic appearance conceal a cleverness, and a confidence, that, for all his mishaps, might yet take him further in politics.' She even raised the seemingly far-fetched notion that her guest might one day become prime minister.

Whoever knew that on the *Desert Island Discs* table there was a crystal ball?

• • •

In her opening remarks, Lawley quoted Boris Johnson as saying that he was 'propelled by an eager mania, a desire, to go on; get on; *have a go*.' This had her guest roundly chortling in the studio. 'You did say it, actually!' she reprimanded him.

'I suppose I must have done,' he conceded.

Lawley suggested that many of Johnson's 'scrapes' were caused by him simultaneously attempting to ride two horses: politics and journalism. She indicated that he'd proved it couldn't be done.

'I think I've successfully ridden two horses for quite a time,' countered Johnson. 'But I admit there have been moments the distance between the horses became terrifying. And I *did*, momentarily, come off.'

'We'll come back to that,' promised Lawley.

'Well, I sincerely hope we won't!'

Lawley: 'But if you had to choose, you'd choose politics?'

'Yes. Of course. I always wanted to do it. I always knew I was going to be an MP and I always knew I'd be very disappointed in myself if I didn't do it ... I had, I suppose, a sense that this was the single most interesting job that one could do.'

At this point, David Cameron had just been elected the Conservative Party leader. Lawley asked if Johnson knew him from Oxford University.

'I do. I did know him. I do remember him. He was younger than me: one of the many traumas I have to bear in my life. We didn't know each other that well.'

Cutting straight to the chase, Lawley asked Johnson if he would like to be prime minister one day. 'Your ex-mother-in-law said, "Boris is very ambitious and always said he wanted to be PM."'

'*Did* I used to say that? Maybe I did. I suppose all politicians, in the end, are like, kind of, crazed wasps in a jam jar, each individually convinced that they're going to make it out and survive. And, in a Darwinian way, the public *needs* politicians to want to get as far as they can.'

Lawley: 'In a Darwinian sense, are you fit enough to survive?'

Johnson laughed. 'Probably not but, in an evolutionary sense, it's vital that everybody should have the delusion that they could.'

After a break for the Beatles, Lawley turned to Johnson's family history. He described his Turkish great-grandfather signing an arrest warrant for young revolutionary Kemal Atatürk. 'The result? He was taken from a bar-ber shop, where he was having a shave, lynched and stuck in a tree.'

Johnson's grandfather had thus fled Turkey and emigrated to England, where he became a farmer in Devon. Boris Johnson initially grew up on this Exmoor farm. 'What was it like?' wondered Lawley.

'It was jolly cold, is the honest truth! We didn't have central heating. We didn't even have electric lights! It was one of those areas of the country that was not wired up to the grid. But it was wonderful. We used to swim in the river, muck about ...'

Lawley detailed Johnson's effortless educational glide through Eton, Oxford and turning down a scholarship to Harvard. 'Gosh! You've done incredible research!' her guest gasped, confessing to being a 'colossal swot' to whom exams came easy.

Lawley pointed out that he had also been the president of the Oxford Union. 'You set your sights on things and go for it? It's what keeps you going?'

'Yes. It's also a sense of, *You might as well do it. There it is: what's life for?* You've got the great dandelion clock of eternity ticking away: *why not*? My ambition silicon-chip has always been programmed to try to scramble my way up this *cursus honorum*: this ladder of things.'

The talk moved on to Johnson's post-university career. Lawley recalled that he had lost his first job, as a trainee reporter at *The Times*, 'pretty quickly', but was then recruited by *Daily Telegraph* editor Max Hastings, who packed him off to Belgium.

'Yes. I was twenty-four, I went to Brussels, and I was the correspondent for five years. And I saw the whole thing change. It was a wonderful time to be there. The Berlin Wall fell and the French and the Germans had to decide what Europe was going to become. This pressure to create a single polity produced *fantastic* stirrings in the Conservative Party.'

Johnson had, he admitted, taken great pleasure in filing a string of anti-EU news reports, which had huge repercussions back home.

'Everything I wrote, from Brussels, I found I was, sort of, just chucking these rocks over the garden, and I listened to this amazing crash from the greenhouse next door, over in England ... having this explosive effect on the Tory party. And it gave me a rather weird sense of power.'

These reports, noted Lawley, had won Johnson a host of journalistic awards and led to him being named the editor of political magazine the *Spectator*. He was given the job by its proprietor, Conrad Black, on the condition that he would eschew any political ambitions.

Lawley: 'Within a year, you were running for [*MP for*] Henley. Was that *dishonest*?'

'Well, it's probably fair to say that I didn't tell them I was going to do it ...' laughed Johnson.

'Right. Well, let's move on to the Ken Bigley affair ...'

Johnson audibly winced. 'Do we *have* to move on to that?'

They did. In 2004, British engineer Ken Bigley was murdered in Iraq by Islamic militants. In an editorial, Johnson's *Spectator* had attributed the 'extreme' reaction to his death to the fact he was from Liverpool: a city, it claimed, which 'wallowed' in 'victim status', as was supposedly also demonstrated by its reaction to the Hillsborough disaster.

A major media uproar followed. Johnson, who, by then, was also on the opposition frontbench, was forced to travel to Liverpool to apologise to the city.

Lawley asked if Johnson had personally penned the fateful editorial: 'Did *you* write it?'

'I take full responsibility for that editorial.'

'Did *you* write it?' she repeated, sensing her Paxman moment upon her.

'I commissioned it, I edited it and I carried the can. And it's well known that editors are responsible for whatever appears in the editorial column.'

Lawley: 'But it would be interesting to find out if *you* penned it or not.'

'It would be. It would be.'

'We're not going to find out?'

'No. No.'

Lawley suggested that the honourable thing for her guest to do, rather than undertake what he described as his 'pilgrimage of penitence' to Liverpool, would have been to resign from the Tory frontbench.

'I think, probably, yes, probably, I mean, no,' replied Johnson. 'What I should have done – I should have resigned from the frontbench and apologised for the things we got wrong.'

Giving her guest a little respite, Lawley played Brahms's *Variations on a Theme by Haydn* before turning to another noteworthy Boris Johnson extracurricular activity ('as if you hadn't got enough on your plate!'). In autumn 2004, he had published a novel, *72 Virgins*, about a homegrown Islamic terrorist attack on Britain. The following spring had seen the 7/7 suicide bombings in London.

Lawley: 'It was chillingly prescient.'

'*Uncanny*, I think is the word,' agreed her guest. 'Four suicide bombers, heading from the north, and the heroine was called Cameron!'

Lawley: 'And, even weirder, it's a comic novel! There's this chap called Roger Barlow, a sort of bumbling Tory MP who rides a bicycle ...'

Seeing where the conversation was heading, Johnson tried to cut her off: 'That's been *grossly* exaggerated.' But Lawley wasn't to be deterred.

'He's – you know what I'm going to say next, don't you? – excessively exercised as to whether the tabloids are going to find out he's having an extramarital affair.'

'I think you've read the novel with *quite* the attention it deserves, Sue!'

Lawley: 'It just strikes me, thinking about you, when your *own* extramarital affair became public ... it's like playing with fire. Why would you do that?'

'Ah,' hedged Johnson. 'I think I'm going to take the Fifth Amendment here. This doesn't come under the category of "just talking about Brahms's *Variations on a Theme by Haydn*."'

'No,' said Lawley. 'It comes under "talking to an MP ..."'

'I'm on a Haydn to nothing here!' muttered Johnson.

Lawley continued: ' ...who got sacked from the frontbench because he fibbed to his leader about whether he was or wasn't having an extramarital affair!'

'Yeah,' dead-batted Johnson. 'All I want to say is, it was very kind of you to read my book. And I notice that you enjoyed it very much!'

Lawley: 'Just do me a little bit of analysis. I mean, you like to play with fire ...'

'Sue!' interrupted Johnson. 'You're a *brilliant* interviewer but, in the immortal words of Sue Lawley, "More music, please ..."'

Lawley, eventually, took pity on her guest in the form of Van Morrison's

'Brown Eyed Girl'. As it faded out, she reflected that Johnson's default mode of dealing with 'accusations of misdemeanours' appeared to be to charm his interrogators. 'Is charm your strongest weapon?'

'It's very, very sweet of you to say this, Sue,' charmed Johnson. 'But what *are* these misdemeanours you keep talking about?'

Lawley: 'You don't want to go back over them, Boris! I mean, I've left quite a few out!'

This elicited a laugh from Johnson: 'For the benefit of your listeners, there are far fewer misdemeanours than there are demeanours! Or whatever they're called!'

Sticking to her theme, Lawley wanted to know if this surface charm was all a bit of a ruse to help her guest get by. The answer gave, possibly, a surprising, illuminating insight into Johnson's capricious, quixotic nature.

'I was very deaf as a child,' he recalled. 'I had terrible glue ear. I could hardly hear anything anyone was saying. I think I must have developed then a certain sort of evasiveness. Often, I couldn't follow what was going on at all. And if you can sort of guess what's going on, but you're not *sure*, it's as well to be a little vague.'

Lawley: 'But you are, at the same time, a comic institution on *Have I Got News for You?* or wherever you crop up. You're highly entertaining. What I'm asking is a question you can't answer: whether you do that in a calculated way, or whether *that's just Boris*?'

'I think the profound truth of the matter is that it would be very, very hard to do it any other way. If I made a huge effort always to have a snappy, inspiring soundbite on my lips, the sheer mental strain would be such that I would explode.

'It's much easier, therefore, for me to try and play what shots I have as freely as I can. Does that make sense?'

'Yes, it does,' said Lawley. 'But, of course, what happens is, maybe, the clever and thoughtful Boris gets lost and people forget he's there. That's the danger, isn't it?'

'Yeah, well, we need to go and find him!' laughed Boris Johnson. 'We need to chivvy him out, wherever he is lurking ...'

• • •

Post-*Desert Island Discs*, Boris Johnson's desire to 'go on; get on; *have a go*' did not diminish. In 2008, he became mayor of London, being re-elected in 2012. He declined to stand for a third term, instead returning to Parliament as MP for Uxbridge and South Ruislip and becoming a driving force behind the Vote Leave Brexit campaign. Appointed foreign secretary by Theresa May in 2016, he resigned two years later over Brexit. When May stepped down in May 2019, he replaced her as Conservative leader and prime minister. Calling a snap general election at the end of the year, he won an eighty-seat landslide majority and oversaw Britain's withdrawal from the EU in January 2020. His handling of the COVID-19 pandemic won, it's fair to say, mixed reviews: he was to contract the virus himself, spending four days in intensive care in April 2020. In July 2022, after cabinet resignations and a revolt within the parliamentary party, Boris Johnson was forced to resign as Conservative Party leader and prime minister, and clamber down from atop the *cursus honorum*. Where he goes next is anyone's guess ...

DISCS CHOSEN

'Here Comes the Sun'
The Beatles
'It's just a fantastically optimistic, happy song'

'Soul Limbo' (theme music to *Test Match Special*)
Booker T and the MGs
'It brings very fond memories of playing cricket in the yard with my brothers. All of whom are better than me at cricket'

'Ich will hier bei dir stehen' from Bach's *St Matthew Passion*
Radio Choir Leipzig with the Dresden State Orchestra

'Start Me Up'
Rolling Stones

❤ **Finale to Brahms's *Variations on a Theme by Haydn***
Berlin Philharmonic Orchestra

'Brown Eyed Girl'
Van Morrison
'You can't have too much of Van Morrison. You can overdose on him'

'Pressure Drop'
The Clash
'Joe Strummer was an avid Telegraph *reader and sent me a letter saying how much he admired a column I'd written about hunting'*

Beethoven's Symphony No. 5 in C Minor
New York Philharmonic Orchestra
'E.M. Forster described this as like elephants walking on the roof of the world'

BOOK
Homer
'I could devote my mind to translating it into English'

LUXURY ITEM
A super-sized pot of French mustard
'Any meat is more or less bearable with mustard'

KIRSTY YOUNG YEARS
2006–18

After presenting close on 800 editions during her eighteen years on the show, Sue Lawley quit *Desert Island Discs* in early 2006. 'It is one of the best jobs in broadcasting,' she acknowledged as she left. 'But I feel the time has come to concentrate on other areas.'

As is the case every time this hugely desirable post becomes available, wild media speculation broke out as to her likely successor. In his 2012 book *Desert Island Discs: 70 Years of Castaways*, author Sean Magee noted that William Hill even opened a book on the subject.

The bookmaker viewed David Dimbleby as the strong favourite, closely followed by Andrew Marr, Sue MacGregor and, surprisingly, a return to the island for Michael Parkinson. One can only fantasise just how much *Desert Island Discs* would have changed had the BBC handed it to Hill's 33/1 outsider: Alan Partridge.

The bookies don't *always* get it right and, in this instance, the mantle passed to a broadcaster they had viewed as a relative long shot. At the end of June 2006, Radio 4 Controller Mark Damazer announced that the new presenter of *Desert Island Discs* was to be Kirsty Young.

Having started out as a continuity announcer on BBC Radio Scotland, then a presenter on TV news programme *Scotland Today*, Young had hosted an STV chat show, *Kirsty*, in 1994. She had then moved south to become an award-winning host of the newly launched *Channel 5 News*.

Young was on maternity leave after the birth of her second child when Damazer broke the big news. Lauding her 'fabulous broadcasting voice', he astutely pinpointed exactly why he felt his new appointment would be the perfect *Desert Island Discs* host.

'She's intellectually curious about people and empathetic with them,' he explained. 'She understands when to press the button and when to release it – when to ask the question, and when *not* to ask it.'

Young arrived with a huge respect for the show, admitting, 'I've loved *Desert Island Discs* as long as I've listened to the radio. There isn't a show on the radio that I'd rather present. I'm completely thrilled to be doing it.'

She also brought a distinct philosophy as an interviewer, which she was to articulate brilliantly a few years into her tenure.

'What's the aim?' she asked. 'For me, it's to strike up an intimacy with the guest that allows them to trust me and, in turn, properly reveal themselves. I want the listener to come as close as they can to meeting them without actually meeting them.

'The best piece of professional advice I was ever given – aged twenty-two, and working at BBC Radio Scotland – was: "*Listen.*" Listen to what people say. It's always good to be prepared but, above all else, be prepared to listen to the answers and take it from there.'

This receptiveness, and the qualities that Damazer had identified in her – intellectual curiosity and empathy – were to make Kirsty Young a fantastic *Desert Island Discs* host. Feeling safe in her hands, castaways happily opened up to her gentle but forensic questioning.

Her first guest, on 1 October 2006, was illustrator Quentin Blake. Two weeks on, veteran war reporter Robert Fisk – who interviewed Osama bin Laden three times – admitted that he had been *driven* to live his life in the world's conflict zones but he had never *enjoyed* it.

The gifted screenwriter Paul Abbott, who conceptualised Channel 4's award-winning drama series *Shameless* around his own dysfunctional upbringing, broke down in tears in the studio but was then transfixed by the caring proficiency with which Young coaxed his story from him.

'I relished the questions,' he says now, reflecting on his desert island adventure. 'They were so clever because they were deep, but phrased very simply. I was sitting there, listening to Kirsty, thinking, *Wow! I wish I could write like that!*'

Holocaust survivor Ben Helfgott told Young that he had never hated the Germans, despite spending three years in a concentration camp as the Nazis slaughtered his family. Unbelievably, he had then moved to Britain and lifted weights for his new homeland at the 1956 Olympics.

The instinctive Young was as at home hearing such tales of unspeakable horror and triumph as she was talking to Ricky Gervais about his wasted years before he hit big with *The Office*. And her 2007 interview with the spirited, thoughtful but troubled George Michael was deeply moving.

Johnny Vegas worried aloud whether he would be able to control the drinking that had been both his blessing and his curse. In 2012, Doreen Lawrence told Kirsty how her whole life since 1993 had been dedicated to trying to come to terms with the murder of her son, Stephen: 'He deserved a life, which was taken from him.'

Martina Navratilova was an ebullient castaway as she reminisced about escaping communist Czechoslovakia, finding political asylum in the US, ruling the tennis world and coming out as gay. By stark contrast, Dawn French spoke movingly in 2012 of her father's suicide.

Young presided over a caring and inclusive island. Steve McQueen talked of surviving a sink school to live a life dedicated to truth and art. In a particularly heart-rending episode, poet Lemn Sissay described how his whole life had been a search for his self, identity ... and name.

In December 2016, Davina McCall spilled out her heart about a troubled childhood, overcoming drug addiction, and being betrayed throughout her life by her beloved but wayward mother. She marvels now at the skills of her desert-island interlocutor.

Young's 'questions will *wind* you,' she reflects. 'It's like being punched in the solar plexus! And it's not because it's too intimate, or personal, or tabloid-y a question, but because it's a question you have hidden in your mind as so dark and deep that you don't want to look at it.'

Global superstars Tom Hanks and Bruce Springsteen both proved very willing to hold their pasts up to the light. The man that rock fans call 'The Boss' talked of the depression that has always plagued him as 'part of my life ... once in a while, Churchill's black dog jumps up and bites you in the ass.'

In January 2017, for *Desert Island Discs*' seventy-fifth anniversary, Manchester United and England football superstar David Beckham rocked up on Young's island for a special extended programme. The extra length was needed for the sheer number of highlights it contained.

Beckham reflected freely on his football obsession as a kid, his travails with Sir Alex Ferguson, posing in his pants – and his somewhat eccentric choice of a purple suit for his marriage to his wife, Victoria, in 1999. 'I looked like the guys out of *Dumb and Dumber!*' he ruefully admitted. 'I even had a top hat in purple as well. Unbelievable! What was I thinking?'

Desert Island Discs had never sounded in better form in August 2018, when Kirsty Young said she was stepping down from the show temporarily to receive treatment for a form of fibromyalgia, a medical condition characterised by widespread pain and fatigue. A fellow BBC broadcaster, Lauren Laverne, would fill in for her on the island.

Nobody remotely imagined that this temporary arrangement was to become permanent.

38

ROBERT FISK

JOURNALIST, WAR REPORTER
15 October 2006

Robert Fisk was the best-known British war correspondent of his generation. Based in Beirut since 1976, he extensively covered both Gulf Wars plus conflicts in Afghanistan, Palestine, Kuwait, Kosovo and Syria. His default mode was living on the frontline.

Fisk's profile was highest during his thirty years as the *Independent*'s Middle East correspondent. His status as the sole western journalist trusted by Osama bin Laden famously led to him interviewing the al-Qaeda leader three times during the nineties.

These encounters were fascinating, but his encounter with Kirsty Young in 2006 showed that there was far more to Robert Fisk, a deeply driven and humane man who freely confessed to never once enjoying a life of war reporting despite feeling it to be his calling and his moral duty.

• • •

This ambivalence towards his role was evident in Fisk's reply to Young's opening remark that, from the outside, he appeared to have lived the life of an action hero.

'No!' he said, firmly. 'I was thinking, the other day, about whether I've actually enjoyed the life I've had, and I think I haven't. I've been *passionate* towards it, but I don't think I've enjoyed it.

'I was sitting on the boulevards in Paris, watching families walking down the street in sunlight. I went back to Beirut, sat on my balcony over the Mediterranean, and thought, *Did I really want these last thirty years of war? Couldn't I have lived a happier, safer, more secure life?*

'If you saw what I saw – which, of course, you don't, because television cuts out the bloodier scenes: "Oh, we must not see the pornography of death!" Well, we *should*, we *should*, because if you saw dogs tearing corpses to pieces, women and children bombed in the desert, you would never support a war again. *Never. Ever.*'

Young touched briefly on Fisk meeting Bin Laden, whom he described to her as 'a rather vain man ... frightened of me, because I was the first foreign journalist he'd ever met.' She asked if he'd liked him.

'I've got so used to meeting these rogues and murderers in the Middle East that I don't have much personal feeling. [*One time*] I said to him, "Here we go again! Another secret meeting with Bin Laden on another bloody mountain top!"'

Promising to return to this topic, Young turned to Fisk's childhood. His father had fought at the Somme in the First World War, and took his ten-year-old son to that battlefield for his first foreign holiday in 1956. The pair had a difficult relationship.

Fisk admired his father for having once refused a direct military order to shoot dead a soldier who had killed a policeman. Yet at home, his dad had been a dominating, dictatorial figure.

'He sent me off to prep school when I was nine years old. I came back after three weeks, weeping not to go back, and my mother pleading in tears. [*He said*:] "He will go back to learn to be a man! *You must grow up!*" And I started to despise that.'

Fisk described, at seventeen, having a Saturday job on the *Sunday Express*, then a spell on the *Newcastle Evening Chronicle* before studying at Lancaster University. On leaving, he joined *The Times*, who sent him to cover the Troubles in Belfast.

Young: 'That was your first taste of conflict. Did it smack you in the chops?'

'Two things did. Belfast was the dirtiest, filthiest, poorest city I'd ever seen. And the British Army was extremely brutal. So was the IRA but, I mean, I'm talking about the *authorities*. I couldn't believe what I was seeing.

'I was seeing dead bodies for the first time. The first time I saw a man shot was a British soldier on the back of a pig: a big, armoured vehicle. I saw him topple out, somersaulting over the back, and [*heard*] the noise of his rifle as it hit the road: a tremendous *crack*. I thought, *My God, this is real! This is not a movie, Robert! Watch out!*'

Fisk described being sent by *The Times* to Beirut in 1976 as their Middle East correspondent. Shortly after arrival, he escaped a kidnap attempt by a gang of armed militias. Young then turned to Afghanistan and his encounters with the CIA's most wanted terrorist leader.

'The first time that you met Osama bin Laden [*in 1993*] was relatively straightforward,' she noted. 'Subsequent meetings were slightly more complex?'

'The second meeting [*in 1996*] ... well, he always asked to see *me* after that. I never asked to see him. I always made a delay to show him that I was not going to be summoned by Bin Laden.

'I got a phone call from Switzerland, saying, "The man you met in Sudan would like to see you again." I knew it was Bin Laden. So, I arrived in Afghanistan, checked into the Spinghar Hotel in Jalalabad, and I waited and waited, day after day. And nobody came.

'Suddenly, one evening I was lying on the bed in the heat, and I heard

[*Fisk knocked the desk*] on the window. I thought, *This is it!* And there was a truck outside with armed men and rocket-propelled grenades.

'We set off, driving for twenty-four hours across the wastelands of Afghanistan. I remember we passed these villages that the Russians had bombed. They were ghost villages, and there were naked children crawling through them.

'Eventually, we crossed a stream at night, and on the other side was a field with trees and lots of military camp beds with armed men lying on them: al-Qaeda. We walked through and sat outside a little hut. And suddenly, in the doorway, was Bin Laden, standing there in his robes.

'The third time was at the top of a mountain in a training camp. The first time, he wanted to talk about the Russian war. The second, he condemned the Saudi royal family for corruption. This time, he was locked on to the West. It was very, very cold. I slept in the tent.'

Young: 'What was the date of that meeting?'

'Nineteen ninety-seven. The last words he said to me was sitting outside a tent on a rock. He said, "Mr Robert, from the mountain upon which you are sitting, we destroyed the Soviet army and the Soviet Union." And he said, "I pray to God that he permits us to turn America into a shadow of itself."

'I was actually crossing the Atlantic on 9/11. The plane turned around, of course, when America closed its airspace. I got back and sat in my hotel room and watched the Twin Towers coming down, again and again: that biblical epic of smoke and fire. And I remember thinking, *My God! New York is now a shadow of itself.*'

Fisk explained that Bin Laden had wanted to see him again after 9/11, but he had been unable to reach him in Afghanistan because of an air raid. Young asked him if it was true that, at one meeting, the al-Qaeda leader had attempted to recruit him.

'Yes,' Fisk said. 'The third time I saw him, he said, "Mr Robert, one of our brothers had a dream." I thought, *My God, I don't like this.* And he said, "They saw you on a horse, coming as a Muslim Imam."

'I thought, *He's reaching out to me! Watch out, Fisk! How do I get out of THIS?* Armed al-Qaeda men were on the ground around us, listening to this man like he was a messiah. And I thought, *I can't offend him, but I've got to get out of this!*

'I said, "No, Sheikh Osama. I am not a Muslim. I am a journalist, and my job is to tell the truth." And he said, "Oh, this is the same as being a good Muslim." Phew! I got out of it, thank God! He got the message that I didn't want to be recruited, and I didn't offend him.'

Young: 'That was how valuable you were to Osama bin Laden. He was inviting you in because ...'

'No, he wanted to make sure I could come back later!' interrupted Fisk, laughing. 'Don't get romantic about Bin Laden. I wasn't valuable to him, nor him to me. He was just another person to interview.'

'Oh, come on!' said the host, incredulously.

'No, he'll live with me for the rest of my life because I interviewed him so many times. He's not actually of great interest to me at the moment. I'll tell you why: because he's totally irrelevant.

'After the atom bomb had been invented you could go around arresting all of the nuclear scientists and it wouldn't make the slightest bit of difference. The bomb was made. Al-Qaeda has now been created. He's created the monster. It doesn't matter if he lives or dies.'

As a fascinating interlocution neared its close, Kirsty Young returned to her first question. 'At sixty, are you wondering if it's all been worth it?'

'I think back to when I was offered the job,' replied Robert Fisk. 'And I remember thinking, *Wow! The possibility of being in the Middle East and covering history!* And I know that I would take the same decision again if I was twenty-nine once more.

'I'm not happy. I don't enjoy my work at all. But I'm passionate about it, and I wouldn't want to live any other way ...'

• • •

Did Robert Fisk get any happier? Arguably not. He stayed in the Middle East, covering further conflicts such as the war in Iraq, the Arab Spring and the Syrian Civil War, writing both dispatches and books about the politics of the region. Increasingly, he became known for his columns, railing long and fervently against the interventions in the Arab world of the US, the West and Israel. After a suspected stroke, he died in hospital in Dublin in October 2020, at the age of seventy-four.

DISCS CHOSEN
'Dies irae' from Britten's *War Requiem*
The Bach Choir with the London Symphony Orchestra and Choir
'This section is meant to sound like the guns of the Western Front'

❤ **Barber's** *Adagio for Strings*
City of London Sinfonia
'A piece of music of utter conviction'

'This was their finest hour ...' (speech, 18 June 1940)
Winston Churchill
'When you listen to this, you think, God, the Bushes and the Blairs are midgets. Here is a real leader'

'Mellow Yellow'
Donovan
'Absolutely synonymous to me of university'

Pachelbel's Canon in D Major
Academy of St Martin in the Fields Orchestra

'The Lord is my Shepherd'
Huddersfield Choral Society
'Every Sunday morning, my father would hum this. And I'd think, Oh God, church again!*'*

'Beirut Hal Zarafat'
Fairuz
'The only great singer for most Lebanese'

'Hatikvah' (the national anthem of Israel)
Slovak Radio Symphony Orchestra
'If only the Israeli government could behave with the dignity and integrity of this piece of music'

BOOK
Le Morte d'Arthur – Thomas Mallory
'The only book that's ever made me cry'

LUXURY ITEM
A violin
'I'd like to see if I can learn to play it again'

39

PAUL ABBOTT

SCREENWRITER, PRODUCER
11 February 2007

Budding writers are often advised to 'write what they know'. If they have endured exceptionally difficult personal circumstances, and are able to capture that harsh, debilitating experience with flair and clarity, the resulting drama or literature can be genuinely staggering.

Introduced by Kirsty Young in February 2007 as 'the defining TV dramatist of his generation', Paul Abbott survived – just – a ferociously dysfunctional childhood. One of eight children in a working-class family in Burnley, he was just nine when his mother walked out on them, followed two years later by his father.

Abbott's eldest sister, who was just fifteen and pregnant when the mum left, then took over looking after the family and somehow raised her siblings despite a domestic environment of poverty, anarchy and trauma. This situation became the template for his ground-breaking, award-winning millennial Channel 4 drama series, *Shameless*.

Paul Abbott had also been the youngest-ever script editor on *Coronation Street* and created acclaimed TV dramas *Clocking Off* and *State of Play*. Unsurprisingly, though, it was his harrowing personal backstory and its adaptation, in part, into *Shameless* that transfixed Young and her *Desert Island Discs* listeners.

• • •

The host opened by asking Abbott how closely *Shameless* had been based on his own early family life.

'Architecturally, it was quite close,' he replied. 'The two parents left and my fifteen-year-old sister – well, she was approaching sixteen, and nine months pregnant – took over the family and became the matriarch.'

Abbott had been nine when his mum left, noted Young. 'Did it happen out of the blue?'

'It happened overnight. It was just ... my dad was bone idle. I only realised later that she had been doing three jobs and doing everything in the house. And she disappeared overnight.

'She just wasn't there in the morning and it was a devastating thing. I thought, at first, she must have died, because a note was left. [*It said*] she was going to come back on a certain day and take the three youngest with her. But she never did. She never came back.

'So, I thought, *Ah, that note was a lie!* And I can't *imagine* what I looked like. But I remember having nightmares every single night about what might have happened to her.'

Prompted by Young, Abbott recalled finding the address at which his mother was now living shortly afterwards. Yet his knock on the door revealed further trauma.

'She answered it, and I remember being really angry at exactly the same time that I was totally relieved that she wasn't dead. She was living with a bloke with a son exactly my age: we were a day apart on birthdays. So, I was swapped. You know, to a nine-year-old, *you've been swapped.*

'I was really shocked recently when my son asked me, "Did you love her?" I mean, oh my God, of course I did. She was the absolute centre of our universe.'

After a music break, Young noted that despite their multiple challenges, the underclass family in *Shameless* – which Abbott stressed was inspired by, but not literally based on, his own – had a real warmth about them. This extended even to the paterfamilias: the amoral, workshy, feckless Frank.

'Absolutely!' her guest agreed. 'Frank is a drug-addicted dipsomaniac who hits his children, takes their [*benefits*] money and spends it on drugs, and everybody likes him! When he's unconscious on the floor, urine-stained trousers, drunk on their money, Debbie [*his daughter*] kisses him on the forehead.'

Young wondered how much Abbott's own father might have objected to being widely considered the template for this character.

'I've gone to great lengths in interviews to say that Frank wasn't based on him, but my dad was *livid* about *Shameless*. [*He said:*] "What if people think it's *me*? What if people think *I* did that kind of thing?" And he didn't. My dad wasn't a big drinker. He certainly never engaged with drugs. In fact, he never moved!

'But his biggest complaint was: "When did *I* ever have long hair?!" To this day, I think he most resents what Frank looks like, not what Frank is!'

In contrast to his mother leaving, Abbott told Young he felt no trauma at all when his dad quit the family home, two years later.

'I was eleven, and there was no real distress when Dad left with his girlfriend. It was a bit of a sigh of relief that there was more room in the house. You got a chair to watch a television, or read a book, or whatever.'

He paused, then laughed.

'I just made that up! We didn't have a television. We didn't read books. And we couldn't claim benefits because she [*his sister*] shouldn't have been looking after us. She was still under eighteen.'

Young: 'If she had tried to get assistance from social services, you would have been broken up? Put into foster homes and council homes?'

'Yeah, exactly that. We were like rats. We had to be invisible to the authorities. We all did small jobs and chipped into a pot. I had three jobs: I worked in a barber's, did a newspaper round and worked in the corner shop.'

'At what age?'

'Thirteen. Fourteen. It was just how it was.'

Abbott described attending school regularly until the age of thirteen, when a vicious sexual assault sent him into a downward spiral.

'The year Dad left, I got quite brutally raped. I didn't tell my sister what had happened because she would have created a fuss and then the police would have been called in and our whole thing would have fallen apart. I started peeling away from school. I couldn't deal with people.'

Asked by Young how he had begun to fall apart, Abbott described playing truant to spend whole days alone to get away from his home that was 'sixteen hours a day, absolutely screaming with noise.

'There was one point that I actually wrote to social services and asked to be taken into care,' he recalled. 'It wasn't that I didn't want to be in the family. I just knew that life was damaging me. I think that was the first point that I realised that I wasn't very well.'

Young: 'What did social services do?'

'They acknowledged the letter and took me to see a doctor to see if I could get a tonic. I got some vitamin C, or whatever, and they dumped me back in the house. In the next two years, I just progressed into foul, foul depression.'

A rare positive note in Abbott's life was struck by a school English teacher who recognised his talent as a writer and, without telling him, entered one of his homework stories in a competition in *Titbits* magazine. It won: 'He gave me a £10 cheque that was in my name, and it was brilliant!'

Young: 'A cheque with your name on. What did you do with that?'

'We cashed it through a bloke named Chequebook Fred. He was the only person we knew with a bank account ...'

Yet this minor encouragement was not remotely enough to alleviate the overall suffering of Paul Abbott's teenage life. At fifteen, he told Young, he attempted suicide.

'I jumped off a car-park roof. I landed three floors down and cracked my leg, and nobody ever knew. And so, for the next year, I was absolutely blind with rage and fury and fear, and I was trying to hold on to all that stuff. And I attempted suicide again, with knives and barbiturates.

'Then I got sectioned: taken into the bin, in the lock-up. It was called Ward Nine, in Burnley, and it was the most shocking thing that had ever happened to me. But on day two, I remember sitting there, thinking, *Oh my God, I'm in the right place. I know I'm in the right place, and I'll get fixed.*'

Young: 'You weren't in a child ward. You were in an adult psychiatric ward?'

'It was like the *Shameless* pub! It was a lock-up and twenty-eight-day sections, so you're in prison. The real criminal thing was standing back and looking at my family from the outside. Looking at me, and them, and us. I knew I had to be independent.'

Abbott described, on discharge, going to life with 'working-class foster parents who were loaded'. Young asked him to define the term 'loaded'.

'Well, they had a car! They had a television! The television stayed where it was put! It was like Penelope Keith, for me. They rescued me in a really casual way. I knew that I couldn't go back and I stayed there until I was eighteen.'

'Were you writing there?'

'Yeah. But I started writing behind my back. I didn't want to look like somebody who was going to be a writer. But it was creeping up on me. It just happened.'

Young recapped how Abbott's nascent writing career had immediately gone into fast-forward. A play for a *Radio Times* drama contest gained the endorsement of Alan Bennett after Abbott wrote to the playwright out of the blue. This led to two further Radio 4 plays and then, at twenty-three, a job as a script editor on *Coronation Street*.

Around this time, Paul Abbott was diagnosed as bipolar. 'Does this, in a way, almost *allow* you to write?' wondered Young.

'I think it *forced* me to write. That was the emotional immunity system kicking in. The extremity of my mood swings became really rapidly productive and became plays, films and things like that ...'

Turning to her guest's personal life, Young noted that he had two 'fairly short' marriages before settling down very happily with his third wife, Saskia, with whom he had two children. Initially, Abbott confessed, he was hugely wary of fatherhood.

'When I first had kids, I was terrified that I would be expected to know what to be as a father, because my dad taught me nothing good to use. I was terrified of what kind of job I'd make of being a dad. But when they reached about seven and five, I realised, I'm not bad.'

Young: 'How did you begin to have confidence as a father?'

'I think it was when I knew that I unconditionally loved them. When that happens, and you get a child, you realise that you have no choice in this.'

'Being bipolar, suicide is a constant presence in your life. It's not that you actually *feel* suicidal but you can't stop thinking about it. It crosses your mind every day and I was plagued by it for a long time.

'The contradiction is when you're walking down the street with your children who are, say, five and three. You look up at a bridge and think, *Oh God, that's high enough. I could get on there!* It's just a thing you can't get rid of. When you're weak, that's when it gets you.

'Except, you know, the love for my family and children is so powerful and so much greater than anything that could make me damage them in that way. They are my immunity ...'

• • •

Paul Abbott, who defied *all* the odds to become the defining TV dramatist of his generation, split from his third wife, Saskia, not long after recording *Desert Island Discs*. He has since remarried and has another son. He continues to write and produce television dramas and films, most notably as executive producer on the movie adaptation of *State of Play*, and three series of the acclaimed Channel 4 police procedural *No Offence* (2015–18). His latest project was *Wolfe*, a 2021 crime-thriller series for Sky. There will be more.

DISCS CHOSEN
'Good Vibrations'
The Beach Boys
'My only memory of my whole family being together in one place'

'Ode to Billie Joe'
Bobby Gentry
'She's just so sultry and so careful'

'Sweet Soul Music'
Arthur Conley
'The big anthem of Wigan Casino when I went out and partied all night'

'Imagine'
John Lennon
'My anthem for realising there was no God'

'Children of the Revolution'
T. Rex
'Every time I hear it, it makes my heart sing'

❤ **'Town Called Malice'**
The Jam
'This taught me how to shout'

'Video Lullaby'
Kids 4077
'A track from my fourteen-year-old son Tom's band. It's two-and-a-half times better than me'

'The First Time Ever I Saw Your Face'
Roberta Flack

BOOK

The Complete Works of Arthur Miller
'*He teaches men how to write women, and women how to write men*'

LUXURY ITEM

Writing pad and pencils
'*This is going to sound really cheap …*'

'ISLE NEVER FORGET …'

'I'd been asked to do *Desert Island Discs* three times before I went on and I'd said no every time because I didn't think I was ready. Then Kirsty took over presenting the show, they asked again and I said yes, because she's great and because I felt I was ready.

'I thought I'd be OK but I got to my first record, the Beach Boys, and I just *cracked*. I said, "It's my only memory of my family being together in one place …" and I properly broke down. Kirsty said, "We don't have to continue with this."

'I said, "I *do* want to continue, but if I sense that you're softening the questions because of what just happened, I'll walk out!" Then I went for a Starbucks to compose myself. I wasn't sure I wanted to go back, but I did, and Kirsty went for my throat, ha ha!

'I really enjoyed the second half of the interview. I sound tense but I relished the questions. They were so clever because they were deep but phrased very simply. I was sitting there, listening to Kirsty, thinking, *Wow! I wish I could write like that!*

'The only thing I regret is saying that I loved my wife because I didn't. We were quite fractious at the time. The words tripped off my tongue and they tasted like paraffin. We split not too long after.

'I don't regret talking about anything else. I wanted to be as honest as possible because otherwise there's no point doing *Desert Island Discs*. It's a piece of archive for my kids now. It was a once-in-a-lifetime chance to put my life on record!

'When it went out, I got a great reaction, I think because I *was* so honest. I've no idea if any of my siblings heard it: none of them have ever mentioned it to me. But I know Paul Weller heard that I chose the Jam because, as a result of the show, he asked me to write the foreword to his book …'

40
BEN HELFGOTT

HOLOCAUST SURVIVOR, OLYMPIC ATHLETE
1 April 2007

It's a widely accepted fact that while Hollywood superstars and A-list British celebrities are the big box-office draw for *Desert Island Discs'* listening figures, it's often the lesser-known castaways who have the most extraordinary stories and make for the most captivating shows.

There are few greater cases in point than Ben Helfgott. Kirsty Young's awed introduction stressed the enormity of his achievements: 'A concentration camp survivor whose journey has taken him from the horrors of Nazi-occupied Poland to the heights of Olympic glory.'

Helfgott had survived the Second World War despite being incarcerated in the infamous Buchenwald concentration camp as his mother, father, sister and twenty-seven other family members were murdered by the Nazis. Sent to Britain after the war, he went on to represent his adopted country at weight-lifting at two Olympic Games.

His simultaneously horrific, humbling and inspirational tale bordered on the miraculous. It also made for hugely emotional, moving listening.

• • •

Kirsty Young began by asking the seventy-seven-year-old Helfgott about his arrival in Britain, in 1945, as one of 732 young concentration camp survivors granted permission to live in the country. How did he feel?

'During the day, anybody who observed us would never have believed what we went through,' he began. 'When we went to sleep, different things happened, because most of us were still living with trauma.

'I was living with a terrible trauma because I kept thinking about my father. I was separated from him on 11 December 1944. And, just like I survived, I expected that he would have survived.

'But somebody told me that he was – together with my father – on a death march [*when Nazis marched prisoners to their execution*]. A few people decided to run away and my father was one of them. They were all caught and they were shot.

'I was living with this horror, you know, and it took me a long, long time to overcome it, because my father was my hero. He did such great things during the war. He defied the Germans at every stage.'

Despite this unbearable tragedy, noted Young, Helfgott had previously said he did not hate the Germans. How did he manage this?

'Well, I've never hated anybody. I just don't know what hate means. I'm easy to forgive. My father was a very liberal-minded person and I grew up in a home where there was no enmity around.'

Young took Helfgott back to what he said was a 'very happy' childhood in his Jewish family in the small Polish town of Piotrków. Yet by 1939, when he was nine, the storm clouds of barbarism were gathering.

'Yes. It was a terrible year because the papers were always full of what was going on in Germany. German Jews were being expelled and came back to Poland. I kept reading the papers and I understood, at that moment, that I am no longer a child.

'My town, Piotrków, was the first ghetto. As soon as the Germans came in at the end of September, there were announcements that all Jews had to move into the ghetto. There were twenty-eight thousand Jews, and my father, right from the beginning, began smuggling flour into the ghetto.'

Young: 'What would have happened to him if he had been found out?'

'He would have been shot.'

'Did your mother support him?'

'No. My mother used to beg him not to do it. He didn't come back for a day or two and we heard people were being shot. I saw how my mother suffered and I joined in with her and begged him to stop.

'My father laughed, and said, "I'd like to see how long you talk like this if you have to live on just potatoes and salt!" Even today, when I think about it, the pain is as great as ever. He was thirty-nine years old and he had so much to live for.'

Helfgott told Young that the Nazis killed the vast majority of Piotrków's Jews. He was one of a small number kept alive to work as slave labour in local factories.

'Deportations started on 13 February 1942,' he remembered. 'They took place over a period of one week, during which twenty-two thousand Jews from the ghetto were deported towards the gas chambers of the death camp. Two-and-a-half thousand were left.

'And then we lived for one year. I was working in the glass factory: my father and I and my little sister, Mala. I had two sisters. One was killed.'

Young: 'Can you tell me what happened to your mother and one of your sisters?'

'My mother and my sisters were in hiding. That meant that they were illegal, because only those who were working were legalised. Anybody else had no right to live.

'The Germans announced that everyone who had returned to the small ghetto should register and would be legalised to work and get rations. So, they did, and they were all rounded up, including my mother and my sister, Lusia, who was nine years old.

'They were all taken, about five hundred and twenty, five hundred and fifty people, most of them women and children, to a synagogue for two weeks. The Germans were deliberating what to do with them. My father managed to get a permit for my mother to be freed, but not for my sister.

'My father begged her to come out but my mother said, "You've got to look after the [*other*] children and I'll look after Lusia." Then a decision was made and, on 20 December 1942, they were taken out to the nearby wood on a Sunday morning and they were all shot.'

Young: 'Were you aware at the time?'

'Absolutely. Within minutes, we knew. I'll never forget when my father came in and I looked at his face. I didn't have to ask him anything. It was terrible. She lived for us. She was the most wonderful mother.' Helfgott, movingly, then chose Sophie Tucker's 'My Yiddishe Momme'.

He was, he explained, to work in the Piotrków factory until 1944, when he got transferred to the concentration camp at Buchenwald. 'We were sent there in order to work at a factory where they were producing an anti-tank weapon,' he told Young. 'But when they called out our names, my father and a few others were left behind. And I was the only boy who was not with his father.'

Young: 'That must have been a horrible shock for you?'

'We travelled for about a day and a half and, during the period, I never stopped crying. I just could not overcome the fact that I was separated from my father. We didn't know at all where we were going. But we came to a place that was Hell.'

Young: 'Describe it to me.'

'Well, when the people returned from work, we just couldn't believe what we saw. They looked like walking dead people. Their clothes were in tatters. Lice was falling off them and their hair was overgrown. They were completely emaciated.'

Asked by the host how he had found the strength of will to endure in Buchenwald, Helfgott recalled that they had had glimmers of light.

'We knew that, any day, we were going to be liberated, because the Germans brought the newspapers with them. We were not far away from Dresden when it was bombed, and we could see the sky in the distance: it was all red. This gave us a lot of hope.'

Young asked if Helfgott could remember the actual moment of liberation.

'I can remember it *vividly*. Early morning of 9 May. It must have been about six-thirty in the morning. I shared a bunk with another boy. He woke me up and said, "We are free!" Of course, I jumped up, I dressed, I ran out ... and that was something very, very special.'

After the Jewish folk song 'Hava Nagila', which Helfgott associated with the founding of Israel in 1948 ('a wonderful feeling!'), Young turned to her castaway's remarkable second life as a four-time British champion at weightlifting.

'It seems utterly impossible, Ben, that somebody who had endured such physical suffering and physical deterioration would manage to rebuild himself!' she marvelled. 'Did you feel it was a challenge, or did it come naturally?'

'It came natural *and* it was a challenge. When I was picked to compete in another country, the British Weightlifting Association was very poor and I had to pay for my fare. I was happy to do it. I was *honoured* that I was representing my adopted country.'

Ben Helfgott captained the British weightlifting team at the Melbourne Olympics on his twenty-seventh birthday in 1956, when he was unable to have any birthday cake lest it take him over his weight for his competition. 'But we had a party afterwards. It was a lovely, lovely day for me ...'

Since then, his life had achieved normality. Married for forty years, he had raised three sons and remained extremely close to his sister, Mala. He'd also been involved with Holocaust Memorial Day and played a key role in establishing a permanent Holocaust exhibition in Britain.

'You seem somehow propelled by the horror that you witnessed, and it seems vital to you that the world must not forget?' asked Young.

'That is absolutely right. I love people. I cherish my friendships. And I cherish love to humanity. That is why, over the years, I have been very closely connected with all the survivors who came to this country.'

'Do you understand the phenomenon of survivor's guilt?'

'Of course! One always feels that one survives because someone else close to him or her did *not* survive, and thinks, *Why me? Why you?* But the fact remains: that is how it is. Those who survived, by lucky chance, have a duty to go out into the world and talk about it.'

Ben Helfgott would, he told Young, always be haunted by his terrible past. Given that, she wondered if he would ever be able to find peace?

'Oh, I have *always* found peace in myself,' he mused. 'I have learned to live with that part of my life, right from the beginning. And the reason why I've been able to carry it out was because I never pushed it away. I live with it. I *want* to live with it. I am at peace.'

• • •

Alongside co-owning a clothes-making business, Ben Helfgott has spent his later life in Britain promoting Holocaust education and travelling the world talking about his wartime experiences. Knighted in 2018, he remains, at ninety-two, a testament to the spirit's capacity to survive even the very worst instances of Man's inhumanity to Man.

DISCS CHOSEN

Elgar's *Pomp and Circumstance* March No. 1 in D Major: 'Land of Hope and Glory'
London Symphony Orchestra
'This represents the glory and majesty of what Britain was'

'Isle of Capri'
Gracie Fields
'In 1939, I kept hearing this lovely, beautiful song'

Max Bruch's *Kol Nidrei*
Zemel Choir of London

'My Yiddishe Momme'
Sophie Tucker
'Every time I hear it, a shudder goes down my back ... I think of my mother often'

'Hava Nagila'
Les Karmon Israeli

Opening of the 1956 Olympic Games in Melbourne
BBC archive recording
'As I marched [at the ceremony], *I thought of my parents'*

❤ **'Nessun dorma' from Puccini's *Turandot***
The Three Tenors
'Serenity ... exemplifying what my family is all about'

Beethoven's Fifth Symphony
Vienna Philharmonic Orchestra
'A call for freedom and for the future'

BOOK
A History of Western Philosophy – Bertrand Russell

LUXURY ITEM
A weight-training bar with two discs

41
RICKY GERVAIS

COMEDIAN, ACTOR, WRITER
24 June 2007

Success and fame came late to Ricky Gervais. Born into a working-class family in Reading in 1961, he had a failed attempt at pop stardom and ten years working in entertainment-industry office jobs behind him before he hit big in 2001 with *The Office*.

Gervais co-wrote, directed and starred in *The Office* as David Brent, a needy, insecure, largely insufferable middle manager in a Slough paper company supposedly being filmed for a fly-on-the-wall TV documentary series that Brent fondly imagined would whisk him to stardom. Instead, it exposed him as a deluded braggart.

By the time Gervais washed up on Kirsty Young's desert island in 2007, *The Office* had been remade for the USA and, in Britain, he had written, directed and starred in acclaimed comedy series *Extras*, and seen his stand-up comedy tours sell out arenas. It appeared that once he had finally become successful, there was no stopping him.

• • •

Young began by describing David Brent as 'the perfect comedy anti-hero' and wondering whether Gervais felt any empathy for him.

'Quite a lot, really,' he replied. 'I think we've all got a little bit of David Brent in us. We all want to be loved, we're all worried about how we're perceived, and we've all got the blind spot. It's monstrous in David Brent but, by definition, we never know about our own blind spot.'

The host quickly turned to her guest's childhood. Gervais had grown up in Reading with three much older siblings, the youngest of whom was eleven years older than him. What had his childhood been like?

'It was very normal. I didn't know that we were poor until I went to university and people spoke like the Queen. I grew up on a working-class estate. My dad was a labourer, my mum was a housewife with part-time jobs. Typical hard-working, working-class family.'

Gervais recalled becoming an atheist at around the age of eight at the prompting of an older brother, Bob. Did his mother mind? asked Young. 'No, not really. I think it was more that Jesus and God were cheap babysitters! *If I'm not watching you, they are!*'

Young wondered where Gervais's sense of fun had originated. 'Was there a family sense of humour? Was it from your father?'

'No, my father was very dry. He said one thing a day. My next oldest brother, Bob, was the one that instigated most things. He just said funny things, and there was nowhere he wouldn't go.

'When my mum died, we were organising the funeral and the vicar said to my brother, "So, tell me about your mother. What was she like?" My brother said, "She was a keen racist." The vicar said, "Well, I can't say that." "Oh, OK, then. She liked gardening ..."

'At my dad's funeral, we were mucking about and laughing, and Bob had to go over to the vicar and say, "Sorry about that but, you know, he was eighty-three. If he'd have been fifty, there'd have been less laughter." And that sums it up. He'd had a good life.'

Young moved on to her guest's aborted pop-star career. Having begun playing guitar in his teens 'because of Cat Stevens', he then became a student at the University of London and formed a two-piece electronic group, Seona Dancing.

'Yeah. It was the New Romantic days – a lot of eyeliner and, *obviously*, I had to sound like David Bowie. I was twenty, and when it was all over, I was *still* twenty!'

'I've seen a video. You cut quite a bit of a dash, didn't you?'

'That's right! People show me pictures of me from then and I go, "Oh, no!" They think I'm embarrassed at the way I used to look. No, no, I'm embarrassed at how I look *now*! I'm jealous of how I used to look. I was six stone lighter! I had a jawline!'

Gervais described going home for Christmas from university and telling his family that not only had he formed a band, but that Seona Dancing had actually secured a deal with a major record label.

'My mum just said, "Rock star is another word for junkie!"' he recalled. 'I told her the advance, and she said, "Mick Jagger bought his mum a house in Wales ..."'

Young: 'So why did you leave behind your ideas of pop stardom and musicianship?'

'I didn't leave them behind! I failed miserably, and had to do something else!'

Gervais described moving into 'the periphery of entertainment' where he managed bands and booked college gigs. This lasted for eight years: 'The last two or three years I was there, we moved upstairs to an open-plan office, which *The Office* is based on.'

Young: 'Then you worked in a radio station, which was where you met Stephen Merchant?'

'Exactly. I was offered a job at the fledgling station XFM. I was allowed an assistant, and Steve's CV was at the top of the pile. He wanted to be a stand-up comedian, he was starting out in stand-up, and I suppose I thought, *Well, I'll show him I'm funny*.

'I had a character called Seedy Boss, and when Steve went to the BBC to do a trainee production course, he had one day with a film crew. He said, "Let's film that character!" and it turned out to be a little twenty-minute *Office*.'

Young: 'Did you know, when you saw it, you had a little bit of gold dust? Did *they* know?'

'I knew it was *different*. We were low-risk. It didn't cost much, and it [*the first series*] went out in July, at nine-thirty on a Monday [*on BBC Two*], so they probably thought, *What's the worst that can happen?*'

Initially only a moderate hit, *The Office* became a phenomenon over the following months via word of mouth. After a break to play Radiohead's 'Bones', Young observed that Gervais appeared to her, 'under it all', to be quite a romantic soul.

'Yeah. Well, we're just here for as long as we're here, and I think that's sad. It's probably because I'm an atheist: *This is all we've got, so you'd better enjoy it*.'

'And you'd better leave something behind that matters?'

'I *do* think like that. I'm conscious of the legacy. I want this work to be as good in twenty years as it is now, or whatever, and I do want to leave something behind, really.'

Young: 'Those are high ideals. You're determined that it's going to be art.'

'Yeah. I always worry about a fat little comedian from Reading even saying the word "art". That's how we're brought up in Britain, isn't it? Worried about being pretentious, or above our station? But I think there's nothing wrong with putting the art into comedy.'

After Gervais chose a song by David Bowie, Young commented that he had actually met his musical hero when he appeared in *Extras*. Bowie had even sung a song about him: 'Little Fat Man Who Sold His Soul'.

'Yeah! "See his pug-nosed face." What a sing-along lyric *that* is!'

Young contrasted Gervais working alongside Bowie, Robert De Niro and Kate Winslet in *Extras* with his years of office drudgery before he made *The Office*. 'Will it become difficult for you to cull your material from reality, because your reality becomes compromised by your fame?'

'Well, my English teacher said, "Write what you know." The first album is easy because it's all of your years' experience. The second album is just the last year, which probably wasn't a normal year. So, yes.'

Gervais moved on from this observation to riff on the differences that fame had made to his everyday life.

'I live in the centre of London, so nobody bats an eyelid. But [*when I won*] the first BAFTA was creepy. There was press ringing my doorbell and I thought, *How do they know where I live? Why do they care?* I didn't sign that deal with the devil!'

Moving on to Gervais's personal life as the interview neared its close, Young noted that he had lived for twenty-five years with his partner, successful film producer Jane Fallon, whom he had met at university. How had she handled Gervais's celebrity?

'Well, it just seems very natural to us because we know that nothing's changed except our bank balance, and when you step outside the door. We haven't changed our values or our outlook or our politics or our beliefs at all.'

Young: 'Your family life sounds a very happy and vibrant one, but you don't want children? That's not something you've chosen?'

'No, no, no!' laughed Ricky Gervais. 'That's a conscious decision. It's just those first sixteen years! I don't want to go through that. I worry about the cat getting out! If I had a baby, I'd watch it all night. I wouldn't be able to sleep.

'Also – they don't give you anything back! Babies? They're *scroungers*! They do *nothing* ...'

• • •

Having tasted success relatively late in life, Ricky Gervais has displayed a ferocious work ethic to hold on to it. Two years after his trip to the desert island, he co-wrote and co-directed his first Hollywood movie, *The Invention of Lying*, followed in 2010 by a very British comedy film, *Cemetery Junction*. Further UK television projects have included *Derek* (2012–14), a black-comedy series set in a care home, and three series of the acclaimed *After Life* (2019–22) about a man struggling, and failing, to come to terms with the death from breast cancer of his beloved wife. He has been the acid-tongued host at five Golden Globe Awards ceremonies, and his vastly successful stand-up comedy career continues to push hard at the boundaries of the forbidden and the taboo. It is safe to say that this 'fat little comedian from Reading' continues to put a lot of art into comedy.

DISCS CHOSEN
'If You See Her, Say Hello'
Bob Dylan

❤ 'Lilywhite'
Cat Stevens
'Off the first album I ever bought. It's just beautiful'

'Anarchy in the UK'
Sex Pistols
'I ran home from school and played it every night for about six months'

'After the Gold Rush'
Neil Young

'His voice is so fragile, like he's worried about what he's got to tell you, but he's going to tell you anyway'

'Bones'
Radiohead
'It does something to my soul and makes me well up'

'Letter to Hermione'
David Bowie
'My single biggest hero in music'

'Galveston'
Jimmy Webb

'Always on My Mind'
Willie Nelson
'This one, out of all the songs, nearly makes me cry'

BOOK
A tabletop book of works of art

LUXURY ITEM
A vat of Novocaine
'And that was Ricky Gervais, the atheist drug addict ...'

42

GEORGE MICHAEL

SINGER, SONGWRITER
30 September 2007

When George Michael washed up on Kirsty Young's desert island in September 2007, he had had spent the previous few years combining being one of the world's most successful and adored music stars with getting himself into a whole lot of bother.

The singer remained a sublime pop craftsman and an idol to millions. After a fifteen-year break from performing, the European leg of his recent *25 Live* comeback had been the year's highest-grossing tour and seen him be the first artist to play the newly renovated Wembley Stadium.

He had also been a tabloid-headline fixture over the last decade. His arrest for an encounter with an undercover police officer in a Beverly Hills public toilet in 1998 had effectively outed him as gay. In Britain, he'd recently been found guilty of driving under the influence of drugs, banned from driving for two years and made to do community service.

It had been quite the rollercoaster for the hugely talented but clearly conflicted and often troubled star, and Young found him not just willing but eager to talk about all facets of his extraordinary life.

• • •

Through all of his travails, Michael had clearly not lost his sense of humour, as was evident when Young began by asking him if he would welcome the solitude of a desert island.

'Right now, I *would*, actually!' he laughed. 'I've just done a year's touring, closely followed by some community service! So, I'm quite ready to be on my own for a while!'

The singer chose a song by Amy Winehouse, telling Young that, like her, he was sure about very little in his life except that he had the ability to create music that people wanted. She asked him to elucidate further.

'I've never said this before but, it's odd, I'm just ridiculously ready to say these things now,' he marvelled. 'I have a huge propensity for guilt, because I was a boy in a Greek family who could do what he liked from an early age.

'The culture is patriarchal and to indulge the boy. I have two wonderful sisters who never got their way as young Greek girls, and I grew up with this terrible feeling of guilt as a small child, knowing that I was always the one that was going to get the easy ride.

'I think I finally realised one of the reasons my life has been so extreme and so destructive is ... it sounds arrogant, but I never had any feeling that my talent was going to let me down. I had a feeling that I had a huge advantage over a lot of other people in the industry.

'In a strange way, I've spent the last fifteen or twenty years trying to derail my own career, and it never seems to suffer. *I* suffer like crazy, terrible things – bereavements, public humiliation, blah blah – but my career just seems to right itself, like a duck in a bath.'

Young switched the conversation to that indulged childhood. Michael talked warmly of his hard-working father, an 'absolutely archetypal 1950s immigrant from Cyprus' who had started out as a waiter and ended up running his own restaurant chain.

By contrast, he said, his half-Jewish mother had 'Victorian values' and 'absolutely no ambition for money'. 'So, being half my mother and half my father, genetically, was never going to be an easy ride!' he sighed.

Born Georgios Kyriacos Panayiotou, Michael confessed he had felt 'a very urgent need for a stage name' when he formed Wham! at seventeen with his best schoolfriend, Andrew Ridgeley. 'The name [*George Michael*] was a creation, but was the persona a creation?' wondered Young.

'Well, I *thought* it was. But at some point, I realised, everything you do is you, even if it's the lies you tell. Even if it's an act, it's part of the real me, isn't it? Because that's what I want people to think I am.'

Wham! got a record deal extremely quickly, when the newly renamed Michael had just turned eighteen. He could not have been more excited.

'Oh, my God, I had £500! I'd never been more flush! I'd been working in a cinema – I went into that office and gave up that job as though I'd just become a diamond dealer!'

Young described Michael's early years in Wham! as the duo had hits such as 'Wham Rap!', 'Club Tropicana' and 'Wake Me Up Before You Go-Go': 'What was life like, going from this boy who wanted fame to the boy who suddenly got it, and then some?'

'For a while, it was just absolutely magical. Playing out your fantasies with your best mate was just a dream. I was supremely confident that I was writing pop classics, to be honest with you.'

Young asked what 'fantasies' Michael was playing out: what his ideal of pop stardom had been. The singer had a very specific answer.

'The image that stuck in my head of what I wanted to be was ... when David Cassidy came to England for the first time, there was a shot of him heading a football on top of the LWT building. Then they panned over the side of the building, and there were just *thousands* of these girls – screaming, obviously, but they couldn't get to him.

'There was all this adulation but they couldn't get to him! Somehow, my desire for safety – because I was quite an insecure child – and my desire for fame were all kind of locked up in that moment.'

Young: 'The insecurity came from what? The way you looked?'

'Just from who I was. I had no physical confidence whatsoever and I looked up to Andrew because he oozed confidence out of every pore. Then, suddenly, we were massively successful, and I went from being Andrew's shadow as a sexually confident being to being the centre of attention.

'I lost all my confidence. I suppose also the realisation that bisexuality was no longer a reality for me. I suddenly felt like a fake and the whole thing turned me into someone who felt like the camera was my enemy.'

Michael described how, after he broke up Wham! and went solo in the late eighties, he remained discombobulated by fame.

'I was twenty-four and still quite afraid. Still not knowing, to be honest with you, how to spend money. I was terrified of my lifestyle, maybe, removing my ability to connect with what I did, and I freaked out. I said, "I don't want to make more videos. I don't want to tour. I have to step back."'

Young: 'To those of us buying your records at the time and watching your videos, it was a very, very heterosexual image.'

'Do you *think* so?' laughed Michael. 'You women, honestly!'

'When I watched the video to "I Want Your Sex", I thought *that* is a very heterosexual man.'

'Oh, I see. Well, it wasn't a *complete* lie. I hadn't stopped having sex with women. But I was already aware that in itself was a lie, because I'd made an emotional connection to a part of my sexuality, and that was clearly gay.'

Young: 'Were you out to some people and not to others?'

'Yes. I had been out to a lot of people since I was nineteen. I wish to God it had happened then; I must be honest. I don't think I would have had the same career, but I think I would have been a happier man.

'I came out to friends and one of my sisters and I said I was going to talk to my mum and dad. I was persuaded by friends, in no uncertain terms, that it really wasn't the best idea: "My God, your dad will hit the roof!"

'Then, very soon after that, everything changed. AIDS [*came along and*] was just not something I was prepared to bring into my parents' life.'

After a break for Pet Shop Boys' 'Being Boring', a song in part about lives lost to AIDS ('All those people I was kissing/Some are here, and some are missing'), Young turned the conversation to the first love of George Michael's life: Anselmo Feleppa, whom he had met in 1992.

'There have only been three times in my life that I've really fallen for anyone,' Michael said. 'And each time, on first sight, I had something that clicked in my head that told me I was going to know that person.

'It happened with Anselmo across a lobby. I didn't understand what was going on: *This is a man in a Brazilian hotel. I'm never going to see him again. Why did THAT happen?*

'This was the first love of my entire life. This was the first person I ever shared my life with. Unfortunately, within six months I knew that he was terminally ill, so it was a very *strange* first love.'

Feleppa died of an AIDS-related illness in 1993 and Michael wrote his next album, *Older* (1995), about him. 'To be perfectly honest, I think it's my best album,' he told Young. 'I think it will probably *always* be my best album and I never want to be that inspired again.'

Young: 'It's a bittersweet situation, isn't it? That your most creative period came out of such pain?'

'I think the album is a beautiful reminder of him. I'd never want to feel that depth of emotion again. I hope he's very proud of it, somewhere.'

The talk touched briefly on Michael's long-running lawsuit with his record label, Sony Music, before inevitably alighting on the fateful day in April 1998 when he came to grief in Will Rogers Memorial Park, Beverly Hills.

'You were in the park in LA,' Young summarised. 'And, in the toilet, you were busted by an undercover policeman because of sexual advances you made to him. You were forced to come out.'

'Well, what was I going to say – it was a one-off?' laughed her guest. 'I always knew it was going to happen sometime. I was going to get outed, one way or another. It took me a good year to admit to myself that it was subconsciously deliberate.'

Young: 'I've read you say it would not have happened if your mother had still been alive?'

'No, it would *never* have happened. I'm not saying the cruising wouldn't have happened, but I'd never have put myself in the stupid position of doing it in America, where I know the level of homophobia.

'I think for me to do that ... I was absolutely tempting fate. I think I was sick of the secret. Now there was no reason to be quiet: my mother was no longer in this world and I was proud of my sexuality.

'[*It was a*] strange way to go about telling the world! But the battle I'd had with the press was so much one of privacy. I felt loath to actually sit and say [*to them*] "I am gay" – the three words they had wanted for years. I think I had to fool myself that it had been dragged out of me.'

Young: 'Did you feel like a burden had been lifted?'

'Oh God, yes, because I'm not a liar! I'm too honest to dye my hair! This was a lie I'd been trying to tell people [*about*] in my own way for years and years, and something in me picked the most difficult way to do it.'

As an intense, confessional, riveting desert island heart-to-heart neared its close, Young mentioned her guest's recent drug-driving conviction and subsequent driving ban and community service. Her question was a simple one: 'Do you think you have a problem with drugs?'

'It depends what you call a problem, really,' hedged George Michael. 'I'm a happy man, I can afford my marijuana, so that's not a problem. I'm constantly trying to smoke less, really. I would like to take less, no question, so to *that* degree it's a problem.

'But – is it a problem in my life? Is it getting in the way in my life? I don't think so ...'

• • •

George Michael was to play only one more tour after his appearance on *Desert Island Discs* and released no further studio albums. His hopeful verdict on the effects of his drug use on his life proved wishful thinking. A year after this broadcast, he was once again arrested and cautioned for possession. In 2010, he was sentenced to eight weeks in jail for crashing his car while driving under the influence of drugs. He served four weeks in Highpoint Prison in Suffolk. On Christmas Day 2016, he died from a heart condition in bed at his home in Goring-on-Thames, Oxfordshire. He was just fifty-three years old.

DISCS CHOSEN
♥ 'Love Is a Losing Game'
Amy Winehouse
'The best female vocalist I've heard in my entire career'

'Do the Strand'
Roxy Music
'It's so original, so sexy and so insistent'

'Crazy'
Gnarls Barkley
'It stands head and shoulders above everything else'

'Smells Like Teen Spirit'
Nirvana
'It changed everything in America overnight'

'Being Boring'
Pet Shop Boys
'If you're gay and you've lost friends to AIDS, you want to hear them honoured'

'Paper Bag'
Goldfrapp
'I'm a real admirer of her voice'

'Gold Digger'
Kanye West
'It's completely brutal, completely sexist, but it's funny'

'Going to a Town'
Rufus Wainwright
'He's really laying into the Bush administration'

BOOK
A book of short stories by Doris Lessing

LUXURY ITEM
An Aston Martin DB9
'On a desert island, who's going to know I've not got a driving licence?'

43

DAME ELIZA MANNINGHAM-BULLER

RETIRED SPYMASTER
18 November 2007

The majority of *Desert Island Discs* castaways tend to be household names. A decent proportion are relatively unknown figures who have lived remarkable lives. It's a rarity indeed to have a guest who prefers, or is required, to *conceal* their identity from the public.

Dame Eliza Manningham-Buller falls into that elite category. When she appeared on Kirsty Young's island in 2007, she had recently retired after five years as the director-general of MI5, the United Kingdom's highly secretive domestic counter-intelligence and security service.

Her tenure had been a demanding one. Taking charge of the agency in the wake of 9/11, when terrorists were altering their methodology and posing a precipitously heightened threat to Britain, she was also in situ during the devastating suicide-bomb attacks on London of 7 July 2005.

In total, Manningham-Buller had worked for MI5 for more than thirty years, including on the Joint Intelligence Committee, which advised the Blair government prior to the 2003 invasion of Iraq. And this fascinating career, she was to tell Young, had been nothing at all like *Spooks*.

• • •

Kirsty Young opened by informing listeners that this was to be the first interview Dame Eliza Manningham-Buller had ever granted. She asked her guest: 'Does it feel strange to be sitting in front of a microphone?'

'No. I've sat in front of microphones, but the idea of it being broadcast to your listeners seems strange because I've only ever spoken to limited audiences. Invited, carefully selected audiences.'

Young: 'For more than three decades, you were very good at keeping schtum. Has it felt an odd way to live your life so privately?'

'Not really. I used to say I worked in personnel. That's a great turn-off: nobody ever asks you questions after that!'

Young pointed out that most people's ideas of the workings of security services are gleaned from watching TV dramas such as *Spooks*. 'We think, I suppose it must be a *bit* like that ...'

'Well, it's *not* like *Spooks*,' laughed the dame. 'In *Spooks*, everything is solved by half-a-dozen people who break endless laws to achieve their results, which they achieve in one episode. For us, it's a much longer, hard grind, and we have far too many things to do at the same time, not just one.'

'Do you watch programmes like that?'

'I don't. I did watch at the beginning, but when the female officer was dropped into a vat of boiling oil in the first series, I thought, *I can't bear any more of this.*'

After a break for Bach, Young turned to the terror attacks on London of July 2005, when four Islamist suicide bombers detonated explosions on tube trains and a bus that killed 52 people and injured more than 700. How had Manningham-Buller first heard about them?

'I was in my office, and at the beginning it was news from journalists. I can remember my heart sinking. We'd prepared for it, we'd exercised for it, so the main focus was to try and support the police in their investigation of these horrible crimes.

'We didn't know at the beginning that it was suicide bombers, so we weren't sure there wasn't a team of terrorists still out there to be found who might do a subsequent one [*attack*]. It wasn't until I got home, late, that the emotional impact of the day hit me.'

Young: 'Was it something you had expected to happen?'

'We didn't necessarily expect suicide bombing, but from a case early in '04 we'd become very concerned about third-generation British citizens who were intent on attacking us. And that remains, I believe, a very current concern as well.'

The host pointed out that two of the terrorists had been known to the security service. How had they been allowed to carry bombs on trains and buses? Manningham-Buller said that a parliamentary investigation was still ongoing, but outlined the scale of the challenges facing MI5.

'It's an unreasonable expectation of the security service that we're big enough, and have resources enough, to anticipate, a year before it happens, what anybody we happen to see in the margin of an investigation – when there's many, many people we're looking at – will do a year later.

'There are too many people with this sort of intention in the UK for us to be confident – as *no* service can be confident – of stopping one hundred per cent. We've stopped very, very many.'

Young: 'You've said as many as one thousand six hundred people?'

'Yes.'

Young turned to Manningham-Buller's family, where 'public service was a way of life'. Her grandfather had been Harold Macmillan's attorney-general and then lord chancellor. Her mother had played an intriguing role during the Second World War.

'Yes. She presented herself as an eccentric woman, breeding pigeons. In fact, what she was doing was training carrier pigeons to bring back intelligence from occupied France and Germany.

'Her pigeons would be dropped in wicker baskets with little parachutes, and they'd be picked up by somebody and sent home with a message around their ankle. One of them got the Dickin Medal: a medal you got for animals doing things bravely in war.'

Young took her guest back to joining MI5 in the mid-seventies, following a chance conversation at a drinks party after leaving Oxford University. 'You must have been one of very few women?'

'There were a lot of women but they were all in very junior roles. You were not allowed, for example, to go out and recruit agents or sources because the view was that no rational Arab – or anybody, really – would want to work for a woman. That changed, quite rightly.'

In the eighties, Young reminded Manningham-Buller, she had liaised in secret with Oleg Gordievsky, the deputy head of the KGB working out of the Soviet embassy in London. She was one of the very few people to know that he was a double agent.

'Yes. He's someone I admire very much, because he believed that the Soviet system was rotten and offered to work for the British, at great risk to his life, for a long time.'

'He said that it was your discretion that helped to save his life?'

'That's generous of him but it was actually the discretion of a number of people who were trusted to protect him.'

Young: 'His point was that one of your colleagues – Michael Bettaney – was passing information to the KGB. If you had mentioned within your office that you were in contact with Gordievsky, that would have been the end of him.'

'Yes. Gordievsky would have been tortured and killed. There are people today in terrorist groups in exactly the same position. It's intrinsic in the job that if there's an agent willing to work for us, then the ultimate important thing is to protect them.'

Young fast-forwarded to the current day. Just before the 2003 invasion of Iraq, Manningham-Buller had sat on the Joint Intelligence Committee that issued a report that any threat to the West from al-Qaeda would be 'heightened by military action against Iraq'. 'Why do you think that very direct warning was not given more consideration by politicians?'

'I don't know the degree of consideration it was given by politicians. But it was right that the committee made that assessment, and that it continues to give dispassionate advice.'

Young persisted, pointing out the irony of politicians fighting a 'war on terror' on behalf of the West seemingly ignoring the strategic advice being given to them by their own security forces.

'Well, I think the real issue was the suggestion, particularly in America, that Iraq had something to do with 9/11, which was completely false. And I think that confusion has been unhelpful in a number of ways.'

'Very diplomatic language,' noted Young. 'Were you feeling that diplomatic at the time?'

'I'm not comfortable talking about anything that might be interpreted as criticising government policy,' her guest stonewalled. 'The advice I gave was given in private.

'Whoever is the government of the day, and I've worked for more than one government, deserves that its public servants give it advice in private and will not subsequently write their memoirs, explaining what they felt, and what they thought, and what those debates were.'

'So, you won't be writing your memoirs?' asked Kirsty Young.

'Most certainly not!' laughed Dame Eliza Manningham-Buller. 'I think it would be not only wrong, but unproductive – and unsellable!'

• • •

Dame Eliza Manningham-Buller told Kirsty Young that she had gone through the 'adrenalin cold turkey' she had anticipated when she stepped down as the head of MI5 but had since 'moved on'. She has continued to do so. Made a baroness in 2008, she has since sat as a crossbench peer in the House of Lords, and had spells as chair of Imperial College London and first female chair of the Wellcome Trust. She has been the co-chair of independent policy institute Chatham House since 2015. During all of this, she has stayed true to her word and not written her memoirs.

DISCS CHOSEN

Sarabande from Bach's *English Suite* No. 2 in A Minor
Angela Hewitt
'A very reflective, peaceful bit of music'

Kyrie from Mozart's Requiem in D Minor
Les Arts Florissants

'I Just Don't Know What to Do with Myself'
The White Stripes
'My eldest stepdaughter tried to bring my husband and me into the twenty-first century by introducing us to the White Stripes'

'Street Fighting Man'
Rolling Stones
'I always thought they had a bit more edge and excitement than the Beatles'

❤ **Schubert's String Quintet in C major**
The Lindsay String Quartet and Douglas Cummings
'The most special bit of chamber music I know'

'Millennia'
Soweto String Quartet
'Wonderfully joyful and quite addictive'

'Do I Love You?'
Ella Fitzgerald
'I love her because she can do anything with her voice'

Beethoven's Symphony No. 7 in A Major
Berlin Philharmonic Orchestra
'I couldn't go to my desert island without some Beethoven'

BOOK
The Rattle Bag – poetry anthology compiled by Seamus Heaney and Ted Hughes

LUXURY ITEM
A large supply of pencils and pens
'Because an iPod would be cheating?'

'ISLE NEVER FORGET ...'
'One of my predecessors at MI5 was asked not to do *Desert Island Discs* after he had left the agency, and I certainly wouldn't have done it had they been unhappy about it. But I decided to do it because I thought it would be fun.

'My sole doubt, which I communicated to Kirsty in advance, was that I didn't want to talk about my family or where I live – for fairly obvious reasons. I wondered if that might be a problem, but she managed to skirt those topics very well.

'It was difficult to choose my music. I love opera but I forgot to select any, and I regret that. I was also apprehensive that choosing the White Stripes might look as if I was trying to be contemporary rather than genuine! But I do like them very much.

'The nicest thing, I think, was that Oleg Gordievsky actually heard the programme. He commented on it afterwards and thanked me for what I said about him. I was very pleased about that.

'I was wary before the show because I'd never done a radio broadcast interview before and *Desert Islands Discs* has such a huge audience. But I enjoyed it very much – and since then I've done the Reith Lectures, which were *far* more frightening!'

44
JOHNNY VEGAS

COMEDIAN, ACTOR, CERAMICIST
3 October 2010

It's logical that we assume that we know public figures through their words and their deeds. But what if that individual has outgrown the image, or the character, that they routinely project, and has come to dislike it – or even to fear it?

Michael Pennington emerged on the stand-up comedy circuit in the nineties, where he developed his Johnny Vegas persona as a bathetic, obese, self-pitying drunk. He then transferred this troubled, alcoholic, self-destructive alter ego to television in programmes such as the 2005 Channel 4 series *18 Stone of Idiot*.

It was a self-disparaging joke that could easily have gone very wrong, but by the time Vegas met Kirsty Young in 2010, he had consigned his heavy drinking to the past and shed a third of his bodyweight. He had survived his grisly creation ... but it had not been easy.

• • •

Young began by quoting Vegas saying he had changed his lifestyle in order to 'reach the ripe old age of forty' – a landmark he had just passed – and be a proper father to his young son. He had also once said he was at his best creatively when 'at odds with the world'. Was this still true?

'I think it was certainly right for Johnny as a character. But I'd run out of anger, and I think people can see when something is genuine and when something's manufactured.'

'How much weight have you lost?' the host asked.

'I'm not sure because I didn't weigh myself before I started. It would've been four stone, or five. I was just judging it by trouser size. M&S are slightly more generous with their sizes, so getting down to thirty-eight inches was a big whoop-and-holler moment from the changing room.'

Young commented that, from the outside, Vegas's stage character was so 'on-the-edge' that you wondered: 'Is it for real? Is this guy absolutely losing the plot here, or is it a beautifully confected, honed stage act?'

'I think what started off as something well-constructed, with absolute parameters, [*got to*] a danger point of other things in my life seeping in where the lines were blurred for the wrong reasons.'

Young: 'Your life started to imitate your art?'

'Yeah. I found popularity through self-destruction. Suddenly, the more you damage yourself, the more people are drawn to you. And that can be quite addictive.'

'You're trapped by your own creation, and that creation is very destructive for you as an individual?'

'It is when you realise that it's not a lifestyle you could maintain.'

After 'Hurt' by Johnny Cash, Young turned to Vegas's childhood in St Helens as the youngest of four children. His mum was a housewife and part-time cleaner. His dad was a joiner – who once cooked his pet rabbit.

'One morning, as we were leaving for school, he went, "Right, whose rabbit's going in the pot today?"' Vegas recalled. 'I thought he was joking because it was such a ridiculous concept.

'We came in from school and he was out the back, cleaning the hutch. I asked where [*the rabbit*] was and he went: "It's there." I looked behind me and it was skinned and hanging up. I couldn't believe it. My sister went berserk – and my mum!

'My dad had always claimed our rabbits were livestock but we'd never eaten one. My dad had [*just*] been laid off. It might have been – not a break-down, but I wonder if it was a man at the end of his tether.'

Vegas described his parents being unemployed for much of the eighties but handling it with 'an amazing amount of dignity'. In a bizarre move, at the age of eleven, he went to a boarding-school seminary. 'How did that come about?' wondered Young, not unreasonably.

'From my saying that I wanted to be a priest from an early age. But I think saying it because I enjoyed the reaction that it got.'

Young: 'At eleven, what are your first memories of the seminary?'

'It really hadn't sunk in what was happening until the first night. You're in this big, imposing school in its own grounds. Horrendously homesick. It was just shellshock.'

'And how quickly did you realise, *Maybe I don't want to be a priest after all*?'

'There was a series of events. It was difficult to go home at weekends, and people saying, "What you're doing is a wonderful thing." And you are quietly going, *It's not a wonderful thing and it's not a wonderful place*.'

Vegas lasted four terms. 'Were you abused there?' asked Young.

'*I* wasn't. And for people who *were*, is it really up to me to drag them into the spotlight and discuss that? But when I left, I wanted to take everybody else with me.'

Once home from the seminary, said Vegas, he struggled to fit into every-day life. 'I wanted to drink cider in bus stops, do everything that everybody else did. I had this thing hanging over me: "That's the priest boy". I just wanted to blend in.'

Young: 'Were you funny? Did you make people laugh?'

'I don't think I was. There were little bits of entertainment. I'd play my nose in class.'

'As a musical instrument?'

'Yeah.'

'What did you play?'

'I played a Hawaiian tune. I had a quiet ambition to get on *That's Life!*'

Vegas left school and went to Middlesex University to study art and ceramics. 'I ran up a lot of debt in my first year. In the second year, the party was over. There was no money, my family couldn't afford to send me any and, suddenly, a friend in need is a pest.

'I graduated, and realised a degree in ceramics is not a commercially successful move. When have I ever gone into the dole and they've had a card up: "Teapot mender"? I sat on the train with my dad, and I just said, "I've made a huge mistake."'

Vegas chose Pulp's 'Common People', saying it mirrored his resentment towards his well-heeled fellow university students. Young commented that in the song, Jarvis Cocker got the girls. 'Did it help at university that you were one of the common people? Did it attract the ladies?'

'It didn't. I'd got to twenty-two without ever having a girlfriend. I thought I was just going to be single: I wasn't a relationships sort of person. I just resigned myself to the fact that women didn't see me in the same way that I saw them.'

Young: 'I imagine that when you started to become well-known on the comedy circuit, that changed?'

'It did.'

'Did that make you cynical?'

'It did, but the relief far outweighed the pessimism!'

In 1997, Vegas was nominated for the Perrier Award at Edinburgh in a major breakthrough. It was the birth of his identity as, said Young, 'the hell-raising, heavyweight comic rarely seen without a pint of Guinness in his hand. That's what people wanted from you?'

'They did. My usual approach was to just get as drunk as possible. I can count on one hand the number of times I've gone on stage as Johnny without a drink.'

Young: 'At its worst, how badly did the drinking affect your life?'

'There was a point after college where there was nothing happening in my life but I wasn't *making* anything happen. I'd always drunk in pubs, to socialise, but this was drinking in a room on your own and blaming the world for not being where you thought you should be.

'Then, oddly, the career took me back towards that path of ... maybe it was arrogant that I thought I could go out and play the hellraiser and then put Johnny back in his box.

'And within my personal life, I went through a separation and a divorce, and I think I was burning bridges with people because I wanted them to know that I was desperately upset.'

'What sort of a husband were you?'

'I don't honestly think it lasted long enough to find out!'

Young: 'Are you not drinking now?'

'I *do* drink now. Drink has served me wonderfully. It helped me create Johnny. I see it as something that's done a lot for me, but that can turn on you at any minute and take it all back.'

Vegas admitted to being 'very scared' that his drinking could get out of hand again: 'In the past, I couldn't say I've come through with flying colours.'

Young turned to a happier topic: her guest's burgeoning side career as an actor in series such as *Benidorm*. How had it happened?

'It was something I quietly wanted to do but, without having the formal training, I didn't really feel confident about putting myself out there and saying, "I want to act!" Because I thought, *If you can't do it ...*'

Young: 'Did you feel self-conscious to be in groups of serious, proper actors?'

'I always have and it's something I've never really got to grips with.'

The host asked what Vegas's parents thought of his TV acting.

'Well, it's really nice to finally do something, like *Benidorm*, that my mum can discuss without bringing shame upon the family!'

Vegas talked of having found love, with a fiancée in Dublin who had made him realise that 'my life isn't best lived on my own'. Yet it was having his own offspring that had given him real ballast in his existence.

'With Michael, I'll love my son until the day I die. Nothing can ever change that. Whether I've struggled with my faith, or drinking, or anything, just that one guarantee has made a world of difference to my life.'

Young: 'You don't want to give up your life to performing, only for him to think, *Well, that's my dad, but I hardly know him*?'

'That's it, exactly. The performance side of your life can be very shallow. I just couldn't forgive myself if he thought he came second.'

As the interview wended to its close, Kirsty Young congratulated her guest on having just turned forty. 'How does it feel?'

'A lot better than I actually expected!' confessed Johnny Vegas. 'There was one point I actually thought, *Will I make forty?* I hope it's the start of a far less traumatic chapter. I'd like my forties to just be a period of focusing on the people closest to me ...'

• • •

Since his *Desert Island Discs* appearance, Johnny Vegas has appeared in more movies, including Sacha Baron Cohen's *Grimsby* (2016) and a fine voice-part cameo in Nick Park's animated *Early Man* as a football-playing caveman with his own catchphrase: 'Champion!' He remains a TV fixture both in comedy series such as the BBC's *Still Open All Hours* (2013–19) and hosting shows such as Channel 4's *Johnny Vegas: Carry On Glamping* (2021). Having survived not just to forty but beyond fifty, he has two sons and continues to live in St Helens.

DISCS CHOSEN
❤ 'Hurt'
Johnny Cash
'It's all about legacy and having a son'

'Dignity'
Deacon Blue

'Love Reign O'er Me'
The Who
'A love song that contained all my frustrations at being every girl's best friend but not the bloke they wanted to kiss'

'Common People'
Pulp
'When I was at college, this song said it perfectly. Thank you, Jarvis'

'Waiting for My Real Life to Begin'
Colin Hay
'It's given me a push to get off my backside and get on with it'

'Domino Man'
The Beautiful South
'It's a tribute to pubs and pub culture'

'There She Goes'
The La's
'I love love songs – I live for love! I'm not a misery guts'

'Vincent'
Don McLean
'If I could create anything as beautiful as a song like this, I could walk away a very happy man'

BOOK

The Ragged-Trousered Philanthropists – Robert Tressell
'I learn something from it every time I read it'

LUXURY ITEM

A pottery kiln
'It's an incredibly therapeutic thing to do'

45
DOREEN LAWRENCE

CAMPAIGNER, ACTIVIST
10 June 2012

Some *Desert Island Discs* castaways have pursued celebrity avidly throughout their lives. Others have become famous by chance. There is a third, smaller category who have reluctantly found themselves public figures as the result of a horrible, catastrophic, life-changing event.

Doreen Lawrence was a south-east London special needs teacher and mother until her life was turned upside-down on 22 April 1993 – the date that her eldest son, Stephen, was murdered by a gang of white youths at a bus stop in Well Hall Road, Eltham. He was just eighteen.

This racially motivated murder made headline news in Britain and his mother began to campaign ferociously against what she perceived as the inefficiencies of the subsequent Metropolitan Police investigation, which failed to reach court after the Crown Prosecution Service stated they had insufficient evidence to bring murder charges.

The Lawrence family was to bring a private prosecution against the main suspects and the strength of public feeling stirred by the murder led to the 1999 Macpherson Report, which was famously to find that the Metropolitan Police force was 'institutionally racist'.

Lawrence had ever since continued to campaign for justice for victims of racist crimes and, in January 2012, finally saw two of the suspects in her son's killing convicted of his murder and jailed. Five months later, she met Kirsty Young for an intensely emotional interview.

• • •

Young began by detailing the ways in which Doreen Lawrence's life had changed since the murder of her son. She had advised the Home Office and police at the highest level; she was on the council of human rights group Liberty; she had been awarded an OBE for community relations.

'How does this sit with you as a person?' she asked her guest.

'It's as if you're talking about somebody else. I don't recognise me. The campaigning was me, because my son was special, and I just wanted everybody to know about him. But all the other things, the OBE – I'd swap all of that just to have my son back.'

In January 2012, nearly twenty years after Stephen Lawrence's murder, two men, Gary Dobson and David Norris, had finally been found guilty of his killing and jailed. 'How did that day feel for you?' asked Young.

'We thought the jury were going to be out longer than they were, so when we were called down because the jury was back, my heart was really beating very fast. During the trial, I couldn't read the jury, I couldn't tell, so my heart was in my mouth.

'When they said "Guilty", I had to hold myself in from screaming out, because I never thought I'd hear those words. I never thought I'd hear that someone was going to be found guilty for Stephen's death.'

Young: 'You'd attended every day of that six-week trial. You must have felt as though you were running on empty. That there was nothing left.'

'Yes. It was a very difficult time. My son was there most of the time with me. It was good having him sitting next to me.

'My daughter came one day and she had difficulty walking through the door of the court. I thought she was following me, and when I looked around, she wasn't there. She [*was saying*] "I just couldn't come in," and she was crying.

'It was a dreadful time – having the press, as well, watching you every minute to see what your reaction's going to be. Like being in a goldfish bowl, constantly. It was a terrible, terrible time.'

Young wondered how Lawrence had felt the morning after the verdict.

'The reality hadn't hit me. I think, even now, I still feel that the reality hasn't really hit me.'

Lawrence had long held that the original police investigation into her son's killing had been blighted by corruption and racism. Theresa May, then home secretary, had announced an inquiry into that investigation after the guilty verdicts. Was Lawrence pleased about this?

'Well, I think the only way we're going to get to the bottom of it is to have a public inquiry to give us the answers we've been looking for over the past nearly twenty years. I'm hoping the review is a stepping stone into having an inquiry.'

Young: 'After the Macpherson Inquiry, you were given a personal apology by the police. Did that mean anything?'

'No, it didn't, because I don't think we should have had to have waited so long for that.'

Lawrence had recently written a book about her struggle for justice for her son, *And Still I Rise*, named after a poem by Maya Angelou. Young wondered how she had found the strength to rise and rise again.

'It was Stephen, I think. Because he deserved a life, which was taken from him. I had this strong sense of truth and justice. I didn't look at it as me campaigning. I looked at it as me trying to get answers.'

Young steered the conversation to her castaway's childhood. Raised in Jamaica by her grandmother – 'a carefree life' – she had moved to the UK when she was nine to join a mother who had emigrated years earlier and thus she did not know.

'The little girl that arrived at the airport,' said Young. 'You were wearing a little yellow cotton sundress and carrying a cardboard suitcase. When you saw your mother, did you even know it was your mother?'

'No.'

'Did you settle in and start to develop a bond?

'I don't think we ever had that bond. In the early days, I think she tried to make that, but I don't think she knew how to.'

Young: 'So, when you came to be a mother yourself, did that help to mould your attitudes to what kind of mother you wanted to be?'

'Oh, definitely! I could never share a joke with my mother and that was just so sad. So I always said to my children, growing up: "You know I'm always here. Talk to me. I want to hear your stories!" And we did. We shared jokes. We shared everything.'

Prompted by Young, Lawrence recalled meeting her husband, Neville, when she was working in a NatWest bank and marrying him at twenty. He was a machinist making leather clothes. Their first child, Stephen, was born on 13 September 1974. 'What sort of baby was he?'

'A very cry, cry baby he was, Stephen! And once he started walking, no more crying: he could just move around. As he grew up, he wanted ... there's so many artist stuff that he wanted to do. Always busy!'

'His ambition was to become an architect?'

'Yes. I mean, he started drawing so very young. He used to make us all our Christmas cards and birthday cards.'

Young: 'And did you enjoy being a young mum at home?'

'I did, because of, when I grew up, not having the unit of a family. I had that with my children. We'd go to the cinema, to the museum, to the park. It was a happy time.'

After a pause for Etta James's 'At Last', Young commented that Stephen would have been thirty-eight that year. Did his mum still mark his birthday in a personal way?

'I visit the spot where he died. There's three times a year that I go: on the anniversary of his death, on his birthday, and at Christmastime. And I bring flowers for him. I stay as long as I can, because I always feel a bit nervous when I'm there.

'I talk to him, tell him the news – not that he can hear me, but I use that time to talk to him where he died. And the [memorial] plaque has been attacked so many times now.'

'Has it?'

'Yes. The second one's down now, because they took an axe and a hammer to it. He would never have been able to rest in peace had he been buried here.'

Young: 'Stephen's buried in Jamaica, next to your grandmother?'

'Yes. I'm pleased I did that. I wonder what it is about Stephen's name that seems to ... it's like they have a fear around his name, and they want to wipe it away. I don't understand because, even in life, Stephen was no problem and no trouble to anybody. And in death he certainly is not.'

Young imagined Stephen learning of his mother's achievements: 'This nearly twenty-year struggle for justice, getting your degree, setting up the foundation, becoming a national public figure. What would he make of that?'

'He would be quite astonished that I've done all of that! At the same time, I think Stephen would have been proud of me. As he was growing up, the things we talked about, and what I'd like to see him do, he'd say to me: "Mum, you know what your problem is? You care too much."

'If only he knew how much I *did* care at the time. When your children are young, you take them for granted. You don't believe anything would happen to them. And when they're *not* there – I could have said to him even more times how much I care and how much I love him.'

Closing a frequently heart-rending conversation, Kirsty Young asked her guest a poignant question. 'The fact that the name Stephen Lawrence stands for something culturally now, a shift in British culture – can you take any comfort from that?'

'Part of me, yes, because I think his name has managed to make so many positive changes,' said Doreen Lawrence. 'If I could turn the clock back, I'd *much* prefer to have Stephen for myself. But I have to live with the fact that he brings a lot more things for other people ...'

• • •

Doreen Lawrence has continued to be an assiduous campaigner. The Stephen Lawrence Charitable Trust, which she founded in 1998, has aided countless community groups and underprivileged young people, including helping them to train as architects. In 2013, she was made a life peer as Baroness Lawrence of Clarendon, and sits on the Labour benches in the House of Lords. In April 2018, at a memorial service to mark the twenty-fifth anniversary of Stephen's murder, Prime Minister Theresa May announced that 22 April would henceforth be designated Stephen Lawrence Day: an annual national commemoration of his tragic death.

DISCS CHOSEN
❤ **'Fallen Soldier'**
Beverley Knight
'She's been very supportive of us. It conjures up how Stephen fell after running all those yards after he was attacked ...'

'Israelites'
Desmond Dekker & the Aces
'We used to have such fun to this, dancing in the school playground'

'Summer Holiday'
Cliff Richard and the Shadows
'I just really remember watching this film'

'Warm and Tender Love'
Percy Sledge
'When I was growing up, it was soothing to fall asleep to'

'At Last'
Etta James
'It meant a lot more to me when Barack Obama became president. For a black man to achieve that ...'

'You Are Loved (Stephen Lawrence)'
Garth Hewitt
'Garth Hewitt wrote this song after Stephen's death. When someone dies like that, you think, do they know that you love them?'

'Mama Africa'
Garnett Silk

'Tears in Heaven'
Eric Clapton
'It's a song for his son, when his son died'

BOOK
I Know Why the Caged Bird Sings – Maya Angelou

LUXURY ITEM
An artist's workshop
'I can create things that remind me of my children and of my young life when I was growing up'

46
AHDAF SOUEIF

WRITER, ACTIVIST
17 June 2012

In the earliest years of *Desert Island Discs*, the castaways had been almost exclusively Anglo-Saxon: predominantly, white British males interspersed with the occasional visiting American superstar. Mirroring societal shifts, the show has vastly broadened its focus over the ensuing decades, becoming infinitely more inclusive.

In June 2012, one week after Doreen Lawrence visited the island, Ahdaf Soueif washed up on its shores. An Egyptian novelist, she had spent her childhood between Cairo and London, then seen her life become closely entangled with the political fortunes of her home nation.

Soueif had been the first Muslim woman to be nominated for the Man Booker Prize for 1999's *The Map of Love* and, at the time she met Kirsty Young, was heavily involved in the Egyptian revolution unfolding as part of the Middle East-wide Arab Spring movement. She spoke about the personal and political sides of her life with equal passion.

• • •

Young opened by quoting Soueif reflecting that 'if she had to locate her Englishness it would be in literature, but when she returns to Egypt, she feels as if she's been holding her breath until she got there.' She then quickly transported her guest to one recent, specific night in Cairo.

On 28 January 2011, a youth-led uprising against the rule of Egyptian president Hosni Mubarak led to violent clashes between protesters and security forces, including in Tahrir Square, Cairo. 'Was there a moment where you thought, *Oh, something important is happening here*?' asked Young.

'I think we all thought that on the twenty-fifth,' said Soueif. 'I wasn't even in Egypt: I was in Jaipur, at a literary festival. I raced back and got back on the twenty-seventh in the evening. Everything was quiet, like the country was drawing a breath.

'The next day, on the twenty-eighth, it all completely broke wide open. Ahead of us in Tahrir, there was smoke and gunfire and thousands and thousands of people. Every once in a while, there would be a surge a few metres forward as friends being killed at the front gained you those metres.

'Your job, as the masses, was to move forward and hold the three metres. That was when it really, really did sink in that this was a battle for the country, we were all part of it, and I was there.'

Young pointed out that Soueif was at the square with her son and her nieces. Amid history being made, was she also afraid for them?

'I *did* feel fear for my son and my nieces but you, sort of ... actually, it's an odd thing but you step away from that because things happen to people.

'We have one thousand two hundred young people who've been killed; we have sixteen thousand who have been subjected to court martial; eight thousand who have had amputations and lost eyes, and so on. It becomes so enormous that, *What fear is it that would be adequate?* Fear becomes not an option.'

After thirty years in power, Mubarak had resigned two weeks later and been replaced by a military junta, who were still in power pending imminent elections. Young reminded Soueif that she had once said that 'optimism is a duty. How optimistic do you feel about Egypt's future right now?'

'I still believe that optimism is a duty. I think that the fight we have on our hands is bigger and will take longer than we had perhaps thought. But maybe you do need wide-eyed optimism to begin with.

'In the revolution, you can't but be a participant. I think even the book I had to produce out of the revolution is a very much a revolutionary act. It is written to push forward the aims of the revolution rather than to comment on them.'

After a music break, Young turned to more personal matters. Was it true that Soueif wrote in English but dreamed in Arabic?

'I dream in both, actually. I write in English because of the fluke of where I first learned to read. We came to England in '55, I was four years old and I lost my Arabic. I learned to read very quickly and I learned in English.

'I read Arabic literature much later. Therefore, I think that my literary language was formed in English whereas I regained my Arabic when we went back to Egypt when I was seven, and Arabic became very much the language that I lived in.'

Soueif's parents were both intellectuals. Young asked if it was the case that her mother had been unable to teach English at Cairo University as she was not, herself, English?

'That's right. It was pre-1952 [*the establishment of Egypt as a republic*], the English department was staffed by British people and you couldn't teach in the English department. So, she found a job as a primary-school teacher.

'My father had graduated from the department of philosophy and they were young and romantic and dissident. My father had already spent a year in jail for being a leftist, so, yes, it was romantic and interesting.'

More music, then Soueif talked of returning with her parents for a second stint living in England when she was thirteen. Homesick, she had an unhappy spell in a comprehensive school in Putney.

'I used to play football at my school in Cairo, in goal, and I was not bad. So, to be on a hockey pitch, in the rain and freezing, and with sticks swiping at your legs ... I was hopeless.

'Then, *the questions*: "Do you go to school on a camel?" "How many wives does your father have?" I had a big rebellion and I said I wasn't going to school any more. It was unthinkable, but I held my ground and I forced [*her parents*] not to extend their sabbatical and to go home.'

Young: 'Did you always know that you would write?'

'No. I had daydreams, like seeing a book with my name on it in a shop window, but I also saw myself doing a flamenco on a stage, so what was more likely than the other?'

When Soueif did start to write, she told Young, happy accidents and chance encounters had seen her find an agent, appear on the cover of the *London Review of Books* and secure a publishing deal. Yet she really emerged into the public consciousness with 1999's *The Map of Love*.

'It was nominated for the Booker shortlist,' noted Young. 'How did that feel?'

'Oh, that felt incredible! Because the book, when it first appeared, got some hostile reviews, so I was not following reviews or literary news of any kind. It was completely amazing! My friends and I were in tears ...'

Through literary connections, Soueif met her husband and the father of her two sons, the poet Ian Hamilton. 'You lived between two places,' Young said. 'How did that work, or *did* it work?'

'The decision was that we would live half the year here and half there, but that didn't work out. Ian would come to Egypt and be very happy for about two weeks, then he'd be restless and unhappy. It became clear it was easier for me to be in England than for him to be in Egypt.'

Young: 'But it was important to make sure that your sons understood Egypt, and that it was as much part of their life?'

'It was *very* important to me that my sons should be Egyptian as much as they were British. They have a very strong and big and loving family in Egypt that they had to be part of.'

Soueif told Young she'd always had three trusted sounding boards to show her writing to first: her husband, her mother (who sometimes translated her work into Arabic), and a friend and literature professor, Edward Said. Sadly, all three had now passed.

Young: 'How much more difficult is it writing, with those three people dead?'

'I've not written a novel since *The Map of Love*.'

Instead, Soueif had thrown herself into political writing, for both the Palestinian cause and chronicling the travails of her beloved Egypt. As the show closed, Young detailed how much that nation had changed before her guest's eyes.

'Your lifetime spans an unbelievable amount of political and cultural upheaval for Egypt. The end of British rule. The birth of the republic. The Six-Day War when you were seventeen. The assassination of Anwar Sadat. And now last spring's uprising. How personally do these things feel to be woven through your life?'

'Totally! I can hardly understand when people, nicely and kindly, want to know how I *personally* am doing, as opposed to me publicly. There isn't really *me personally*, separate from the larger picture.'

Young: 'Your mother died in 2007. She didn't live to see the uprising in Tahrir Square. Can you imagine what she might have made of it?'

'I think she would have been delighted!' enthused Ahdaf Soueif. 'I was constantly wanting to go home and tell her, you know, talk to her about it, describe it to her, ask her. My father is overjoyed: he's eighty-eight and it feels like he's lost ten years since the revolution happened. He watched it unfold, and he is full of hope ...'

• • •

In more recent years, Ahdaf Soueif has felt less optimistic about Egypt's future as the country, under long-term President Abdel Fattah el-Sisi, has arguably moved in a more repressive direction. She says her current attitude is summarised by an Antonio Gramsci motto: 'The pessimism of the intellect and the optimism of the will.' In 2020, she was arrested in Cairo for pressing for the release of political prisoners during Egypt's COVID-19 pandemic. Along with her family, she continues to campaign fervently for a freer and more democratic Egypt.

DISCS CHOSEN
❤ 'Rag'een'
Eskenderella
'When the revolution happened, they were in Tahrir ...'

'Emta el-zaman'
Mohammed Abdel Wahab

'She Loves You'
The Beatles
'The song that started a whole new era of consciousness in every one of us ...'

Mozart's Bassoon Concerto in B Flat Major
Stepan Turnovsky with the Vienna Mozart Academy
'So romantic and so hopeful'

'Sawwah'
Abdel Halim Hafez
'The big heartthrob singer when I was sixteen'

'Hotel California'
The Eagles
'A track from years of driving my kids around'

'Zahrat El Mada'en'
Fairuz
'A classic of Arabic music'

'Seeret el-Hubb'
Umm Kulthum
'The great Egyptian diva'

BOOK

Keepers of the Flame – Ian Hamilton
'He would read me the chapters as he finished them and I thought it was amazing'

LUXURY ITEM

Blank lined paper and smooth, coloured biros
'I only work things out when I write them down'

'ISLE NEVER FORGET ...'

'When I was asked to be on *Desert Island Discs*, I felt surprised and flattered and like something had fallen into place: *Ah! Now I'm a serious person!* I love how the show is serious but not confrontational. It's a brilliant concept, and very pleasant to potter around on a Sunday morning and hear a résumé of somebody's life.

'I wasn't apprehensive: I was really looking forward to it. I knew I'd be reaching people even more directly than through my writing. People are actually *listening* to you, and there's something very empowering and human about that.

'Kirsty had this calm tone when she spoke to me and she drew me out. I was grateful. I'm so used to combative interviews, and having to fight my interviewer on Egypt or Palestine. Nice to be treated kindly for a change!

'People I knew were so pleased to hear Umm Kulthum and my choices of Arabic music on Radio 4 in a normal context and not being treated as "funny", "exotic" music. One minute it was "Hotel California" – the next, it was Fairuz.

'I usually worry about hearing my interviews back but I listened to my *Desert Island Discs* and I liked it. It's one of the nicest things I've done, and maybe my media appearance which has had the most resonance ...'

47

MARTINA NAVRATILOVA

TENNIS SUPERSTAR
8 July 2012

It's widely accepted that top sportspeople's athletic brilliance is not matched by their interview techniques. Myopic focus on their chosen sport, and years and years of repetitive practice, can render them less than scintillating when they get behind a microphone.

This accusation could not be levelled at Martina Navratilova. Arguably the greatest female tennis player of all time, the Czech superstar also boasted a jaw-dropping backstory and a broad cultural hinterland, both of which she displayed to memorable effect on *Desert Island Discs*.

Navratilova swam ashore in July 2012 and told a transfixed Kirsty Young and her listeners about defecting from behind the Iron Curtain when still a teenager, adapting to life in the West, being outed as gay – and, along the way, finding the superhuman strength and resolve to win fifty-nine major tennis titles, including eighteen Grand Slam singles crowns.

All this and a great sense of humour, too! By common consensus, it was one of the all-time great *Desert Island Discs* episodes.

• • •

Kirsty Young began by marvelling at the fortitude that had seen her guest play at the highest level of tennis for thirty years, including winning her last Grand Slam tournament just before her fiftieth birthday. As a girl, Navratilova's father had told her to play 'aggressively, like a boy'. 'I already did!' she said.

Her father had also told her when she was eight that she would one day win Wimbledon. Young asked for her earliest tennis memory.

'I really didn't have a forehand until I was seven, because I was too little,' Navratilova recalled. 'I played with my grandmother's racquet and it was too big to hold with one hand, so I had to just hit two-handed backhands.

'But I think my father realised that I was amazingly gifted. My left arm – he used to call it my golden arm.'

Young took Navratilova back to her first Wimbledon singles title, when she beat Chris Evert in the final in 1978. Her guest laughingly remarked that the cash prize that year – £17,000 – was the same sum as female players now got for losing in the first round.

Young: 'And when you won, where were your parents?'

'Well, my family couldn't be with me because I'd defected in 1975 and my family couldn't travel to me. I could travel to them, but I'd never get out again, so *that* wasn't an option. I didn't even know if my parents were able to see [*the final*] on TV.

'As it turned out, they *did* watch it, on German TV. They drove to the German border in Pilsen in the west Czech Republic. Regular Czech TV wouldn't show it because I was *persona non grata* in those days. And I spoke to them on the phone a couple of hours later.'

It was, she said, 'emotional and sad' to be separated at that moment of triumph: 'It's just about being with your family, the people that you love. That's what I'll never forgive the communists for. They destroyed so many lives. You can never get those years back.'

Young took her guest further back: to being born in Czechoslovakia in 1956. 'What are your earliest memories of life at home?'

'I was in the mountains. I grew up in the Krkonoše mountains because my father was the keeper of a lodge. So my mum was there with him, then my parents divorced when I was about three-and-a-half.'

Navratilova said she continued to live with her mother while her father, who had no car, once or twice a year took all-day journeys by train, bus, tram and foot to visit her. 'He stopped coming when I was nine. Finally, I said, "Mum, where's my father?" And she said, "Oh, he passed away a year ago."

'Mum wasn't very good at telling me bad news, so she kept it away from me for as long as possible. It turns out he killed himself over a woman he was in love with who left him.'

In the meantime, Navratilova had inadvertently helped her mother to meet her next partner – Mirek Navrátil, the stepfather that the tennis star loved from the start and was to call 'Dad' as he coached her. She met him as he laid a court at her local tennis club.

'He would take the clay to the court in a wheelbarrow. I would get in and he would take me around in the wheelbarrow. He was like, "Oh, you're always smiling! What's your name? Where's your mum?" That was how they met ...'

Young commented that there was no word in Czech for 'tomboy' but asked if the young Navratilova had been one nevertheless.

'Definitely! Always, always! Always wanted short hair, always hated wearing skirts. To this day, I will not wear a skirt, except when I play tennis. In a skirt, you can't run properly – catching a train, catching a tram, riding a bicycle – a skirt just doesn't work!'

Young: 'You became famous for this incredibly honed, powerful physique as a tennis player. As a little girl, you must have looked very athletic?'

'I was very athletic from the get-go. I ran everywhere or rode the bike, and swam in the river or skated on it in the winter. In the third grade, a teacher was explaining how the bicep works and she picked me to show the class because I had more defined biceps than the boys. Go figure!'

Young took her guest forward to her first trip to the West, for a tennis tournament when she was thirteen. What did she remember of it?

'Oh, that was in Germany. Big cars! It was close to an American army base, so there were a lot of old Chevrolets and Cadillacs. I'd never seen a car like it: I thought it was amazing. And the *food* – the variety, and things I'd never seen before! I never saw a fresh pineapple.

'I wanted to experience it all. To this day, if I go to a shop and see a fruit I've never seen before, I buy it. I have to try it.'

Navratilova had also witnessed the oppressive nature of the USSR at first hand when Soviet tanks rolled into Czechoslovakia in 1968.

'It was extremely depressing. It's like you're in jail and you're almost on the other side of the wall and then, *boom!* Another huge wall shows up and you know you're never going to get out of the prison.

'I was at a tennis tournament with my best friend and her father called and said, "Don't go outside – there are tanks in the street." So *of course* we went outside and checked it out, and were throwing rocks at the tanks. But it wasn't very helpful ...'

Navratilova recalled how her family had first contemplated escaping Czechoslovakia when she played her first Wimbledon in 1975.

'My whole family – my parents and my sister, who's six years younger – were talking of leaving Czechoslovakia. But my father was not sure of himself. What is he going to do? How is going to provide? He doesn't speak English. So, we didn't do it.

'We went back to the Czech Republic and [*people*] said, "Oh, my God, you're back!" Because rumour had it that we had defected. Because of that, they didn't want to let me out of the country again.

'The US Open was coming around the corner and they said, "You're not going because we don't want you to travel any more." It was like, *what*? The Czech Tennis Federation got behind me and they ended up giving me the visa just before the tournament. That was when I knew I wasn't going to come back.'

Young: 'Did you have that conversation with your parents?'

'Well, I spoke to my father, and he said, "Don't tell your mother." And he said, "If you're not going to come back, don't come back if we ask you to. If you stay, stay. Because they may ask us to tell you to come back – but don't."'

'Why did he want you not to tell your mother?'

'Because he knew it would break her heart.'

Young enquired about the process of seeking political asylum in the US. What questions had the Americans asked her?

'Well, everything. If I was a communist? If my father was a communist? I assured them that I was *not*, and my father actually got thrown out of the Communist Party for not toeing the line and my parents did labour camp and were political prisoners, in a way.

'"I want to be number one." That's all I remember saying. "I just want to be number one.'"

Newly based in the US, Navratilova initially looked a long way from that goal. 'I just ate everything in sight!' she recalled to Young. 'I was twenty pounds overweight, maybe twenty-five, a year after I left Czechoslovakia.'

'I lost at the US Open, the first round. I was burned out from tennis and exhausted. I didn't have anybody to turn to. I didn't have any place to go: I couldn't go back to my family. I didn't have a coach for five years. I didn't think I needed one.'

Navratilova recovered her legendary sense of purpose in time to win Wimbledon in 1978. When she won it again, the following year, she was reunited with her mother for the first time in four years.

'The Duchess of Kent intervened because she had read the story of how in '78, when I won, I couldn't be with my family,' she told Young. 'So, she implored the Czech government to let my parents out. They made a concession and let my mother out for Wimbledon.'

After a pause for Ella Fitzgerald, Young moved the conversation on to the topic of Navratilova's sexuality. 'I was going to say, in 1981 you came out, but you *didn't* come out: you were outed?'

'I *was* outed. I had wanted to come out years before but I couldn't: it would be a disqualifier for being a US citizen. I wanted to after I got my citizenship, except my then-girlfriend was in the closet and she was well-known – Nancy Lieberman, the basketball player.

'She didn't want to come out, but then a reporter outed me anyway. The WTA [*Women's Tennis Association*] said, "We can't have any more scandals about sexuality!" because there was a scandal about Billie Jean King, and I would've been coming on the heels of that.

'So, to this reporter, I said, "I don't want to come out because it would really hurt our sponsors." And the headline was: MARTINA DOESN'T WANT TO COME OUT BECAUSE IT WOULD HURT THE SPONSORS. I mean, *really*! So that was how I came out.

'But I wanted to come out – it was other people that were keeping me in the closet.'

Young: 'Your parents were absolutely fine about it?'

'No, initially they were upset, but then my father read some books on it and educated himself and realised it wasn't his doing and it wasn't my doing. It was just that I was born ... I mean, he accepted it and just wanted me to be happy. And the same for my mum.

'As for the fans – that was difficult, because I definitely got some jeers and boos and whistles that I wouldn't have gotten had I been straight.'

Young put it to her guest that she had often had a very rough deal from the press. Navratilova agreed, while sounding stoical on the subject.

'I never had a chance! I left a communist country and defected: that's controversial. And then being gay – again, through no doing of my own, I'm controversial by just *being*. That's the cards I was dealt.'

Fast-forwarding to the current day, Navratilova told Young that she was now in a relationship with a partner who had two daughters and so was a parent: 'It's difficult but it's amazing.' She had also, two years earlier, gone public about having breast cancer.

Young: 'You've described it as your own 9/11. Why did you decide to go public?'

'That was one of the bravest things I did! I was keeping it quiet before I had the surgery but, afterwards, I realised how much difference I could make in women's lives by speaking out about having mammograms. Because I skipped four years! I didn't know I'd skipped four years, but I did. I was lucky I caught it when I caught it ...'

Having covered an exhaustive range of profound topics during an enthralling programme, Kirsty Young closed with a little light relief. In 2008, to mass amazement, Navratilova had gone into the Australian jungle as a contestant on ITV's *I'm a Celebrity ... Get Me Out of Here!*

'Why on earth,' wondered the host, not unreasonably, 'would a woman who's won fifty-nine Grand Slam titles decide that she was going to spend time having burrowing cockroaches and orb spiders crawl across her face so she can get a meal for the night?'

'Well, I didn't know that was going to be the case!' laughed Martina Navratilova. 'I was told it was more like camping with some side trips, and I love camping. I didn't know I would be completely deprived of food – I lost eleven pounds in three weeks – and I couldn't bring anything with me!

'My luxury item was my pillow that my mum made. And, of course, once you're there, you can't quit, because that's not in my nature. So, you just get on with it. But it was *miserable* – I was hungry for three weeks ...

• • •

Martina Navratilova has enjoyed a happy post-tennis retirement with her partner, former Miss USSR Julia Lemigova, living between homes in Aspen, Paris and, primarily, Florida. The couple married in 2014. In recent years, she has investigated the issues surrounding trans women being allowed to compete in women's sports, including presenting a documentary on the subject for the BBC in 2019.

DISCS CHOSEN
'Bad Romance'
Lady Gaga
This song came out at the beginning of my relationship. It was pretty rocky at the start so it resonated with me!'

'L'amour est un oiseau rebelle' from Bizet's *Carmen*
Maria Callas with the Orchestra of the National Opera of Paris
'Her voice is not the best in the world but it certainly is the most colourful'

'Dancing Queen'
Abba
'It's happy music – puts you in a good mood every time'

'Nessun dorma' from Puccini's *Turandot*
Luciano Pavarotti with the London Philharmonic Orchestra
'He was my mum's hero, so this is a tribute to her'

'Love Is Here to Stay'
Ella Fitzgerald
'When all else fails, love will be around'

'Crying'
k.d. lang and Roy Orbison

❤ **'Vltava' from Smetana's *Má Vlast (My Homeland)***
Polish National Radio Symphony Orchestra
'The river that I grew up on, Berounka, flows into the Vltava'

'Un bel dì, vedremo' from Puccini's *Madame Butterfly*
Maria Callas
'It's sad but gives you a sense of spirit and hope'

BOOK
The Fountainhead – Ayn Rand
'It's about the human spirit and doing what you feel is right'

LUXURY ITEM
Her pillow
'The same thing I took to I'm a Celebrity ... Get Me Out of Here!'

48
DAWN FRENCH

COMEDIAN, ACTOR, WRITER
23 December 2012

Christmas 2012 brought to the desert island a much-loved figure who, warned Kirsty Young, 'if's she's not careful, may be moments away from being given the queasy-making status of national treasure'. And, whether she liked it or not, this was clearly only a matter of time.

Dawn French had earned her place in the nation's affections over the course of a thirty-year career in TV and film comedy that had taken in *The Comic Strip Presents*, many series with comedy partner Jennifer Saunders and, for nearly twenty years, the lead role in the BBC's *The Vicar of Dibley*.

French's life had not been not-stop laughs, as was evidenced during a conversation that touched on the suicide of her father and her divorce, after twenty-five years of marriage, from fellow comedian Lenny Henry. Even so, the star's ready wit, natural ebullience and *joie de vivre* still made the episode a joy.

• • •

'If you like funny, then you like her,' declared Kirsty Young, introducing her guest, before wondering if Dawn French ever found it a pressure, in her everyday life, to be expected to make people laugh all the time?

'I guess it is, but it's the most fun you can have with your clothes on – and even with your clothes off – laughing, isn't it? It's the glue that has bound the family I grew up in and the family I've raised.'

Young delved into that early family life. French was born in Anglesey, where her father was in the RAF. In fact, a photo existed of her, at four years old with her family, meeting the Queen Mother at a military base.

'Yes. We were chosen, I think, as a safe option. A nice, ordinary family. Because when the royals visit any kind of base, of course, they go and see the officers. And we were the oiks down the other end.

'My mum cleaned our house for six weeks. I had new shoes, a little tartan skirt, did curtseying practice and we bought new china. And, for some reason, I absolutely expected a) for her to arrive on a unicorn and b) wearing a crown, please.

'But she came in a lilac hat. *What was she thinking of?* And when she smiled, no word of a lie, she had black teeth. Now, when you're four, people with black teeth are *evil* – witches, or something. So, you know: no unicorn, no crown, and black teeth! Please leave now!

'I was terrified. I didn't want her in our house. I was clinging to my dad's leg like a randy terrier!'

Young: 'You say that you were the oiks. What was your dad's position in the military?'

'He became a sergeant in the RAF. He refused a commission, and I think that says a lot about him and about my family, actually. Very aware of class and how we don't really belong in "that other class".

'We were a working-class family but my parents were so determined that we would lift ourselves out of the working class that they had all sorts of pretensions, really. They sent us to public school and my mum used to come to speech days in a special hat with a buckle on the front and speak in a posh voice.'

Young: 'You had a pony as well, didn't you?'

'I had a pony, but it wasn't the kind of pony that enters gymkhanas. I had a pony that had a disease called sweet itch, that meant that every spring all of its mane and its tail fell out and it was covered in scabs.

'I *did* try gymkhanas but I wasn't suitable. The horse wasn't suitable. In one race, my dad had made the girth out of an old tyre, and as we were bobbing along, I started to slip round and round and round until eventually I was riding the horse upside-down. And that's not right.'

Young commented that French had been a working-class girl receiving a middle-class education. 'When you were at school, did you feel like one of them, or never quite?'

'Never quite. Never quite. Most of the girls there were from moneyed families. So, if I went to their homes, they had beige carpet and sinks in the corner of their bedroom. I'd never seen the like!'

After a pause for James Taylor, French talked more about her early family life, and how comedy was as its core.

'The main performers were me and my dad. Everything in our family was done through jokes and humour. There was a lot of sarcasm and teasing. My dad would say, "Ooh, now it seems to be *Dawn* talking the loudest! Everybody look at *Dawn*, because she's got something to say which is more important than everybody else!"'

When French was nineteen, she went to study at the Central School of Speech and Drama in London. Young asked for her memories of her first few days there.

'Well, my dad had just died – sadly, he committed suicide two weeks before I went to college. I was late for the start of term. And I was full of grief, obviously, but trying to cover it up. My mother had insisted that I go to college as planned.'

Young: 'You've written – incredibly honestly – that the feelings you had towards your father then were: *How dare you steal our happiness? You lied when you said you'd always be there for me!*'

'Yes. I think, initially, there was huge anger and sadness. I don't have that anger any more because I understand the kind of altered state he would be in, with massive depressions that he'd lived with ever since he'd been a young man.

'I did not know until much later that his first attempt on his life was when he was sixteen. In fact, all credit to him and my mum that when it *did* eventually happen, my brother and I were so shocked, because we'd had no idea that he lived like that.'

Young: 'How did the family structure repair? You were very close to your dad. When he wasn't there, how did the family structure readjust itself?'

'Well, interestingly, we were a square and we became a triangle. That's it. The sides join up and you're still strong.'

'Your mother must have been an incredibly strong person.'

'Absolutely amazing. She was a survivor and a coper.'

After a break for Etta James's 'At Last', which had recently been played at the funeral of French's mother, Young turned to happier matters and asked her guest about first meeting Jennifer Saunders at the Central School of Speech and Drama.

'According to Jennifer, when she first noticed you in college, you were wearing a corduroy skirt?' the host enquired.

'Yes. It was an A-line corduroy skirt – a further offence! I remember that she was very cool, very sophisticated, quite *posh*, I thought, and very beautiful. And I think she was sort of out of my league, and a little bit lofty.

'So I just decided that she wouldn't be one of the people that I would get to know. Then we had to share a flat, and I realised that she was *so* many other things besides.'

French described bonding with Saunders over some of the more outré and preposterous exercises that the college tutors inflicted on them.

'One day, we entered a studio and the whole class were asked to wrap themselves in newspaper with Sellotape. We had to help each other. The lights were lowered and we had to be reborn out of our "eggs" and have no language and have to learn to communicate with each other.

'Well, this was just *silly*! I couldn't enter into it at all. I stayed in my "egg" for a very long time because I knew, the minute I came out of it, I'd be out of control with laughter, especially if I caught Jennifer's eye, which I *did*. And we were asked to leave the class because we were ruining it for everybody else.'

Young commented that much of French's comedy in the past had been based on her physical size, including dressing up with Saunders as two fat men and as ballerinas. She was now much slimmer. Did she worry she had lost a comic tool?

'No. I think if you've got comedy chops, you've got them, whatever size you are. But if you've got the gift of a bit of extra heft, use it! And there is something about me controlling what people will laugh at when it comes to my physical shape.

'I think, *I'd like to decide what you find funny about my fatness*, if you like. For me, there's a dignity in that. I don't need you to be laughing at the fatness of me in a cruel or bullying way. I think I've always wrestled that control into my domain.'

French had recently filmed a *South Bank Show* about 'the aesthetics of fat' and, noted Young, done a 'very sexy' photoshoot for *Esquire* 'nude, with an artfully draped bedsheet around you'. This daring exercise, regretted her guest, had led to unwanted consequences.

'I did *not* expect the photo to be scanned in the *Sun* with a poll for people to ring in and say whether they'd like to do it with me or not, and whether it's sexy or not!'

Young: 'What was the poll result? I bet it was a resounding yes!'

'I didn't want to look, thanks! I didn't want to look!'

Towards the end of the interview, Young turned gently to the delicate topic of French's divorce from Lenny Henry in 2010. She suggested the couple had been Britain's answer to Brad Pitt and Jennifer Aniston.

'Oh, *were* we, now?' laughed her guest, sounding decidedly sceptical.

Young: 'Yes, you were. I think you were the nation's sweethearts. People liked that [*you were together*].'

'Well, I'm glad they liked it, because it was great.'

Young asked if this public approval had, in itself, been a pressure.

'Yeah. I think one of the reasons why people invested in it a bit is, you know, a black man, a white woman. Lots of racism came hurling at us and we tried not to be too bothered about that.

'But he lived, and probably still lives, with a certain amount of that at all times, and I've got a mixed-race daughter who also lives with a certain amount of it at all times. And it's just shocking.'

French said that the couple had separated 'in the right way: it was a tribute to the way we had been married'. Young asked how they had accomplished that difficult task.

'Kindness. That's all I can say. We knew the marriage was untenable, and we were sad about that, so we hunkered down. We went home to Cornwall and we walked on a beach and we drank a lot and we talked a lot. We laughed a lot – oddly! So those last few months of our relationship were pretty much like the first few months.'

French described the awkwardness of being single and attempting to date again in her fifties, but described an epiphany when she suddenly realised: 'I don't need a bloke to be happy! And then, of course, *bang*! I met somebody else!'

She was, she explained, now happily ensconced down in Cornwall with her new man, Mark. 'So, it's a life together, is it?' asked Kirsty Young.

'I think so,' replied Dawn French. 'Yeah, I think so. I hope so ...'

• • •

It looks to be. Dawn French married her new partner, charity executive Mark Bignell, in April 2013, and the couple still live in Cornwall. She has continued to make TV and film appearances, including three series of Sky drama *Delicious* in 2016–19, and a deeply amusing cameo in *Absolutely Fabulous: The Movie* (2016). Christmas 2022 finds her starring in *Jack and the Beanstalk* at the London Palladium alongside Julian Clary. As Kirsty Young prophesied, her unwanted status as a national treasure has long since been secured.

DISCS CHOSEN
'Bring Me Sunshine'
Morecambe and Wise
'That's exactly what they did'

'Ne Me Quitte Pas'
Alison Moyet
'A very, very close friend ... she's singing in French and I find it incredibly moving'

'You've Got a Friend'
James Taylor

'Just A Gigolo/I Ain't Got Nobody'
Louis Prima and Keely Smith with Sam Butera and the Witnesses
'Lenny and I often played this on a Sunday and danced around the house'

'At Last'
Etta James

'Kinky Boots'
Patrick Macnee and Honor Blackman
'Jennifer and I have this on our warm-up tape for our shows'

❤ **'Song to the Siren'**
This Mortal Coil
'My new chap, Mark, brought me this. You would fall in love, wouldn't you, with somebody who gave you this song?'

'One Day Like This'
Elbow
'A massive, wonderful, joyful anthem'

BOOK
Puckoon – Spike Milligan
'It is ludicrous and funny and the genius of Spike Milligan rings through it'

LUXURY ITEM
Nobby, her daughter's teddy bear
'She won't be happy about it, but it smells of her and it would be a great pillow'

49

ZADIE SMITH

NOVELIST, ACADEMIC
22 September 2013

Zadie Smith's debut novel, *White Teeth*, was a major publishing event of the year 2000. Written while Smith was still at Cambridge University, its multi-layered narrative won numerous awards and established its young author as a defining fiction writer of her generation.

Set in her native north-west London, *White Teeth* told the later-life story of two old wartime friends from different ethnic backgrounds, yet was largely concerned with the dynamics of multicultural Britain and its historical treatment of immigrants from the Commonwealth. It had profound themes yet was a fantastic page turner.

Many authors who rocket to success at such a precocious age struggle to follow it up and become one-hit wonders but, thirteen years later, Smith rocked up on Kirsty Young's desert island with a string of acclaimed novels and short stories and a flourishing academic career behind her. She was also deeply entertaining.

• • •

Kirsty Young opened by explaining that Zadie Smith had been born in Willesden, north London, to a Jamaican mother and British father, and now divided her time between there and New York, where she taught creative writing. How did this work?

'I go to New York to work,' replied Smith. 'It's a great place to work in that nobody does anything *except* work. But when I'm there, I can't say I'm full of ideas. I can't *stop* writing when I'm in London.'

Young turned to the prodigious success of *White Teeth*, listing some of the literary awards it had accrued, including the Whitbread First Novel Prize, the *Guardian* First Book Award, the James Tait Black Prize and the Commonwealth Writers First Book Award.

Despite this, she added, Smith now said that reading the first twenty pages of the book 'induced nausea' in her. Why was this?

'I don't think that's a very unusual thing to say,' demurred her guest. 'Imagine picking up a letter that you wrote at twenty-one, or a diary or a journal. What's your reaction? It's as if somebody else wrote it! But as I get older, I feel fonder towards it. I think of it as a book that young people really like, and that's great.'

Young commented that on *White Teeth*'s publication, Smith had found herself posited as a poster girl of multicultural Britain: as 'a brilliant, educated, beautiful, capable, literary young woman of colour'. People wanted to draw attention to her 'to prove the liberal ideal was fine'.

'But it's not proof enough, is it?' Smith demurred. 'Kanye [*West*] has a great line about "being the black spot on a domino". It's not enough, just one or two people out of a comprehensive school of two thousand. That's no kind of success.

'I was never interested in being held up as that kind of example, or in the idea that I'd been rescued or saved from a class that you need to be rescued or saved from. I don't feel that way. I love the community I come from and I hope I'm still a part of it.'

Young complimented her guest on the T-shirt she was wearing for the interview. 'Tell us what it says on it?'

'It says: BLACK NERD. It's from a T-shirt shop in New York where you choose what you want written on it. I chose BLACK NERD: that's what I am! It's good to be a black nerd. I enjoy it.'

Smith chose Billie Holiday and 'Easy Living'. As it faded out, Young told listeners that her guest had been singing along in the studio and had a beautiful voice. 'You used to earn money with it?'

'Well, I'd sing a bit in the lobbies of hotels at Christmas and in old people's homes when I was in school. I didn't like the performance bit – that was the problem!'

Young: 'You were born slap-bang in the middle of the seventies. What are your first memories?'

'I think my earliest memories are, kind of, knocking around Willesden and Kilburn with my slightly odd-looking parents.'

'Odd? Why?'

'It wasn't that they were mixed race, actually, because that was as common as grains of sand around Kilburn. It was the age gap, which was quite severe. I had a very young mother and what I thought was a very old father at the time.'

'What was the actual age gap?'

'Thirty years.'

'Oh, it *was* a big one!' acknowledged Young. 'And you didn't mind him being older?'

'I think ... I *did* mind. It would be untrue to say I didn't mind. I was very concerned about it. My earliest memories, really, were always thinking, *Well, when is he going to die?*

'It's my personal psychological theory about myself that a lot of my writing instinct came out of that concern, because it's not a normal thought to always be thinking about death when you're five, six, seven, eight!'

Young: 'Can you tell me about life at home? What do you remember?'

'My brother might say differently but I was the oldest and my memory was of my parents at war, basically. They were just always at war.'

'Were they at war, like, "We can't pay the bills!" Or was it, "I really don't like you!"?'

'They just didn't like each other! It was just terrible, but they really liked us, and I always felt that. So I always felt, kind of, sympathy for them.

'We'd be in a car going to Cornwall, and they'd be screaming at each other, but I was always aware of the fact that, *At least they're trying to get us to Cornwall.* They were united in the idea of giving us a happy childhood.

'When they got divorced, everybody was relieved. My dad lived around the corner. It was a much better arrangement – we were still close but we didn't have to have the yapping!'

After a burst of Bob Dylan, who Smith noted was a rare artist able to unite her warring parents in admiration, Young commented that her guest had been born not Zadie but Sadie. At what age had she changed her name?

'I was about fourteen. I never did it by deed poll: I just wrote it every-where. It's a stupid reason! There was a boy I really liked whose name began with Z, and I thought it would help if I changed my name.'

Young: 'What were you like as a little girl?'

'I was very bookish, obviously. I was awkward. Very self-conscious. I looked pretty funny. I had crazy teeth and didn't know what to do with my hair and, I guess, I was kind of a big kid.

'And I made a decision early on that I wasn't going to get involved with social things: *If they don't like me, or whatever, I'm just going to go to my room and read everything.*'

Smith was to find the bookish life she craved. After leaving school, she studied English Literature at Cambridge. 'You say you had the life of Riley there?' asked Young.

'I did! It *was* a life of Riley! You weren't at home, there's no one to tell you what to do, you got to read all day long! It was incredible! Instead of being one nerd, you were surrounded by nerds! Although, being one of four black nerds wasn't much fun ...'

Young: 'Did you get a lot of male attention?'

'No! The opposite! I was a minor stalker of other people. I looked like one of the Thompson Twins. I was crazily dressed: skirt down to my ankles, a series of very big hats. I was primarily trying to date my husband, who was not at all interested.'

Young: 'This is Nick Laird? How did he fob you off?'

'He says that I used to go to his room and just sit there all day and half the night, just hoping that something would happen. At about 4am, he would say, "Well, I really need to go to bed now!" and I would shuffle off. That went on for ages.'

'When did he change his mind?'

'Long after we were out of university! It was good, because we were friends for a really long time and it's good to be friends with someone you're married to. It's a good basis!'

Young noted that Smith had written her third novel, the Orange Prize for Fiction-winning *On Beauty* (2005), just after she had married Laird. She had taken their union as an unlikely springboard for the book.

'You were newly married,' the host said, 'yet in writing the book, you wanted to explore the landscape of a long marriage: of this couple who had been married for thirty years. What did you discover?'

'I discovered that there's something very odd about someone who just gets married and then thinks, *Yes, but what's this going to be like in thirty years?*' Smith laughed. 'There must be a part of me that's always trying to make the future safer by imagining it.'

Young: 'You didn't learn anything in the process? As you imagined this world for this couple, you didn't think, *Ah, maybe that will happen?*'

'No,' confirmed Zadie Smith. 'I think when I look back over my earlier books – and I think this is very true of young writers – they are full of aphorisms: little moral sentences. Young people are full of that sort of stuff. They're very certain they think they know what's going on.

'As you get older – in my experience, anyway – that all disappears. I don't write aphorisms any more because I have no idea what's going on. The person who wrote *White Teeth* was a know-it-all at twenty-two. That's how you are. The older you get, the less sure you are ...'

• • •

Anything but a literary flash in the pan, Zadie Smith has continued to write critically acclaimed novels and short stories that play out among the joyous, contrary hubbub of multicultural Britain. In 2022, her debut play, *The Wife of Willesden*, won the Critics' Circle Theatre Award for Most Promising Playwright. With her novelist/poet husband, Nick Laird, and their two children, she still lives between north-west London and New York, where she is a tenured professor in the creative writing faculty of New York University. We assume that she no longer dresses like one of the Thompson Twins.

DISCS CHOSEN

'Mo Money Mo Problems'
The Notorious B.I.G.
'It was in the middle of Clintonia in America: just an enormous feeling of optimism'

'Easy Living'
Billie Holiday

'I love female vocalists. I wanted to be one, when I was younger'

'To Ramona'
Bob Dylan

'Human Nature'
Madonna
'When you go on Desert Island Discs, *you don't expect to be choosing Madonna! But I have to try to be honest'*

'Pop Life'
Prince and the Revolution
'It's a song about the mess of human life ... a joyful thing'

Confutatis from Mozart's Requiem in D Minor
Chœur et Orchestre de Paris
'It plays a large part in On Beauty'

'Unorthodox'
Wretch 32
'His voice is perfectly north London'

❤ **Prelude to Wagner's *Tristan and Isolde***
Berlin Philharmonic Orchestra
'As a work of art, I find it perfect'

BOOK
À la recherche du temps perdu – Marcel Proust
'I've never finished it but I'm going to have a lot of time on the island'

LUXURY ITEM
Goggles
'I was torn between goggles and running shoes, but I think goggles so I can swim'

50

STEVE McQUEEN

ARTIST, DIRECTOR
21 September 2014

It takes sublime talent and supreme dedication to forge a reputation in any of the contemporary arts. By the time Steve McQueen surfaced on Kirsty Young's desert island in September 2014, he had ascended to the apex of not just one but two major creative fields.

After surviving a rudimentary school education, McQueen thrived at art college. In 1999, he won the art world's prestigious Turner Prize with an exhibit including *Deadpan*, a recreation of a 1928 Buster Keaton stunt that saw him stand stock still as the wooden wall of a house collapsed on him, its empty window frame passing right over him.

McQueen also worked in sculpture but filmmaking was his true love. In 2008, his feature-length debut, *Hunger*, about IRA hunger strikers, won the Caméra d'Or award for first-time filmmakers at Cannes. Three years later, erotic drama *Shame* gained critical acclaim. Then came *12 Years a Slave*.

Released in 2013, this stark dramatisation of the 1853 autobiography of Solomon Northup, an African-American kidnapped in Washington, DC in 1841 and forced to spend twelve years as a slave in Louisiana, was a breathtaking cinematic tour de force. It was to scoop best picture at both the Academy Awards and Golden Globes.

It was a hell of a CV for a lad who had found himself in the duffers' class at school in Shepherd's Bush, and McQueen detailed this extraordinary journey to Young with humour, humility – and burning passion.

• • •

Kirsty Young began by admiring a phrase that Steve McQueen was wont to use – that he wanted to make 'films that are essential'. 'What *is* essential to you in a movie?' she asked him.

'Truth,' her guest replied. '*Whatever* that is. There are many truths: you can smell it. There's a sort of universality to it. *That's* the kind of films I'm interested in: the kind of art I'm interested in.'

Young wondered if McQueen saw art and filmmaking, rather than two different disciplines, as all part of one creative endeavour.

'Yes, absolutely. There's no differentiation of film and art, for me. It's just art: it's one thing. It's as if film is the novel and fine art is poetry. It's the same thing, but saying it in different ways.

'You're led by the idea and what it wants to be. How it wants to represent itself. Sometimes it wants to be, you know, a photograph or an artwork or within a film. Other times, it wants to be a narrative feature film.'

Had it meant anything to McQueen, Young asked, to be the first black director to win best picture in the eighty-six-year history of the Oscars?

'It's not important to me at all. There's nothing I think black people can't do. It's of no consequence to me. "So what?" as Miles Davis says.'

Young moved on to the film that had won McQueen that honour. His wife, Bianca Stigter, had first shown him the 1853 memoir that had inspired *12 Years a Slave*. How did he feel when he first read it?

'*Wow!* I couldn't believe it. At the same time as reading it and being amazed by it, I was angry at myself: how did I not know this book? And how wasn't Solomon Northup's name known throughout the world? And that's why I decided I had to make this into a film.

'There was a girl who lived in Amsterdam, Anne Frank, who wrote *Anne Frank's Diary*, and it was amazing to me that it echoed that. Obviously, I knew *her* name but I did not know *him*, and I wanted to let the world know about it.'

Young: 'Horrific and beautiful: the film is both of those things. It is shot with such majesty that the horror is magnified.'

'The fact of the matter is, I am not interested in manipulating people. The complete opposite. I'm interested in a truth ... I cannot put a filter on life. It's about not blinking.'

In his acceptance speech for the best-picture Oscar for *12 Years a Slave*, noted Young, McQueen had said his life had always been full of strong women. 'Tell me about your mother.'

'She's great. She's strong. I mean, goodness gracious, without her I wouldn't be sitting here talking to you now, I'll be honest! She always told me: "Do what you want to do."'

McQueen was born in Shepherd's Bush in 1969. A few years later, his mother had demonstrated this discussed strength by buying a house in leafy Ealing for the family to move to, without telling his father. 'How did that go [*down*]?' asked Young.

'Not well! But my mother wanted to get out of a certain area and when we moved to Ealing, it was middle-class living, so the environment was amazing. You could use your imagination: you had these massive parks where you could make things up. Before, it was concrete: an estate.'

Young: 'In your home environment, were there pictures on the walls?'

'No. My father was more of a person to get a trade. Work was about making money, and that was it.

'I remember taking him to the Turner Prize and him saying, "What's this all about?" In his high-pitched, West Indian [*voice*], when he gets excited: "*What's it all about?*" Even then, he wasn't really buying it. My mum was just very, very proud.'

Prompted by Young, McQueen described his unpromising, dispiriting school career. Hindered by dyslexia, he was placed in a class of students not expected to go on to college. 'I was in a manual-labour situation, and that was it. My future tied up when I was thirteen years old. End of.'

Defying those negative predictions, he enrolled at Chelsea School of Art after leaving school. It felt, he told Young, like the Promised Land.

'Art was my salvation. My foundation course at the School of Art was the first time I could breathe. Stupid ideas, daydreaming, falling asleep, not going in sometimes, finding a book ... wow!'

'What did your dad feel about you going to Chelsea School of Art?'

'Listen, I think my dad would have been happier if I was a mechanic or worked for London Transport! When you grow up in a certain way, or are institutionalised in a way, you obviously don't think certain things are possible for your children.'

Young: 'What was the first piece of film you ever made?'

'Travelling from Goldsmiths Art College back home, on a Super 8 camera.'

McQueen had progressed to Goldsmiths after Chelsea to study fine art. He became interested in film there, and found the college environment both liberating and intimidating, he told Young.

'You're told, "You're free, do what you want!" and your first reaction is, "Yippee, fantastic! Oh my God, this is amazing!" But, after a while, you have a nervous breakdown, because you've never had that freedom before.

'Somehow, you learn through your own devices to build yourself to make, in some ways, your own language in order to produce ... to sort of navigate yourself in what you want to do within art. And it's crazy. It's wonderful. Scary.'

McQueen's next move, narrated Young, had been to film school in New York. It was not a success. 'After four months, you left?'

'It was very difficult. It was a very competitive film school and, no, it didn't work. NYU was a place that was very narrow ... it *was* teaching you to make film, in a way, but it felt almost like a Chinese circus, where you come out and you do the splits.

'I remember lying in bed on the phone to my mum and the sensation of having tears come out of your eyes and roll back into your eyes. I said to Mum, "I have to leave. I have to come back."'

Young wondered if McQueen had encountered that 'narrow' way of thinking again in more recent years when Hollywood executives wanted him to repeat the approach of his successful films and 'make that movie another five times'. How did he resist that pressure?

'Easy! I don't need money. When you don't need money, you're free: you can do what you want to do. The only thing they can offer you is money and if you don't need it, you don't want it, then there's nothing there. No enticement.'

After a music break, Young commented that McQueen tended to tackle difficult subject matters: IRA hunger strikes in Belfast, racism in the US Deep South. Did he ever encounter antagonism from locals who were keen to put these memories behind them?

'Slavery was something that no one wanted to talk about,' he agreed. 'But I remember our first [*12 Years a Slave*] Q&A, we were promoting the film in Florida, half an hour from where Trayvon Martin was killed [*in 2012*].

'A woman stood up and said, "I thank you for making this movie. I want to share this with everyone. I discovered this ten years ago, but I never spoke about it – my father, in the fifties, was poisoned for teaching kids how to read!" And the movie was a platform to allow people to have these conversations that had been buried very deep inside.'

Young: 'One of the things that propels you is you can't stand injustice. Is it very exhausting, a great drain on you, to follow through on that sensation? It's not an easy path you have chosen, artistically?'

'It's a pleasure! It's an honour! It's a privilege! I can do it – wow! I'm an artist. I try things through art. That's about it.'

Young touched briefly on a further McQueen project. In 2003, he had been embedded with British troops in Iraq as an officially appointed war artist. Initially, he had found the project challenging.

'I was filming out there, but I failed,' he told Young. 'It didn't add up at all. I remember sitting on the edge of my bed, feeling very frustrated – then I had an idea of making stamps with dead servicemen on them.'

McQueen reached out to the families of servicemen and women who had died in Iraq. Slowly but surely, 93 per cent of the people approached had agreed and given him images of the fallen. 'Then we went to Royal Mail, and *that's* when things didn't progress.'

McQueen explained that he had wanted this 2006 artwork, *King and Country*, to become actual postage stamps: 'I loved the idea of it going under the radar of the media and recognising this person, who had died for the country.' However, the postal service had declined the idea.

Young: 'Why?'

'You'll have to ask Royal Mail! They told me no, and I don't know why. I'm still waiting for an answer, so many years later.'

Wrapping up an engrossing dialogue, Young told her guest that he had been far more affable company than a lot of people had led her to believe was likely: 'They said, "Oh, I wonder what *he* will be like!"' And McQueen's answer was hugely telling.

'I'm a black man. I'm used to that!'

'Is that what it is?'

'Shall I say anything more? I'm a black man – what do *you* think? Before I walk in the room, people make a judgement. I don't care.'

'Does that make you annoyed?' wondered Kirsty Young.

'Totally not,' declared Steve McQueen. 'I wouldn't be talking to you if it did! I'd be in jail locked up somewhere, where a *lot* of people are, to be quite frank ...'

• • •

Since being cast away, Steve McQueen has continued to work across art forms and genres. In 2018 he co-wrote and directed a well-received crime thriller movie, *Widows*, starring Viola Davis and based on a 1983 British TV series written by Lynda La Plante. Two years later, he created and directed an acclaimed five-part BBC/Amazon Prime anthology film series, *Small Axe*, dramatising the lives of successive generations of Caribbean immigrants to Britain. He was also knighted for his services to film. In 2021, he co-directed *Uprising*, a BAFTA-winning three-part BBC documentary series focusing on seismic events within black communities in Britain in 1981, from the New Cross fire to the Brixton riots. In all these projects, McQueen's quest for the truth has continued to play the defining role.

DISCS CHOSEN
'Rock with You'
Michael Jackson

'Raspberry Beret'
Prince
'It's as if James Brown and the Beatles had a baby'

'Too Much Too Young'
The Specials
'The first people I looked up to – they were so cool'

❤ **'Blue in Green'**
Miles Davis
'This is going to be played at my funeral'

'Hell Is Round the Corner'
Tricky
'He was trying things out, experimenting ... genius'

Aria from Bach's *Goldberg Variations*
Glenn Gould
'It's a scent, I know it, so personal yet so foreign ...'

'This Woman's Work'
Kate Bush
'It evokes so much – it's art'

'Power'
Kanye West
'An artist who is pushing the medium'

BOOK
The Fire Next Time – James Baldwin
'Similar to a lot of the records I've played – it's all or nothing'

LUXURY ITEM
A compass
'To give me some idea of where the bloody hell I am'

51
LEMN SISSAY

POET, AUTHOR, BROADCASTER
11 October 2015

Some *Desert Island Discs* guests are an open book. They arrive on the island willing to shine a light into the deepest recesses of their life and soul. Others are more guarded. But what happens when a castaway, for more than half of their life, had absolutely no idea *who* they were?

Such was the fate of Lemn Sissay. Born in Wigan in 1967 but then taken from his Ethiopian single mother, he was raised (and renamed 'Norman Greenwood') by Christian foster parents who suddenly, when he was twelve, put him into a care home and abandoned him.

Alone in the world, he bounced around Lancashire's children's homes until, at seventeen, he left the care system and was given two pieces of paper: his birth certificate giving his real name, Lemn Sissay, and a 1968 letter from his birth mother to social services, pleading for his return.

From that point, Sissay's life had been a quest to find his real family and discover his true identity – but this search for himself had not stopped him becoming one of Britain's most gifted young poets, including being appointed official poet of the 2012 London Olympics.

By the time he arrived on the desert island in October 2015, Sissay was an acclaimed writer and broadcaster and had recently been appointed chancellor of Manchester University. Yet, as he told Kirsty Young, one huge question still hung over him: *Who am I?*

• • •

Greeting her guest, Young attempted to fill in some of his remarkable backstory. His mum came to England from Ethiopia to study in 1966. When she fell pregnant, she was sent to a mother-and-baby home in Lancashire. Her son was born. They were instantly wrenched apart.

'In the mother-and-baby homes, the nuns would make the women feel extremely guilty about the situation they were in,' said Sissay. 'And social workers would pressgang women into signing adoption papers.

'They might say to the woman, "We will sort out you seeing your child once a year." But they never got to see them. The social worker gave me to foster parents and said, "Treat this as an adoption – he's yours forever."'

As a baby, Sissay was given the first name of his social worker, Norman Goldthorpe, and the surname of his very religious white foster family,

Greenwood. What did he make, Young began to ask him, of his 'foster parents – in practice, adoptive parents ...'

'Mum and Dad!' Sissay interrupted her. 'They were my mum and dad!'

Young: 'Tell me about those early years with Mum and Dad.'

'Early years with Mum and Dad were going to church; hot summer's sticky tarmac roads; the flower park across the road. And magical summers in Scotland. We were half-Scottish and my grandfather was Duncan Monroe and wore a flat cap and loved me to bits.'

'Were you a happy little boy?'

'I was *so* happy! I thought the world smiled, and I didn't realise it was me smiling and the world smiling back at me. It was this great rhythm, this great bounce, between me and the world. I really, really loved having a family.'

After Sissay demonstrated his love for Scotland by choosing 'Amazing Grace', Young brought him to the cataclysmic event of his young life: being defenestrated from the family he adored.

'By the late seventies,' she said, 'your foster family – technically, but really your adoptive family – had three children that they'd given birth to, and they wanted you to leave?'

'Yes. I was twelve. I was right on the edge of adolescence. Because I was the eldest, they had not had an adolescent before, staying out late with my friends, or taking biscuits from the biscuit tin without saying "Please" or "Thank you!"

'So, they basically put me into care, into children's homes, and said they would never write to me or contact me again.'

'I'm scarcely able to get a handle on where to begin on this,' admitted Young, wondering how the young boy had made sense of it all. Sissay admitted he had *not* – but recently, after twenty-five years, he had got hold of his official papers from the authorities. They had contained clues.

'It's clear from the files that the foster parents blamed me for ... let me say this calmly.' He paused. 'Basically, I was [*seen as*] a threat within the family. I was a Trojan Horse: the devil was working inside of me. They were extremely religious.'

Young: 'What do you make of your adoptive parents' decision now?'

'I reserve the right to be emotional about what happened to me. You know, I reserve the right to feel. But I totally forgive my foster mother and father and entire family.'

'How do you manage that?'

'Because of what they did to me, I refused to believe in any higher power. But now I *do* believe that there is a God greater than my understanding and I have to trust that, and in trusting that, I can forgive.'

After a break for Górecki, Young commented that many abandoned children in the care system turn to alcohol, drugs or self-harming. Few of them find solace in poetry. How had Sissay come to do so?

'Well, I was in care *with* those children,' stressed her guest. 'I'll show you these tattoos. Fortunately, I'm black, so you can't see them.'

'The ones which you self-tattooed?'

'Yes, with Indian ink.' Sissay showed her his arm. 'I have "DA" here, which was my first girlfriend. This was self-harm: stabbing a blunt needle into your arm to write things that will be there forever.'

Young gently steered her guest back towards poetry by quoting W.H. Auden's definition of the artform to him: that it is 'articulating with words feelings that people cannot quite grasp and name'.

'That's a very beautiful description!' admired Sissay. 'Because poets are translators of the spirit and we feel a need to do that. I was a poet when I was thirteen.

'I made a BBC radio documentary where I went back to those children's homes. A cleaner said that I was always in the corner, writing away with my pen, scrumping up the paper and throwing it out. And I needed to *know* that was what I did when I was a child.

'To be able to write something that nobody had ever seen before was proof to me that I was alive. I can look back at my poems and say, *That is what I did think then*. Because I didn't have any family to tell me ... to argue with me about what I thought.'

Young: 'Our families are our sounding boards. Words became yours.'

'Absolutely.'

Young moved her guest's story forward. When he left the care system at seventeen, Sissay had moved into a flat and self-published his first book of poetry, *Perceptions of the Pen*. How had he done this?

'Dole money. I sold them for £2.95 to striking miners and their families. I sold out and then I printed some more. It meant so much. And then I came to Manchester to use those resources to find my family.'

Having, when he left care, been given the 1968 letter written by his mum, Yemarshet Sissay, pleading to have her baby son returned to her, Sissay tracked her down to the Gambia, where she was working for the UN. Their reunion was not a blissful one.

'When I found my mother, I looked like my father, the last time she saw him. If you're an adopted child, you forget you're the embodiment of the man who impregnated [*your mother*], and you're the same age, so you actually *look* like him.

'Do you know the first thing most people think when they find their family? *I don't want anything from you. Don't worry, Mum. I just want to see you.* I was twenty-one, in the Gambia, and I used to lie on the beach all day because she was at work and trying to avoid me.'

At that point, Sissay told Young, he had learned that his father had died in 1974 but had been a charismatic, ebullient figure. 'You are your father's son,' replied the host. The comment hit her guest hard.

'Not many people in my life say, "You are your father's son!" he said, softly. 'Just so you know. I don't hear that, because I don't have family. It's nice, but discombobulating to hear. In a good way ...'

After a break for Prince, Kirsty Young attempted to encapsulate her guest's scarcely believable life story to date, and asked him how it had helped to light his creative spark.

'You've spoken so eloquently about your life's work, which has been constructing your truth, and understanding yourself and your experience by curating your past,' she said. 'Has it worked?'

'The most important lesson I learned is to let go of it all,' concluded Lemn Sissay. 'To let go of the family, to let go of anybody who doesn't want to talk to me, and to accept anybody who does.

'It's not to hold on to this narrative and, sort of, *hug the bruise*. I am not defined by my scars but by the incredible ability to heal. You have to live in the present, which means I can laugh, and I can be scatty, and I can be depressed, and I can be *blah*, but I have to live in the present – not in the past, and certainly not in the future.

'And I find that the most powerful place to be. It's the only place to write from ...'

• • •

After he stopped by *Desert Island Discs*, the odyssey of self-discovery on which Lemn Sissay was engaged picked up pace. In the same year he appeared on the show, he was finally given all of the official documents covering his years in foster care and care homes, and was able to piece his brittle young life together. He compiled this knowledge into a bleak, heart-rending yet ultimately oddly life-affirming autobiography, *My Name Is Why*, in 2019, and won the PEN Pinter Prize, awarded to writers who take an 'unflinching, unswerving' view of the world and 'define the real truth of our lives and societies'. In 2021, Lemn Sissay was awarded an OBE for his services to literature and charity.

DISCS CHOSEN
'Taitu'
Yegna featuring Aster Aweke
An inspiring piece of music about the empowerment of women in Ethiopia

❤ **'Says'**
Nils Frahm
'This will lift up the sun at sunrise and lower it at sunset'

'Amazing Grace'
The Royal Scots Dragoon Guards

Górecki's Symphony No. 3: *Symphony of Sorrowful Songs*
Jerzy Katlewicz with the Polish National Symphony Orchestra of Katowice

'Cold'
Annie Lennox
'Every word is from me to my mum when I was twenty-one in the Gambia'

'Bridge Over Troubled Water'
Aretha Franklin
'This is about Black America'

'Nothing Compares 2U'
Prince
'Mr Prince – cool and a great musician'

'Better Not Look Down'
B.B. King

BOOK
The Koran
*'Because if I ever get saved by Muslim people in a boat, I'll go, "Look, I've got a Koran!"
And if it's Christians, I'll go, "Look, I've got a Bible!"'*

LUXURY ITEM
Pen and paper

'ISLE NEVER FORGET …'
'When I was asked to be on *Desert Island Discs*, I wasn't sure that I had earned the right. I thought of it as being for interviewees who were out of reach, in the stratosphere – your Rod Stewarts!

'I made a decision that I would give everything to the show and I would trust the process. I'd be an open book. I wouldn't try to curate my story. Wherever the conversation took me, I would go there and give Kirsty the information she wanted. That was the best way to make it work.

'*Desert Island Discs* caught me on this very singular journey I was on. It shone a massive spotlight on to this dark area that I was mining. I think it showed the world: *Wow, can you see this guy here, underneath the earth, digging for his family?*

'I split my life into pre-*Desert Island Discs* and post-*Desert Island Discs*. My programme got such a lot of attention that people could see that some wrong had been done to me. It made everybody realise what I was doing. It was magical and very powerful.

'It was one of the best experiences of my entire life. I had spent years running and running and running. The whole world was a blur. Then *Desert Island Discs* ran along at my side, and it said, "I see what you're doing, and it's OK! It's all good! Now, what music have you got on your headphones?"'

52

KEITH RICHARDS

GUITARIST, SONGWRITER, ROCK AND ROLL DEITY
25 October 2015

A serial societal rebel whose life's mission appeared to be perennial consumption of Jack Daniel's, cigarettes, sex, drugs and rock and roll, Keith Richards was arguably an unlikely candidate for longevity. Had he crashed and burned back in the sixties, few would have been surprised.

Well, maybe the devil has not just all the best tunes but the greatest resilience. Richards swaggered on to Kirsty Young's desert island at the age of seventy-one, in 2015, with more than half a century as the Rolling Stones' talismanic guitarist and co-songwriter behind him.

'If one single living person could be said to personify rock and roll, it is surely him,' acknowledged Young before going on to grill her guest on his famously debauched lifestyle, selling his soul to the blues, and his love–hate relationship with Mick Jagger. The twinkle in his eye was audible throughout.

• • •

Young opened with a consideration of Richards's lifelong image as an eternal rebel. 'Rebellion is a natural part of being young,' she mused. 'But at nearly seventy-two, does it come quite so naturally?'

'No,' chuckled Richards, before adding, in his inimitable nicotine rasp, 'I watch *other* people rebel now, really!'

The host wondered if there was a danger he was perceived as a bit of a cartoon, a 'sort of one-dimensional person'.

'That's the image, and it's a bit like a ball-and-chain. I recognise I'm in that sort of jail but, at the same time, I do love old Keef and I love the way people cotton on to him and say, "Go for it!" It's part of me, even if a lot of it's in the past.'

After Richards's first musical choice, almost inevitably Chuck Berry, Young took him back to his childhood. Her guest gave his mother, Doris, the credit for filling his family home with music.

'Doris, bless her heart, was a genius in the early fifties with the BBC dials,' he said. 'Because, what did you have? The Light Programme, the Home Service and the Third Programme?

'Doris would know where there would be half an hour of good music: Ella Fitzgerald, Sarah Vaughan, Billie Holiday, Louis Armstrong. I grew up listening to them because she had unerring aim on the dials.'

As an only child, Young asked Richards for his memories of being a boy. She understood that camping holidays had been involved?

'Yeah, we went camping. I was the third one on the tandem. They had a little seat built for me on the back. Mum and Dad would be pedalling to Dorset, or whatever, and I used to sit in the back and get sunstroke ...'

Another key family member, noted Young, was Richards's fiddle-playing grandfather, Gus Dupree. 'Something of an unconventional sort?'

'Yeah. He was the father of seven daughters! I was [*like*] the boy that he didn't have. He was more like a dad, or a friend, than a grandfather.

'He'd take me to music shops. We'd always go in around the back. We'd never go in the front door! I'd be in the back of these music stores for hours, watching people making and repairing guitars and violins. The smell of the glue. It just seemed like magical stuff going on.'

Young: 'Did he ever give you an instrument to hold, or play?'

'He teased me with a guitar! It was on a shelf that I couldn't reach, and he said, "If you can reach it, you can have it." So, I'm devising all sort of ways: putting books under the joint, loading cushions on it, just to try and get up there to it. Finally, I made it.

'He said, "OK, sit down." He showed me the rudiments of "Malagueña". He said, "If you can get your fingers around there, possibly you can be a guitar player." I worked at that "Malagueña" like mad and he let me have the guitar. To me, it was the prize of the century!'

Young wondered how Richards had first met his musical partner and foil, Mick Jagger. The pair went to the same primary school but only really became friends, Richards explained, after a fateful encounter on a train in 1961.

'I was going to Sidcup Art College and Mick was going to the London School of Economics. I'm sitting in a carriage and in walks Mick, who I hadn't seen in years. [*I said*:] "Oh wow, man, what's that under your arm?"

'He pulls out *The Best of Muddy Waters* and *Rockin' at the Hops* by Chuck Berry. American pressings: you can't get those recordings in England at the time. He said, "I send away to Chicago for them." I mean, *Wow! This man's organised!*'

Young: 'Was your writing partnership always an easy one?'

'Not always – but in the early days, *very* easy. It was like being on a factory line. I mean, "Satisfaction" is number one all over the world and Mick and I are going, "Fantastic, man!" Then there's a knock at the door and it's the record company: "Where's the follow-up?"'

The genesis of 'Satisfaction', explained Richards, had been remarkable. It was all down to his habit of sleeping with his arm around his guitar, with a recent invention, a cassette recorder, on his bedside table.

'Somehow, in the night, I got up and laid down the basic framework for "Satisfaction". The only way I knew that something had happened was I looked at the [*machine*]. I knew I'd put a brand-new tape in but the reel had gone the other way, [*meaning*] it was recorded.

'I thought maybe I'd hit the button in the wrong position in my sleep. So I roll it back, and listen back, and there is this very weak, faint idea of "Satisfaction". The riff, the first verse and the second, and then forty-five minutes of me snoring! By a miracle, captured on that little machine.'

After a blast of his 'great friend' Etta James, Young probed deeper into Richards's relationship with Jagger. 'You have said working with him is like working with Maria Callas and he can be a bit of a diva. How would he describe *you* to work with?'

'You'd better ask him!'

'Oh, I knew you'd say that!'

'In probably the same way, actually. No, Mick and I have a great relationship except when we don't, and that's when you hear about it.

'With Mick, I've always felt it's like a brother thing. What brothers *don't* fight occasionally? And we are always fighting for the right reasons. We just think that our version is more right than the other's.'

Young wondered what had kept the Rolling Stones going for more than fifty years. 'Why have you stuck together? You don't *need* to do it ...'

'I think it's because – especially on the last tour – we still think we're getting better. I mean, we could be fooling ourselves, but from the response from the audience, and the way I'm feeling and the way the boys are playing, there's the promise of more. And who's going to jump off a moving bus?'

Young turned to her castaway's well-documented history of drug use and abuse. How do drugs affect an artist's creativity?

'I think I should say there is no correlation between drugs and music, and how you perform it – but this is a lie. Some people can handle things and others can't. If the drugs become more important than the music, you've lost the battle.

'I've never felt that it did anything to my creativity, and it kept me up a lot at night, looking for the stuff! [*But*] it was something I had to stop, because I realised some experiments go on too long.'

Young reflected that many parents warn their kids off drugs. 'How does Keith Richards have that conversation with his offspring?!'

'I don't talk to them about it. If they bring it up, I will, but none of my kids have shown any interest in drugs at all. I haven't given them any talking to: "Don't do what Daddy did!" and all of that!'

Richards reflected that his first long-term partner, Anita Pallenberg, was his 'partner-in-crime' for much of his drug taking. Young asked him to revisit the worst moment of their relationship: the cot death of their son, Tara, in

1976, while he was away on tour with the Rolling Stones. 'Has that healed over time, or is it always there for you?'

'It was *such* a shock. I got a phone call in Paris, and I thought, "I'm going to go mad if I don't do this show tonight." Maybe it was just a sense of self-preservation. Because if I didn't go on the stage, I'd probably have shot myself.'

From this awful tragedy, Young turned to the happier business of Richard's thirty-year marriage to Patti Hansen. 'You married her on your fortieth birthday. And I'm wondering why such an unconventional soul as Keith Richards wanted to put a wedding ring on his finger?'

'I was in love with the woman. We'd been together two or three years and I saw the possibilities of what could happen if we got married. She is very maternal, as well. I thought, *If you're going to have more babies, this is the one I'd like to be the mother.* And it turned out to be true.'

Young: 'It can't be a breeze being married to a rock star. How has she dealt with the groupies?'

'I think she just blasts them out of the room! No, I know that if there's some groupie there, and Patti Hansen there – forget about it!'

Turning next to Richards's reputation for being indestructible, despite his often-self-damaging lifestyle, Young mentioned his nickname of 'The Man Who Death Forgot' and ran through a few of his health mishaps over the decades.

'You were very seriously electrocuted once during a soundcheck ...'

'Ah, that's par for the course!'

'You were concussed very badly when you fell off a ladder in your library and a lot of books fell on top of you ...'

'Yeah, I broke three ribs and punctured my lung!'

'You fell out of a coconut tree in Fiji, which resulted in two seizures and a blood clot on your brain ...'

'Ha! I'm accident prone, I guess!'

'Do you feel indestructible, or like your life is hanging by a thread?'

'Indestructible!' laughed Richards. 'If I can go through all that, I just think, *What more can they throw at me? What more can I throw at myself?*'

After a blast of Vivaldi, the host moved on to her castaway's distinctive look. 'Does Johnny Depp pay you royalties for nicking your image?'

'No. In fact, he was the first one to tell me: "You know I've nicked most of your moves?" "Oh, Johnny, feel free!"'

This insouciant charm had made the interview a rare delight. As it began to wind up, Kirsty Young attempted to get her guest to evaluate the seismic changes the sixties in general, and the Rolling Stones in particular, had wrought on British society.

'There was an entire shake-up of the establishment,' she said. 'With the perspective, and maybe even a little bit of the *wisdom*, you have now, what do you think that time in British cultural history actually changed? Do you feel like there was a permanent and significant shift?'

'I don't know if we did *anything* except do what generations do, which is to rebel,' concluded Keith Richards. 'And, of course, it was not that new, really! The music I play, and the Beatles played, which was part of the sixties revolution, was all taken from great American music ...'

• • •

Now seventy-eight, Keith Richards lives between his homes in Connecticut and the Turks & Caicos Islands, and Redlands, the Sussex mansion he bought in 1966. Despite the 2021 death of drummer Charlie Watts, the Rolling Stones roll on: in summer 2022, they commemorated their sixtieth – yes, sixtieth – anniversary with a tour of European stadia. A year after going on *Desert Island Discs*, Richards commented in an interview that, when his time comes, he'd like 'to croak, magnificently, on stage'. The only possible hurdle to this scheme is if he is, indeed, indestructible.

DISCS CHOSEN
'Wee Wee Hours'
Chuck Berry
'A great inspiration to me ...'

'You Win Again'
Hank Williams
'Hank was like listening to a blues singer. He was real'

'My True Story'
Aaron Neville
'One of the best voices in the world. And I'm playing guitar in the background'

'Sugar on the Floor'
Etta James
'I've got to have a soul diva in this list'

'Are You Lonely for Me Baby'
Freddie Scott
'Possibly the classic rhythm and blues record of all time'

❤ **'Extra Classic'**
Gregory Isaacs
'A song where I met my old lady'

First movement from 'Spring', Vivaldi's *Four Seasons*
Nigel Kennedy with the English Chamber Orchestra
'I'm thinking – desert island, NO seasons!'

'Key to the Highway'
Little Walter
'Top of the line rhythm and blues'

BOOK
Doctor Dogbody's Leg – James Norman Hall
'A collection of stories about a sailor with one leg. Every time he turns up, he gives you a different story about how he lost it'

LUXURY ITEM
A machete
'I have several machetes and I happen to know how handy they can be on islands'

53
RT HON. NICOLA STURGEON

SNP LEADER, SCOTTISH FIRST MINISTER
15 November 2015

Politicians can prove divisive castaways. The nature of their role means that their partisan supporters may be equalled, or even outnumbered, by listeners who are sorely tempted to write them off in disgust before they have even sat down and chosen their first record.

Nicola Sturgeon was not like that, opined Kirsty Young. Introducing the Scottish National Party leader and Scottish first minister in November 2015, the presenter marvelled that her fellow Scot was 'that rare and fascinating animal – a politician admired even by many who strongly disagree with her politics'.

It was a bold claim but it seemed highly justifiable as Young and her guest discussed Sturgeon's humble roots, her politicisation in her teens, the SNP's sweeping successes in that year's general election, the pros and cons of Scottish independence ... and, most importantly of all, ice-skating to Duran Duran in Irvine.

• • •

Young began by observing that the last twelve months in Nicola Sturgeon's political life – losing the Scottish independence referendum, becoming SNP leader, then 'decimating' Scottish Labour in the general election – had, from the outside, looked like a rollercoaster.

'It's been a rollercoaster from the *inside*, as well!' laughed the first minister. 'I came out of September 18 utterly devastated. I'd given my heart and soul to trying to win a Yes vote. We had come very close, closer than many people thought we might. I was in floods of tears.

'Then Alex Salmond told me he was going to step down the day after the referendum and there was no changing his mind. I actually tried very *hard* to change his mind. So suddenly, out of that exhaustion and devastation, I just saw my entire life change before me.'

Young moved on to the recent Westminster general election in which the SNP had, remarkably, won fifty-six out of fifty-nine Scottish seats. 'How was it for you?'

'Well, you know, it was euphoria! I've campaigned for the SNP all of my adult life and many, many times it seemed as if defeating Labour in the heartlands was just an impossible task. So, for suddenly that to happen was a huge moment of euphoria.'

Turning to Sturgeon's first musical choice, Cilla Black, Young teasingly asked if she had compiled her own list of records (rather than it being done by an adviser or spin doctor). Her guest's answer was emphatic.

'For better or worse, this is all me! And some of it – you can probably guess which ones – I might take some time to live down when I get back home to Scotland.'

In a conversational exchange that has since been severely overtaken by events, Young mused on the imminent Brexit referendum. Sturgeon argued that, should the UK vote to leave the EU and Scotland vote to remain, another independence referendum could be justified.

'I think Scotland *will* become an independent country,' she declared. 'I've believed that for a long time. I probably believe it more now than I did before the referendum.'

This belief, she stressed, was not rooted in hostility towards England: 'It upset me during the referendum campaign when I came up against people living in England who felt what Scotland was doing represented a rejection. Nothing could be further from what I believe in.

'My grandmother was English, from just outside Sunderland, and she was a big SNP supporter. She had this belief that Scotland should be an independent country. So I detested the sense that we were arguing for rejection of England as a country or as a people.'

Young turned to Sturgeon's background. When she was born in Irvine, Ayrshire, in 1970, her dental-nurse mum was just seventeen and her electrician dad was twenty-one. 'What are your very early memories of home life?' asked the host.

'Stability. Security. My mum and dad were my world when I was wee. If I look back now, and think about what my mum and dad instilled in me, it's nothing short of remarkable, in some ways.

'They were really young and their life experiences were limited. Nobody in either of their families had ever gone to university, yet they managed to raise this wee girl that had a belief that aspiring to go to university was something I should take for granted.'

Young reflected that Sturgeon had hit her teens in the eighties under Thatcherism, 'when people in Scotland were finding that Westminster in no way reflected the votes that they were putting in the ballot box. Did you find yourself connecting with politics as a reality that was impactful upon people's lives?'

'Absolutely! For me, my political awakening was all about what was happening around me. I remember me and all my friends thinking that if your dad lost his job, he might never work again. [*At school*], there was a sense you might end up without a job or a future.

'That all created a sense of hopelessness, it seemed to me, being inflicted by a government that most people in Scotland hadn't voted for and would *never* have voted for. That's what provoked me into politics.'

After a pause for Duran Duran, Young turned to a local institution that had been of huge importance to both of them as teenagers.

'Let's talk for a moment about Frosty's Ice Disco at the Magnum Centre [*in Irvine*]. There are very few opportunities for me to raise this on *Desert Island Discs*! Would you get the crimpers and eyeliner out and head down?'

'We are clearly of the same vintage, Kirsty! Yes, it was dayglo yellow or orange or pink legwarmers! The ice rink had a Saturday-night disco called Frosty's, where we used to skate round and round to Wham! and Duran Duran and Culture Club.'

Yet alongside these teenage pursuits, Sturgeon was becoming heavily politicised. She first stood for the SNP, in a no-hoper seat, at the age of twenty-one, in the 1992 general election. She then graduated in Law in Glasgow and became a solicitor, first in Stirling and then in Drumchapel.

'I learned a lot in that job,' she said. 'I learned very directly the issues and problems and challenges people come up against in their everyday lives and that, probably more than anything, equipped me for the job of being a member of Parliament.'

Sturgeon became an MSP in 1999. She admitted she could occasionally feel intimidated by aspects of the job – then, and even now.

'I'm first minister of Scotland but I still regularly feel overwhelmed by things I'm dealing with. Never more so than in a constituency surgery with someone at their wits' end because of a benefits problem, or dampness in their housing, or a partner trying to take away their kid.'

Her normal recourse, she told Young, was to vent her stress at home to her husband, SNP chief executive Peter Murrell.

'He bears the brunt of most of it! I'm quite hot-headed, impulsive – it doesn't last very long, thankfully, but if I'm confronted with a big problem, I go, "Oh, my goodness, what am I going to do about it?" He is very calm and doesn't get flustered – exactly what I need.'

Sturgeon and Murrell did not have children. Young mentioned that this had sometimes been weaponised against them by political opponents. 'What do you make of that?'

'It can be very hurtful, if I'm brutally honest about it. Because people make assumptions about why we don't have children and, frankly, people who make those assumptions know nothing of the reality of it.

'The assumption some people make, that I made a cold, calculated decision to put my career ahead of having a family, is not true. It never has been true. Sometimes things happen in life, and sometimes they don't.'

Politics, of course, is a rough business. Young reminded Sturgeon that not-terribly-complimentary labels hung around her neck by elements of the media had included 'nippy sweetie Nicola' and 'the most dangerous woman in Britain'. She also made an interesting observation.

'You've voiced annoyance about the amount of commentary about your appearance and your style,' she told her guest. 'Yet recently, you chose to appear in a seven-page spread in *Vogue*?'

'I don't mind saying, I struggle a bit with this,' admitted Sturgeon. 'On the one hand, I want politics to be accessible. But I'm equally of the view there is too much focus on what women wear and what their hair is like. That would be fine if it was applied to men as well.

'So, yes, I'm under no illusions that sometimes I might appear to be, and feel myself to be, a wee bit conflicted and contradicted on that ...'

After Kate Bush and 'Wuthering Heights', Young asked her castaway for her thoughts on the political truism that it is lonely at the top.

'I absolutely agree! The most eye-opening thing about my experience of the last twelve months is just how true that old cliché is. I had been Alex Salmond's deputy for ten years so I went into the job thinking I'd been so close to it for so long, I knew all there was to know about it. But nothing quite prepares you for that moment when you've got to take the first big decision. I remember that feeling in my stomach when I realised that I was having to take it, and the guy next door wasn't there any more to pass it over to.'

Young closed the interview by remarking that her guest freely admitted to not being 'a naturally gregarious person'. As first minster, did she ever have to put on a front to compensate for shyness?

'Less so now, I think,' mused Nicola Sturgeon. 'But in the early days of my career that was definitely, definitely an issue. I think I would don the persona of Nicola the politician and that was how I overcame the shyness.

'As I've got older, that divide between the real me and the politician me has definitely disappeared. So what you see now is the real me, for better or worse ...'

• • •

Under Sturgeon's leadership, the SNP were returned as the largest single party in the Scottish Parliamentary elections of both 2016, when they formed a minority government, and 2021, when they entered into a power-sharing agreement with the Scottish Greens. In 2022, she surpassed Alex Salmond's record to become Scotland's longest-serving first minister. Nicola Sturgeon's canny prediction regarding the Brexit referendum – that the UK might vote to leave the EU, and Scotland to remain – came true, and her government has proposed holding a second referendum on Scottish independence in October 2023.

DISCS CHOSEN
'Step Inside Love'
Cilla Black
'I had a childhood obsession with the wonderful Cilla Black'

'Freedom Come-All-Ye'
Pumeza Matshikiza
'A famous Scottish protest, anti-imperialist song'

'Ordinary World'
Duran Duran
'I'm just an eighties girl at heart'

'Letter from America'
The Proclaimers
'A soundtrack to my political awakening, and mentions my home town'

❤ **Robert Burns's 'My Love Is Like a Red, Red Rose'**
Eddi Reader
'Played just before Peter and I took our vows at our wedding'

'Wuthering Heights'
Kate Bush
'As a teenager, I played it incessantly while reading Emily Brontë'

'Sisters Are Doin' It for Themselves'
Eurythmics and Aretha Franklin
'It speaks to the feminist in me'

'(Something Inside) So Strong'
Labi Siffre
'The ultimate upbeat, optimistic, motivational song'

BOOK
Complete works of Jane Austen

LUXURY ITEM
Coffee machine
'The one thing I cannot do without in the morning is my injection of caffeine'

54
TOM HANKS

ACTOR, FILMMAKER
8 May 2016

There's always a slight element of risk whenever a bona fide Hollywood megastar strolls down the desert island beach. Will they open up and take the show's central conceit seriously, or is there a danger they may find it all a tad beneath them, like dear old Tallulah Bankhead?

Tom Hanks did anything but coast through his episode. A Tinseltown deity who had sprinkled his Midas touch over everything from *Big* to *Philadelphia*, from *Sleepless in Seattle* to *Forrest Gump*, from *Apollo 13* to *Saving Private Ryan*, he nevertheless threw himself into the show with relish.

Hunkering down in the sand with Kirsty Young in May 2016, he opened up about his frequently displaced childhood, his motivations to act, and whether all dramatic art is essentially a consideration of a deep human need not to be lonely. It was fascinating stuff.

• • •

Hanks began by teasing Young as she marvelled that her extensive research for the show had failed to find anybody with a single bad word to say about him. 'Oh, you've got to dig a little deeper!' he chided. 'I'm disappointed with the BBC that they can't come up with *someone*!'

Hanks paid tribute to a school drama teacher, Rawley Farnsworth, and to the director of *Forrest Gump*, Bob Zemeckis: 'I didn't know it, but Bob was making a movie about Vietnam-America!' Young then asked about her guest's eventful, frequently itinerant childhood.

'My father got out of the navy and he was working in a coffee shop in Berkeley, California, and there was a cute waitress,' he began. 'And they got married, had four kids and it lasted eleven years. But in the midst of that eleven years, they realised they had absolutely nothing in common. So they broke up.

'Mom could not afford to have four kids. My younger brother had just been born, so my dad took the three of us. He married another lady who was *also* a waitress in a coffee shop he was working in, and that lasted a couple of years.'

Hanks was seven when his parents split. Young asked how the kids coped with it.

'We were confused, because nobody explained anything to us. No one said, "Hey, listen, *you* guys are great! *You* haven't done anything wrong! Give us a couple of moments and we'll figure out what we're going to do ..." No one ever said that to us.'

As a boy, he lived in five houses in ten years. Young: 'This was to do with your father's employment?

'Yeah. He was in the restaurant business. It's very vagabond. He'd get a call at night from a buddy who desperately needed a head chef. My dad would say, "I'll be there at 8am!" and we'd pack a car and drive from Sacramento to my aunt's house in San Mateo, California. My dad would start the next day.'

Young quoted Hanks saying he had survived this constant upheaval by learning to act in 'whatever way was expected of him'.

'Well, I was never intimidated by a new atmosphere. I actually saw it as an adventure: *OK, we're living in an apartment now, with no lawn, and we had been in a ten-bedroom house out in the country. Well, there are advantages to this!*

'I didn't have a problem being the new guy in the classroom. I could make friends pretty quick: size up who was good and who was bad.'

Young: 'How much did you see of your mother, Janet?'

'I didn't see much of her until after my dad was divorced and they had made some peace between themselves. She lived in Red Bluff, a small farm town in northern California. And we were living in Oakland – as urban a place as you can possibly be.

'So, on school vacations, I'd get to go and be all, "Let's ride our bikes down to the river and go swimming! Hey, the county fair is coming!" I ended up having this exposure to small-town life that I thought was just as cool as big-town life.'

After a pause for Dusty Springfield, Young complimented her guest on the equanimity with which he had coped with his childhood upheavals. Had they helped to fire his creativity?

'Yes, because when you're eight, and you're living in a big house in a housing complex somewhere, and there's a pack of people all over the place, you learn how to navigate yourself. I ended up seeing examples of human behaviour and the human condition that impacted me.

'Some of my best friends were a Mexican family and they ate frijoles and their names were José and they spoke Spanish to their mum. [*And*] I had one brilliant teacher, Mrs Castle, who could engage my addled, attention-deficit-disorder eight-, nine- and ten-year old brain.'

Young: 'What do you think Mrs Castle saw in you?'

'I think she saw an energy and an interest in me that other kids did not have. I chewed up school like a delicious meal.'

Choosing the theme from Kubrick's 1968 movie *2001: A Space Odyssey*, Hanks identified seeing the film as 'the *Wow!* moment of my life: going from a kid trying to figure out what's interesting in this life, to a young man yearning to be an artist. How's that?'

Young: 'Did you make a plan, and think, *It's acting for me?*'

'No. I started asking myself a whole different set of questions: *How do I find the vocabulary for what's rattling around inside my head?* And I started going to the theatre, by myself, to see plays that I had no idea even existed.'

Young remarked that Hanks was by then a young teenager, emerging from a far-from-settled childhood. Had he been able to articulate his feelings? 'What *was* rattling around inside your head?'

The question seemed to throw her superstar guest. Hanks didn't speak for a few seconds. When he did, he sounded dumbfounded: 'Ah, *what* you've done to me!'

Young: 'I can only apologise!'

'No, it's all right. What it was, was the vocabulary of loneliness.'

Young: 'That comes up all the time. Every movie I watch you in seems to come down to a man's struggle with loneliness.'

Hanks responded by describing, at twenty, working with a director, Vincent Dowling. 'He was talking about Chekhov and said, "All the great plays are about loneliness." And it was a lightning bolt! I said, "*That's* why I'm here. *That's* why I went to the theatres by myself."'

Young: 'And is this how come a twenty-one-year-old aspiring, smart, relatively ambitious actor finds himself married and suddenly with two kids?'

'Yeah.'

'Quelling the loneliness?'

'I think so. I had kids very young. My son, Colin, was born when I was twenty-one, and my daughter, Elizabeth, four-and-a-half years later. By then, I thought I was rolling along with the natural order of things. Progressing towards my badge. My certificate of achievement.'

That first marriage ended. Hanks moved to LA and, in 1988, married his second, current wife, Rita Wilson. 'Yes. Two more kids!' It was also the year that he received his first Oscar nomination, for *Big*.

Young: 'Was it a coincidence that everything came together at that time? Or were you starting to feel you could walk in your shoes and fit them?'

'I would say that, by that time – I'm twenty-seven, twenty-eight – I've experienced enough bitter compromise that I overcame. There was stuff that should have destroyed me and it did not.

'You end up meeting that other person and it's: *Oh, she gets it. Guess what? I don't think I'm ever gonna be lonely any more!* That's what I felt when I met my wife.'

Young: 'You talked about beginning to want to act. Has the process of making it helped what was inside? Has it been a way for you to deal with the layers of your early experience?'

'You know, in some ways, I viewed it as having gone into the ministry! It *is*. Selfishly, it's a constant exercise in self-examination – but, beyond that,

Shakespeare said you've got to hold the mirror up to nature. And I think that's what our job is.'

Young moved on to Hanks's long relationship with Steven Spielberg. 'I heard that, for many years, you held back from working with him because you were friends. Is that true?'

'Yeah. We met socially because our wives are friends, and we had kids around the same age, but I never worked with him as my boss. And the first time we did, we had to have a conversation about that very thing.

'We did *Saving Private Ryan*, and he said, "Listen, we're friends, but on the set, I've got to be able to tell you whatever I have to tell you, and I can't be worried about hurting your feelings." And I said, "Dude, you're my boss on this!" And the air was cleared.'

Young: 'What do you and he do when you hang out?'

'We talk about movies, and new stuff. But I can never discount that this is the guy who made *Close Encounters of the Third Kind*!'

The conversation moved on. Selecting 'Once in a Lifetime' by Talking Heads, Hanks commented that that band's *Stop Making Sense* concert movie had been one of his first dates with Rita Wilson 'as a regular guy – because it was complex'.

Young: 'Complex because of your level of fame by that time?'

'No. The level of my place in life. We had met, and we really liked each other, but we had to put a kibosh on it because, socially, I had to get through an awful lot of stuff.

'One part of it was that I had to realise that, just like my dad, I was a divorced guy now, with kids. And that took some analysis in order to get through.'

Hanks mused on the nature of fame. The strangest bit, he reflected, was that 'because you're quote-unquote famous, you are viewed as being an authority on things. And I'm not an authority on anything outside of the best root beers or typewriters.'

As an engrossing episode neared its end, Young complimented her guest on being in such good physical shape as he stood on the verge of turning sixty. Hanks professed himself unconcerned by this landmark.

'Now – sixty? Well, both of us now, we're empty nesters. The kids are gone, and when that happens – *pff!* You're twenty-four again, man! Nothing is expected of us but to keep ourselves entertained. So, sixty means nothing to me!

'I went to see a neurologist and he said something so profound that I've since told everybody. He said, "Never retire. Do less, don't work at the same pace, but never give up that pursuit of the spark that has always fascinated you." So, I'm always reading, and *trying to get involved*, and being open to other people's inspiration ...'

• • •

Tom Hanks clearly took his neurologist's advice to heart – apart from the bit about working less. In 2022 alone, he starred in three major movies, including playing the lonely (that word again) puppet-maker Geppetto in *Pinocchio* and Colonel Tom Parker in *Elvis*. Over his forty-year career, he has won two Oscars, four Golden Globes and seven Emmys, and his movies have grossed close on $10 billion worldwide. And he *still* took *Desert Island Discs* incredibly seriously.

DISCS CHOSEN

'Relax-Ay-Voo'
Dean Martin and Line Renaud
'It has the most unhip lyric I have ever heard: "Let's put on our sneakers and slacks and relax-ay-voo ... "'

'There's a Place'
The Beatles
'To me, this was the birth of the Beatles'

'Doodlin''
Dusty Springfield
'She stirred my loins in ways that I didn't quite understand'

❤ **Strauss's Also sprach Zarathustra (theme from *2001: A Space Odyssey*)**
Vienna Philharmonic Orchestra
'This is the big magilla here!'

Soundtrack to *How the West Was Won*
MGM Studio Orchestra
'This is the soundtrack for America'

'Once in a Lifetime'
Talking Heads

'Mama Said Knock You Out'
LL Cool J
'There is something about the anger and joy inside this song'

'Layla'
Derek and the Dominoes
'The most beautiful recording ever made'

BOOK
A World Lit Only by Fire – William Manchester
'A book about the Dark Ages'

LUXURY ITEM
A Hermes 3000 manual typewriter and paper
'Made in Switzerland – indestructible'

55

DAVID NOTT

SURGEON, HUMANITARIAN
5 June 2016

Tom Hanks is a global superstar who would be recognised if he walked down the street in just about any town on Earth. He was a tremendous castaway – and yet, arguably, the appearance on the show of a largely unknown medic, three weeks later, was even more memorable.

A London-based NHS surgeon, David Nott regularly takes unpaid leave from his day job to perform operations in the world's war and crisis zones. Over the past twenty years, this humanitarian calling has taken him to Darfur, Sierra Leone, the Congo, Afghanistan, Gaza and Syria.

Operating on the victims of conflict in makeshift theatres on the very frontlines of war, Nott has saved innumerable lives – not to mention putting his own at risk many times. It was hard to listen to him talking to Kirsty Young without your mouth falling open.

• • •

Young opened an extraordinary encounter by quoting her guest saying saving lives while being so close to death was 'an amazing adrenalin buzz – it's not enjoyable but it's euphoric, like a drug.' She asked him to elucidate.

'I've operated in operating theatres and outside you can hear gunfire, and the sounds of bombs dropping, and you really have to concentrate on the patient,' Nott replied. 'It's the fact that it's so intense, and dangerous, and difficult that gives me the incredible adrenalin buzz.

'Being involved in the middle of it all, and very close to people who are being injured, and next door to people being shot, you realise that life is so precious and important, and to try and preserve it is a wonderful thing.'

Nott described the difficulties of operating in these 'surgically austere environments' with few medical resources – and the risk that anything could happen at any moment, as he had found in Syria in 2013.

'Our hospital was on the frontline,' he said. 'A patient lost two litres of blood from a chest drain. I was with a Syrian surgeon and as we did a thoracotomy, the door flew open and six fighters came in with AK-47s. The Syrian surgeon told me, "Just don't say anything."'

Young: 'You literally didn't dare open your mouth for fear of them finding out that you were British?'

'I didn't say a single word. One of the fighters came up, who was in charge of this group, and I suddenly realised that this was an ISIS fighter we were operating on, and the rest of the group were from ISIS.

'My colleague [*told them:*] "You mustn't disturb the senior surgeon who is trying to stop the bleeding on your colleague." I remember, so vividly, my legs shaking like jelly. They stayed in for about twenty minutes with their guns all pointed towards us on the floor.

'Then all of a sudden, something happened outside and six of them left. The senior guy stayed in and he was happy we'd stopped all the bleeding.'

Young: 'Do you care who you operate on?'

'I *don't* care who I operate on. That person – maybe I'd saved his life, maybe he might have changed his mind about things. We're all human beings.'

'All the things we know about what Islamic State are capable of,' Young persisted, 'and you *still* say, "This is a life worth saving"? He may well have gone on to kill many more people.'

'Exactly, but I don't know that and you don't know that. Nobody knows that. He may find out that he was operated on by a Christian surgeon in a hospital. I hope he *does* find out.'

Young delved into her guest's childhood. Born to a Welsh nurse mother and an Indian medical student father, he had spent his very early years at his grandparents' home in Wales. A lonely child, he built hundreds of Airfix model planes, a hobby that he part-credited with giving him the dexterity required for surgery.

Having been pressured to become a doctor by his father – 'he used to chase me upstairs to work, and sit in my room and watch me studying!' – Nott qualified and became a neurosurgeon. Young asked him about his first trip to a war zone, in Sarajevo in 1993.

'I remember the Ilyushin aircraft doing a nosedive into the airport. We got picked up by a bulletproof vehicle which took me to the hospital in the city centre. It was called the Swiss Cheese because it had so many holes in it. And I thought, *Why are you shooting at hospitals?*

'We didn't know much about trauma at the time. Patients would come in and, unfortunately, die on the operating theatre because it was so cold. And one particular time, I was operating on a young lad who'd had a fragment injury to a major blood vessel in his abdomen.

'I was operating with an anaesthetist and a scrub nurse and somebody else when a rocket hit the hospital. The lights went off and it was pitch black. Ten minutes passed. Nobody came. Fifteen minutes later the lights came on. And I was the only person in the operating theatre!

'Everybody had left, because they realised if the hospital had been completely destroyed, we were all going to die. But nobody had told *me*. That was a major moment for me: realising that you probably have to look after yourself sometimes rather than the patient.'

Young: 'Are there times when you have had to exit mid-operation?'

'I was in Gaza in 2014 during the Israeli–Palestinian conflict, working in one of the big hospitals in Gaza City. There was a little girl that came in, of about seven, who had her ... evisceration, it's called, where the bowels are hanging out of the abdominal wall.

'She had severe fragmentation injuries. Her fragment had gone into her bladder, her stomach, her spleen and so on. I prepared her with iodine. Somebody came in and said, "David, we need to go *now*. We need to leave the hospital because it's going to be blown up in five minutes."

'I looked at her. At the time, I had no family, I had no siblings, I had nobody. I was thinking, *OK, I'm on my own here. Am I going to leave this little girl on her own to die in the hospital?* I made a conscious decision that I wasn't going to, so I stayed with her.'

Young: 'You must tell me. What happened to the little girl?'

'All the staff in the operating theatre left. I looked at the anaesthetist and said, "Do you want to go?" He said, "No, I'll stay with you." The two of us stayed and operated, waiting for the bomb to explode on to the hospital. Nothing happened. I've got a picture of me and the little girl.'

After a pause for the Rolling Stones' 'Gimme Shelter', Young marvelled at how calmly her guest recounted his harrowing experiences. They must, she speculated, have had an effect on him. Had he suffered from PSTD?

'I *do* suffer, there's no doubt about it. It takes me about three months to get over a mission. More recently, I've suffered more severely. When I came back in 2014, I had almost psychotic post-traumatic stress.'

Nott gave Young a particularly striking example of this. Newly returned from Syria, he was invited to have lunch with the Queen.

'I came back around 15 October and, ten days later, I found myself sitting in Buckingham Palace with the Queen. She was sitting on my right, and when it came to my turn to start talking to her, she said, "I hear you've just come back from Aleppo?"

'I said, "Yes, I have." And I'd just come from ... the hospital being blown up; everything around me being shelled; coping with children who had been really badly damaged. And I didn't know what to say to her. It wasn't that I didn't *want* to talk to her: I just couldn't say anything.

'She picked this up, and said, "Well, shall I help you?" I thought, *How on earth can the Queen help me?* And all of a sudden, the courtiers brought the corgis, and they went under the table. She asked a courtier, "Can we open up *that* please?" and under a lid were a load of biscuits.

'She got one of the biscuits, broke it in two and said, "OK, why don't we feed the dogs?" So for twenty minutes the Queen and I, during this lunch, just fed the dogs. And she did it because she knew that I was so badly traumatised. The *humanity* of what she was doing was unbelievable.'

As the interview neared its close, Young commented that Nott had said earlier that he had no wife and family. Now, he had both. How had that happened?

'It was remarkable. I was in Gaza and thinking that I was going to die. I was in one of the shelters, and it felt like the apocalypse. The shelter that we were in was shaking and I thought, *I'm not going to survive this.*

'I'd met a girl at a charity event a few weeks earlier and thought, *God, she's nice*, but I thought nothing of it. And I thought, *Hang on, I don't think I'm going to survive this ... I'll send her an email.* So, I did. I wrote: "I met you, and I just want you to know that I think you're very nice."

'I would *never* have done that had I not thought I was going to die! So, she sent me an email back, saying, "Well, why don't we meet up?" I met her outside a tube station and it was love at first sight. I had three weeks with her until I went off to Syria.'

Nott and his wife, Elly, now had a daughter, Molly. Yet the surgeon told Young he had not been around for the whole of the pregnancy.

'When Elly was twenty-eight weeks pregnant, there was an earthquake in Nepal. She is so utterly supportive; she could see me itching. And she said to me, "David, if you really need to go, *go*. I'll be here and I'll call you if anything happens." So, I went off to Nepal for three weeks.'

Nott then chose Debussy's 'Clair de Lune', 'which is all about Elly and how, when I came back from Syria after six weeks, she was at the airport, waiting for me ...' His voice faltered as he broke down. Young kindly helped him out: 'Shall we just listen to it?'

As Debussy's strains receded, Kirsty Young attempted to pin down the urge behind her guest's humanitarian missions. There were, she said, many doctors and surgeons in Britain's NHS who all did their best for the patients they had. 'What's going on in *your* head that makes you think, *Well, I've got to leave this and take it somewhere else?* Because you're doing good where you are.'

'I *am* doing good where I am,' concurred David Nott. 'But, then again, there's lots of other people who can do my job. Out there [*in the war zones*], with the knowledge that I have, if I *don't* go, those patients will die.

'If I stay here, I'm not hugely, one hundred per cent, required. Whereas there, I am. And *that's* the difference.'

• • •

Shortly before going on *Desert Island Discs*, Nott and his wife, Elly, set up the David Nott Foundation to provide surgical training for doctors and nurses working in war and disaster zones. Their courses focus on relevant skills such as treating gunshot wounds and vascular surgery, and have, to date, been held on the frontlines in Yemen, Libya and Iraq. Inevitably, as soon as Russia invaded Ukraine in 2022, David Nott headed to that war-torn land so that he could help to train surgeons.

DISCS CHOSEN
'Myfanwy'
Treorchy Male Voice Choir and the Jonathan Price String Ensemble
'I remember my grandparents singing each other this song'

'Gadael'
Triban
'It's "Leaving on a Jet Plane" in Welsh. My mother introduced me to it'

'Stairway to Heaven'
Led Zeppelin

'Cavatina' (theme from *The Deer Hunter*)
John Williams
'One of my great films of all time'

'Gimme Shelter'
Rolling Stones
'I take it with me when I go on my visits'

'Fix You'
Coldplay
'I've been around the world fixing people and I got to the stage where I needed fixing myself'

'Clair de Lune' from Debussy's *Suite bergamasque*
James Rhodes

❤ **'Good Golly Miss Molly'**
Little Richard
'It has to be about Molly ... and it's the best rock and roll one can ever listen to'

BOOK
Kallimni 'Arabi Mazboot (Arabic textbook)
Samia Louis
'I really want to learn Arabic'

LUXURY ITEM
Fishing rod
'I'm going to catch that elusive salmon which I've never caught'

56

LEVI ROOTS

CHEF, ENTREPRENEUR
17 July 2016

Many *Desert Island Discs* castaways have been famous for almost their entire lives. Yet there is a strong case that the most intriguing life stories, and thus episodes, belong to the guests who have found fame, success and public profile relatively late in life.

Before he went on the BBC's *Dragon's Den* in 2007, Levi Roots was a struggling Brixton musician who, as a sideline, sold his Reggae Reggae BBQ jerk sauce at Notting Hill Carnival each year. Roots sang on the TV show, seduced two dragons into investing in the sauce ... and his life turned around.

By the time he loped on to Kirsty Young's island in 2016, Roots had seen his cottage industry expand to a £30-million business with more than fifty product lines and even a Reggae Reggae Sauce restaurant. It was all the more impressive since, as he told Young, it had been built from such unpromising beginnings ...

• • •

After Roots and Young exchanged a few Caribbean cooking tips, the host turned to the incredible transformation in her guest's life: 'Do you ever look at it and say, "How? What? Wait a minute, how did *this* happen?"'

'I do. Every day, because I thought I was quite rubbish in the *Dragon's Den*, personally. I'm scared to look at the programme now to see how rubbish I really was.'

After Root's first musical choice, Stevie Wonder's 'Master Blaster (Jammin')', Young complimented him on being a 'sharp-dressed man' and described his studio attire to the listeners.

'You are in a bespoke suit. You have wonderful jewellery on, some of it encrusted with diamonds. You've got beads in your hair. Is it true you have thirty-five Ozwald Boateng suits?'

'Yeah. That's the only thing I spend my money on! But I do think it's important that you have to look the part when you're in business, especially for someone like myself, with my background. If you want to inspire others, you've got to be able to inspire your own self.'

Young: 'You became a Rastafarian when you were eighteen. You'd been brought up, before then, as a Christian?'

'Yeah. It was about finding myself. I was a bit lost before Rastafari came into my life. My father gave me the name "Keith Graham" and I looked it up and saw it was Scottish. And I didn't feel Scottish! Where did I fit into the world? And it was the music of Bob Marley.

'I started to listen to his albums and I got the drift of what Rasta was saying: *you are African, and you should have a name that identifies with who you are.* And I wanted to be Levi Roots, not Keith Graham.'

A blast of Marley followed, then Young turned to Roots's childhood. He was born in Jamaica in 1958, the youngest of five children. As was the custom, his parents emigrated to England, intending to build a life there then send for their children.

Roots was left in the care of his grandmother, Miriam. 'Do you have memories of early family life?' asked Young.

'Indeed. I have beautiful memories of my wonderful grandma. To me, she was mum, dad and granny and everything in one, because I was a bit young when my parents left. I was four.

'My grandfather had a little farm. We were so poor: I don't remember she ever going to a supermarket. Everything that went into the pot she could send me out in the garden to pick, or send my grandfather to catch a chicken.

'It was what we call yard food: food that was grown in the yard. Yet even though we were a poor family, her skill was using spices to make a delicious meal. It would draw the neighbours from miles around when she was cooking!'

Roots's elder siblings left, one-by-one, to join their parents in London. His turn came when he was ten and a half.

'My suitcase arrived, finally. I'd seen my brothers' and sisters' suitcases arriving every year but I didn't think it would happen to me. I was too close to my grandma: I never thought I would leave her. It was one of the saddest things I remember as a child.

'She was saying: "Look after yourself! When you get to the UK, eat fresh food!" And I never saw her again. She died four or five years after me coming to the UK, and our memories is what I try to keep alive in my products and my sauces.'

Overcome by emotion, Roots found it hard to speak – 'Oh, God!' as he played Dionne Warwick's 'Walk On By' for his nan. And when he arrived in London, he told Young, life was not easy. His father, in particular, was 'a stranger' to him.

'I didn't know this man, so I struggled when I came over. I didn't get the attention that I thought I deserved or I wanted from him. And I don't think he knew what to do with me.

'I'd see his fantastic Wolseley car outside, big and everything, and my secret wish was that one day, my dad would say, "Come on, son, let's go for a drive, just the two of us, and eat and have a chat!" But it never happened.'

Unable to read when he arrived in London, Roots knuckled down and studied hard with his mother's help. When he left school in 1976, he became a lathe operator. He also had his first child. 'How did you cope at the time?' asked Young.

'I coped by having fun! I'd left home and was involved in music. I'd met the great Lloyd Coxsone and his sound system and he'd said, "Hey, you're an eighteen-year-old kid! Come along and I'll produce you!"'

Roots did two years in his engineering job but the pull of music was too strong. 'I felt like I didn't belong pulling on a lathe machine. I belonged on a stage with a microphone in my hand. So I gave up the job, to my father's shock, and joined the circus – in my case, the sound system.'

This was also the time, commented Young, of the Brixton riots. 'As a young Rastafarian living in Brixton, what do you remember?'

'Ooh, I remember terrible housing. I remember lack of jobs. I remember a police state ...'

'A police state? Those are strong words!'

'Yes. And, most importantly, I remember the stop-and-search laws, the scourge of all black boys and girls. You didn't have to do anything to get into trouble. The police could be intrusive and stop and search you, and you could spend the night in a police prison.'

Young: 'This happened to you repeatedly, did it?'

'Of course! Absolutely! And I was rebellious, like many youths back then. You wanted change.'

Young fast-forwarded to 1986. 'In your late twenties, you were running a youth and community centre in Brixton. You were convicted of unlawful possession of a firearm and conspiracy to supply Class A drugs. You say you were a good prisoner. What *is* a good prisoner?'

'A good prisoner is one that *finds* himself or herself. Being incarcerated gives you that opportunity to find the elusive self. I don't think I turned to be good overnight: it's having the time to become good. Because you went in bad. That's why you're there in the first place.

'I made the metamorphosis from Keith, the part of me that got me into trouble and was unfocused, and it allowed the Levi part of me to come through: the person that loves to cook and to sing and to articulate.'

When Roots came out of jail, he focused on his longstanding side business of making and selling jerk sauce, remembered from his grandma's cooking, at Notting Hill Carnival. At a food trade show, a BBC producer asked him to go on *Dragons' Den*. He had never heard of it.

Young: 'And you told your family. What did your kids say?'

'My kids' words was: "Dad, no one with three-foot-long dreadlocks is going to be no dragon-slayer on *Dragons' Den*!" They were thinking that Dad on TV with a guitar, on a show about finance and enterprise, was not going to be cool for them!

'But if you've got kids and they think that you're not cool to do something, what do you do? You do it just to prove them wrong!'

Young recapped that Roots's *Dragons' Den* appearance had not been a total success. He messed up his figures and his financial presentation. Yet he charmed two dragons into investing, and just weeks later, his sauce was on the shelves in Sainsbury's.

'Did you walk into a Sainsbury's and buy some?'

'I did! I did!'

Reggae Reggae Sauce was a phenomenal success from the off and had not stopped growing since. Yet after Beyoncé's 'Single Ladies', Young turned to Roots's own, rather active past romantic life.

'You're a father of eight by seven different mothers. You've never been married. Tell me about that.'

'Lord! How long have you got? I love my kids. They're the most valuable thing that I have. And I've now learned how to be a proper father.

'I do think I was rubbish in my earlier years. My young son now is three-and-a-half, and my last child before him is twenty-eight. I do remember all of these moments when I should have been there that I wasn't. There are a lot of memories [*of*] missed opportunities that come floating by.

'But I do think, the way I've lived my life since then – hopefully, they'll look at that and be very proud that their father has managed to be able to do these things for them.'

Kirsty Young offered some closing thoughts: 'You are someone with a lot of charisma and you seem very at home in your skin. When you think about the time in prison, and the young man who didn't have the father he needed – does where you are now feel a good place?'

'I am the best of me,' answered Levi Roots. 'I do think I've got to that point where I'm able to focus. I know what I can give. So, in my skin at the moment, I *do* feel fulfilled ...'

• • •

Six years on, Levi Roots's Reggae Reggae Sauce empire continues to grow and diversify via new product lines and tie-ups with companies such as KFC. As a philanthropist keen to help young people not to make his own early-life mistakes, Roots speaks at scores of schools, youth centres and prisons every year, and is an ambassador for the Prince's Trust. In 2021, he was appointed chair of St Pauls Carnival in Bristol. He now owns even more than thirty-five Ozwald Boateng suits.

DISCS CHOSEN

'Master Blaster (Jammin')'
Stevie Wonder
'It is so Jamaican but it is still Stevie'

'War'
Bob Marley and the Wailers
'A massive inspiration for me'

❤ **'Walk On By'**
Dionne Warwick
'It sounds like my grandma singing. She had a great voice'

'Many Rivers to Cross'
Jimmy Cliff

'Respect'
Aretha Franklin
'I'd like to send this request to my mum'

'Declaration of Rights'
The Abyssinians
'Anyone who knows my life in sound system will say, "Yeah, this is a Levi Roots style!"'

'Single Ladies (Put a Ring on It)'
Beyoncé
'On a desert island, I'm going to need a party-vibes feeling'

'Mama Africa'
Garnett Silk
'A lot of people thought he would've been the next Bob Marley'

BOOK
Long Walk to Freedom – Nelson Mandela

LUXURY ITEM
His guitar
'I don't think I could leave that behind ...'

'ISLE NEVER FORGET ...'
'I'm a music fan, so I've loved listening to *Desert Island Discs* over the years, but I never in a million years thought I'd end up on there! I thought it was meant for big movie stars and rock stars, not a sauce man from Brixton!

'Normally people avoid asking me personal questions – it's rare to get interviewed by someone proper, like Kirsty! I didn't mind talking about going to prison because I use that experience now to inspire young kids. But I was *very* apprehensive at being asked about my family.

'I'd never talked about my father before. It's not the Caribbean way to *go deep* about your parents and your family. But I know how deep this show goes and, if I'm asked a question, I will always answer. So, I did, even when it made me feel queasy.

'How did it compare to *Dragons' Den*? On *Dragons' Den*, I got to do what I love best, which is sing. *Desert Island Discs* was like the bit after I stopped singing on *Dragons' Den*, when I had to answer questions and I was like a rabbit in the headlights!

'After I'd been on *Desert Island Discs*, I felt nervous my family might have disagreed with me saying some things. But later, I felt happier that those things were out of me now and I had talked about them. And I loved talking about the music!'

57
DAVINA McCALL

TELEVISION PRESENTER
11 December 2016

Some public figures are so warm and ubiquitous that you can feel you know them like a much-loved friend. It's only when they appear on a forum such as *Desert Island Discs* that you realise there may be far more depth and darkness to them than you had imagined.

In 2016, there were few more high-profile and high-octane presenters on British TV than Davina McCall. Her effervescent energy and risqué sense of fun had enlivened prime-time reality and game shows from *Streetmate* to *Big Brother* and *The Million Pound Drop* to *The Jump*.

McCall seemed a perennial fount of positivity, yet her trip to Kirsty Young's island saw her share tales of a chaotic childhood, parental neglect and betrayal, and overcoming potentially life-ruining drug addiction. There had always been, it was clear, a lot going on behind that upbeat front.

• • •

Young began by commenting that all three of Davina McCall's children with her husband, Matthew Robertson, had been born in September. Was this *really* to avoid clashing with recordings of *Big Brother*?

'It's true,' confessed McCall. 'I loved *Big Brother* so much that the idea of anybody else presenting it was, like, over my dead body! So I told Matthew, "We are *not* trying for a baby until after December." And there we are – three birthdays in September!'

The conversation moved quickly on to McCall's childhood. Her parents, Andrew and Florence, had met on a ferry from France to England. Her mother was young, French, reckless, and had alcohol and drug issues. 'How did that affect her behaviour as a mum?' asked Young.

'She would just forget me. When I was about eight or nine, I nearly drowned. I was hit on the head in the sea by a little boat. I choked. A woman saw it, waded out to me, lifted me out of the water, and hugged me. I remember hugging her really tight and calming down.

'I remember standing on the beach, thinking, *Shall I go and tell Mummy?* Then thinking, *Well, there's no point. She won't mother me.* She always, kind of, came first. We always worked around her.'

The parents had divorced when McCall was three. Her father was granted custody of her, while her mother returned to France with her elder sister. The young Davina went to live with her dad's parents in Surrey.

'How much was explained to you about what was happening?' asked Young.

'Nothing, actually. I knew that my mum had gone somewhere and I didn't know why she hadn't come back. And I felt guilty, because I loved my granny so much, but I thought, *She probably doesn't want me here.* So, it was very confusing.'

In her school holidays, McCall would stay with her mum's parents in France. 'Do you have memories?' asked Young.

'Yes. My mum's parents were pretty solid but Mum would come and go in chaos. I thought she was kind of brilliant: leg-crossingly embarrassing but exciting. She had no boundaries for me, so I could go out whenever I wanted.

'I could wear whatever I wanted: high heels, make-up. Do anything, and I mean *anything*. I thought at the time it was great, but I look back now and it was *so* destructive.'

McCall recalled living 'two lives' – a solid existence in England with her grandparents, punctuated by pockets of wildness in France with her mum.

'I couldn't really talk about what was going on in France. I wanted to protect my mum: I was worried people might not let me go back if I told them what was happening. I wanted to see her ... but I knew what was going on was pretty mad.'

Young asked if any particularly outrageous events stuck in her mind.

'We were out once and she was in an electric-blue floor-length fur coat and she wasn't wearing anything underneath it. She would just flash people because she thought it was funny, and I was dying inside.

'Guys giving her interest, and her loving the interest, but me hating the interest that these men are giving her and feeling protective but feeling vulnerable and needing protection myself. And not knowing where to get it and seeing people pity me.'

'How old were you?'

'Ten. Eleven.'

At thirteen, McCall moved out of her grandparents' to live with her father and stepmother in London. She took to it immediately.

'I loved Shepherd's Bush – it had reggae sound systems in the streets! It was so exciting and it felt like being reborn. Unfortunately, I think I was already careering slightly off the rails. I was already smoking and, sort of, drinking.'

McCall initially did well at school but then stopped working and flunked her A levels. 'I fell into a job at [*model agency*] Models 1, on the men's desk representing male models, which at nineteen years old was the best job ever!

'But all the time I was trying to either sing or do something musical. I was running nightclubs at the weekend and clubbing. Everything was kind of pointing towards trying to get a career in music.

'I just wore the most amazing clothes, I used to go out in next to nothing.

I went out once in a body-glove swimming costume and a pair of Timber-lands, and that was it.'

McCall was taking drugs recreationally, said Young, then 'the fun turned into something else. By your late teens, what was the reality of your drug use?'

'I thought I had it all under control but it was white-knuckling: "Right, I'm *definitely* not going to do anything until Friday night!" Then Friday night would turn into Thursday night, just to see me through. And the weekends were getting longer and longer.

'I'd carefully stayed away from alcohol, because I could see my mother was an alcoholic. I thought, *I'm being really good, so I'll take a few drugs instead. I mean, what kind of common sense is that? Ridiculous!* I ended up a complete mess.'

Young: 'When you were a complete mess, what did your life look like?'

'Until the last year, you wouldn't have *known* my life was a complete mess. I mean, I had a job. I didn't steal. I didn't inject. These things made me different from those awful drug addicts over there: *I'm not as bad as THEM, so it's OK, I'll carry on!*'

'And what was the turning point?'

'When I realised people knew I had a problem with drugs. My best friend, Sarah, said to me: "You know, you're the topic of every dinner party I go to: what an absolute mess you are. I know you're lying to me. I know you're taking heroin. I can't hang out with you any more."'

Young: 'What did you do when she said that?'

'Got really angry. Swore at her – "What kind of friend are *you*?" Got in her face and left. And then just cried non-stop for about eight hours. I thought, *This is it. I've got to stop.* I had nowhere to go except to stop. So I did. I went to a meeting that day.'

'That day?'

'Yes. I took a bunch of flowers to my friend, feeling sick and awful, and said, "You're right. I'm a mess and I'm going to change." And I went to a meeting that night at six o'clock. I thought they were all going to go: "Junkie scum, get out!" But they were really nice. And that was *it*.'

McCall secured a job at MTV that was to lead to her hugely successful presenting career. Fast-forwarding, Young wondered how much what had happened to her as a child had influenced how she initially tried to be a mum to her own kids.

'I was constantly just trying to be perfect. I was so uptight and tense. I thought I was being so relaxed but, looking back, I gave myself such a hard time about everything. I was desperate not to repeat the same mistakes, and *to be everything.*

'But you *can't* be everything all the time. It's impossible. Also, Matthew needs attention, and I need attention, and there's life. I had to work. So I had to let go of the reins a bit. I became a bit of a control freak. It was exhausting.'

Young: 'Did your relationship with your mother repair at some point?'

'For a moment. Nanoseconds. When I married Matthew, she'd been clean and sober for a while and we'd been speaking. I said, "I'd love you to come to the wedding," so she did. And before, we went to a meeting, sat together, both cried, held hands, and it felt like ...'

Young: 'An AA meeting?'

'Narcotics Anonymous. It was what I'd always dreamed of: my mum supporting me and me supporting her. It was beautiful. We had a great time at the wedding, and Matthew and I popped over to Paris as part of our honeymoon to see my mum.

'Six months later, Matthew took me to Scotland for my birthday. On the day of my birthday, a piece came out in the paper and it was a headline something like: MUMMY – I NEED A MEETING!

'She'd sold the story about me and her going to Narcotics Anonymous. I'd *never* talked about going to NA: it's an anonymous fellowship. And she sold pictures of our honeymoon. And it was terrible, the worst: like being stabbed in the heart and she twisted it hard.

'And she did that a couple more times. She sold a couple more stories and I kept going back and trying to build bridges again. And I'd think that *this* time, it would be different.'

Young: 'Did it end with an acceptance by you that this simply cannot be repaired?'

'I was in counselling when she got really sick at the end, to try to come to terms with the fact that my mother will never mother me. I got the news that she was very, very poorly and I lay in bed with my palms facing upwards and said out loud, "I forgive you. *I forgive you.*" Then a few days later, she died.

'My sister and I hugged each other, we cried a bit, and then she said, "I feel relieved." And I said, "So do I." For the first time, we could stop hoping that our mother could be anything other than what she is, and we could just live with her memory. And remember her more fondly ...'

It was a harrowing tale, but Davina McCall had bounced back, and then some. For her last disc, she chose 'Angel' by Sarah McLachlan, which her husband had introduced her to: 'I fell in love with *her* as I fell in love with *him*, and this was our music. I probably shouldn't say any more.'

Young: 'You've got a very cheeky look on your face?'

'It was our sexy music, if you need to know, Kirsty ...'

• • •

A year after her *Desert Island Discs* appearance, Davina McCall was to separate and divorce from her husband, Matthew, after seventeen years of marriage. She has continued to host TV reality and game shows including

This Time Next Year and *Davina McCall's Language of Love* (which attempts to match-make couples with no shared language) and is now a judge on both *The Masked Singer* and *The Masked Dancer*. There have also been projects with greater gravitas: her Channel 4 documentary *Sex, Myths and the Menopause*, bursting the many taboos surrounding female midlife changes, preceded a book, *Menopausing*, on the same topic.

DISCS CHOSEN
'Our Mutual Friend'
The Divine Comedy
'Neil Hannon is just a genius'

Overture to Tchaikovsky's *The Nutcracker Suite*
Duke Ellington and His Orchestra
'The most brilliant big band version'

'Your Kiss Is Sweet'
Syreeta

'One Nation Under a Groove'
Funkadelic
'From when I started really beginning to enjoy music'

'Can You Feel It (Can You Party)'
Todd Terry
McCall: 'Could you feel it?'
Young: 'I could, just about ...'

'Jig of Life'
Kate Bush
'Every single track, every breath she takes, is magic'

'Never Let Her Slip Away'
Andrew Gold
'In memory of my lovely sister – we played it at her funeral'

❤ **'Angel'**
Sarah McLachlan

BOOK
Still Life with Woodpecker – Tom Robbins
'A love story set on a pack of Camel cigarettes'

LUXURY ITEM

A bath

'I find true peace in my bath. My children know that when I'm in the bath, I'm out of bounds'

'ISLE NEVER FORGET ...'

'Until recent years, I've always considered myself a TV lightweight. I've always done easy-going entertainment shows that are a bit of fun. And I looked at *Desert Island Discs* as a highbrow, intellectual programme, and thought I'd literally be the last person in the world they'd want on.

'So, when I got invited, I looked over both of my shoulders and thought, *What, me? Huh? Are you sure you've got the right person? Is there not a brain surgeon in Massachusetts called Davina McCall that you've mistaken me for?*

'I felt safe with Kirsty. She is an extraordinary interviewer. She's just amazing at drawing out bits of people that you'd never normally get to see. She does all of the research first, then she asks questions that get right under the skin.

'Her questions will *wind* you. It's like being punched in the solar plexus. And it's not because it's too intimate, or personal, or tabloid-y a question, but because it is a question you have hidden in your mind as so dark and deep that you don't want to look at it.

'I knew I could go on and either be light and fluffy or be *real*, and I decided to be real. I enjoyed it. It felt good. And when I listened to it, I didn't spend the next two days on the sofa with my legs crossed and a pillow over my face, thinking, *Why did I say THAT?* I wasn't embarrassed by it.

'What I enjoyed most about *Desert Island Discs* was I felt maybe people saw another side of me. They may have formed an opinion of me as one person – and I *am* that person: annoyingly enthusiastic, and a bit lewd – but I also have another side that most people don't get to see.

'The production company that I made *The Jump* with gave me the best present ever. I used to DJ, so I love a good record box, and they gave me a record box with the vinyl versions of all of my desert island discs in it. *AND HOW COOL IS THAT?'*

58

BRUCE SPRINGSTEEN

SINGER, SONGWRITER, AMERICAN ICON
18 December 2016

Bruce Springsteen has spent fifty years being the musical voice of the American everyman. He is, as Kirsty Young reflected, 'the bard of blue-collar America'. So it should be no surprise that he pitched up on the desert island and turned out to be a straight-down-the-line regular guy.

Springsteen arrived having just published his autobiography, *Born to Run*, and was thus in reflective mood. He was fascinating talking about his insecure childhood in New Jersey and the insatiable drive that made him turn to writing and playing music as 'something that would cut me out as different'.

The man rock fans call 'The Boss' is such a global megastar that some of the story he recounted was known, but much of it wasn't – not least his surprising descriptions of his recurring depression which, even now in his later life, would still sometimes settle on him. By the end, you knew Springsteen a little better than you'd always thought you did.

• • •

Kirsty Young opened by referencing the title of Springsteen's memoir, *Born to Run*, named after the signature song he had written at the age of twenty-four and that he still played at every show. 'What does it mean to you now?'

'It takes you back, it takes you forward,' he replied. 'I suppose the show builds to it. It's a cathartic moment and it's still something I find a lot of satisfaction in playing.'

Young took him back further still, to his early 1950s childhood in New Jersey, living with his parents and grandparents and surrounded by aunts and uncles. 'What are your earliest memories of that time?'

'It's always the church, the church, the church. It was the centre of our existence. What I remember most is just the tall steeple at the end of the corner and the red bricks of the church.

'It was our second home: you lived there every Sunday and Friday. We saw every wedding, every funeral, because we lived next door so there was always a show going on. Somebody was always either getting married or getting dead! It was an enormous centre of my childhood.'

Young: 'It all sounds idyllic, but you say you grew up among "very ill, secretive people with disturbing, unpredictable behaviours"?'

'Yes. There was a lot of illness that runs through my family, on the Irish side particularly but even somewhat on the Italians' also.'

'And the behaviour might be what?'

'Depression, and a mental illness that just swept through my family and gets passed on down.'

Springsteen described how his Italian mother, Adele, and her two sisters were a fount of 'endless optimism ... they always decided life was worth living ... they insisted on joy and beauty'. Another major shaping influence was his paternal grandmother, who indulged him endlessly.

'She'd had a child, my father's sister, who'd died, aged five, in a traffic accident around the corner from my home. It put her in bed for several years. When I came along, that was the first new child in the family since that had happened, and it gave me quite a bit of licence.'

Young: 'What did she let you get away with?'

'I was doing a lot of strange things when I was a young kid. I was staying up until 3am and waking up at three in the afternoon!'

After a break for the Beatles, Young moved to Springsteen's teens. He was a regular at Friday-night Young Men's Christian Association dances, doing 'the Monkey, the Swim, the Jerk, the Pony, the Mashed Potato ... how did you learn the dances and what did you look like?'

'I'm sure a complete fool!' laughed her guest. 'But before I played the guitar, I realised that girls love to dance, so I'd spend a lot of time at home in front of the mirror, practising the different dance moves.

'I would use my mother's hair clips to pin my hair down then I'd sleep on it *exactly right* on the pillow – I had curly Italian hair, but I'd pin it down till it was as straight as Brian Jones's. Black chinos, black shoes, pointy toes, red socks, red shirt and my hair *just so*, and off I'd go.'

Prompted by Young, Springsteen described his first ever show in a teenage band, at the local Freehold Elks Club. Most groups in those days merely played instrumentals, he recalled, like the Shadows, but he would risk vocals on the Beatles' 'Twist and Shout'.

Young: 'Did you feel at home on stage from the very beginning?'

'I did. I was nervous when we first started but, at the same time, it was a very singular place and I was seeking that out – some place that was going to cut me out as different.'

After a pause for the Rolling Stones, Young turned to Springsteen's factory-worker father, about whom her guest had said, in his memoir, 'he loved me but he couldn't stand me.' 'Those are powerful words,' she commented. 'Why do you think he felt the way he felt?'

'My dad had a gruff exterior but inside he could really be quite soft. The qualities he had on the inside were the things I wore on the outside and they were just difficult for him to deal with.'

Young: 'Seeing your sensitivity reminded him of the things he was trying to ...?'

'Yeah, might have reminded him of his own frailties or fragility. So it was just a terrible cross-current of emotions that went on between us. We sorted through some of it as we got older but it was sad when I was young.'

Another major figure in Springsteen's life, commented Young, was Jon Landau. A music critic, he waxed lyrical in a review of a 1974 Boston gig: 'I have seen rock and roll's future and its name is Bruce Springsteen.' It was to raise the young singer's profile enormously.

'Did you like it or did it irk you?' asked Young. 'It's quite a proclamation, isn't it?'

'Yeah, that's for sure! Initially it was a little ... difficult, but it's all funny now.'

Springsteen was to hire Landau as his manager, and his co-producer on albums such as 1975's *Born to Run*. 'You've said you wanted to pen a record like the last record you'd ever need to hear,' said Young. 'That's quite an ambition for a young man!'

'I was twenty-four. I *was* an ambitious young man. I'd been playing for ten years, and I thought, *Well, I've been around a bit, I've seen a lot. I think I'm one of the most distinctive musicians I've seen at my age.* And I had a lot of confidence and a certain vision.

'I wasn't so much a revolutionary as an alchemist. I had Duane Eddy in my head, Roy Orbison, great Phil Spector records, the physicality of Elvis. And I said, *Somehow, I'm going to mix all these things together and make the greatest record that was ever heard.*'

Following a burst of Van Morrison, Young remarked that Springsteen's subject matter – on his landmark 1984 album *Born in the USA* but also at all points of his career – was 'ordinary people grinding out their jobs; trying to make difficult relationships work; being short of money.'

'People who have had pain and difficulty in their childhoods often make a success of themselves by not going there any more,' she said. 'Yet, in order to write about the things that you do, you've always gone back. Is there a price to pay in mining your past for your current creativity?'

'I think you work on the thing that's eating away at you,' Springsteen mused. 'Why couldn't people take their eyes off Brando? Something was always eating at him. Why can't you take your eyes off Dylan? There's something eating at him.

'A lot of my work is drawn from the period of my life where I'm trying to go back and make sense of things that were unfathomable at the time. I go back and I put my father's clothes on and I walk out on stage and I present some vision of him and myself to my audience.

'*Why* am I doing that? I'm trying to find the piece of it that would lead to a certain sort of transcendence over those circumstances I grew up in.'

Young moved the conversation to her guest's romantic life. His wife of twenty-five years, Patti Scialfa, had joined his group, the E Street Band, in 1984. How important was it that she was also a musician and performer?

'Patti is a great songwriter and a very distinctive and original voice. She gets to show about one-hundredth of that with the E Street Band!

'She joined the band just literally days before we went on tour in 1984, then it was three or four years later when we got together as a couple. It was a lovely beginning to what's been a very beautiful relationship.'

The couple had three children, explained Young, and before the birth of the first, Evan, in 1990, Springsteen's father drove hundreds of miles to see him. 'Why was he doing that, and what happened?'

'I was going to be a father and he had some things that he wanted to say, which was very unusual for my dad. He must have felt pressed to come down and give me ... a bit of a warning as to where he felt he went wrong.

'He said he felt he hadn't been present enough for me and he hadn't, perhaps, been quite as good to me as he might have wanted to be. It was a short conversation because my dad's not much of a talker, but it was a pretty meaningful one.'

Young asked what becoming a father had been like.

'It opens your heart, your mind, your life up to a world that was present but that previously you had not recognised or seen. So, suddenly, you get this beautiful flooding of another vision of life and of what life can be.

'It changes the way you see everything. It changes the way you write, the way you think. You step outside and fill your lungs: it feels like more air. It has been, and continues to be, an incredible thing to experience.'

Kirsty Young remarked that her guest was such an American hero that even Barack Obama had joked, 'I'm only running for president because I can't be Bruce Springsteen!' So, had he had any doubts about writing so honestly, in his memoir, about an ongoing battle with depression?

'If you're writing an autobiography, you have to open your life up to a certain degree,' explained Springsteen. 'You agree to show them your mind and how it works, and the things that have affected you that have shaped your music.

'It's just something that's been part of my life. It was more difficult for my pap and other family members, who suffered with it a lot. I've had to deal with it as time's passed and it's usually OK. But, once in a while, Churchill's black dog jumps up and bites you in the ass.

'I've developed some skills that help me dealing with it. Sometimes, it's just naming it! Patti's very helpful and sometimes it's just time, or the correct medication. The right drugs can really help ...'

• • •

The all-American hero Bruce Springsteen continues to rage hard in his never-ending quest for artistic integrity and authenticity. In 2017, the year after his *Desert Island Discs* appearance, he began his *Springsteen on Broadway* residency at a small New York theatre, performing songs and reminiscing about his life and career. Prodigious reviews and ticket sales saw this production extended from its planned eight-week run into the following year, and then repeated in 2021. At the age of seventy, he co-directed his first film, *Western Stars*. To date, he has sold more than 150 million records worldwide.

DISCS CHOSEN

'Hound Dog'
Elvis Presley
'It hit me like a thunderbolt and still sounds great to this day'

'I Want to Hold Your Hand'
The Beatles
'The song that inspired me to play rock and roll music'

'It's All Over Now'
Rolling Stones
'When I got thrown out of my first band, I learned this guitar solo'

'Madame George'
Van Morrison
'Astral Weeks made me trust in beauty and gave me a sense of the divine'

'What's Going On'
Marvin Gaye
'From start to finish, it's a masterpiece'

'Out of Sight'
James Brown
'Pure excitement, pure electricity, pure get-out-of-your-seat, move-your-ass, sweat-filled, gospel-filled, raw rock and roll rhythm and blues'

❤ **'Like a Rolling Stone'**
Bob Dylan
'The snare drum that opens the song feels like somebody kicked open the door to your mind'

'Baby I Need Your Loving'
Four Tops
'Motown was an incredible part of my youth'

BOOK
Woody Guthrie: A Life – Joe Klein
'It changed my way of thinking about what you might be able to do with popular music'

LUXURY ITEM
His guitar
(He was not allowed his first choice: a chef)

59

CAITLIN MORAN

JOURNALIST, NOVELIST, DRAMATIST
22 January 2017

Bruce Springsteen had started out as a volatile young dreamer driven to document and champion the working class that spawned him. A month after his visit, the desert island welcomed a contemporary precocious young talent on a similar mission via a very different route.

Caitlin Moran was one of eight siblings raised on benefits and home-schooled on a Wolverhampton council estate, yet had gone on to become an award-winning newspaper columnist who had also written five books – the first by the age of sixteen – and a successful TV sitcom.

All of these ventures drew heavily on her own life and personal history and had made her an icon to teenage girls throughout Britain. Yet as she told Kirsty Young, this precipitous rise had made her even more determined to focus on, and tell the tale of, her own humble roots.

• • •

Young opened by commenting that Caitlin Moran was a star columnist – on *The Times* – and one of that particular vocation's signature notes tends to be rage. 'What's *your* purpose when you write?'

'Rage is very bad for the complexion!' demurred Moran. 'No, I don't like rage. I like to walk around the snooker table of topics and come at it from a different angle. My favourite one is to simply *Boggle*.'

Young: 'You are forwardly a feminist. You're left-wing in your views. It is your purpose to change people's minds?'

'I'm totally metropolitan liberal elite. I've had a T-shirt made with that written on it because I think they're all brilliant words.'

Young: 'You also write about things like masturbation and abortion and menstruation. There's nothing you think should be off limits?'

'I always felt that these were things I wanted to talk about. It took me a while to realise that you open up your newspaper and read about war all the time. We're reading about millions of people dying – yet being able to write about masturbation is seen as wrong?

'Very few people are writing about benefits, or being working class, or shame, or being fat. Mental illness. All the things I like to write about. It's an empty field. I get to be first. Yay!'

After a break for the Beatles, Young turned to Moran's early home life. Her dad was a would-be rock star. 'How much did he believe he would still make it?'

'It was always pending. When we watched *Only Fools and Horses* and Del Boy would go, "This time next year, Rodders, we'll be millionaires" – that was very much the mantra in our house.

'He'd been in a band. They were signed to a record label and being produced by Bowie's producer, Tony Visconti. He was on the scene, he was a hot young man, and then the band broke up and he came back to Wolverhampton and had all these kids and retrained as a fireman. And then a washing-machine repair man.

'Then he developed arthritis and we had to go on to benefits. And he was still: "Next year, I'll be back in the music business. We'll be in London, living in a huge house. I'm going to make it." He was *furious* that he wasn't playing Live Aid!'

Young: 'Your father and mother met when she was at Sussex University and she dropped out to marry him. What are you earliest memories of your mum as a mum?'

'She was always pregnant, because she had to pump out eight kids. She would have a baby, come back and be quite ill, and when the baby was about two, she'd hand it over to me and the rest of the kids, and go off and have another baby.'

Moran explained that, living in a three-bedroom council house, she and her seven siblings, 'the best people in the world', were incredibly close. This was just as well as, she said, she had no friends at junior school.

'I couldn't read yet but I knew that books were a shield that would keep you safe and a door to escape through. So I was "reading" *The Railway Children* upside-down – because I couldn't read – while everyone else was running around, having fun, playing knicker chase and kiss chase.'

Young: 'What are your most pungent memories of poverty?'

'*Pungent* is the right word. It's primarily smells: boiling potatoes. The combination of hot dust and chip fat on a curtain. *Towels*. When you're poor, you don't know what a dry towel is. They're wet all the time, because you're sharing them with so many people.'

Moran won a scholarship to Wolverhampton Girls School but she lasted only four weeks there. 'Why?' asked Young.

'It was – they were all posh. They'd all had tutors and been to prep schools. They'd been taught things like algebra, and I hadn't. And there was immediate bullying.

'There was a girl who hated me straightaway because I was fat and weird. I'd read enough books about bullying to know that this would continue for years, and what you should do was punch the girl in the face. But I had a very poor left hook, so I left the school instead.'

She was not to attend school again. Instead, aged thirteen, Moran won an essay competition run by Dillons bookstore and judged, among others, by *Times* journalist Valerie Grove. Moran wrote her first novel and sent it to Grove, who forwarded it to a publishing house.

Delighted when they published it, Moran was less pleased to be given an advance of only £1,800: '*That's* not going to support my whole family and jet my life off to London!' At seventeen, she moved to London alone and began writing for *Melody Maker* ... and sexually adventuring.

Young: 'You enjoyed a couple of years of what you brilliantly termed *rumpeteering*. You call them your "sex quest years". What did you learn that we can broadcast?'

'Absolutely nothing! What I learned particularly is that you can't try to recreate things you've seen in the video to Madonna's "Erotica" with a very scared twenty-three-year-old man in a south London bedsit!

'When you start dripping wax on to his genitals without warning him in advance, he will scream, "What are you doing? Are you insane?" You'll both sit there trying to pick dried wax off his pubic hair, you'll end up having to shave it off, and it'll be quite lopsided for a while.'

Young: 'When you meet young girls at signings, how do they respond to you? Because this is new. It's not been written about before.'

'Two years ago, I did a stand-up tour where it was me on stage for two hours talking about my life. It would be funny and truthful and sad. And then afterwards I would do a signing that would go on for three or four hours. Four, five, six, seven hundred people queuing up to meet me.

'I'd hug every single one, I'd sign everything and we'd talk. I would get a lot of girls crying. It gets to the point when you've met thousands of people over a couple of months that, as they walk towards you, you can *see* their stories.

'You can see the girls who are self-harming. You can see the girls who eat too little and are starving themselves. You can see the girls who eat too much to crush down their feelings.'

Young asked whether, in Moran's own teenage years, writing had felt like a release.

'I've just always found it ... the easiest single thing I can do is to write. It sounds weird and perverted but my mouth waters like I'm about to eat something delicious. Writing is beautiful. The hard bit is the sitting.'

After a pause for Madonna's 'Vogue', Young commented on her guest's extraordinary life trajectory. 'You were sixteen. A size twenty-two. Your house had rats. You had no GCSEs or friends. You're now a fantastically

successful columnist. You've published five books. You look to be a size ten
…'

'Well, twelve,' Moran interjected, modestly.

'Do you feel like a survivor? Like you've survived something?'

'No. The reason that I write these things is that this is how most people
are. We are all fragile things. We fake it until we make it. We present public
faces but, underneath, we are all dealing with massive things. Everyone has
got problems.

'Everyone is surviving, and you just try and do the most fun version of
that. Always look for the joy in it. Because the ultimate purpose of life is to
experience as much joy as possible.'

After David Bowie and 'Rock 'n' Roll Suicide', Young remarked that her
guest's sitcom, Channel 4's *Raised by Wolves*, had won the Rose d'Or at Cannes.
This stellar success, and her consequent comfortable lifestyle, raised an obvious question.

'You've described it [*the sitcom*] as a sympathetic portrayal of the working
class. How much does keeping in touch with where you came from feel
important to you, now that you live the life of an, as you say, metropolitan
elite star journalist and writer?'

Moran paused. 'What's the best way to put this? Leading the life that I do,
and living where I do, means it's impossible *not* to write constantly about
being working class, and council estates, and weird kids, and the people who
don't get written about.'

Young: 'Impossible because … what? You feel you wouldn't be doing your
duty?'

'Because living in medium-middle-class Oxbridge white male London,
you're living in a world where everyone presumes that's normal. That anything outside that is *other*, and *let's go and look at these lives for twenty minutes,
underneath this rock*, in a kind of Attenborough way.

'It's not understanding that those lives, the working-class lives, lives on
benefits, weird kids, autodidacts, the humour, the intelligence, the joy, the life,
is the normal experience. That's how most people *are*. And yet those lives are
treated like a special case.'

Young: 'According to government figures, forty-three per cent of newspaper columnists are privately educated. Seven per cent of the population
is privately educated. Writing in *The Times*, do you feel like an exotic
species?'

'Well, they have been amazing to me!' marvelled Caitlin Moran. 'I mean,
my God, to be given a column in a national newspaper at seventeen! They
have been incredibly supportive for the last twenty-five years, because they
basically hired a mad child in a hat from Wolverhampton!

'I keep constantly being told, "Why don't you write for the *Guardian* instead?" Well, because their readers *know* this stuff. I'm writing to judges, I'm writing to MPs, I'm writing to people whose minds I want to change. And I should be showing them what this life is like.'

• • •

Having followed up her 2011 memoir, *How to Be a Woman*, with *How to Build a Girl* in 2014, Caitlin Moran also wrote the screenplay for the 2019 movie adaptation of the latter. She has since written *How to Be Famous* and *More Than a Woman*; her next book will be *What About Men?* – titled after an audience question she invariably gets asked whenever she gives talks about feminism. No longer a mad child in a hat from Wolverhampton, she writes multiple weekly columns for *The Times* and communes daily with her 874,000 (and rising) Twitter followers.

DISCS CHOSEN
❤ **'Twist and Shout'**
The Beatles
'In our house, the Beatles were our Jesus'

'Wuthering Heights'
Kate Bush
'When I saw Kate Bush, it was the first time I thought, Oh my God, that could be me! *Primarily because she appeared to be wearing a nightie and was spinning around and around on the spot'*

'Weekender'
Flowered Up
'It's all about how one night can change your life, and how horribly wrong it can go'

'Not the Girl You Think You Are'
Crowded House

'Vogue'
Madonna
'She wasn't alternative – she was trying to be supreme'

'Rock 'n' Roll Suicide'
David Bowie
'At one point he was so thin that his teeth looked fat'

'Common People'
Pulp
'We've got thirty seconds more of class war, haven't we, here?'

'Gotta Work'
Amerie
'Halfway through, you're like, "Yes! Work! Work is amazing!"'

BOOK

The Secret Diary of Adrian Mole aged 13¾ – Sue Townsend
'It's working class, written by a woman, and line-by-line the funniest book ever written'

LUXURY ITEM

A solar-powered laptop. not connected to the internet
'I can write characters and I would be able to talk to them, so I wouldn't be lonely'

'ISLE NEVER FORGET ...'

'When they rang to invite me to go on *Desert Island Discs*, I went into pleasurable, mild shock, coupled with an unedifying triumph. Let's face it – it's the cultural equivalent of getting a knighthood. My last similar thrill was being asked to write my entry for *Who's Who* (where it said 'Education' I just wrote 'None').

'I know Kirsty was a bit frustrated that I didn't want to discuss sad or dark things from my life, or childhood – no mystery there, she literally said it on the show – but I have a policy of never talking about anything negative in my life until it's over and I've solved it, so I'm in a position to share useful advice, rather than just, basically, *whine*. I'm whine-intolerant in myself. It brings me out in a rash.

'Also, I believed very firmly that I simply wasn't famous enough to cry on *Desert Island Discs*. If you're Tom Hanks, of course you can cry. You're Tom Hanks! At my level of fame, however – I'd say I was 7.5 per cent famous *at a push* – I'm afraid my internal, no-nonsense Welsh nanna just categorises it as "attention-seeking". You can only cry when you've got an Oscar. Those are the rules.

'I didn't get *any* feedback from my family. I never tell them when I do anything, and we all basically pretend my job doesn't happen, which I think is totally correct and healthy. But what was pleasing was other working-class people saying to me, "It was so good to hear someone talking about *class* like that on Radio 4."

'The last ten years, particularly with social media, have been so good for talking about race, feminism and LGBTQ issues, but the one thing we do *not* yet talk about in this country is class. I think that's the next, and last, big civil rights conversation that we need to have – and it intersects with all other inequalities. Lack of money and social mobility underpin nearly every problem. It makes our country palpably weaker. Often the best *don't* succeed. They can't. They're stuck in the "wrong" postcodes.

'I haven't listened back to my show. I never watch or listen to *anything* I'm on. If it's TV, I might watch a bit back to check that my hair looks big enough, or if it's gone flat in the middle – but that's as far as I'll go, because otherwise I'll sit there going, "That was the wrong word!" or "You've mis-pronounced 'hyperbole' *again*." That was the only bad thing about doing *Desert Island Discs* – I couldn't listen to it the week I was on. I spoiled it for myself.

'Oh, and I just listened to Kathy Burke's episode again, because it's excellent.'

60

DAVID BECKHAM

FOOTBALLER, BUSINESSMAN, PHILANTHROPIST
29 January 2017

A special occasion demands a very special guest. And for *Desert Island Discs'* celebratory seventy-fifth anniversary show in February 2017, Kirsty Young's island played host to a man who, at the time, was arguably the most famous Briton on the planet.

Introduced by Young as a 'footballer, global brand, humanitarian', David Beckham had long surpassed mere football stardom to become recognised and revered worldwide. His career as one of Manchester United's greatest ever players and his 115 England caps had been only the start of the story.

When Beckham began dating Spice Girl Victoria Adams in the late nineties, the ultra-glamorous couple immediately became the international media phenomenon known as Posh and Becks. Twenty-five years and four children on, the widespread fascination with them had not faded.

David Beckham, to say the least, had experienced ups and downs but, as he told Young, his dogged determination, and his love for football and for his family, had survived all the slings and arrows that the tabloids and the wider world could throw at him. This was genuine must-hear radio.

• • •

Kirsty Young began what she called her 'post-match analysis' with the observation that no other footballer had ever had a movie made named after their signature skill: 2002's *Bend It Like Beckham*.

'I want to just try to get a sense of what it is like to be able to bend the ball like that,' she said. 'As your toe touches the leather, is there a sweetness in it?'

'Yes,' replied Beckham. 'As soon as you've hit the ball, and you know you've hit it well, you know that it doesn't matter if it's one of the best goalkeepers in the world. You know that it's going in.'

That ability had won Beckham vast amounts of honours, including his 115 England caps, 59 of them as captain. Young asked where he kept all of his trophies and awards.

'I have all of my caps at my house. I have my medals in a safe at the bank because they're so precious to me, and they're for my children in the future. And I have so many pairs of boots, because I always used to keep my boots after a game ...'

'How many pairs, do you think?'

'Oh, my goodness! Over a thousand pairs of boots.'

'And where are they?'

'I keep them in storage. In boxes.'

'I bet that competes with Victoria's shoe collection, doesn't it?'

'It *does*, actually. It does.'

Young turned to Beckham's childhood, growing up in Chingford, Essex, with his hairdresser mother, gas-fitter father and two sisters. 'What's your very, very, very earliest memory?'

'My mum taking me to football all the time. My dad was working so my mum did a lot of the training sessions and games at the weekend.

'And my dad – day after day, week after week, we used to go over to the park right near our house. There was a goal there with no nets, and he used to say, "OK, hit the crossbar. Hit the crossbar." We'd do it for hours and hours.

'I remember my dad going out at six in the morning and coming home at seven-thirty, eight at night – sometimes later. My mum would make dinner for us, then at nine she would have her old ladies come in and she'd do their hair until eleven or twelve at night.'

Young suggested that his dad had been a hard taskmaster. Beckham agreed. Had it been, the host asked, 'tough love'?

'Without a doubt it was tough love. I remember playing for Ridgeway Rovers on a Sunday morning. If I had a bad game, he would tell me, and he'd go through every minute of that game on the way home. I was seven, and every single detail, he would go through.

'I remember turning round to him sometimes and saying, "Yeah, I'm so sorry. I didn't mean to." But when I look back on it, I think that was exactly how I needed to be taught.

'He always loved football. He had trials for Leyton Orient but he was one of those players ... he was always offside. Always offside! But when I started playing, he gave up playing for his Sunday league team and he focused on me.'

Beckham described, at the age of ten, his parents paying for him – 'it was really expensive' – to attend a Bobby Charlton Soccer School in Manchester, overseen by the great man himself. Young wondered if, as he grew older, he had been able to indulge in normal teenage activities.

'Were there local discos?' she asked. 'Was there cider in the park? Was there a fag in the bus shelter?'

'There was never ever a fag in the bus shelter because of the football. And whenever my friends were down the corner shop, hanging out, drinking, I was in, watching *Match of the Day* and preparing for the game that I had on the Sunday.'

Young described a fateful event in Beckham's life. Alerted to his talent by his appearance at Bobby Charlton's Soccer School, but unknown to him, Manchester United sent a scout to watch him play in Essex. This emissary was highly impressed.

'I remember my mum saying to me, "Lucky you played well today." I was, like, "Why?" and she said, "Because there was a Manchester United scout here and he's asked you to go up to Manchester for a trial." And I just burst into tears.

'It was all I'd ever wanted. Manchester United was my dad's team; was *my* team. I was training at Tottenham and Arsenal at the time. I had to choose between the two, so I chose Tottenham, because my grandad was a season ticket-holder for forty years. But Manchester United was my team. So that was my opportunity.

'I was fourteen. I was sat in a room with Sir Alex Ferguson. I ate with the team before their game. He took me into the office and I was signing a contract for Manchester United.'

Beckham became, noted Young, one of United's famous 'Class of '92', alongside Ryan Giggs, Paul Scholes, Gary and Phil Neville and Nicky Butt. 'Try to describe how it felt to be there.'

'To be honest, at the time, we never felt that there was something so special going on. We had a really tough youth team manager – Eric Harrison – that kept us all in line. And, obviously, Sir Alex Ferguson.

'We all had jobs. I cleaned eight of the first team players' boots. Nicky Butt cleaned the showers, Paul Scholes cleaned the toilets and the changing room. Gary Neville and Phil would be picking the dirty kit up.'

Young jumped forward to a formative moment in Beckham's career: a wonder goal he scored in the first game of the 1996/7 season, against Wimbledon at Old Trafford. 'You've said in the past that it was "the goal that would change my life".'

'Yeah,' agreed Beckham. 'And I didn't realise, at the time, *how* much it would!'

Young: 'This was a goal from your half. You were almost exactly on the halfway line ...'

'I was. I just remember the ball falling to me, and thinking, *Yeah, why not?* And I hit it. It started to the left then it came back and I thought, *This has got a chance! It's got a real chance!*'

Young: 'And there seemed to be silence as people watched it cruise through the air.'

'There *was* silence. It was amazing. My mum, my dad and my younger sister, Joanne, was actually behind that goal. I've got a photo at home where the ball's literally going in the back of the net and my parents are standing up, which is amazing.

'The best part of that day for me was Eric Cantona came up to me and said, "What a goal!" And he was a hero of mine. Usually, I would have been doing interviews on *Match of the Day*. But the manager told me: "Do not speak to anybody. Get on that bus with the team."

'That's one thing with Sir Alex Ferguson – he prepared us for the future. I scored that goal at a really young age so I probably wasn't prepared to talk on *Match of the Day*. The manager was, like, "Nope – you don't talk to anybody!"'

Beckham selected 'Something About the Way You Look Tonight' and explained that Elton John was to sing it at his wedding day to Victoria in 1999 but had a heart attack on the day: 'We christened the kids a couple of years later and he performed this song in our house. It's a very special song for us.'

As Elton faded away, Young moved on to how Beckham had first met Victoria: 'You've said, "My wife picked me out of a football sticker book and I chose her off the telly." That's very funny, but is it actually true?'

'I don't know whether it's true on *her* side, because she was never into football. Everyone at the time had their favourite Spice Girl, and I remember seeing Victoria on the telly and she was dressed in this black catsuit – shiny, and ...'

Young: 'It didn't leave much to the imagination, as I recall?'

'No, it *definitely* didn't, which is one of the reasons why she became my favourite Spice Girl!'

'Your wife wrote a letter to her young self in *Vogue* magazine very recently, and said, "Love at first sight *does* exist." Was it love at first sight for you when you saw her in the players' lounge?'

'Without a doubt. *Without a doubt.* I'd seen her the week before and I must have caught her eye because then, the week after, she came to another game. She was obviously there for a reason and I was hoping *I* was the reason. And, apparently, I was.

'I went into the players' lounge ... and I spoke to her for about twenty-five minutes and got her number, so it worked.'

'And so Posh and Becks were born!' said Young before wondering, with their extraordinary levels of celebrity, how they ever managed to go on any dates.

'At the beginning, [*their manager*] was very protective of the girls and wanted to keep it quiet. So, every time I went on a date with her, we just used to sit in a car park and talk.

'I had an amazing bright blue BMW. I spent my whole pay packet from Adidas on this car but I was still living in lodgings. I drove down and picked her up. I remember having sunburn, because she turned up with this aloe vera plant she gave me, which I thought was really sweet.

'We used to sit in a Harvester car park and just kind of, you know, kiss, of course, and spend time together. And that was how, the first two or three months, before anybody knew, we used to spend our time.'

Young gently teased the suddenly bashful Beckham by asking for his fondest memory of what she comedically described as his 'very low-key wedding'.

'It was a ... well, yeah,' he replied, sounding a tad lost for words. 'It was ...'

Young: 'There were *doves*. There were *thrones*. You threw a lot at it!'

'Yeah, we *did* throw a lot at it. It was the thing to do around that time.'

'When you look back at it now, your his-and-hers purple matching outfits ...'

'Yeah, that was bold,' conceded Beckham. 'Victoria's was pretty nice. Mine, I'm like: what was I thinking? I look like the guys out of *Dumb and Dumber* when they went to that party in ridiculous outfits. I even had a top hat in purple as well. Unbelievable! What was I thinking?'

Young: 'You sold the rights to *OK!* They said they sold five-and-a-half million copies. That's extraordinary! The world was watching.'

'Yeah. To be honest, I was always a private person, and in Victoria's world then, everything they did was scrutinised. And all of a sudden, we were together. So, there was an opportunity for even more media to talk about us or take pictures of us.'

Young remarked on the solidity of the couple's relationship. In 2004, they had sued the *News of the World* for libel for claiming that their marriage was a sham.

'The case was settled out of court, and you said, "*Nothing* will break me and Victoria up." And you have been together for nineteen years, amid all that scrutiny and hoo-ha. A highly public partnership. Why has your marriage been successful?'

'I think because we're a strong family unit. We've got strong parents. We were brought up with the right values. You make mistakes over the years. We all know marriage is difficult at times. And it's about working through it.

'People have talked about, "Do we stay together because it's a brand?" Of course not! We stay together because we love each other. We stay together because we have four amazing children.'

Young steered the conversation back to football and, specifically, her guest's famously sometimes-troubled relationship with his legendary Manchester United manager, Sir Alex Ferguson.

'He wrote in his autobiography that you were the only player he had managed who *chose* to be famous,' she noted. 'That is a carefully chosen phrase from a man who knows what he's getting at.'

'Yeah, carefully chosen words,' agreed Beckham.

Young: 'I know you're reconciled now. But, when you didn't get on, what was the crux of the problem?'

'I was young at the time. There were certain decisions that I made back then that were wrong decisions.'

'Like what?'

'I think the manager felt I was driving down to London too many times during the week – which I wasn't, actually. There was so much media attention around Victoria and me, people were thinking I was living in London and driving up to Manchester to train, which I would never have done. I'm very professional.

'One time, Victoria was in Ireland. I had a day off so I flew over. I didn't feel that I needed to tell the manager what I was doing. As I was coming back, at six o'clock in the morning, for training, I was sat in the lounge and the manager walked in.'

Young: 'What did he say?'

'He didn't say anything. He didn't talk to me. So, I knew that I was in a little bit of trouble. And I can understand the manager thinking, *OK, maybe he's not looking after his body!* Or, *He's not resting as much as he should do!*'

Young focused on the infamous moment after a 2003 Manchester United match when Ferguson had kicked a boot in the dressing room and 'it clocked you right on the nut'. The next day, the story, and a photo of Beckham's scarred forehead, were ubiquitous.

Young: 'I don't know if you actually had stitches on the eyebrow?'

'I did. It was a butterfly stitch.'

'So, the next day the world sees that stitch and knows ... how badly it's going.'

'Yeah. Well, we'd just lost the game to Arsenal, our massive rivals at the time, and the manager felt that either one or two of the goals was my fault. At the time, I was young and I argued back. And when you argue back with the manager, it *doesn't* go well.

'The manager walked towards me and he kicked a pile of clothes that were on the floor. There was a boot [*under them*] and it came flying towards me. It hit me in my eye and my eye started bleeding straightaway.

'We said at the time, he could never do it again – even though he does think he's one of the best strikers of all time in the game! It was a freak accident, but an opportunity for the media to say this was the end of my Manchester United career.'

Young remarked that Beckham's time at the club had, indeed, ended that same year. 'You were on holiday in the States when you saw that statement from United that they were going to sell you to Barcelona. It was the first you'd heard of it. What was your reaction?'

'Shocked! And I was devastated, because we'd just won the league that season ...'

'And you've said you never would have left? You'd have stayed there till your last playing day?'

'Without a doubt. *Without a doubt.* Because Manchester United was my team. I had no aspirations to actually leave Manchester United.

'I was hurt. I was angry. I flew back to London ... and that's when I spoke to my agent and said, "If I am going to move, I want to move to Real Madrid."

Within a day, I was sat with the president of Real Madrid and we agreed that that's the club where I was going to go.'

Young: 'You said you felt hurt. How long was it before the hurt healed?'

'I didn't watch Manchester United play for three years. I couldn't. I spoke to Gary – Gary Neville – every weekend after games, but I honestly didn't watch a Manchester United game for three years.'

After a break for the Rolling Stones, Young turned to the undoubted nadir of Beckham's football career. At the 1998 World Cup in France, he was sent off for a petulant kick at an opponent as England were knocked out by Argentina. He immediately became a tabloid hate figure.

'The press went into meltdown,' recapped Young. 'You received death threats. People sent you bullets in the post. I have seen the picture of an effigy of you hanging from a lamppost, which turned my blood cold. What helped you through that tough time?'

'My family. Manchester United. Sir Alex Ferguson was the first person to call me after that game. He said, "Son, get back to Manchester. You'll be fine." That gave me the strength to get through probably the toughest time that I've been through in my life.

'I remember getting off the plane and walking through the terminal. A journalist and a camera crew were following me, and they were, like: "You've let your grandparents down, you've let your sisters down, you've let your nation down and you've let yourself down.

'It was *such* a difficult time. Not just for myself because I knew, once I was in Manchester, I was protected. I had the support of the fans, every single game. Every time I walked to take a corner, the whole stadium stood up, clapped and sang my name. I get emotional talking about it.

'It was more difficult for my grandparents. They were seventy years old and being doorstepped by journalists, saying things that I don't want my grandparents hearing about their grandson. My *parents* were going through it. My *sisters* were going through it.'

Young: 'How did you protect your family?'

'The only thing that I could do to protect them was to say, "Don't open the door to those people. Don't talk to them."'

Beckham spoke movingly of the satisfaction that he now got from his work as a goodwill ambassador for UNICEF, raising funds and travelling to the world's most deprived areas. He also described his and Victoria's efforts to protect their four children from the glare of celebrity.

'We can't control the exposure that they get,' he said. 'They are always going to get attention. I find it unbelievable [*the media*] can criticise an eleven-year-old, a fourteen-year-old, a seventeen-year-old, *a five-year-old*! That's bullying. And we'll always support our children, no matter what.'

As Young guided an utterly compelling special desert-island encounter to its close, she turned to more light-hearted matters. 'You're not afraid of sending yourself up,' she complimented Beckham, before identifying a perfect recent example of this willingness.

'I've watched the spoof underwear ad you just did with James Corden, where you were both in your pants. And *you* came off better in that particular comparison.'

'Well, I know,' agreed her guest.

'You are forty-one now. Are the underwear shoots a thing of the past?'

'I enjoy the skits, because I trust James and what he does,' answered David Beckham. 'But as far as the underwear ads – I don't think I'll be doing them any more just because, yeah, I'm forty-one years old now.

'I'm sure people are fed up of seeing me in my underwear over the years, anyway. So, I think it's time to step back and maybe let Brooklyn do them at some point ...'

• • •

In recent years, alongside his humanitarian work for UNICEF, David Beckham has become a businessman and entrepreneur. He is co-owner of Inter Miami CF, who played their first US MLS game early in 2020, and, in England, of Salford City, alongside his Manchester United 'Class of '92' ex-teammates and friends. Nor has his celebrity status in any way waned: at the time of writing, he has no fewer than 74.2-million Instagram followers.

DISCS CHOSEN
❤ **'Every Time We Say Goodbye'**
Ella Fitzgerald
'It used to be playing every time I walked in my grandad's flat'

'What a Fool Believes'
The Doobie Brothers
'My dad used to sing this really loud but he was tone deaf'

'I Am the Resurrection'
Stone Roses
'There was so much going on around Manchester – Oasis, Stone Roses and the Haçienda. I only went there once because the manager [Sir Alex Ferguson] knew where we were every minute of the day'

'Something About the Way You Look Tonight'
Elton John

'*No Es Lo Mismo*'
Alejandro Sanz
'*It reminds me of my four years at Real Madrid*'

'Wild Horses'
Rolling Stones
'*Such a strong, powerful song by one of the best bands of all time*'

'The Girl Is Mine'
Michael Jackson and Paul McCartney
'*My special song with my little girl, Harper*'

'Si tu vois ma mère'
Sidney Bechet
'*It reminds me of Paris, of France, and such an important moment in my career – when I retired [after playing for Paris Saint-Germain in 2013]*'

BOOK
Mallman on Fire – Francis Mallman
'*He teaches you to cook anywhere so I thought, if I'm on a desert island, I could rustle up something*'

LUXURY ITEM
His England caps
'*Very precious to me. People always say, "Oh, you actually get given a physical cap?" and you do – an amazing velvet cap with gold trimming*'

61

BILLIE JEAN KING

TENNIS PLAYER, CHAMPION OF EQUALITY
15 July 2018

As the old Wild West aphorism goes, the pioneers get the arrows and the settlers get the land. In women's sport, there has been no more dogged pioneer for progress, and spirited backhand-volleyer of hostile incoming arrows, than the great Billie Jean King.

A tennis force of nature, winning thirty-nine major titles between 1961 and 1980, King nevertheless fought many of her hardest battles away from the court, both for gender equality and pay equity within her sport and, later, as a high-profile and passionate campaigner for women's rights and gay and lesbian rights.

It has been a life of struggle rewarded with prodigious victories, be it vanquishing opponents over the net or overcoming entrenched forces of reaction within society. It would all have ground a lesser woman down – yet the irrepressible King fetched up on Kirsty Young's island, in July 2018, still sounding implausibly positive.

• • •

Young opened by observing that in 1967, when Billie Jean King won the singles, doubles and mixed doubles at Wimbledon, her prize was a £45 gift voucher. It was little surprise that she became a campaigner – and yet those particular seeds had been planted a long time ago.

'I had an epiphany at twelve years old,' King told her. 'I was sitting at Los Angeles Tennis Club, daydreaming, and I started thinking about my tiny sport of tennis and that everybody who played wore white shoes, white socks, white clothes, used white balls and was white.

'And, at twelve, I asked myself, *Where is everybody else?* And that's what started me fighting for equality. That was my moment of truth.'

After Aretha Franklin's 'Respect', Young turned to her guest's childhood: 'You were brought up in Long Beach, California. Your dad was Bill, a firefighter. Your mother, Betty, was a homemaker?'

'My parents were good citizens. They were risk-averse because they were Depression children. My dad served in the Second World War. Basic, kind, hard-working, very strict but very loving parents.'

'Dinner was on the table at five-fifteen, and you'd better be there?'

'Yes! My brother and I would be running down the street: "Hurry, hurry, we've got to be on time!"'

Young: 'Long Beach is a very outdoors life? You've got the weather ...'

'We were eighteen miles south of Los Angeles, on the coast. Obviously, we didn't live *on* the coast because that's the rich kids. We lived on 36th Street, so thirty-six blocks from the ocean. Which still made it very easy to go.'

Young asked if it was true that King had first got into tennis when she was ten.

'Yes. In fifth grade, my best friend, Susan Williams goes, "Do you want to play tennis?" I go, "What's tennis?" She says, "You don't know what tennis is?" I go, "No. What do you do?"

'She said, "You get to run, jump and hit a ball." I said, "Those are my three favourite things in sport! I can't wait, let's go!" She belonged to a country club, because her dad worked for Shell Chemical and had a great job.'

King adored the sport from the get-go. After taking free lessons from a local coach, she recalled to Young, 'I told my mom, "I know what I want to do with my life. I want to be the number-one tennis player in the world."'

Young: 'You said that? For real?'

'*Absolutely* for real! I was jumping up and down on the car seat, which I'm not supposed to do. That's why I remember it.'

Young asked her guest exactly what it was she loved about the sport. The reply could hardly have been more enthusiastic.

'I loved to hit the ball. There's nothing like running, feeling the wind in your hair, and when you hit the ball on the strings, it is just magic. Oh my God, it is *so* much fun! It just feels great.

'You have to bring all of yourself to be great in something anyway, but you have to *truly* bring all of yourself in tennis. It's upper and lower body. It's footwork. It's hand–eye. It's just the *best* feeling.'

King's father said she could buy a tennis racquet only if she could find the money herself. She began an intensive local fundraising campaign.

'I went to all the neighbours. They were so sweet. They made up jobs for me and they would give me a quarter or a dime or a nickel. I'd keep saving it in a mason jar in the cupboard. I had $8.29 and could not wait any longer: "*Please* can we go and get my racquet?"

'I walk into Brown's Sporting Goods and say, "I want a racquet. What can I get for $8.29?" This guy starts laughing and says, "We can figure this out." I loved purple and he had a purple racquet with purple strings and purple felt. I used to sleep with it. Oh my gosh, I was so excited!'

In 1958, King won the under-fifteen Southern Californian Championship. On the days she lost, she confessed, she was not great company at home.

'I'd be so furious! My dad would go, "OK, calm down. Did you try your best?" "*Of course* I tried my best! Are you *kidding*?" He'd say, "Are you practising too much? Are you burned out?" "No! I'm *not* practising too much!" "Do you need to practise more?" "YES!" I mean, I was crazed. My poor parents!'

King got a coach, Frank Brennan, who told her, "You're going to be number one in the world one day." Based in New Jersey, he invited her to stay with him and his family, which allowed her to spread her wings outside of California and enter – and win – tournaments in the east of the US.

In 1961, she arrived at Wimbledon for the first time, aged seventeen, to play women's doubles. She and her partner, Karen Hantze, won the title. Young asked her for her first impressions of SW19.

'It was elegant, which I liked. I love tradition. I was just in awe. I still am. Every Sunday, I used to go out before the matches would start, and sit up in the Centre Court and just take it all in. Just be thankful that I had a chance to play there.'

King entered her imperial period, winning the Wimbledon singles title for three years from 1966 to 1968. However, she had also already become an activist, trying to improve female players' pay and conditions: 'I was trying to change the game. We always had meetings going on!'

Young: 'It's interesting you credit your former husband, Larry [*King*], with being the person who began to introduce you to feminism?'

'Oh, in a big way! We were walking hand-in-hand at Cal State University and he said, "Do you know why you can't get a grant or a scholarship for this university? You're the best athlete here! *I* get a tennis grant and I'm the seventh guy on a six-man team!"

'He said, "You can't get that because you're a girl, and that is wrong." And boy, when he said it, that was a crystal ball, sitting right there!'

King's campaigning for gender equality in tennis led to the sport's most infamous encounter: 1973's Battle of the Sexes. Young recapped how it had come about.

'Bobby Riggs, who was fifty-five and had been number one back in the thirties and forties, challenged you to this match, as a self-confessed male chauvinist pig, saying that he could beat you. He didn't. You won, very decisively. How did you feel?'

'I felt so relieved. When he jumped the net, he said, "I underestimated you." I think that's what a lot of people feel about women. Don't underestimate anybody. Ever. Ever. My dad taught us that.'

By 1971, King's activism had begun to pay dividends, said Young. 'You'd become the first female athlete ever to win $100,000 in prize money in a single season. But your private life was highly complicated?'

'I had asked Larry for a divorce in 1969. He said no. He said no *forever*. I still couldn't get a divorce even in the eighties. We remain good friends now but I still loved him, too – shoot, man, it's confusing!'

Young: 'You were struggling with the nature of your sexuality, having come from a home where you've said your parents were homophobic.'

'Yes. It was just *so* confusing. In those days, back in the sixties and seventies, no one talked about it. Even gay people didn't talk about it!'

King was to be publicly outed in 1981 when she had a relationship with an assistant, Marilyn Barnett, who then sued her for palimony. Young asked her what consequences ensued.

'I lost all my endorsements overnight. Today, that would not happen. I was thirty-seven, I was just about to retire and have these lifetime deals and be able to make some money. Some real money. Because I didn't even make $2 million in my whole career.

'I had to argue with my lawyer and my publicist for forty-eight hours straight. I said: "I want a press conference." "No, you cannot do that, no one has *ever* done that!" They finally gave in. All the media were there.

'I walked in. Larry was there. My parents came up: they didn't know what was happening. Well, they *did* but they *didn't*. It was terrible. It was all shocking to them. I felt so bad for them. I said, "I *did* have an affair with Marilyn Barnett." You could have heard a pin drop.

'It was probably a good thing in some way, that I got outed, because when would I ever have come out? I don't know. What I didn't like was how it affected some of the people I loved. *That* was the hard part.'

King told Young that it had taken her years of psychotherapy to come to terms with her sexuality: 'They saved my life ... I was only comfortable by the time I was fifty-one.' However, this hard-won wisdom meant she could advise Martina Navratilova when she faced the same dilemma in 1981.

'Martina came to me and said, "I'm going to get outed by a newspaper guy. What do you think?" And I said, "Control your message. You need to come out yourself, if you're ready." But nobody can tell somebody else when they're ready. Your body tells you. It's a magical moment.'

In contrast to those dark, confusing days, Young pointed out that King had now been with her partner – and former tennis doubles partner – Ilana Kloss for nearly forty years. How had the gains in societal attitudes been made?

'It's been the courage of the LGBTQ+ community. It's been one by one by one. Plus, lawsuits. Just getting it out there and changing legislation. It's all about inclusion. You let everybody live the way they want. Who cares as long as we're good people and don't break the law?

'There are still seven countries where you would be killed, and about seventy-two where we would be in jail, for sure. So, we have a long way to go. But as far as Britain, and America, and a lot of the world, it's so much better.'

As she wound things up, Kirsty Young reflected that, in 2009, President

Obama had awarded King the Medal of Freedom: America's highest honour. 'And you were moved by what he said to you?'

'Well, it was the first time any president had mentioned the LGBTQ community, or sexuality, *ever*. So, that meant a lot to me. And I was thrilled that day.'

And even the young Barack Obama, it transpired, had been inspired by Billie Jean King's 1973 Battle of the Sexes.

'The president [*told me*] he was twelve years old when he watched the King–Riggs match. He said that it had really changed his life, and how he raised his two daughters. And *that's* what happened from that match when I played Bobby Riggs ...'

• • •

Billie Jean King continues to be viewed both as an all-time tennis great and a revolutionary figure, both within the sport and in wider society. Later in 2018, she was to marry her four-decade partner, Ilana Kloss, in a ceremony in New York conducted by the city's former mayor, David Dinkins. In September 2020, the Fed Cup, the leading women's international tennis team tournament, was renamed the Billie Jean King Cup in her honour. And in June 2022, on the fiftieth anniversary of her French Open title, President Emmanuel Macron awarded her the French Legion of Honour. Not bad for a girl who once asked, 'What's tennis?'

DISCS CHOSEN
'Respect'
Aretha Franklin
'It made women stand up a little straighter'

'Ain't No Mountain High Enough'
Diana Ross
'She sang it when they named the entire facility of the US Open after me'

'Winds of Change (Mandela to Mandela)'
Nona Hendryx
'She's mentored a lot of people in music'

'World in Union' based on 'Jupiter' from Holst's *The Planets*
Katherine Jenkins with the Crouch End Festival Chorus

'If I Dare' (from the movie *Battle of the Sexes*)
Sara Bareilles
'From the movie about one little sliver of my life'

'You Don't Have to Say You Love Me'
Dusty Springfield
'She's one of the all-time greats'

❤ **'Philadelphia Freedom'**
Elton John
'Elton said, "I want to write a song for you." Philadelphia Freedom was a tennis team I played on'

'Hey Jude'
The Beatles

BOOK
Oh, The Places You'll Go! – Dr Seuss
'It doesn't matter what age you are – it's inspirational and it's lovely'

LUXURY ITEM
Scrapbook of family photos
'People are everything'

LAUREN LAVERNE YEARS
2018–

Kirsty Young had been receiving treatment for her fibromyalgia while intending to return to *Desert Island Discs* when her condition eased. In July 2019, she announced that these plans had changed.

'Having been forced to take some months away from my favourite job because of health problems, I'm happy to say I'm now well on the way to feeling much better,' she said. 'But the enforced absence from the show has altered my perspective on what I should do next, and so I've decided it's time to pursue new challenges.'

So it was just as well that her replacement presenter had been rising to the task remarkably adeptly.

Lauren Laverne was unique among all *Desert Island Discs* hosts in that her life and career had been steeped in music. Sunderland-born, she had been the teenage singer and guitarist in Britpop-era band Kenickie, who had enjoyed four top-forty singles and a top-ten album.

Laverne had then begun a media career, spending five years as a DJ on XFM London before leaving to focus on co-hosting *The Culture Show* on BBC Two. She also joined BBC Radio 6 Music in 2008 and still presents that station's breakfast show, as she has done since 2018.

Having impressed during her *Desert Island Discs* stand-in stint, Laverne was confirmed as Kirsty Young's replacement in the immediate wake of her predecessor's resignation. She had already been demonstrating an extremely sure touch in her early weeks in the show.

A February 2019 encounter with fellow north-easterner Bob Mortimer was a joy as her guest recounted battling crippling shyness before he met his comic partner and 'soulmate', Vic Reeves. 'He's a genius, total genius, so to find someone like that, and to work with them every day – it's amazing,' he enthused.

Pat McGrath told her how, unable to find make-up for people of colour in stores during her penurious childhood, she had gone on to build a billion-dollar cosmetics empire. The veteran punk poet, John Cooper Clarke, recounted being given an unlikely break by Bernard Manning.

A charming and likeable presence, Laverne was rapidly putting her own stamp on this challenging job, but not all commentators were satisfied. Kirsty Young was a big act to follow and, in August 2019, a silly-season minor media storm blew up around her replacement.

Critical reviews in the *Sunday Times* and the *Spectator* speculated that *Desert Island Discs'* fifth full-time host might not be up to the job. The latter dismissed Laverne as 'lightweight and uncerebral' while also, oddly, huffing that the show had become 'more politically correct'.

It was a curious assault with little or no supporting evidence – and yet it was not unprecedented in the show's history. A timely and informed counter-weight article in the *New Statesman* pointed out that, over the years, many new *Desert Island Discs* hosts had been similarly criticised.

Under the headline HOW POLICING *DESERT ISLAND DISCS* BECAME A NATIONAL TRADITION, Rachel Aroesti defended the 'coolly competent, chronically genial' Laverne and explained that Kirsty Young had been likewise dismissed as 'too nice' and 'lowbrow' on replacing Sue Lawley.

Young herself also spoke up, recalling those early bad notices. 'I knew it was coming, but it's not very nice being hit in the face with a concrete slab,' she reminisced to comedian John Bishop on his TV chat show. 'And that was what it felt like!'

The Laverne criticisms fell away as soon as they began, but not before many listeners leapt to the host's defence. Famous names including Matt Lucas, Irvine Welsh, Robert Webb and Caitlin Moran took to social media to lavish praise on the briefly beleaguered presenter.

Typical was the intervention of musician Nitin Sawhney. 'A great inter-viewer has compassion, empathy, interest in their subject, sharp wit, and an ability to extract the heart and soul of a personal journey,' he tweeted to Laverne. 'All traits of yours.'

As the ensuing months unfolded, it was clear that Sawhney's supportive message was bang on the money, especially when Laverne met Sabrina Cohen-Hatton, who had spent two years living on the streets before becom-ing a senior and transformative figure in the British fire service.

'Lauren was an incredible interviewer!' Cohen-Hatton enthuses now. 'She really brought out the best of the stories as well as the worst of them. I was sat there in tears at one point. My eyes were streaming, and Lauren was starting to cry.'

Equally tear-jerking was Laverne's charged encounter with screenwriter and producer Russell T Davies. Her castaway talked about taking eight years out from his successful writing and producing career to become a full-time carer for his partner, Andrew, who was fighting a terminal illness.

'Thinking about this interview today, for the first time I realised that those eight years were our happiest years,' he told the host. 'They were so intimate and so honest ... just that care: the love. I'm talking about love here. That's the word: *love*.'

Former footballer Ian Wright was unable to control his tears when he told Laverne of an abusive boyhood and the mentor who saved him. 'Gosh, man, I'm so sorry to the people who are listening!' he apologised to the nation in a show that quickly went viral. 'I've just turned into this bumbling, crying guy!'

Thankfully, tears weren't a prerequisite for a powerful episode. Sir Keir Starmer showed the human side behind his sometimes stiff-seeming public image. Sir Cliff Richard returned to the island after sixty years and marvelled at how cool he'd sounded first time around.

Laverne's natural warmth established a fine rapport with Malala Yousafzai, who had survived being shot in the head by the Taliban in her native Pakistan to become a global campaigner for girls' education. Sophia Loren oozed charm and style because ... she's Sophia Loren.

At the end of 2021, Richard Osman made headlines on *Desert Island Discs* when he told Laverne about his life-long food addiction. The effervescent Oti Mabuse then enthused about her love for 'the magic of *Strictly*' shortly before she quit the BBC's prime-time dance show.

As we hit the high summer of 2022, *Desert Island Discs* proved yet again that it has a pulling power beyond any other radio programme. U2 singer Bono used his visit to the island to tell Laverne, and the world, of the existence of a half-brother whom he had kept secret for twenty years.

A week later, global megastar Adele recalled how she was 'always chosen third!' by the teachers at the BRIT School. And then Kate Moss, the fashion icon who never speaks, turned up to chat about Croydon, modelling, and why she's happily binned nightclubs in favour of garden centres.

The biggest names in popular culture, washing up on the island to open up to a receptive host about all aspects of their lives: business as usual on the world's longest-running radio interview show. As *Desert Island Discs* heads into its ninth decade, it is in very good shape and very good hands ...

62

BOB MORTIMER

COMEDIAN, PRESENTER, ANGLER
3 February 2019

Sometimes a performer will meet a comic partner and click with them straightaway. As Lauren Laverne noted, Bob Mortimer met Vic Reeves in a room over a pub in 1986 and 'the pair have barely stopped, or been apart, since'. It's almost like a showbiz version of love at first sight.

Yet by the time Mortimer fetched up on the desert island in February 2019, he was also carving himself a parallel solo career outside the long-standing double act, including appearances on the panel game *Would I Lie to You?* and launching a cult football podcast, *Athletico Mince*.

He also teamed up with another noted comedy sidekick, Paul White-house, for *Mortimer & Whitehouse: Gone Fishing* ... and all this after surviving heart surgery in October 2015. He had had quite the journey and it was one that he was happy to relate in amusing detail.

• • •

Lauren Laverne opened by observing that Bob Mortimer's name had for years been inextricably linked to that of Vic Reeves, 'who you call by his real name, Jim Moir. Is it true that you live quite close to each other?'

'We do,' replied Mortimer. 'We see each other most days. I spend my days in his kitchen, writing with him and laughing.'

'What's a typical writing day like you for you?'

'I arrive at nine-thirty, we talk about TV and then it drifts into coming up with funny ideas. I'm the typist, which is important if you analyse comedy duos. I think it means I'm the weaker member. And we finish at two o'clock.'

Laverne commented that the pair initially had hardly used scripts. Her guest agreed.

'On [*Vic Reeves*] *Big Night Out* we'd just have a list of props. We'd send through an instruction [*to the studio*] – "We need the world's smallest puppy inside the world's largest diamond!" – with no more explanation. Then we'd just see what was there when we arrived.'

Mortimer and Reeves had recently done their first live tour together in twenty years. Laverne asked how much things had changed for them.

'I have to admit that for the first fifteen years of touring, I don't think we ever did a show sober.'

'What was it like [*this time*]?'

'It's more scary. You don't have the bravado that drink gives you, but I think we did better shows. When we first started doing *Big Night Out*, in a room above a pub, it was just an excuse for drinking, really.'

Laverne: 'You describe yourself as naturally very shy. That might surprise people.'

'Yeah. My shyness probably defined the first thirty years of my life, really. It's a crippling thing: it can be very lonely, knowing you've got things to say but you daren't say them.

'So, I've had this gift that I'm on television so people come up to me and say hello. They make the first move, so I've learned that it's OK to talk to people and contribute and try to have your voice heard.'

Laverne turned to Mortimer's childhood in Middlesbrough. Were there any clues that he might become a performer?

'I don't think so. I was one of four boys: the youngest. My dad died when I was seven and it's often the way that one of the kids will take on the role of being mum's little helper. My memory of my early years is hoovering, painting and taking washing down to the launderette.'

Laverne: 'What was Middlesbrough like in the sixties?'

'It's a place I remember very fondly. The Cleveland Hills, to go and frolic in. In my teen years, there was plenty of work. I worked in a chicken factory, in a steel foundry, and on the bins for a year.'

Mortimer described enjoying being a binman because it made him fit ('so I could wear short-sleeved T-shirts!') and he'd be finished by noon. Laverne asked him to say more about his dad dying.

'I just remember coming home, being ushered away by a policeman and not knowing what was happening. Then, a couple of weeks later, being told my dad had died, and crying, and being very sad about it.

'Then forgetting about it, really, and thinking that it hadn't affected me at all. But then, later in my life, realising it was the defining moment of my life. It's defined my personality.'

'How so?'

'If something so precious has been taken from you, you can feel very insecure. I think they call it "compulsive helping". Just to make sure people aren't going to abandon you, you make them really rely on you.'

Laverne turned to her guest's boyhood dreams. 'You were a passionate footballer with aspirations to play professionally. How serious were you about it?'

'It was what I was going to do. I captained my school team three years earlier than I should have, and played for Middlesbrough's youth team. But at the age of sixteen, I went into a shed at the training ground and was told they weren't signing me on. And football was my life.'

Laverne: 'How did you cope?'

'I felt a little bit resentful towards football, actually. I didn't play again until I was in university.'

Mortimer flirted with joining the North Eastern Electricity Board to train as an electrician, but instead stayed on at school then enrolled to study law at Sussex University. It was not a happy experience.

'It wasn't something I really wanted to do and it never suited me. In my heart of hearts, I knew it didn't. On the first day, there was a little card, saying, "Welcome! All the law students are having a drink tonight!" So, I went down.

'I thought appropriate dress would be my Middlesbrough football shirt and a Levi jacket but they were all in black tie. I instantly thought, *Ah, this probably isn't going to be for me.* Throughout my entire three years at Sussex, I never spoke to another law student.'

Laverne: 'How is that *possible*?'

'We talked in tutorials and so on, but as soon as they finished, I was away back to my room to listen to my records.'

Mortimer graduated and became a solicitor in south London, where he helped high-rise tenants suffering from a cockroach infestation: 'I was on the front of the local paper as the "COCKROACH KING". I were right proud!'

Laverne: 'What was your life like at this point?'

'I was doing my work and living in a homeless hostel. Then one day an old acquaintance from Middlesbrough appeared at my door and said, "Do you want to go to something tonight called *Vic Reeves Big Night Out*?" I did, because I didn't know a soul in London!

'We went to a tiny room over a pub. Jim was on stage in a Bryan Ferry mask, with planks attached to his feet, tap-dancing and making high-pitched wails. I was hooked instantly. I got introduced to him and I started going every week.

'His friends would all do something in the show. I think the first thing I did was go up and give him a cheque for seven million pounds for helping out daft kids. Then I came on with a helmet on and I was the man with the stick.

'We eventually started writing it together and transferred from a pub to a little local theatre. One night, Michael Grade and Alan Yentob were in the audience, unknown to us, and asked if we'd like to go on the telly.'

Mortimer took twelve weeks off from his job as a solicitor to give comedy a go. He didn't expect to require any longer.

'We didn't think there was any chance of it ever being recommissioned. We just thought it was a lovely little thing to tell our kids that we were once on the telly. But it hit a note with enough people that that became what I wanted to do.

'I'd found a passion at last, and a soulmate in Jim. He's a genius, total genius, so to find someone like that, and to work with them every day – it's amazing.'

Laverne: 'What did your mum think about your comedy career? You risked disappointing her by giving up the law?'

'Yes. She was very proud that I was a solicitor. Every time I phoned her up, it was: "When are you going back to the law?" It only stopped when I launched the Cadbury Boost bar on TV and she realised that I probably *was* going to be able to make a living.'

After a break for the Beautiful South, which reminded Mortimer of the surrealist 2004 comedy series *Catterick*, his favourite TV project to that point, Laverne turned to a weightier matter. In 2015, he had suffered serious heart problems. 'What happened?'

'I went to see my GP because I had a little pain in my chest. He sent me to the heart specialist. Four days later, I was on the operating table. Sadly, you don't get any warning with heart disease. You just drop.'

Laverne: 'What did you do?'

'Got married! I had to get a special licence to be married quickly. Just myself, my wife and my two boys. Then we went to a café for a cup of tea and my last bacon sandwich, and then I went to hospital for my operation.'

Mortimer explained that the scare had made him 'more certain of what I wanted to do'. He launched his *Athletico Mince* football podcast. A friend, comedian/actor Paul Whitehouse, also had an idea for him.

'Paul, bless him, was very worried that you can go two ways after heart surgery. You can either get scared and just shrink on to your sofa or you can engage with life again. I was in danger of taking the first option.

'Paul kept asking me, "C'mon, let's go fishing!" until eventually I did, and I absolutely *adored* it. I discovered something I'd lost from when I was young: just a purposeless day with a friend, chewing the fat and immersing yourself in the countryside. And I got addicted to it.

'The show came from that. We started going fishing together, and Paul mentioned to someone at the BBC: "You could maybe film it?" That's what we do: we just film it. There's no preparation at all.'

Laverne: 'Did its success take you by surprise?'

'Absolutely! If I'd had my choice on the day that it was being broadcast, I'd have had it pulled. It's so gentle and nostalgic that I just couldn't see what would motivate anyone to watch it! But there you go.

'It ties back to my health. I don't think I'd have done that show before my health problems. But, after them, I wasn't going to miss an opportunity like that.'

As the show meandered to a gentle close, Lauren Laverne asked her guest what he had learned from his career. 'What advice would you give to someone who wants to be a comedian?'

'Well,' considered Bob Mortimer, 'the thing that's served myself and Jim quite well is just doing what makes each other laugh, and never asking that question: "Will other people find it funny?" I think people should just return to, you know, *do what makes you laugh ...*'

● ● ●

Two years after he appeared on *Desert Island Discs*, Bob Mortimer published his autobiography, *And Away* ... It included the nugget that, in his Cockroach King years as a solicitor in Peckham, he was once mugged by one of his own clients, who then recognised him and apologised. He continued to represent this errant soul. Surrealist humour has clearly always been his bag.

DISCS CHOSEN
Ralph Vaughan Williams's *A Sea Symphony*
BBC Symphony Orchestra and Chorus
'It's the track Jim and I play before we go on stage and have done for thirty year. It's a very intimate moment: me and Jim, backstage, scared stiff'

'On My Way'
Free
'I went to see them when I was thirteen and fell in love with them'

❤ **'Down to You'**
Joni Mitchell
'My heroine. I saw her at Madison Square Garden and cried for the first ten minutes. There she was, in front of me, this amazing woman'

'It Must Be Love'
Madness

'The Punk and the Godfather'
The Who
'I went to university in Brighton because of Quadrophenia*'*

'Hot on the Heels of Heartbreak'
The Beautiful South
'Me and Morwenna [Banks] *sang it in* Catterick*'*

'Some Fantastic Place'
Squeeze
'I've asked Jim if he'll sing this at my funeral'

'King of the Rodeo'
Kings of Leon

BOOK
My Secret History – Paul Theroux
'I can find different lives in there'

LUXURY ITEM
His pillow
Mortimer: 'It's thin, soft and luxurious and has a lovely moisty smell to it'
Laverne: 'The smell of your own head.'
Mortimer: 'It must be my head, yeah.'

63

PAT McGRATH

MAKE-UP QUEEN
19 May 2019

Fashion and beauty are hermetically sealed worlds, and notoriously difficult to break into. To go from a provincial childhood of poverty to become the most influential make-up artist in the world, and to build a business worth a billion dollars, almost beggars belief.

Pat McGrath has achieved those extraordinary milestones. Raised by a fashion-obsessed single mother in Northampton, she quickly formed a passionate interest in style and beauty, and an inventive, idiosyncratic approach towards how to decorate and present herself – and others.

Those obsessions had consumed her throughout her life and career and made her, as Lauren Laverne marvelled, 'the most prolific runway make-up artist of all time'. And marooned on the desert island in May 2019, McGrath made it sound like it had all been one great big, fun adventure.

• • •

Laverne began by asking her guest to give some idea of the logistics of working on a major fashion show.

'We're talking eighty-seven suitcases, sometimes one hundred team members, five to six motorcycles, eight cars, four vans,' replied McGrath. 'The team travel thirty thousand miles per season. I look at it as like an army.'

'It's military precision. The show goes on at ten am. We'll have started at four am. I'm like a general marching around the tables, going, "Eyebrows on! Skin done! Lips on!" The adrenalin is magical.'

Laverne: 'When you've got a model or a client in the chair, there is something very intimate about touching their face and changing the way that they look?'

'Yes. You're very close with whoever you're making up. You have so much fun and they always open up to me. I love to give advice!'

'You'll come straight out and say what you think?'

'*Oh, darling, pack your bags! Order the car! There's plenty more where that came from!*'

Laverne: 'What about when you get the chance to make up one of your heroes?'

'Well, I'm always very nervous, but I do a dry run where we get all the timings perfectly. I'm shaking inside and then I get my act together once somebody arrives. And, in the end, just turn it into a light, fun day.'

Laverne asked her guest to describe her signature look: 'Like many people who work in fashion, you love black?'

'My signature look is making my skin look beautiful. I love mascara. I put on layers of it, a little bit of eyeliner, shimmering highlights on the cheek-bones. I like very simple beauty. My obsession is putting make-up on other people. That's my canvas and that's my joy.'

After a pause for David Bowie's 'Life on Mars?', Laverne asked McGrath where her childhood interest in fashion and beauty had originated.

'From my mother. She was *obsessed* with make-up and clothing. She'd take me to buy the patterns for the clothes, then to the fabric store to choose the remnants, then to the make-up store: *hours* of choosing the make-up!

'Back then, there weren't the colours that were right for dark skin, so there'd be one colour a week that was right. She'd say, "We've found it! *Now* we can go food shopping!"

'I'm really grateful to her for inspiring me and making me who I am, but back then I used to *beg* her not to take me. I was crying but I was the youngest and I had to go. She'd be like, "Get your coat!" Isn't it *amazing* that that became my obsession?'

McGrath described her mother, Jean, also hoarding vintage dresses and constantly changing her hair colour and style. Yet, noted Laverne, her guest had described her childhood before as very difficult and hard.

'Basically, we had no money. I think it was very difficult and hard for *her* but she didn't let *me* know that it was difficult and hard. For me, it was a little bit of a wonderland, because she let me go with her on these imaginary journeys of glamour.'

McGrath recalled, as a girl, using lipstick as eyeshadow – 'fairly futuristic!' – and her mum overcoming the dearth of make-up designed for black skin by making up her face with cocoa powder. She also formulated her own very first beauty product.

'I made a moisturiser for my dolls and myself. I mixed oil and water, whipped it, put it in the fridge and it looked like a cream. I packed it all over my face. I was shining like a Belisha beacon for months!'

Laverne: 'To what extent did you experience racism?'

'Growing up in the community, and going to church, you have a really solid base around you. My mother was like, "Oh, look at that person – they're racist! *Poor things!* Anyway, let's go shopping!"

Inevitably, McGrath shifted her gaze outside of Northampton. As an art student, she would get the train to London and go to the late-eighties havens of the Blitz Kids and New Romantics such as the Wag Club.

'My mother didn't approve so we lied and told her we were going to art galleries. I'd come home, my clothes full of sweat and smoke, and she'd say,

"They smoke so much in those galleries!" And I'd say, "Yeah, it's terrible, Mum!"'

McGrath progressed to going to London 'to stalk celebrities, because I was obsessed with the Blitz Kids'. Outside Radio 1 one day, she had a chance, life-changing encounter with DJ Janice Long.

'Janice came out and said, "Oh my God, look at your make-up!" I'd got my lipstick on my eyes and my cheeks were really burgundy. She said, "I'd love it if you could do that on me!" I went, "Is that a job?" She said, "Yes, it *is* a job." And I found my calling right there and then.'

Moving to the capital, McGrath took day jobs in a King's Road shoe shop and then at the Department of Transport to fund a heady nightlife of clubbing. Back at the Wag Club, she had a chance encounter with Kim Bowen, fashion director of *Blitz* magazine.

'I had tied thousands of rags into little braids so it looked like I had a fabric hat on. Bomber jacket, sneakers, hoop earrings, and she came up and said, "Wow, I love your look."

'She said, "What do you want to be?" and I said, "A make-up artist." She said, "OK, I'm shooting this weekend and I'd love you to come and watch." And I'd go and watch her shoot for *i-D*, the *Face*, *Blitz*. I'd just soak it all up. It was the best schooling ever.'

Laverne: 'And you and your friends would pretend to be fashion editors to get into fashion shows. Did you have fake IDs?'

'We'd have fake *Vogue* cards. It'd be me and Edward Enninful and we'd pretend to be the editors of Jamaican *Vogue*. Back then it was easier to get in. We'd sneak in, or rip the side of a tent.

'In the end, all the PR firms knew us, and were like, "This is ridiculous! You are in Italian *Vogue*'s seats and you need to get out!" And we'd be, like, "*No!*" Defiant. We felt like we deserved to be there.'

McGrath attempted to balance her day jobs with working as a freelance make-up artist before resolving to give up the former to concentrate on the latter. As soon as she did, she told Laverne, she was invited to tour Japan with singer Caron Wheeler and her band, Soul II Soul.

'I went to Japan. I was scared and I was shaking but it was a miraculous moment in my life and an incredible trip. And that's how *that* began.'

After a break for Malcolm McLaren's 'Madam Butterfly', Laverne rewound to McGrath's partner-in-crime when she was gatecrashing fashion shows. Edward Enninful was now the editor of British *Vogue*.

'What do you remember about him when you first met?' asked the host. 'Because he was only eighteen back then.'

'Yeah, he was a baby! I'd been working in the industry for quite some time and someone said, "There's a new young lad at *i-D* magazine, Edward. Let's pop in and see him. We went to the office and there was this shy, quiet young boy who never spoke.

'And I walked in *with my loud self* ... he always blames me that I'm the one who made him loud, because now we're both booming voices, screaming at each other all day!'

Laverne: 'He says you always had the confidence to create trends rather than follow them. He remembers you demanding a yellow eyebrow in *i-D* during the very bare-faced grunge era?'

'Oh, yes, I remember that! I demanded the yellow eyebrow and then I changed my mind and called him up and he said, "It's too late, it's gone to press." I was begging for mercy: "You've *got* to get rid of it!"'

'But it's about freedom of expression. Make-up: you can do anything you want. That's what I believe. You wash it off at the end: it's not permanent. It's always best to push yourself and have fun with it.'

Laverne: 'You once said fashion is an industry where the real insiders are all outsiders?'

'I think everyone within the industry are obsessive people. They are obsessed with the perfect pleat or the perfect hairdo: coming up with new ideas. And I always think the people in the industry are very geeky and not what you'd expect.

'It's like me running around like Darth Vader, all in black, with probably not much make-up on. I always think that the insiders are outsiders: the ones who probably were not the coolest at school.'

Laverne reflected that her guest's first and strongest influence, her mother, Jean, had died in 1992. 'What do you think she'd have made of your career today?'

'Oh, she would have been so proud! I think she would've been with me at most of the shows – probably directing! She would've been pointing out mistakes or how we could do things better. I would've loved her to have been there ...'

As a tantalising glimpse into the often-impenetrable world of style and beauty came to a close, Lauren Laverne wondered if there was still a skinny-and-white bias in the fashion industry.

'I mean, really and truly, that was the standard of the fashion industry when I was growing up, but I'm so happy to see the changes that I'm seeing now,' asserted Pat McGrath.

'We have models from all different social backgrounds, weights, body types, religious backgrounds. Shows that are over fifty per cent women of colour. It just wasn't there for such a long time, and now it is just fantastic to see. *Beautiful!*'

• • •

Pat McGrath no longer needs to rip open the sides of tents to get into fashion shows. Launched in 2015, her Pat McGrath Labs beauty company is now worth a cool billion dollars and is the biggest-selling line of beauty products in Selfridges. In the 2021 New Year Honours list, she was made a dame – the first make-up artist ever to receive this honour.

DISCS CHOSEN

'The Boss'
Diana Ross
'As a little girl prancing around the room, she was the icon'

'Life on Mars?'
David Bowie
'The androgyny, the bleached eyebrows, the colour, the clothes, the fearless use of gender – he's every make-up artist's dream'

'The Rain (Supa Dupa Fly)'
Missy Elliott
'She's different from everyone else and she celebrates her differences'

'Fade to Grey'
Visage

'Madam Butterfly'
Malcolm McLaren
'Malcolm McLaren's always been a huge inspiration'

'Prelude and Rooftop' from the soundtrack to *Vertigo*
Bernard Herrmann
'The song I played when my lipstick, Matte Trance, was launched'

'All Is Full of Love'
Björk
'I worked on Björk when she was in the Sugarcubes. She's extraordinary, she's fabulous.'

❤ **'La Vie en Rose'**
Grace Jones
'A ground-breaking legend. When I think about the strength and beauty of Grace Jones, I think of my own heritage with pride'

BOOK

Polaroids – Andy Warhol
'Andy was the first: instant glamour, instant fame, instant gratification. This book is like the genesis of what we're living in now'

LUXURY ITEM

Her make-up
'I'd be on the island in full beat, with lots of colours on my cheekbones, dancing to "La Vie en Rose" over and over again'

64
JOHN COOPER CLARKE

PERFORMANCE POET
21 July 2019

They call him the Bard of Salford. Born into a working-class family in the immediate post-war years, John Cooper Clarke was inspired by a school English teacher to become a poet. He wrote his first creative verse at the tender age of twelve and has never looked back since.

Clarke started out reading his poems in northern clubs in the seventies. The advent of punk rock gave his career a major boost as he recited his spiky, attitudinal words at gigs by the Sex Pistols, the Fall, Joy Division, Buzzcocks and many more, consequently finding himself dubbed punk's poet laureate.

Punk is long gone, and a crippling heroin addiction dimmed his creative spark in the eighties, but John Cooper Clarke rolls on. His idiosyncratic, vivid verse gets everywhere, from Arctic Monkeys songs to episodes of *The Sopranos*. And, when he rocked up on Lauren Laverne's island in July 2019, at the august age of seventy, it was a very big deal for him.

• • •

Laverne opened proceedings by asking her guest a crucial question: 'What makes a good poem?' Appearing loath to answer ('It's the kiss of death, isn't it, to over-analyse what you do?'), Clarke was far keener to share how excited he was to be invited on to the desert island.

'I've revised this list [*of records*] for sixty years,' he claimed. 'I've been a fan of the show for that long. I'm not even joking! If I might explain how important I feel this show to be: poetry is forever, so is *Desert Island Discs*.

'For me, *Desert Island Discs* has all the finality of a suicide note without the actual obligation of topping yourself. As you can see, I'm a coconut-half-empty kind of guy on this desert island!'

After Clarke's opening music choice, Laverne asked if it was true that his engineer dad, George, had once given him some life-shaping advice.

'Well, there were two pieces of advice I've never forgotten. One was never work for nothing, even if it's a flaky job like I've got. And never leave a bookie's with a smile on your face.'

Discussing his childhood, Clarke described his dad as 'a funny guy and a real good geezer' and his mum, Hilda, as 'a living saint' who was 'hyper-literate' and would withdraw five books at a time for both of them from the local library. She was also his 'movie date'.

'We had an arrangement: for every two or three gangster movies, I'd have to go see three what they call "women's pictures": *The Best of Everything* or *Peyton Place*. I could always find something to enjoy in them.'

'What was Salford like in the fifties?' wondered Laverne.

'Our apartment gave out on to what was the busiest crossroads in the north of England – pre-motorway, so it was all commercial traffic. Real chocka. I loved it. I didn't know any different.'

This polluted environment possibly contributed to Clarke contracting TB at the age of seven and being sent away to a relative in Rhyl to convalesce. 'How did it go?' asked Laverne.

'It was great! I was more or less feral. I was turfed out of the house at ten am and not expected back until teatime, so I'd knock around the fairground and make myself useful. They'd be playing rock and roll as you work – Gene Vincent, Elvis, Everly Brothers, all the good stuff.'

Clarke admitted to hating school: 'I've never been a team player. On every school report I ever had was "no team spirit".' Yet he found his English teacher, John Malone, an inspirational figure.

'He was a rugged outdoor type but with a weakness for the Romantic poetry of the nineteenth century, which he conveyed to the entire class. And it was quite a tough school. Put it this way: we had our own coroner.

'But he imparted his love of Romantic verse to the entire class until it became a hothouse of poetic competition to the point where it was a badge of honour to use polysyllabic speech at all times. I was the best at it, and that's where I flourished.'

Laverne: 'Which poets did you love?'

'The one that struck me first was Edgar Allan Poe. We had to learn them off by heart, Michael Gove-style. Really, it's the only way to do it. The way poetry works is it sneaks up on you thirty years later.

'You're not going to understand it. It was written by a forty-year-old guy and you're twelve. Just learn the words, and then, thirty years later, *Wow!* It's amazing how it makes its mark.

'Then, on reading up on Poe, I found that his entire body of work had been translated into French by Charles Baudelaire, so I resolved to read his poetry in translation. Ever since then, Charles Baudelaire has been, without a doubt, my number-one guy poetry-wise.'

Laverne: 'After school, you took jobs as a printing compositor, a lab technician at Salford Tech and a firewatcher on Plymouth docks. Yet you were convinced that poetry as entertainment would work?'

'I was convinced: *if the poetry is entertaining enough, why doesn't it belong in the entertainment business?* You can take it back to the days of Edwardian music hall. Sentimental, nature-boy stuff would really fly in the music halls of Whitechapel.'

Laverne: 'But when you would tell people you wanted to be a poet ...'

'They'd all say: "Nobody makes a living out of *poetry!*" I'd say, "What about Philip Larkin?" "He's a librarian!" "T.S. Eliot?" "He was a bank clerk!" They all had these other jobs.'

Clarke took inspiration from a whimsical poet, Pam Ayres, winning TV talent show *Opportunity Knocks*. 'For a year, the British public were voting her back. I was like: *There you are! Why not me? She writes about her life; I write about mine.*'

Yet his first break into live performance came from a most unlikely source: lewd northern comedian Bernard Manning, who also owned the Embassy Club in Manchester. Clarke recalled asking him for a gig.

'He said, "What is it you do?" I said, "Poetry, Mr Manning." He said, "Oh, they don't like poetry 'ere! Half of 'em can't bleeping read!"'

'Well, I'd just written a poem, "Salome", set in the Ritz in Manchester, which I knew Bernard would've known very well. I'm going to have to bleep myself here! It's about a punch-up that kicks off and this woman, Salome Maloney, gets dragged into it.

'A line is: "*When the punch-up was over, she was lying on the deck / She fell off her stiletto heels and broke her bleeping neck!*" As soon as he read that, he said, "Oh yeah, that'll fly! All right, I'll give you a chance!"'

The gig at Manning's club was not a success, reported Clarke: 'I was met with the poet's worst enemy: indifference.' Yet he found more receptive audiences when he began performing at punk-rock gigs.

'Once it took off, it was great! It wasn't all dodging bottles and phlegm. That didn't last very long. Some of them liked it and some of them didn't. Howard Devoto, who was then the singer with the Buzzcocks, convinced me I should be playing punk venues.

'He pointed out the concerns in my poems were singing from the same hymn sheets as punk rock. For me, poetry is the shortest way to convey something really big. That's what my poems had in common with the lyrics of John Lydon and Joe Strummer: broadly social, abrasive at times, yet with its own kind of feral attraction.

'The lyrical style of punk rock I found a great kinship with, specifically the Ramones, who I thought were sensational lyricists: "*How the hell am I gonna tell 'em, I ain't got no cerebellum?*"'

Seizing on this similarity, Clarke had a top forty hit with 'Gimmicks' and began making albums of his poetry. He judged it only a partial success: 'When I hear my poems with music, it sounds to me as if one of my feet has been nailed to the floor!'

After the demise of punk, his own fortunes also took a dive: 'I never stopped working, but I was doing smaller joints and I wasn't writing as much as I should have done.' There was also another, deadlier reason for this.

Laverne: 'By this time, you'd developed a heroin addiction that lasted seventeen years. How bad did it get?'

'Well, *that* is the centre of your universe. There was always something better to do than write a poem. I mean, every drug addict is virtually the same person. I needed money more than ever so I had to work.

'The glamour was flaking off with every new job. I really felt like I was selling my sorry arse at times. There used to be a tedious saying among hippies: "If you're not part of the solution, you're part of the problem." I was very much part of the problem.'

Laverne: 'Were you scared for yourself at any point?'

'No. I don't remember fear being a factor. But when I quit, I felt really badly done to.' Clarke laughed. 'I didn't *want* to quit.'

'Really? Why?'

'You feel you're doing it for society, or something. Know what I mean? I thought I was doing everybody a favour. Everybody was worried about me. What can I say? Who wants to be a source of anxiety to everybody they know? You're just trouble.'

Clarke chose a song by former Velvet Underground singer Nico, with whom he shared a flat during a period of joint heroin addiction. Laverne asked her guest how hard it was to begin writing poetry again once he had shaken his habit.

'It took a long time to get back into it. I'd got out of the habit of writing poetry. But I think it was a good thing. The poetry I write now is so markedly different and superior to everything that was around before that.'

Laverne: 'How did it feel to know you still had the touch? You could still do it?'

'Well, marvellous, because I really did think that you can lose this, and now I *know* that you can. I don't let *anything* escape now.'

Laverne described Clarke meeting his second wife, Evie, at the end of the eighties, drawn by their shared love of Baudelaire. The couple had a daughter, Stella, in the early nineties. 'What is parenthood like?'

'If I'd known how much fun it is having a kid, I would've had seventeen of them! I was very, very late to it – forty-five – and all my life, my mates have had kids and they'd be saying, "Don't have kids!" I wish I hadn't listened to those miserable people!'

Prompted by Laverne, Clarke reflected on the late-career profile boost he had received from one of his poems being used over the end credits of *The Sopranos* in 2007 – and, separately, from hooking up with the Arctic Monkeys.

'I was doing a show at the Boardwalk in Sheffield, and the proprietor said, "Would you just have a word with these lads – big fans of your work?" And they'd done my stuff at school! Shy schoolboys, very polite, nice kids – but I knew they had something. And I couldn't be happier with their cover of "I Wanna Be Yours".'

As an absorbing interview rolled to a close, Clarke wished his parents could have heard him on *Desert Island Discs*: 'It would have impressed the hell out of them!' And he reflected that his long, erratic career might even have opened some doors for others.

'I think I've created a platform. It's a legitimate thing now – to write poetry, and read it in public. This Baudelairean idea of having an idle life and yet contributing, somehow, to the quality of everyone's life is just the best that I could ever have hoped for, really!"

Lauren Laverne asked what her guest might say to a young poet after advice. And John Cooper Clarke had some closing words of wisdom.

'You have to be idle to write it. A pen, a notebook and idleness: *those* are the three requisites for the manufacture of poetry ...'

• • •

The Bard of Salford has released seven albums, published two volumes of poetry, and, in 2020, wrote an acclaimed autobiography, *I Wanna Be Yours*. On its publication, Kate Moss admiringly noted that 'John Cooper Clarke uses words like Chuck Berry uses guitar riffs ... he's the real deal, funny and caustic, the velvet voice of discontent.' The *Sunday Times* reviewer took a more direct route: 'Any autobiography that features both Bernard Manning and Nico is unlikely to disappoint.'

DISCS CHOSEN
'A Quiet Place'
Garnet Mimms & the Enchanters
'A reminder that it's not all beer and skittles living in the inner city'

'Whole Lotta Shakin' Goin' On'
Jerry Lee Lewis
'The greatest piano player that ever lived'

'I Wonder Why'
Dion & the Belmonts
'I went to see Dion in 1961 and he was the best-dressed and most handsome man I'd ever seen'

'Skylark'
Ella Fitzgerald
'She sings beautiful songs beautifully'

'I'll Keep It with Mine'
Nico
'A very mysterious tune. Enigmatic isn't too big a word'

'Moonlight in Vermont'
Frank Sinatra
'What's life without Sinatra? Nothing'

'The Black Hills of Dakota'
Doris Day
'The first woman I fell in love with, at a very early age'

❤ **'How Great Thou Art'**
Elvis Presley
'The greatest singer that ever lived'

BOOK
Against Nature – Joris-Karl Huysmans
'The way he talks you through a painting is better than going to an art gallery'

LUXURY ITEM
A boulder of opium twice the size of his own head
'Whose law am I breaking? I'm not going to be worrying anybody …'

65
DR SABRINA COHEN-HATTON

FIREFIGHTER, PSYCHOLOGIST
29 September 2019

Some people have overcome almost impossibly abject and desperate personal circumstances to achieve their goals and realise their heart's desire. Their stories are so impressive that they sound like testaments to the sheer strength and durability of the human will.

Dr Sabrina Cohen-Hatton landed on Lauren Laverne's desert island in September 2019 as chief fire officer of West Sussex and with a PhD in psychology gained studying the on-the-job decision-making of firefighters. After eighteen years in the service, she was one of the most senior firefighters in Britain.

Yet Dr Cohen-Hatton had ascended to these precipitous heights from almost unimaginable depths. After tragedy struck her family in her early teens, she was homeless and slept rough in her native south Wales for two years, surviving abuse and attacks and the indifference of the authorities.

Determined to become a firefighter, she was rejected by the first thirty-one stations she applied to, then endured abuse and hostility from male colleagues before becoming a senior and pioneering figure within the service. She brought a truly inspirational tale to *Desert Island Discs* and related it with articulacy and passion.

• • •

Lauren Laverne began with a key question: 'After almost twenty years in the fire service, what is it that you love about your job?'

'*Everything!*' answered Cohen-Hatton. 'Probably, for me, the privilege of being trusted by people to know what to do when they're literally having the worst day that they've ever experienced.'

The host commented that the female, diminutive Cohen-Hatton did not fit the stereotypical image of a firefighter. Which was what?

'I think nine times out of ten, if you ask people to imagine a firefighter, they imagine some tall, dark, handsome, hunky calendar model. The reality is – and I say this with love, I really do! – I've seen far more firefighters who look like Ed Balls than Tom Hardy!'

After Cohen-Hatton chose, fittingly, Alicia Keys's 'Girl on Fire', Laverne wondered how one of her guest's life passions had triggered another. 'Working as a firefighter sparked your interest in psychology. How did that happen?'

'I had a really harrowing incident. My husband and I were firefighters on neighbouring stations. One day I was called to an incident where a firefighter had been severely burned. There was a one-in-four chance that it was him.

'It was horrendous. I got on the truck and for the entire journey it was all I could think about. We got there, I jumped off, and all I could see was this pair of legs sticking out with a huddle of firefighters around them. I couldn't tell who it was. I couldn't see anyone's face.

'I remember grabbing the oxygen cylinder to run over. I bit down on my lip so hard to stop myself crying that I've got a scar there to this day. Then I saw Mike stand up, and I felt this overwhelming sense of relief that it wasn't him. But, also, a sense of guilt, because the guy who *was* injured wasn't just a colleague – he was a friend.

'I started to look at what we could do to stop it happening to anyone else. What I found was incredible – eighty per cent of injuries across all industries happen from human error! In *my* world, that meant people getting hurt. And I started looking at what we could do to help reduce that.'

Cohen-Hatton explained that there had been no previous research into the specific pressures affecting decisions made by firefighters in high-stress situations. However, as a firefighter poised to begin a psychology degree, she was ideally placed to fill that gap.

'Because I had that dual role, I was able to access that environment and got some really rich, valuable data. And we found that eighty per cent of the decisions people were making were intuitive, gut decisions.'

Laverne moved on to her guest's childhood. Her Moroccan father, an immigrant from Israel, was 'a maths genius with a photographic memory' who was utilising those talents in a casino when he met her mother, a croupier. The attraction between them was instant.

'They were absolutely head over heels in love: idolised each other. They settled in Cardiff, had me and my brother, and ran a pizzeria after my dad had finished playing cards.'

Cohen-Hatton was only three when her dad was diagnosed with a brain tumour. It affected his personality, taking away 'part of his soul' before he died when she was nine. His death devastated her mother.

'She really suffered with her mental health: it broke down terribly. The business went under and we lived in abject poverty for a long time. We grew up on benefits and were on the at-risk register from nine or ten. The social worker was round all the time, which would stress Mum out and make things even more volatile.

'It got worse and worse and, when I was fifteen, I found myself sleeping rough because it was a better alternative to the one that I was experiencing. And I don't blame my mother in any way, shape or form, because she was ill.'

There began what Cohen-Hatton described as 'some really, really dark, difficult times' in her life. 'I started off sleeping rough in the doorway of an abandoned church. There were a few others there as well. Which, in a way, gave you comfort: it wasn't only you.

'I had a stray dog: we befriended each other and he used to sleep by my feet. People might look at homeless people and think, *Why do you have a dog? You can't even look after yourself!* But that dog was my rock and my protection.'

This was never more evident, she told Laverne, than the night that she and her dog, Menace, slept in a subway.

'I woke up with some drunk guy urinating on my sleeping bag, laughing hysterically, and his mate was laughing. And Menace jumped out of the sleeping bag, and ... let's just say, I don't think that guy will be urinating on anyone any time soon!

'But it felt dehumanising on so many levels. I remember being hungry all the time. One time, I started eating out of a bin by a hotdog stand. I remember waiting by the bin for someone to chuck half a hotdog in, and then quickly darting in and grabbing it.

'People were looking at me with disgust: *How can you eat out of a bin?* And I can remember firing back a look: *How can you let your fellow human be so hungry that you'll stand by and look on in disgust when they're eating out of a bin?*

'People would walk past you like you're not there; like you're a ghost. It's funny: if someone falls over in the street, everyone will rush to pick them up, because you don't want to see someone suffering.

'But you have someone sat on the side of the street, with no food in their belly and no hope, and you walk past like they're not there. That is someone's son or daughter there. Possibly someone's mother or father. They're a *person*.'

After the local council refused to put her on the housing list as she was already homeless ('They prioritised people who were about to *become* homeless'), Cohen-Hatton found succour selling the *Big Issue*. After two years of sleeping rough, she managed to rent a flat.

She also began applying to be a firefighter. 'What was it particularly about the fire service that appealed to you?' asked Laverne.

'The idea of doing something to help other people. I suppose, in a funny kind of way, I wanted to rescue others in a way I felt like no one had been able to rescue *me*.'

Having been rejected by thirty-one fire stations, Cohen-Hatton was accepted by the thirty-second and joined the South Wales Fire and Rescue Service. She was eighteen, five feet one-and-a-half, and the only woman in her station.

Laverne: 'How did the other, male, firefighters react to you?'

'It wasn't brilliant. My first six months, I wasn't even allowed my own name. They called me something derogatory, which I certainly couldn't say on the BBC.

'They'd say to me, "There's no place for women in the fire service. No offence to you, Sab!" After a while, I'd get fed up, and I'd be like: 'Well, I don't think that *morons* should be in the fire service. No offence to you, mate, but here we are!"'

Cohen-Hatton survived early workplace bullying such as having her boots filled with rubbish to establish herself in the station. Having resolved not to date a firefighter ('you become mess-table gossip'), she promptly fell in love with, and married, a colleague, Mike.

In nearly eighteen years in the fire service since then, she told Laverne, she had seen progress being made in tackling such sexist attitudes, and in areas such as helping firefighters to deal with PTSD – a particular danger after major disasters such as 2017's Grenfell Tower fire.

'It was the most harrowing event, I think, that any of us have ever experienced,' she recalled. 'I wasn't there on the night, but I ran our welfare centre debriefing the crews as they came off the next morning.

'And then I was in charge of the scene for two days when we were dealing with the body recovery. I haven't spoken about it publicly, and I won't do ... but that scale of incident raises wider questions about mental health in the emergency services.'

As a heartening interview with one of the most inspirational castaways in *Desert Island Discs*' eight-decade history closed, Laverne noted that her guest had recently written her memoir, *The Heat of the Moment*. She had also become an ambassador for the *Big Issue*.

'I wonder what the current generation of vendors made of reading what you'd gone through, and where you've been since?' the host mused.

'I hope that they can take something from my experiences,' said Dr Sabrina Cohen-Hatton. 'Because I've been in the position where you feel you've been written off; where you feel that society has put you in a place, and you're confined by what people expect of you.

'And I wanted to say to them that you *can* break out of that, and that doesn't have to be the case. So I hope that, if it's done anything, it's inspired some hope for people who perhaps, at one point, didn't have any ...'

• • •

In addition to her day job as chief fire officer of West Sussex Fire and Rescue Service, Dr Sabrina Cohen-Hatton continues to be an agent of change in Britain's fire service. Her research is widely acknowledged as having helped to shape national fire-service policy and increased the efficacy and mental wellbeing of the country's firefighters. In 2020, the *Big Issue* – the magazine that she credits with 'saving her life' – named her its Top Campaigner in its Top 100 Changemakers list.

DISCS CHOSEN

'Girl on Fire'
Alicia Keys
'My little girl, who's nine going on nineteen, loves this track'

'Mi Gente'
J. Balvin & Willy William
'I did some work in South America and discovered reggaeton'

❤ **'Bankrobber'**
The Clash
'It reminds me of my father. He'd always find a way around the rules'

'Samaritans'
Idles
'It's about the toxicity of macho masculinity'

'Anarchy in the UK'
Sex Pistols
'When I was fourteen, I had an anarchy symbol tattooed on my back, which I later had removed'

'Don't Look Back in Anger'
Oasis
'It reminds me of my darling, long-suffering husband, Mike'

'Local Boy in the Photograph'
Stereophonics
'It nods to my Welsh roots. You don't get much Welsh-er than the 'phonics!'

'54-46 Was My Number'
Toots & the Maytals
'I love proper old-school Jamaican ska music – and the power of perspective in this song'

BOOK

The Old Man and the Sea – Ernest Hemingway
'Such a powerful story of hope and resilience and mental toughness. It really resonates with me'

LUXURY ITEM

A family photo album
' ...that also dispenses an unlimited supply of ice-cold gin-and-tonic'

'ISLE NEVER FORGET ...'

'It felt a real honour to be asked to go on but I must admit there was a point initially when I thought, *I don't think I'm important enough to be on* Desert Island Discs. *What if I don't have enough interesting to say? And I have terrible taste in music!*

'But doing the show was unbelievably great. I loved it. I went in with a couple of friends who are big fans of the programme. Lauren was an incredible interviewer. She really brought out the best of the stories as well as the worst of them.

'I was sat there in tears at one point. My eyes were streaming and Lauren was starting to cry. My friends were sat in an adjoining room, listening in. We met at the end and *their* eyes were red and puffy as well. We all ended up in floods of tears.

'I've always found my homelessness difficult to talk about. It's always a bit of a risk to decide to bare all and show the world. But I know there are still loads of people, especially young people, who are in exactly the same position today as I was then.

'We talked for three hours. We went over our allotted studio time. There was a lot they could have used but the show was beautifully produced and authentic to my experience. And, after it was broadcast, people were so kind! Really, really warm and lovely.

'I got so many messages from people that I've now got a little folder of them on my phone. When I'm having a bad day, and I wonder if I should have talked about those things, I just look through that and I remember that it's already helped people.

'It was a lovely experience and one that I will always remember. To have your personal story recorded in history, which *Desert Island Discs* does, is really exciting. And it was the first time the punk band Idles had been played on BBC Radio 4, so *that* was a bit of a coup!'

66

LIN-MANUEL MIRANDA

PLAYWRIGHT, COMPOSER, ACTOR
6 October 2019

Lauren Laverne had a very pertinent question: 'How does a musical theatre-loving, hip-hop nerd from Manhattan start a theatrical phenomenon, and reshape American attitudes towards the birth of their nation, by telling the story of the country's first bureaucrat?'

Lin-Manuel Miranda had the answer. Since its 2015 premiere, his rap-based musical *Hamilton*, telling the story of American founding father Alexander Hamilton, had made $1 billion, won eleven Tony Awards, a Grammy and a Pulitzer Prize, and been described by Michelle Obama as 'the best piece of art that I have ever seen in my life'.

Not content with conceptualising and writing *Hamilton*, Miranda had also played the leading role on Broadway. Yet, as he related to Laverne, a whole host of racial and cultural influences had fed into this American success story ... and it had all started with *The Pirates of Penzance*.

• • •

Laverne opened by asking Miranda about this formative experience of appearing in a high-school production of the Gilbert & Sullivan comic opera at the age of fourteen. He played the Pirate King.

'It was my first time auditioning for the school musical,' he recalled. 'To be a freshman and get a lead role felt like a coup: an enormous vote of confidence. Also, it just felt like, *Oh, OK, I could be good at this!*

'I remember working so hard: Gilbert & Sullivan isn't easy! And I just remember the applause at the end of that thing feeling like the most gratifying sound I'd ever heard. I've been chasing that ever since.'

Laverne listed her guest's vast range of professional activities: actor, musical director, composer, MC, playwright. 'And one of your many talents is freestyle rap, [*including*] once with Barack Obama in the Rose Garden ...'

'That was a not un-stressful experience!' laughed Miranda. 'It was their idea, actually, and I said, "OK!"

'I remember saying to the president, "If you could start slow and speed up, that would be more dynamic ..." And he cut me off mid-sentence: "We're just gonna do what we're gonna do!" I was like, "OK!"

'So it was scary, and probably not my best freestyle, but it was the best I could do in that moment, with the Leader of the Free World!'

After a break for Liza Minnelli's 'Cabaret', Laverne turned to *Hamilton*'s genesis. The hip-hop musical was based on a biography of Alexander Hamilton by Ron Chernow. 'What was the moment that you thought: *THIS is the idea. This is going to fly?*'

'At the end of the second chapter of reading the book. This guy is a wordsmith and he used words to get himself out of his circumstances. And, in that moment, I thought, *Well, that's hip-hop.* Words were his passport to everything, and that's what my favourite MCs do.

'I understand that it is incongruous, the notion of these Founders with this very contemporary form of music, but I thought it made sense for the fact that Hamilton really *wrote his way* into everything. It seemed a unique way of telling it.'

Laverne: 'It features actors from many different backgrounds telling the story of an immigrant to America?'

'Tommy Kail, the director, said, "This is the story of America then, told by America now." I didn't realise what a big deal that was until you see it on stage, in the opening number, when they sing the word "Time" at the top of their lungs. And how thrilling that is!'

Laverne turned to Miranda's childhood. His political consultant father and psychologist mother had emigrated from Puerto Rico to Inwood, at the very northern tip of Manhattan Island in New York City.

'It was like a tiny Latin American country. We moved there when I was one, in 1981. Everyone spoke Spanish. Even the businesses that weren't Latino-owned spoke Spanish, because that was the clientele.'

Miranda recalled winning a scholarship to, and studying at, a top publicly funded school in uptown New York, and spending his summers in Puerto Rico with his grandparents. These varying life perspectives, he said, were invaluable.

'The best recipe for a writer is being a little out of place everywhere. In my neighbourhood, I'm the kid who goes to the fancy school; in Puerto Rico, I'm the kid who speaks Spanish with a mixed-up gringo accent; at school, I'm the kid who lives way uptown.

'That's a great recipe for making a writer, because you're always kind of thinking about which part of yourself to bring into the conversation. *Which part of me is most applicable to the people I'm around?*'

Miranda described loving his elite school, Hunter College, but finding it intimidating: 'I was very aware that the kids around me were smarter and swimming in deeper waters than me.

'So I learned a couple of things. I learned very quickly that funny is a currency. Then I was like, *All right, I'm never going to be as good in math and science. I'm just going to double down on this passion of mine. Film and theatre: these are things that I love.*'

Laverne: 'You were also enormously sensitive to music as a kid. How did this manifest itself?'

'In me making an ass of myself! I would get very emotional over music. I now realise that that is a strength and a superpower, but as a kid, when your class listens to "Bridge Over Troubled Water" and you're struggling to hold it together because you think the song is so sad, it's tough.

'My parents tell a story of, as an infant, I would start crying if it was a minor-chordy-type song.'

Laverne: 'But now you know it's a superpower? One you've harnessed?'

'Yeah, I think so. Music is one of the only things that pings off neurons on both hemispheres of your brain and does things to us chemically that we don't even understand ...'

Laverne remarked that YouTube footage existed of the young Miranda, in his bedroom, dancing to 'Footloose'. 'Your camera was a constant companion as you started growing up. Why?'

'It's easier to film something than to be a part of it. It's easier to film a conversation than have a conversation. And it really became a crutch for me in high school. I was the kid who brought the camera everywhere and I was making movies with my friends.

'I remember seeing *Rent* on my seventeenth birthday. There's a fight between Mark and Roger, where Roger says [*Miranda sings*]: "Mark *lives* for his work, Mark *loves* his work, Mark *hides* in his work." And Mark is the character who has been holding a camcorder the entire play.

'[*Roger*] is calling him out for using his video camera as a crutch, to distance himself from his friends, some of whom are dying. And *I* felt called out, in the back row of the mezzanine of the Nederlander Theatre. It's as personal as a musical ever felt to me. That one moment.

'I started writing musicals there and then. It was the first time I saw a contemporary musical about people who wanted to be artists; were scared of selling out; were scared of dying. I was scared of *all* of those things. That's when my career as a writer of musical theatre began.'

Laverne: 'You wrote your first musical, *In the Heights*, at just nineteen. It opened on Broadway with you in the lead and won four Tonys: an amazing achievement. What did you find most difficult?'

'Patience! I was so impatient for a production that I think that, had it not been for [*director*] Tommy Kail, a far worse show would have made it to production and I wouldn't be sitting here talking to you!'

Laverne mentioned that, after the astronomical success of *Hamilton* in 2015, Miranda had been given an august American award named the MacArthur Genius Grant. 'How do you feel about the term genius being applied to you?'

Miranda laughed. 'I mean, I've known too many *actual* geniuses! Do I count myself among them? I think I work very hard. I think I am talented. I do not think that is the same thing.'

Laverne: 'What do your parents make of what you've achieved?'

'Well, my mother will tell you, "I know since he was in the womb that he was brilliant!" She tells this story about me kicking her in time to the music *in utero*. It gets younger in the pregnancy every time she tells it!'

As the engaging conversation drew to a close, Laverne turned to her guest's recent new role as a campaigner for his native Puerto Rico. He had visited the island after it had been devastated by a hurricane in 2017. 'What did you find?'

'I found an island struggling with challenges no major American city has ever had to face – and with less help. The island of blue tarps as you're landing, instead of roofs! My aunt and uncle lived on generators in their town for five months, just to have electricity at night.

'It just wouldn't happen on the mainland. It was a stark reminder of the colonial status of this island. And the horrible body count that we knew to be much higher than the president [*Trump, had said*], who fixed it in his mind at sixteen and refused to think about it again.'

In a gesture of support and solidarity, he had even staged a production of *Hamilton* in Puerto Rico, again playing the lead role. 'How did it feel to perform that role on stage there?' asked Lauren Laverne.

'Oh, man! It was one of the toughest and yet most triumphant months of my life. Tough because the stuff that we're dealing with is all stuff Puerto Rico's dealing with. It's a colony dealing with what the hell it wants to be. And here is this show about a colony struggling with what the hell it wants to be. So, on that level, it was very complicated.

'I had a great moment. It was January 16, which is my birthday, and we finished the matinee. I got offstage and took my wig off and I was, like, half-naked. The stage manager says: "You have to go back out. They're not leaving and they won't stop cheering."

'So I went back out in a bathrobe and, like, bowed, and the entire audience sang "Happy Birthday" and I was a mess. I can't *talk* about it without crying. At that moment in Puerto Rico's history, they needed just a day of good news. That's what *Hamilton* was sort of able to be.

'And the reception! You know, because I always felt like an outsider on the island – the embrace of it healed something in me that I didn't even know was incomplete ...'

• • •

In 2019, the same year that he washed up on the desert island, Lin-Manuel Miranda acted in a BBC TV adaptation of Philip Pullman's *His Dark Materials*.

Two years later, he made his movie directorial debut with *Tick, Tick... Boom!* – a musical drama based on the stage musical of the same name by Jonathan Larson. The acclaimed film and its star, Andrew Garfield, scooped many awards, including a Golden Globe and Academy Award nominations. Meanwhile, in both New York City and London, *Hamilton* continues to run and run.

DISCS CHOSEN

'Cabaret'
Liza Minnelli
'The way her voice perfectly cracks on the last "B" in "cabaret" ... it's really alive, and I get goosebumps every time'

'The Crane Wife Part 2'
The Decemberists
'They're at the forefront of expanding the vocabulary of what rock music and pop music can do'

'El Padre Antonio y el Monaguillo Andrés'
Rubén Blades and Seis del Solar
'The album I remember most in my parents' vinyl collection'

'Passin' Me By'
The Pharcyde
'I'm crazy about their voices'

❤ **'What You Know'**
Ali Dineen
'Al Dineen was my seventh-year student when I taught at Hunter'

'On the Radio'
Regina Spektor
'She's a genius ... it's just a miracle of a song'

'Déjate Querer'
Gilberto Santa Rosa
'He'd be our Tony Bennett ... an old-school salsa crooner. He sang this song at our wedding'

'Rosa Parks'
OutKast
'I think Andre 3000 and Big Boi are the Lennon/McCartney of hip-hop'

BOOK

Moby Dick – Herman Melville

'*It's my wife's favourite book so it would be the closest thing to having my wife with me*'

LUXURY ITEM

Coffee

'*And I'd love milk and sugar, if you'll allow it ...*'

67

RUSSELL T DAVIES

SCREENWRITER, PRODUCER
3 November 2019

It's widely accepted that the portrayal of gay people in British television drama improved immeasurably around the time of the millennium. And if any one individual could be heralded as the prime mover of this much-needed shift in sensibilities, it would be Russell T Davies.

Davies emerged in 1999 as the writer, director and producer of *Queer as Folk*, the ground-breaking Channel 4 drama series chronicling three highly sexed men's adventures in Manchester's gay village. After a six-year stint rebooting *Doctor Who* for the BBC, Davies then declared that he would write exclusively gay dramas.

His subsequent career had featured TV triumphs such as *A Very English Scandal* – a dramatisation of a scandal that consumed the Liberal Party leader Jeremy Thorpe in the 1970s, starring Hugh Grant as the troubled politician – and dystopian BBC/HBO sci-fi drama *Years and Years*.

Yet when Davies fetched up on Lauren Laverne's island in late 2019, he also discussed the lengthy career hiatus when he had been the full-time carer for his late husband, who had been living with a terminal disease. It was an encounter with all the drama, pathos and humanity of one of his own award-winning productions.

• • •

Laverne and Davies began by discussing the dramatist's most recent productions, *A Very English Scandal* and *Years and Years*, before the host asked her guest a key question. Why was he happy to be seen as 'a gay writer' rather than a general writer of dramas?

'After *Doctor Who*, I said, "I'm going to write gay stories from now on,"' Davies replied. 'And it's what I've done. I did a series called *Cucumber*, I did the gayest version of *A Midsummer Night's Dream* for the BBC that you could ever see; *Years and Years*; and now I'm working on a story about AIDS in the 1980s.

'It's my joy: it's what I think about. I don't even need to analyse this. These are the ideas that I have without even thinking about it.'

Laverne: 'Apart from your own identity and connection with that, as a writer – why?'

'Well, it's unexplored territory. It still is. Any sense of queerness, any sense of otherness, is still very, very new as a society. We've always been there, behind the scenes, making the sensible decisions!

'But now, as an out society, we are less than fifty years old, really, and that's nothing. There are things that we've felt, things that we've said, emotions in our hearts that have not been put on the screen yet, or on the page. It's wonderful: it's rich, open territory.'

When Laverne turned to Davies's childhood in Swansea, he revealed that his two teacher parents, while raising him in a bookish household 'with the full *Encyclopædia Britannica*, taking up a whole shelf', also had 'an enormous respect for television'.

'It was never switched off. If a visitor came, it would be left on. I think visitors were interrupting: "*Stop interrupting my television!*" And, strangely, I was allowed to watch anything.

'In the seventies, and maybe even late sixties, I was allowed to watch all sorts of nine pm *Play for Today*s. I was allowed to watch *I, Claudius*, and I was thirteen then! There were people in school [*saying*], "I'm not allowed to watch that!" And I'd go, "Ho-ho: what you're missing! Wow!"'

Davies told Laverne that his first creative passion had been not writing, but drawing.

'I used to churn out cartoon strips. I'd draw *Doctor Who* strips and my own comic strips. I loved *Peanuts*. I'd draw stuff like that. I tried to do my own Marvel-type comic strips.

'Then, when I was around sixteen, a careers teacher told me that I'd never work in graphics or design because I'm colour blind. Which turned out to be wrong, but that changed the whole path of my life.'

By his mid-teens, Davies had discovered another passion: 'I was clever and I sailed through school, but I was living for the West Glamorgan Youth Theatre.'

Laverne: 'Why did you love the theatre?'

'Oh gosh, it was just a properly creative space. It taught me punctuality, it taught me discipline; it taught me endeavour; it taught me how to work hard; it got me writing for the first time. Putting on a play teaches you teamwork like nothing else.'

Davies described playing Bottom in a Youth Theatre production of *A Midsummer Night's Dream*: 'I gave my Bottom to Swansea!' Laverne wondered what acting had given him that was 'useful and valid'.

'It made me *feel* drama. We put on *The Crucible*. To have been onstage, to have been acting in something and to have felt that touching an audience – I have to believe that carries over into my writing, in some way.

'I think I write *big stuff*. Dramatic stuff. It makes you laugh; it makes you cry. I'm sure that was part of that training in youth theatre.'

After school, Davies studied English at Oxford, having 'a nice time' but finding the course a little underwhelming: 'I think I could have skipped those three years.' He left with no obvious career path open to him.

'I didn't really have a concept that you could be a television writer. I kind of presumed I'd work in television, but behind the scenes. Three years running I applied to *this building* for the training scheme. Three years running I was turned down. *Me!* I mean, come on, Lauren!'

Yet Davies found an alternative route to the BBC. Working on a theatre production in Cardiff, he heard of a BBC producer 'looking for someone to work with children: £50 per day.' Applying, he was taken on to work on kids' programmes such as *Why Don't You?*

'I was a multi-camera studio director. I did OBs [*outside broadcasts*] on location. I was greedy for it. I loved all that!'

The experience led to a job at Granada TV in Manchester, where Davies spent weekend evenings in Canal Street in the city's gay village. 'And, twenty years ago, your landmark series, *Queer as Folk*, came out,' recapped Laverne. 'Did it feel like a particularly personal piece of work?'

'It did. It was right from the heart. Whether anyone would watch it was unknown to us but I feel so lucky to have been the one to write that show because it's kind of obvious. There was a street full of gay men and women escaping their lives on Friday and Saturday night.

'I'd been living in Manchester. I'd seen that street begin to grow. There was a couple of gay pubs and venues that became what is now Canal Street.

'I used to love going on my own. If I bumped into friends, I'd be peeved and move clubs! I was that strange, tall man, standing on the edge of the dancefloor, not dancing, just watching: smoking, and watching it all happen. Just the lights, the smoke ... *it's a stage*, a dancefloor.

'You'd watch these people, who were bank clerks, or unemployed, or teachers, or nurses, a lot of them with a different life at home – maybe a closeted life. Just standing in those lights, in that smoke, dancing and kissing and being themselves for a couple of golden hours. Wonderful!'

Laverne: 'It was, to say the least, sexually frank, *Queer as Folk*. Were you nervous how it would be received?'

'No. We loved it. I mean, it was about sex, about the sexual urge: men sometimes at their best but sometimes at their lowest, as well. That's what was driving those characters: the need for sex, the need for *expression* via sex.

'I never dreamt we'd get away with what we got away with! It went much further than I imagined it would and I was really delighted.'

Laverne: 'One of the characters was fifteen. That caused a lot of controversy.'

'Yeah. That was what I was starting to see on Canal Street: the arrival of the first fifteen-year-olds. The gay teenagers.

'Here's a thing. When I wrote that, an out gay teenager was a miracle. They barely existed. Now, I gave a talk at a Manchester school the other week. The out boys in their sixth form are so numerous they are doing a float for the Gay Pride march next summer. What a different world! That's got to be brilliant, hasn't it?'

The conversation moved on. A lifelong *Doctor Who* fanatic, Davies had in 2003 been asked by the BBC to revive the show, dormant since 1989. 'How much did that take over your life?' asked Laverne.

'It was my whole life for five or six years. I mean, *every weekend*! We used to transmit on Christmas Day, so even Christmas Day was loaded with trans-mission fever! But it was like giving an alcoholic a free bar.'

Laverne: 'An interesting simile, but not necessarily a good thing?'

'No, indeed! It was too much hard work, in a way! I still think I'm tired, in some ways, after all those years. I still think, *Gosh, I haven't quite recovered from that!*

'We invented *Torchwood*. We invented *The Sarah Jane Adventures*. I was the executive producer on six shows at once, at one point. I'd sit there watching episodes of *Totally Doctor Who* at four in the morning, just to sign off every last second.'

Laverne: 'Why did you want to bring it back?'

'I think it's brilliant. I loved the BBC putting it on at seven o'clock on a Saturday night. We moved it into the family home to get mum, dad and kids watching which, at the time, wasn't being done at all.'

After a pause for a Neil Hannon song from a *Doctor Who* Christmas epi-sode, Laverne switched back to her guest's personal life. In 2009, Davies had moved to America with his partner, Andrew. 'Your plans were put on hold when he became ill. What happened?'

'He began having a lot of headaches. He went for a scan and it was glio-blastoma multiforme, which is very, very bad: a grade-four cancer. They gave him eighteen months to live and he lived for the next eight years. He was extraordinary.'

Laverne: 'You moved home, and ...'

'Yes. I gave up work for a few years and I became his carer. I mean, he had seven craniotomies: seven operations on his head. The whole thing affected his motor functions.

'He was *compos mentis* and he could walk. He just needed that extra care. It was hard, and it was also an honour to be the person doing that. And, think-ing about this interview today, for the first time I realised that those eight years I cared for him were our happiest years.'

Laverne: 'Why were they your happiest?'

'They were so intimate and so honest. Everything else just falls away and there's no nonsense and it's just you and him. I wish I could tell you we had the most profound conversations but, more often than not, you'd just find us watching *The Chase*, or something.

'Just that care: the love. I'm talking about love here. That's the word: *love*. And to be able to be like that, where he was properly cared for, he was properly cherished, and that made me feel good as well.

'I actually miss that. If you'd asked me at the time what it's like to be a carer, I think, in year four, I'd have said, "It's driving me mad! I wouldn't mind a bit of freedom!" Now I've *got* the freedom, I would chuck it away in an instant to have five more minutes watching television with him.

'It's been hard and sad, but I was lucky. He was the nicest man in the world. "Nice" sounds such a bland word, but when I gave the eulogy at his funeral, I just said, "The world turns under the march of all the nice people."

'Niceness is a very fine quality to have in life, and he had it in spades. He was so polite and so kind and so loving towards people. How lucky was I? He will be in every good man I write now ...'

• • •

Russell T Davies has continued to write many, many good men. In 2021, the 'story about AIDS in the 1980s' that he had mentioned to Lauren Laverne came to fruition in *It's a Sin*, a five-part drama series about the tragedies wrought by the deadly HIV pandemic. The opening episode was to attract the biggest ever audience for a Channel 4 drama launch: when the series was released to the network's streaming service, All 4, it was viewed 6.5 million times, making it the platform's most binge-watched show ever. Davies will also return to be *Doctor Who*'s showrunner in 2023. They really should have let him on that BBC training course.

DISCS CHOSEN
'Sugar Mountain' from TV series *Rock Follies*
Julie Covington, Charlotte Cornwell and Rula Lenska
'Women being bold and brilliant and strong'

Dinicu's *Hora Staccato*
Jascha Heifetz and Emanuel Bay
'Writing A Very English Scandal, *I played this more than 10,000 times'*

'Three Wheels on My Wagon'
The New Christy Minstrels
'The very first record I ever owned. I did love songs with stories ...'

♥ **'Gloria in excelsis' from Bernstein's *Mass***
The Norman Scribner Choir

'Wuthering Heights'
Kate Bush
'She once wrote to me and invited me round for tea, and I was so terrified, I didn't go. I didn't even reply!'

'Hold That Sucker Down (Builds Like a Skyscraper mix)'
O.T. Quartet
'The greatest club track of all. It's like being out clubbing!'

'Song for Ten'
Neil Hannon

'Mr Blue Sky'
Electric Light Orchestra
'This was played at our wedding'

BOOK
Asterix and the Roman Agent – René Goscinny and Albert Uderzo
'You can see everything I've ever written in this book'

LUXURY ITEM
A box of black Ball Pentel pens
'I will just draw and draw and draw with those ...'

'ISLE NEVER FORGET ...'
'Selecting my records for *Desert Island Discs* was a joy. It's a rare chance to sit and think through my entire life. And I didn't choose my *favourite* records. I chose things that trigger memories of certain parts of my life – where I was, and *who* I was.

'You're talking about music that touched your soul and is *bound into you*. I've been stopped in the street about it. A marvellously rude neighbour of mine in Swansea just said, "What awful records!"

'When I went on the show, I feel as if I made friends. I've stayed in touch with the producer and the production team. I still text Lauren. It's a very intimate atmosphere. There's a genuine kindness to the show.

'Was I happy talking about Andrew? I think that you can't do the show unless you are prepared to open up and reach that level of introspection. I think that's what the best episodes do. *Desert Island Discs* exists for that kind of honesty and that kind of depth.

'I went on thinking that I don't *have* to talk about it on the radio, and I don't want to try, but Lauren led me towards it so gently and tenderly. There was so much truth and faith that it felt entirely natural. I didn't think, *Should I have said that? Did it go too far?*

'When young writers come to me for advice, I tell them that *anyone* can write about chases, and explosions, and monsters, and detectives, and murders, and ghosts. But all you have to do, all you *must* do as a writer, is to understand the human soul.

'You have to understand psychology: why people do things, where they are from, what built them, what they're capable of. That's what *Desert Island Discs* does. It lays open a person's life. And there is nothing more dramatic, or interesting, or beautiful than that. It's the ultimate drama.

'Having said that, I've never heard my episode. I can't listen to my own voice for five seconds! I'm delighted that other people think my episode was nice, but I am confident I will never listen to it ...'

68
IAN WRIGHT

FOOTBALLER, BROADCASTER
16 February 2020

With its platforming of household names and the often-intimate and intro-spective nature of its discourse, it's no surprise that *Desert Island Discs* often produces what the Americans like to call 'water-cooler moments': memora-ble broadcasts that, the following morning, have work colleagues asking each other, 'Wow! Did you hear *that*?'

Ian Wright's visit to Lauren Laverne's island in February 2020 was a clas-sic example. As a footballer, Wright was a goal machine, banging in 128 goals over seven seasons to become Arsenal's all-time top scorer, as well as winning thirty-three caps for England.

Wright was a divisive figure, playing with a swagger and a hot temper that could appear near to arrogance. He seemed to enjoy being a *bête noire* for opposing fans. Yet his visit to *Desert Island Discs* revealed an individual way more complex, sensitive, vulnerable and self-questioning than most observers had previously imagined.

During a candid and confessional exchange, Wright was reduced to tears as he discussed an abusive childhood, a guardian-angel school teacher who had rescued him from potential self-destruction, and early setbacks and wrong turns that had included a prison term before his eventual, belated rise to become a true English football great.

Ian Wright's episode is up there in the *Desert Island Discs* pantheon as one of the most moving, heart-on-sleeve encounters in the show's entire history. As those water-cooler conversations revealed the next day, there was scarcely a dry eye among the millions who heard it.

• • •

The first clue that Ian Wright might prove a highly emotional castaway came right after Lauren Laverne's introduction, when she referenced the building-site foreman who had allowed him time off work to have a trial for Crystal Palace when he was twenty-one.

'It makes me well up, Lauren,' her guest confessed.

'You're welling up just at *the intro*?' she boggled.

'Yeah. It was a time when Palace had offered me a trial two times by then and I turned them down twice because I had a young family. Sean was three-and-a-bit and Bradley was just born [*both were also to go on to be Premier League footballers*].

'I couldn't afford to go for another trial and another rejection and give up this good job what I'd finally got, where they were going to teach me a trade. But he [*the foreman*] said to me, "Listen, I'll keep the job for you and you go and see how you can do."'

Asked by Laverne to name the highlight of his later, long career at Arsenal, Wright chose his first league game, at Southampton in 1991, when he played alongside a childhood friend, David Rocastle.

'We grew up on the same estate,' he recalled. 'I'd known David since he was five and I was nine. He was an inspiration to the whole estate because, at fifteen or sixteen, he got signed by Arsenal as a youth player.

'He used to always meet me. I'd be coming back from the youth club, not doing anything – I was eighteen, nineteen at the time – and he'd always dig me out about wasting time: "You should be playing! You should be trying to get in!"

'It's difficult for me to speak about him because he was always looking out for me. So [*in his first league game for Arsenal*] I scored a hat-trick and David scored the other goal. And it's the best football match I've ever played in.'

Laverne: 'He died tragically young, didn't he?'

'Thirty-three. [*Non-*]Hodgkin's lymphoma. Even with the Premier Leagues, the FA Cups, the golden boots ... all I think about is the fact that I played with him for a year as a professional.'

'I'm not surprised you're so emotional talking about him,' empathised Laverne before taking Wright forward a few years to a different match: the 1997 game against Bolton Wanderers when he got his 179th goal for Arsenal and became the club's all-time top scorer.

'I'd never been so nervous in my entire life,' confessed Wright. 'Literally forgot how to shoot. My legs turned to lead. And when I went home that night I couldn't sleep. I felt a sense of accomplishment.

'It took me back to the fact that I'd got so late into the game. People don't realise, I was twenty-eight when I got to Arsenal. It was hard to comprehend what I'd done. But I would have given all of that up for another twenty years with my dear friend.'

After a pause for music, Laverne came to another career highlight: Ian Wright's first cap for England in 1991.

'It's strange to think back to it now,' he marvelled. 'Playing for England with a side that's not long come back from the Italia 90 World Cup. Gazza and Lineker and Waddle and Barnes: all these great players I watched in that tournament.

'And now I'm among them! I remember almost floating on air when I went into the first camp and they were all there, all doing normal things like swearing and eating sandwiches.

'When we got to Wembley, I could feel it all welling up. To go in and see your boots, under the number nine for England – people are looking to see how you're going to react. Gazza said, "Ah, look at Wrighty, he's going to cry!" If he hadn't said that, I probably *would* have burst into tears.'

It was when Laverne moved on to Wright's childhood that it began to emerge *why* he was so volatile and emotional. Born in 1963, he was raised in Brockley, south London, by his Jamaican immigrant mother, Nesta, and a stepfather.

'It wasn't a loving place to be. I didn't feel like people cared, apart from my brother, Maurice. My stepfather was a very big, growly voiced, gambling, weed-smoking, angry man. I was afraid of him.

'So, when I was young, I was very angry. If anything happened, I'd get a smack. When I played football, if it got to a point I couldn't deal with it, I'd lash out. That's how I felt – a very angry and confused little guy.'

Laverne: 'Your dad left when you were very young [*eighteen months*]. What contact did you have with him after that?'

'You might see him in two years or after five years. I remember when I was eleven, twelve, the whole estate used to go on family trips to Littlehampton or Margate. Everybody used to get dressed up, and I didn't have any decent trousers.

'Someone got a message to him: "Ian's going to a trip on Sunday and he hasn't got any trousers to wear." And the message came back: "Yeah, I'm gonna come and give you the money to go buy trousers." So, you've got to understand, *my stomach* ... because I just didn't see this guy.

'Saturday comes and I'm literally beside myself. They said he's coming at half past nine in the morning. I was sitting in our block of flats on the little plinth-y thing by the entrance. I was there from half past nine in the morning, and he got there at quarter past five.

'I just remember, *the emotions* – I can't tell you the emotions I went through. Because if he didn't turn up, I don't know what I would have done. I would never, ever have had anything to do with him again.'

Turning to music, Wright chose Ike and Tina Turner's 'River Deep – Mountain High'. Yet this was not a song that brought him pleasure.

'When you see Tina Turner's film, and what she went through, then what I saw my mum go through – I remember this record would come on and my mum would just cry. Because I'd seen what she'd been through with my stepdad.

'She was, like, four-eleven and he was six-four and I used to see him lift her ... *do stuff to her*. When my stepfather was really manhandling my mum, my brother used to cover my ears so you couldn't hear it. This song takes me back to that place. It's a *horrible* tune for me.'

Laverne: 'Why is it important to you to represent that experience?'

'Because I have to own it and deal with it, as hard as it is. My mum came through it, with my help as well. It's part of my life.'

When Wright was eight, he explained, football was his only solace. 'It was the one thing I was good at. I'd practise my left foot, practise my right foot, practise my heading. I was so happy when I played!'

School was a less happy environment. With a short attention span, and unable to concentrate on his lessons, he was often sent to stand outside the class room by his exasperated teacher. He was there one fateful day when a teacher, Mr Pigden, walked by ... then stopped.

'I was so scared of him because he was really strict. I wouldn't look at him. He looked at me, then he went inside the classroom, said a couple of things to the teacher, then came back out and said, "Come with me." And that changed my life.'

Laverne: 'Mr Pigden was so important to you that you dedicated your autobiography to him. How did he treat you? Engage with you?'

'Well, I know he loved me. I don't know *why* he chose me. I'm so glad that he did. Once he came in, everything was so much better.

'He was the one who taught me about Jimmy Greaves: "Ian, *pass* the ball into the goal. Score beautiful goals!" He gave me responsibility. I used to collect the registers from the teachers, then they made me milk monitor. I really liked that.

'I just felt important. He'd put me back into the classroom and then my writing got better. He wouldn't let me play football if he heard I'd been naughty in class. He just gave me a feeling like *I had some use.*'

Wright mentioned a highly emotional video, filmed in 2010, that had shown him being unexpectedly reunited after thirty years with Mr Pigden, whom he had mistakenly believed dead. It had since been viewed on YouTube more than 2 million times [*now, nearing 5 million*].

'I just ripped my hat off my head! I said to him, "Oh my gosh, I thought you were dead!" And he said, "Well, I'm very much alive, Ian!" He said how proud he is of me, and I hugged him. I felt like I was seven again.

'We kept in touch from then on. He was one of the youngest pilots in World War II, so he was chosen to do a flyover of Buckingham Palace. And he said he was more proud of the fact that I played for England than him flying over Buckingham Palace ...'

Wright's voice quavered and he burst into tears in the studio. 'Oh, Ian,' said Laverne, simply. He attempted to collect himself and carry on.

'Gosh, man, I'm so sorry to people who are listening! I've just turned into this bumbling, crying guy! But he changed my life by recognising, when I was stood outside that classroom, that *I needed more.* And he gave it to me. He was the greatest man in the world.'

Wright composed himself as Laverne played Bob Marley. The host then commented that he had left school at fourteen and got a job as a plasterer. 'What about your footballing ambitions at this time?'

'I went for a trial with Orient, went for a trial with Charlton, had trials with Millwall. It was really horrible because I'd be walking off the pitch and I was never getting picked. It was demoralising.'

His life took a turn for the worse, said Laverne, when he went to jail in 1982. 'You were imprisoned for non-payment of fines and driving without a licence. You were in Chelmsford Prison for eighteen days. What was the effect on you?'

'I got put into a cell – BAM! – and when the door closed, I realised where I was. And I literally cried from the first day to the last day. It made me realise: *I can't do this*. So, when I came out, it was a case of finding a job to pay me and focusing on getting a trade.'

Three years on, Wright was working as a labourer when Crystal Palace made their third offer of a trial. He was unsure whether to accept.

Laverne: 'I understand you talked it through with your son, Bradley, who was about eight months old at the time?'

'When the day came, I remember, I was having a bath, and Bradley was crawling around in the bathroom, mainly trying to eat the bubbles out of the bath. I was having to stop him.

'I remember saying to him: "*This is it*. Another chance for me. What happens, though, if I don't make it again? People are going to say, 'You're not good enough!' again. All I want is the best for you and your mum. For us to live somewhere nicer. I want to be a footballer so bad."

'I was speaking like that to an eight-month-old baby. It was amazing. I felt so free! I went to this trial and said, "I'm just going to do what I do, because I've been rejected doing what I think they *want* me to do." And I scored three or four goals in the game. I was going to make it.'

Signed to Crystal Palace, Wright's goals powered them to promotion after four seasons. In 1991, aged twenty-eight, he moved to Arsenal for a then-record £2.5 million.

Laverne: 'Can you sum up how you felt, signing for such an important club?' Laverne asked.

'Well, leaving Crystal Palace, for a start, was a shock. I never asked to leave. I was happy at Palace. It took a while for it to sink in that I was at Arsenal Football Club with my friend, David Rocastle.

'Everybody was scrutinising. People saying, "He's not going to be good. Once he's among better players, we'll see what he's about. But once I was around better players, I actually just slotted in and got better. I went to another level with Arsenal.'

Wright freely admitted that this had gone to his head.

'I think what happens, with the amount of praise you're getting ... you say, *Listen, I'm invincible!* You start feeling that you're breathing different air. You start to think you're a bit special.'

Laverne: 'A little bit too big for your boots?'

'Absolutely! I went through that. And, if I'm going to be honest, it's not my proudest years. I caused a lot of problems for a lot of my family. I made some terrible decisions and done some terrible things.'

'How did you start to tackle that?' wondered Laverne.

'I needed therapy. I got to a stage in my life where you're not hearing the word "No" too frequently because you're doing so well. And that's dangerous to the point you're obnoxious. I was not in a good place.

'I went to see this wonderful woman. When I first started to go to speak to her, she recognised: "You're not telling me the truth. Why have you come here? If you want to waste money, go and do it somewhere else. I've got too many people who need help. You're wasting my time."

'She said that, and I burst into tears. And then I just poured out and the therapy was the best thing that ever happened to me, because what I realised was a lot of it stemmed from my youth and when I was a child.

'I remember, she said, "Can you remember the first hug you got from your mum? Can you remember any time when your stepdad showed you ...?" And I literally couldn't remember anything like that.'

It was this therapy, Wright said, that had triggered the self-knowledge that had helped him to find greater peace of mind later in life. Laverne asked how it had affected his familial relationships.

'You talked earlier about becoming a dad when you were very young. You're now a father of eight kids from several relationships. What do you hope your kids have learned from you?'

'Do as I say, not as I do! I was very young and I don't regret any of my past. I know I'm a decent man now. I can look at myself in the mirror and know that ...'

'We've spent a lot of time today looking back,' summarised Lauren Laverne, as this enthralling football highlights show neared its close. 'What about looking forward? What are your hopes for the future?'

'To be honest, I feel like I'm in an unbelievable place,' reflected Ian Wright. 'I've got an unbelievable woman who married me. And with every-thing I went through, to get to marry someone like my wife, Nancy ... I know someone's looking out for me.

'I don't feel like there's much I want now. I've done all the material stuff. I'm in a place now where it's more about *the substance of things*. I don't want to waste words. I don't want to waste time.'

• • •

Ian Wright's tumultuous, tear-jerking *Desert Island Discs* excited more media reaction and general admiration than almost any programme in the show's venerable history. Two-and-a-half years on, he remains a huge figure in the football world and a characteristically, entertainingly frank and heart-on-sleeve pundit on shows such as *Match of the Day*. In 2021 he co-wrote a novel, *Striking Out*, aimed at children and teenagers and inspired by his troubled early years. In April 2022, he was inducted into the Premier League Hall of Fame.

DISCS CHOSEN
'Duettino – Sull'aria' from Mozart's *The Marriage of Figaro*
Orchester der Deutschen Oper Berlin
'I know people would never guess [I'd choose] *this one ...'*

'Looking for You'
Kirk Franklin
'He's a pastor. I'm not particularly religious but I'm God-fearing ...'

'River Deep – Mountain High'
Ike and Tina Turner

'Redemption Song'
Bob Marley and the Wailers
'It's a powerful song for me'

'Mysteries of the World'
MFSB
'Transcendent ... a beautiful record, a gorgeous song'

❤ **'Endlessly'**
Randy Crawford
'Shola Ama sang this song at our wedding'

'Crown'
Stormzy
'He caught what it means to be successful as a black person'

'Just Fine'
Mary J. Blige
'For me and Nancy – I'm at my happiest when we're out dancing to this song'

BOOK

The Curious Incident of the Dog in the Night-Time – Mark Haddon
'*I really loved reading that book*'

LUXURY ITEM

Golf club
'*A seven-iron with some golf balls*'

69

BRIAN COX

ACTOR
29 March 2020

In sixty years as an actor, Brian Cox has done almost everything. He has won an Olivier, played King Lear at the National and appeared in more than 100 films. Yet this redoubtable thespian was seventy-two years old before he took on the TV role with which he was to become synonymous.

When Cox rolled up on Lauren Laverne's beach in March 2020, he had already spent two years in HBO's compelling *Succession* as Logan Roy, the amoral, Machiavellian trash-media mogul believed by critics and viewers to be a close approximation of Rupert Murdoch.

Succession depicted the volatile, volcanic Roy as being the product of a difficult and penurious childhood in Dundee. A fascinating *Desert Island Discs* interlocution revealed that the charming, easy-going Cox had that background – but little else – in common with the screen monster that he had helped to create ...

• • •

Lauren Laverne opened by observing that, over his lengthy career, Cox had played both good guys – Churchill, Sir Matt Busby – and bad: the first ever incarnation of Hannibal Lecter in 1986 movie *Manhunter* and, of course, Logan Roy. 'Are villains more fun to play?'

'Well, obviously, the devil has the best tunes,' her guest chuckled. 'And at one point in my life, about twenty-five years ago, I suddenly thought, *Why am I playing all these nasty people?* And I worried for a bit. But it didn't last more than ten minutes!'

Laverne turned quickly to the heinous Logan Roy, a part for which Cox had recently been awarded a Golden Globe. 'Is he based on anyone in particular?'

'Not really. Everybody thinks he's based on Conrad Black or Rupert Murdoch. They all have theories who it is. I think Logan and I have one thing in common: we find the human experiment rather disappointing.'

'There's a misanthropy that you share?'

'Oh yeah! I flirt with misanthropy all the time. But I'm an optimist, so I always come down on the good side.'

Laverne: 'I read that when you're out in public, a lot of people want you to repeat some of Logan's more choice lines. What has been the most peculiar request you've had?'

'It was at a very serious #MeToo event with Ronan Farrow, which I was invited to by Rosanna Arquette. As it ended, I found myself surrounded by a lot of ladies asking: could they video me telling them to eff off?'

'What did you say?' laughed Laverne.

'I said, "Is that *really* appropriate at a #MeToo meeting?" But I think that's also to do with the kind of confusion that we live in at the moment, and it's also what the series is about.

'People kind of love the naked ambition of somebody like Logan, but at the same time, they go, "Oh, we love to hate him!" But actually, they love to love him as well. It's kind of complex.'

After a burst of music and a discussion of Cox playing Churchill in the 2017 film of the same name ('Wonderful material to work on – a great man in doubt!'), Laverne asked her guest about his earliest memories of acting. His reply was both bleak and illuminating.

'Well, my dad died when I was eight and my mum had a series of very severe nervous breakdowns. So she had electric shock treatment and she was institutionalised for a lot of my childhood. But before that, my life was blissful. Really very happy.

'The thing my dad used to do at New Year was we had a window recess that was curtained, and a coal bunker. My sister May – a flamboyant singer – used to say, "Presenting Brian Cox!" She would swing open the curtains and I would do [*Al*] Jolson impersonations.

'I'd do Jolson impersonations, with the movements and everything. And of course, at one in the morning, there'd be a lot of drunken people in the room, but they were so giving. And I thought, *Wow! This is good!*'

Cox's father, the youngest of thirteen, had initially worked in a mill, but then ran a small Dundee grocery shop. 'What was he like?' asked Laverne.

'He was just sweet. He was kind. He was warm. He had a lovely chuckle. He was the centre of the community – but, unfortunately, people were poor and he gave out a *lot* of credit.

'He had pancreatic cancer and died within three weeks of his diagnosis. We were left with debts and my mum had a breakdown and it all went belly up. It was horrific.'

Laverne: 'You were just eight. It must have been an extraordinarily difficult time?'

'Yeah. I just went into survival mode and that's what's sustained me throughout my life. In this current [*COVID*] crisis, I'm in survival mode.'

'And what's that like?'

'Really, you just keep in touch with yourself. You keep in touch with your inner person. And you keep in touch with that wee boy.

'I teach drama, and I say to my students, "Always carry a picture of yourself as a child. That's who you are. Never forget it. That person of wonder, person of amazement, person of joy, is who you are. The rest is just propaganda that you've had to deal with."'

After a pause for k.d. lang, Cox described hard times after his father's death and his mother's breakdown, sleeping many-kids-to-a-room at his sister's house. 'Your attitude to money must have been influenced by what you experienced as a kid?' mused Laverne.

'Yeah. I've always had issues about money because we didn't have any. When my mum came out of hospital, finally, she got a small job but she mostly lived off her widow's pension. It would come on a Friday and sometimes, on a Thursday night, we wouldn't have any food.

'I would go across to the fish-and-chip shop, and we would get batter bits from the back of the pan, and that would be our tea on a Thursday night. It sounds a cliché but it instils in you a sense of the value of stuff. I'm a bit cautious. I can be a bit parsimonious at times.

'I did the Bill Maher show last week in the States, and he kept saying, "Why are you a socialist?" And I said, "You Americans, you don't know the first *thing* about socialism. You conflate it with reds under the bed. I'll tell you why I'm a socialist – *poverty*. When you know poverty, *then* you know about how we have to take care of our people."'

After a break for the Beatles, Cox recalled falling in love with acting via seeing productions at the Dundee Rep. After he left school, he blagged a job at the theatre mopping the stage and shifting scenery – and then became 'probably the worst stage manager there's ever been'.

Laverne: 'The worst?'

'The worst. I was *terrible!*'

'Why so bad?'

'I'd be on the book [*the script*] in the prompt corner. I'd be on page twenty and the actors were on page forty. Suddenly there's a pause on stage, and then there's a tap on my shoulder. I turn, and the actress says to me, "Telephone!" I said, "For me?" and she said, "No! On stage!"

'I was supposed to make the phone ring. I was *hopeless*. I'm surprised they didn't fire me.'

Wisely eschewing stage management, Cox went to drama school in Edinburgh then joined repertory theatres in London and Birmingham. 'It was a wonderful, wonderful experience. I was ambitious but it was all about the work. I just wanted to get better.'

Laverne: 'Some of the performances, like *Titus Andronicus* at the RSC, have gone down in theatrical history. How did it feel to get that triumph under your belt?'

'Well, it was odd because, when I was a kid, I wanted to be a movie actor. The generation of Albert [*Finney*] and Peter [*O'Toole*] and Tom [*Courtenay*], they did movies, but it became a different class of person doing movies in the seventies and eighties.

'I did two plays that brought me to America, they were very successful and, out of that, I got this film, *Manhunter*. But then my marriage fell apart so I realised I'd have to go back to London and be present for my kids. So I joined the RSC, and it was the best move I ever made.'

Despite this, Cox moved back to America in the nineties. Laverne noted that he had, at this point, described trying to break into Hollywood as like 'wrestling with a blancmange'.

'Yes. [*People are*] always very sweet, very nice, but fickle as everything. You can't really take any of it seriously. And you shouldn't.

'I went to Hollywood in the seventies and the *farce-ness*, the glibness of the life, was something I really couldn't handle. I didn't succumb. So I just came back and did my work. As my old friend, Fulton Mackay, used to say, "Follow your mercenary calling and draw your wages."'

Like Logan Roy, Brian Cox had by now long left Dundee behind and had been for years happily settled in New York. As she cast him away on the island, Lauren Laverne wondered if his native Scotland drew him back, as he grew older. 'Do you miss it?'

'I do. I'm there a lot, actually. It's God's country. It's beautiful. There's nowhere like it. *Nowhere like it!* It's just incredible ...'

• • •

In addition to a slew of upcoming movie projects, Brian Cox continues to wreak havoc as Logan Roy in *Succession*, which was filming its fourth series during the summer of 2022. Shortly after appearing on *Desert Island Discs*, he was asked to explain the Waystar RoyCo patriarch's toxic and dysfunctional relationship with his warring offspring. 'I asked Jesse [*Armstrong, series creator and chief writer*] very early on, "Does Logan love his children?" ... And he said, "Oh, yes, he really *does* love them!" So, given the fact that Logan *is* locked into his children in that way, you come to realise that they are just a source of deep, deep disappointment to him ...'

DISCS CHOSEN
'Bridge Over Troubled Water'
Johnny Cash
'It's an incredibly moving rendition of the song ...'

'Saturday Night at the Movies'
The Drifters
'This is my childhood. I spent more than Saturdays – I was Every Night at the Movies!'

'The Air that I Breathe'
k.d. lang
'I didn't know this Canadian lassie. Then I heard her and thought, Wow!*'*

'Get Back'
The Beatles
'I want their rock and roll side'

'La quête'
Jacques Brel

'Both Sides Now'
Joni Mitchell
'You hear a woman who's lived'

❤ **'God Only Knows'**
The Beach Boys
'A terribly romantic song for my wife, Nicole'

'Don't Get Me Wrong'
The Pretenders
'She's a friend and she is the original rock chick. I love her to bits'

BOOK

In Search of the Miraculous – Pyotr Ouspenskii
'It's about man's quest for consciousness, and being conscious'

LUXURY ITEM

A very, very good sewing kit
'I'm imagining I'll have some clothes that I need to repair ...'

70

PROFESSOR DAME ELIZABETH ANIONWU

NURSE, PROFESSOR
31 May 2020

As Britain reeled beneath the onset of the worst global pandemic in decades in spring 2020, it felt entirely appropriate that *Desert Island Discs* welcomed a woman heralded by Lauren Laverne as 'one of the most influential nurses in the history of the NHS'.

The first COVID-19 lockdown necessitated Professor Dame Elizabeth Anionwu's visit to the island being conducted remotely, yet it was no less memorable for that. A mixed-race child born out of wedlock in the 1940s, her childhood had included harrowing years being subjected to punitive abuse by the nuns who ran her children's home.

Anionwu had risen above this desperate beginning to enjoy a forty-year nursing career, pioneering the treatment of sickle-cell disease patients and becoming the UK's first sickle-cell specialist nurse and a professor of nursing. It was an inspirational tale in the midst of a global medical emergency.

• • •

Deep into COVID lockdown, the seventy-two-year-old Professor Dame Elizabeth Anionwu was self-isolating due to asthma. Lauren Laverne welcomed her, figuratively, to the island, and asked how she was getting on.

'My twelve-year-old granddaughter is FaceTiming me like nothing on earth!' she reported. 'I think it has helped me avoid sinking into any depression with what is going on. Human contact is really valued right now.'

Laverne: 'What have you made of the Thursday-night clap for carers?'

'I think it's ... showing people's solidarity,' said Anionwu, diplomatically. 'But NHS staff are really being valued right now, and they have to continue with that in more ways than one, shall I say?'

Laverne remarked that a disproportionate number of NHS staff who had lost their lives in the pandemic, possibly as high as 60 per cent, had been of BAME heritage. 'What are your thoughts about that?'

'All the deaths are absolutely tragic, but as a black nurse, I am so scared for my colleagues. There's a history of black and minority ethnic health professionals not being valued as much as they should be. I want them to be listened to and paid more – as *all* NHS staff should be.'

After a music break, Laverne turned to Dame Elizabeth's personal story.

Her mother had won a scholarship to Cambridge in 1944. There, she met a Nigerian student. 'What happened?'

'Well, *I* happened, Lauren! I was the outcome of their short affair, and it was a huge shock for my mother. She came from a deeply religious Catholic family. It was my maternal grandmother who realised she was pregnant, during a trip back home to Stafford.

'All my mother would say was that the father of the baby was a fellow student: nothing else. When my grandparents came to visit my mother and me at the mother-and-baby home run by Irish nuns, before they let them into the room a nun said, "Ah, to be sure, the baby's a little dark!"

'This was their first realisation that the father of the baby wasn't white, as they had assumed. I can only imagine the waves of shock that everybody went through!'

Laverne: 'What would your mother have been feeling?'

'I think absolute shame, and stigma, and letting people down, because there must have been so much joy when she got that scholarship. She was the first one to go to university, and study classics, and she was doing brilliantly, apparently.'

Her mother dropped out of Cambridge and decided it would be best for her daughter to be raised by the nuns. 'But she was determined that you weren't to be adopted,' said Laverne. 'To what extent were you aware that she intended to come back for you?'

'I always grew up knowing that my mother wanted to make a home for me. Even though I spent nine years in the children's home, she visited me regularly. I never had a sense of rejection by her, and I know that has helped me enormously through my life.'

Nevertheless, Anionwu's time in the home was marked by vicious and arbitrary punishments that she admitted were still 'seared in her brain'.

'I was a bed-wetter. They would drape the urine-soaked sheets over our bodies, we'd have to put our arms up under the sheet, and the punishment was that we had to keep our arms stretched out.

'You can't do that for very long, and if your arm dropped, there was a nun on the other side of the sheet with a ruler, who would whack you. I just thought it was so cruel!'

Laverne: 'Were there many other children of colour at the home?'

'Not until I was eight. For most of the time, I was the only child of colour. I washed my face ten times a day with Lifebuoy soap to [*try to*] be like my friends.'

Yet there was, the dame explained, one 'wonderful' nun in the home – and this sister had set her on the course that was to define her life.

'She used to run the sick bay. I had very bad eczema and so I'd go for daily dressings. Cold tar paste! It would be very cool when the bandage went on, but when I had to go back for the dressing, I'd peer around the door to see if the nun with the white habit was there.

'The nun with the black habit would just tear off the bandage and it would hurt and I would cry. But the nun with the white habit would use distraction therapy and she would say words like "bottom"!

'I would burst out laughing, she would take the bandage off and I would not feel a thing. I thought she was the most wonderful person on earth! Later on, before I left the convent, I realised she was something called a *nurse*, and I decided that's what *I* wanted to be.'

Anionwu was nine when her mother married and took her out of the home to live with her and her new husband, Ken, in Wolverhampton. 'How did you get on?' asked Laverne.

'Initially, it worked out, but I only stayed there for twenty months because of a change in my relationship with my stepfather. He was being teased by his mates in the pub about having a half-caste child at home and, when my mother wasn't around, he started to physically abuse me.

'One day he hit me. I went sprawling and hit my eyebrow on the wall. I bled, it was painful, and my mother was distraught, because this was the revelation that he'd been physically abusing me for some time. I'd never told her.'

Her mother sent her to live with her maternal grandparents in northern England. 'It was a very traumatic period of my life. Initially, I was angry with my mother: *Why didn't she protect me?* But as I grew older, I realised she was trying her best to make a home for me.'

In 1965, aged eighteen, Anionwu began nurse training at Paddington General Hospital in London. She then decided to become a health visitor. With a few months to kill before her course began, she got a job in Paris with 'a wonderful medical family', teaching English to their children.

'I became friendly with a French Benin midwife who was quite active politically. I told her the story about washing my face ten times to try to become white and she said, "I know the very book you should read: *Black Skin, White Masks* by Frantz Fanon."

'I read this book about why people want to be white instead of black, in terms of colonialism. And the scales came off my eyes: *I'm a brown-skinned person and I don't know anything about my African heritage!*

'When I came back to London, the first thing I wanted to do was to get involved with black community activities, particularly health issues. And that was when I realised that there is this condition called sickle-cell anaemia.'

After attending lectures by haematologist Dr Milica Brozovic, Anionwu worked with her, becoming the UK's first specialist sickle-cell nurse in 1979. Laverne asked her to summarise the medical condition.

'It's an inherited disorder of the haemoglobin inside the red blood cells.

And it's characterised by mild-to-incredibly-severe episodes of pain, suscepti-
bility to infections, and anaemia. It can affect virtually every organ in the body.'

Laverne: 'What kind of understanding did people have of it back then?'

'*Zilch*. I never had any lessons about it in my nurse training or my health
visitor training. This was starting to build up deep-seated anger in me.

'By the time [*sufferers*] – children as well as adults – went to A&E, they were
rolling around in pain. It is the most horrific pain that people can have. Most
of the patients were young, and black, and many health professionals thought
they were drug addicts. *Can you imagine?*'

Pioneering awareness of the condition, Anionwu helped to found a
national charity, the Sickle Cell Society. As the illness disproportionately
affects the BAME community, she admitted that she perceived racism at play
in the lack of resources assigned to its treatment.

'When you're talking about health inequalities, there's still some way to go
to get conditions on an equal footing, so that families do not feel that they're
getting a lesser quality of care simply because of the colour of their skin.'

After another music break, Laverne returned to her guest's personal life.
In 1972, she had discovered that the father she had never met was living in
London. She went to meet him. How did it go?

'It was fantastic. I used to ride a scooter in those days and I had to go up
the North Circular Road. I remember parking the scooter, going to the front
door and the nerves really kicked in!

'Pressed the doorbell, he opened the door and, Lauren, I was like Mini Me! He
was darker, he was male, he was larger than me. He just gave me this enormous
bear hug, and welcomed me, and I met my stepmother. It was just wonderful.

'He was very erudite. He was an ambassador before the Nigerian Civil
War, very educated, a very dry sense of humour. In fact, we discovered we had
the same sense of humour and the same love of music. That was wonderful.

'I never called him "Dad", initially. It was my stepmother who, after a few
weeks, said, "You know, he's your father! Call him 'Dad'!" *Hmm? OK!*'
Anionwu was to travel to Nigeria with her father to meet his, and her, family
there.

In 2017, she was awarded a damehood for her services to nursing – and
for a successful twelve-year campaign she had waged. This battle was for a
statue of Mary Seacole, the British-Jamaican nurse who treated British soldiers on the battlefield in the Crimean War, to be placed at St Thomas's
Hospital in London. It was erected in 2016.

'It was the first statue of a named black woman in the UK,' noted Lauren
Laverne. 'People might be shocked by that. Why is it important that she's there?'

'Mary Seacole is part of the history of Britain,' replied Professor Dame
Elizabeth Anionwu. 'She was of Jamaican-Scottish heritage. The fact that
she is brown-skinned should not be important, but it *is* important.

'It's a wonderful, wonderful monument, whatever background you are from, but can you *imagine* how important it is for groups of individuals who don't always feel accepted? I took my granddaughter down: she was there at the unveiling.

'A few months later, she was staying with me. I took her on the London Eye, then said, "Is there anything else you want to see?" And she asked, "Can we go and see Mary again?" Oh, the joy in my heart ...'

• • •

Professor Dame Elizabeth Anionwu officially retired in 2007 and hasn't stopped being busy since. Her 2016 memoir, *Mixed Blessings from a Cambridge Union*, was widely acclaimed and, in addition to the Sickle Cell Society, she is a patron of charities including the Nigerian Nurses' Charitable Association UK, and an honorary adviser to England's chief nursing officer's BAME strategic advisory group. Six months after she visited the island, the dame made the BBC's annual '100 Women' list.

DISCS CHOSEN
'Faith's Song'
Amy Wadge
'My love song to NHS professionals'

'The Rakes of Mallow, Girl I Left Behind'
The Gallowglass Ceili Band
'I absolutely adored Irish dancing'

'Manman'
Leyla McCalla
'An homage to my wonderful mother'

'A Te, O Cara' from Bellini's *I Puritani*
Andrea Bocelli
'It would cheer me up immensely'

'Missa Bilban'
The Jamaican Folk Singers
'I heard this when I went to Jamaica to learn more about sickle cell'

❤ **'I Wish I Knew (How It Would Feel to Be Free)'**
Nina Simone
'She was a feisty woman and I love her to bits'

'Nnekata'
Flavour N'abania
'My Igbo name given me on my first visit to Nigeria is "Nneka" – it means "My mother is supreme"'

'My Girl'
Otis Redding
'We should call it "My Girls": for my daughter and my granddaughter'

BOOK
Dreams from My Father – Barack Obama

LUXURY ITEM
Trampoline
'I've always wanted to jump and jump and jump and jump on a trampoline. It's the inner child in me ...'

'ISLE NEVER FORGET ...'

'*Desert Island Discs* is perfect for me because I love music and I'm very nosy about people's lives. It's one of my favourite shows and so I was shocked to be asked to go on: I opened the email and I went, *What?!* I replied immediately!

'I wasn't worried about the conversation because I love conversation – especially about myself! – but I *was* nervous beforehand because the show is such a big part of British culture. And, thanks to COVID, I had to have all the equipment in my flat and be my own audio technician!

'I found it very moving at times. Lauren is a very astute interviewer because she picked up that it was emotional for me to talk about how much my mother had done to try and provide a home for me, and how I was subjected to physical abuse by my stepfather.

'By the same token, I wasn't embarrassed to talk about my humiliating treatment in the children's home. Maybe once I would have been, but by then I'd written about it in my memoir. And once you've done *that*, it's out there.

'I felt proud to be on the programme and the feedback that I got was incredible. When I listened to the show back ... well, I hadn't realised previously that my favourite word is "wonderful"! I mean, *how* many times did I say it? But other than that, I enjoyed it very much ...'

71
SHARON HORGAN

WRITER, ACTOR, PRODUCER
26 July 2020

If Russell T Davies reinvented the way that gay men were portrayed in British drama series in the twenty-first century, there is a compelling argument that Sharon Horgan was a similarly revolutionary force on the way that women are depicted in sitcoms and comedy dramas.

From 2006 to the current day, the prolific Irishwoman has created and co-written a succession of scabrous TV comedies, including *Pulling*, *Catastrophe*, *Motherland* and *Divorce*, that feature thoroughly modern women living their best lives … on the verge of a nervous breakdown.

The writer and actor's career appeared to be one lengthy, effortless, uninterrupted triumph, but she explained to Lauren Laverne that there had been plenty of wasted opportunities, false starts and self-doubt during the many years it had taken her to become an overnight success.

• • •

Laverne began by quoting Horgan saying there was 'a lot of overlap' between her complex, anxious female comedic creations and herself: 'I'm still a mess, and there's still just a mess at the heart of all my work.' 'Why are you drawn to writing about this mess?' she asked her guest.

'Oh, well, I don't know that I'd know what else to write about, really! I've never been great at working things out, or talking. You can tap it into your laptop and it feels easier than saying it out loud.

'I think, generally, I'm trying to explore parts of my life I haven't fully worked out. I've recently started having therapy and doing the normal person's route, rather than making a TV show about it! But for years, I didn't want to do that. I wanted to … hold on to the mess.'

Laverne: 'There is often a crossover between things that happen in your own life, or the lives of those around you, and what ends up on screen. Do your friends and family need to be careful? Are you a watcher?'

'Oh, yeah, I'm a watcher. I'm a comedy dogger! Sometimes, I get angry with myself: I think, *Be in the room, don't be thinking what you can do with that thing!* Because it feels sort of … *cheeky*, I suppose.

'I used to do it in what was not the right way. I just squirrelled away the stories and then they'd turn up on the screen. Now, I'm very open and honest with people. If they're telling me something I know for a fact is going to go in somewhere, I tell them.'

After David Bowie's 'Rock 'n' Roll Suicide', Laverne turned to her guest's background. Her Kiwi dad, John, and Irish mum, Ursula, ran a turkey farm in County Meath. 'How would you describe your childhood?'

'I mean, it was great! There was a lot to love about it, but there were stressful elements, because it was a turkey farm and my parents made all their money at Christmas.

'So Christmas, which is supposed to be, I guess for most kids, a time of joy and anticipation, was just kind of us watching our father have a slow heart attack. He would start smoking again every Christmas, and my mum would be literally covered in feathers.

'They would spend two weeks in a shed trying to get it all done. Then on Christmas Day, they would just sleep. They would just fall asleep and they would sleep for days. But they still managed to buy the presents and make the dinner ...'

Laverne: 'You're one of five. Were you competitive as kids?'

'Yeah. I just wanted to make them laugh. I knew that that was a way to focus attention on me. My dad's very funny, very dry, but cracking my mum up – well, I'd do anything for that!'

Horgan was a convent schoolgirl, 'under the thumb of an actually quite psychotic nun'. 'What was your time there like?' asked Laverne.

'There was this constant fear running through you. It was very fire-and-brimstone, and it built up a really nice, juicy level of guilt and shame in you at an early age. If you had any streak of boldness in you at all, it was terrifying, because you were *always* going to get caught.'

'And did you? You were one of those girls that couldn't help yourself?'

'Yeah! I got caught drinking wine in the classroom. Someone smuggled it in. We couldn't even get the cork out. We just put a compass through it, so it was literally drips. I got in trouble for drawing a smiley face on a uterus in science class ...'

As a teen, said Horgan, she had written poems and 'angsty monologues' and performed them to a friend. It filled her head with big ideas.

'I remember telling my mother – this is very embarrassing – that I was going to win an Oscar one day, so she'd better hold on to her hat. She was very nice about it, but she *did* tell me I might need to set my sights a little lower.'

After school, Horgan went to art college in Dublin, took a drama course at weekends and danced with a rock band. In 1990, aged twenty, she moved to London. Initially, it was an underwhelming experience.

'I tried to get into all the drama schools in London but I had no joy. So, I spent my twenties doing not very much, really. It was a bit grimy and dark. I was squatting for a big portion of it. I went to Kilburn, worked in a job centre, and left after six-and-a-half years ...'

Laverne: 'Why did you leave?'

'That's such a brilliant question!' laughed her guest. 'Why did I *stay*, Lauren? I *hated* it there. I was so bad at my job but I stayed there and I sort of expected promotion: *Why aren't I an executive officer! I've been here five years!* And they were, like, "You don't *do* anything!"'

'One day, the manager asked if I'd clean up the back of the job centre because someone had made a mess. I went outside and it was human faeces. Someone had taken a crap outside the job centre! I quit very, very soon after that.'

Having got an Equity card by 'putting on a Punch & Judy show', Horgan did a degree funded by work as a waitress and in a Camden Town bong shop. More importantly, she went to the pub one night and bumped into Dennis Kelly, an old friend from a London youth theatre.

Laverne: 'You started writing together, and that drew the attention of the late BBC comedy producer Harry Thompson, and that led to BBC Three commissioning *Pulling*. What was that moment like?'

'It changed *everything*. I've genuinely never had the same level of excitement as when Harry called me and said our treatment has been commissioned. I can remember him laughing down the phone at me because he couldn't believe the pitch of my excitement.

'I had done shows as an actor, but this was *my own thing*, and Dennis's thing. We had this freedom creatively, which, as it turns out, is really hard to hand back once you get it.'

Laverne said that she had loved Horgan and Kelly's description of *Pulling* as '*Sex and the City* with kebabs'. 'It just puts you there so neatly – and you were writing characters that you weren't seeing elsewhere?'

'Yeah. I mean, you genuinely weren't seeing female characters overall being that funny, or being allowed to be really flawed and messed up. And it was exciting to have this opportunity to put female characters who were selfish, or drunks, and that was OK.

'Previous to that, in sitcoms, the female characters were eye-rolling, put-upon women who had to put up with selfish children who were their boyfriends. There's nothing really fun to play in that, and I think it's not that fun to *watch*, either.

'And I've always known women like that [in *Pulling*]. I've always *been* a woman like that!'

Pulling won critical acclaim and was commissioned for a second series. In 2014, Horgan set up her own production company, Merman. One of its first projects, noted Laverne, was *Catastrophe*, 'echoing your own experience of getting pregnant quite early in a relationship'.

Horgan agreed the series had contained 'hard, confessional truths. It's partly getting it off your chest: admitting that being a mother doesn't *always* make you happy.

'We had an episode of *Catastrophe* where the character thought that they might be carrying a baby that had a chromosomal abnormality. *I* had that experience, and I felt at the time that if I wrote about the fear, and all the complicated feelings that surrounded it, in the right way, it could be really helpful.'

After *Catastrophe*, Horgan went to New York to write and co-produce comedy-drama *Divorce* for HBO. It meant many weeks away from her husband, Jeremy, and their two daughters. She didn't take to it well.

'Oh, I lost my mind completely! I've got OCD from it. I sort of developed anxiety. I would lie in bed at night, feel my heart going, and think, *Oh, I'm about to have a heart attack!* It was only afterwards that I realised it was anxiety.

'Every couple of weeks, I'd go back, or they'd come over, but it was still *ridiculously* long and painful. Jem brought them over for Christmas and I was up for being the best Christmas mum in the land.

'We were in Austin, Texas. They had a trampoline in the back garden. I was jumping on it with my girls and I just broke my ankle. I cracked a bit of bone off and it was terrible. I was back on set and I was even *more* annoying, walking up to people on crutches, giving notes ... *ah, Jesus!*

'It was awful. It was a choice we made as a family, and lots of good things came out of it, but it certainly messed me up for a while. And I wouldn't want to do it again.'

Laverne: 'You and Jeremy are now amicably divorced and co-parenting. What kind of mum are you? Fun mum, on the trampoline?'

'I mean, I was fun mum for years. I *entirely* thought that was my role. But that changes a bit when you co-parent. Everything changes, and you take on a lot more roles. I'm much more practical than I was. I think that's a positive thing.

'When you bring anything like that into your kids' lives, it's tricky. When you turn their world upside-down. But it balances out, and everything's sort of eased back. It's lockdown and it's weird, but I like being here, and I'm here all the time.'

As a characteristically chaotic but compelling conversation with a one-off comedy talent came to a close, Lauren Laverne inquired of Sharon Horgan: 'What keeps you going when life gets *especially* messy?'

'I think I still have a mad love for what I do,' she ventured. 'I don't know if I still get the same kind of buzz from my *own* stuff, but I definitely get a buzz when we get something picked up that's the first show they've written. A mad buzz!

'Sometimes it's a bit much – and I *know* I take on a bit too much – but it's because I'm genuinely excited. It's all stuff that I truly love, and with people I really admire ...'

• • •

Shortly after being capsized, Sharon Horgan starred opposite James McAvoy in *Together*, a BBC2 comedy-drama by her *Pulling* co-writer, Dennis Kelly, about a long-standing couple coming apart during COVID lockdown. She then played Nicolas Cage's ex-wife in his big-budget, self-effacing Hollywood movie, *The Unbearable Weight of Massive Talent*. In 2023, Horgan and Michael Sheen will be a married couple fighting for the life of their apparently terminally ill daughter in BBC drama *Best Interests*. It's all a serious amount of success for somebody who reckons she is 'still a mess ...'

DISCS CHOSEN
'Rock 'n' Roll Suicide'
David Bowie
'I think David Bowie asking me to give him my hands and telling me I'm not alone, on a desert island, would really help ...'

'The Queen Is Dead'
The Smiths
'The Smiths were my punk in Ireland'

'Kid's Song'
Mic Christopher

'Telephone Thing'
The Fall
'The Fall were the soundtrack to my misspent twenties'

'The Only One I Know'
The Charlatans
'They get better all the time'

'Everything Goes My Way'
Metronomy
'I danced in one of their videos, and I can't really dance'

'The Suburbs (Continued)'
Arcade Fire

❤ **'Moments of Pleasure'**
Kate Bush
'A really good song to cry to. I've cried to it a lot'

BOOK
The Sun Also Rises – Ernest Hemingway
'It just transports me, and that'd be good on the island'

LUXURY ITEM

A laptop, to use just as a word processor

'I'll adapt The Sun Also Rises *and maybe a couple of stories from the Bible ...'*

'ISLE NEVER FORGET ...'

'I was very flattered to be asked on *Desert Island Discs*. I was also really surprised because it's like the radio version of *This Is Your Life*, and I still feel as if I'm just starting out. I know that's bonkers but it's also true.

'I got very nerdy choosing my songs. It was a tortured process. At one stage, I had a document on my phone, one on my laptop, and lists in my notebook and on scraps of paper. I found myself completely at sea with the enormity of it. Then a producer told me, "Don't think of it as your *favourite* songs, but ones that can chart a narrative."

'It was COVID lockdown so I did the show from my attic in Hackney. I felt pressure because it's such a special show for so many people. Because I was so nervous, I started off like I was going to have a heart attack! It was like I had anxiety mixed in with stage fright.

'Because I *make* shows myself, I was worried about the content! It was ridiculous: I was over-thinking the whole thing. But then I got really into it. Lauren is very easy to talk to, and good at asking the right questions to get interesting answers out of you, so you kind of stop worrying.

'Once I relaxed and started enjoying it, it was nice to take a trip down memory lane. The only time I ever do it is with my brothers and sisters when we're all drunk. You don't sit around thinking about the past, but sometimes it's really nice to do it. It puts life into perspective.

'I was surprised that I got emotional. I started talking about my kids, and my big life changes, and, *Oh shit!* I felt something happening to my voice! I could feel a tremor, and I was nervous that anyone else could hear it. I had to take a breath and pull it together.

'It's weird. I'd assumed I'd just be talking about music and telling funny little anecdotes. I didn't think for a minute that I'd be getting deeply into my life – which was pretty crazy, because that is *exactly* what the show does! And that's why people love it.'

72

SIR KEIR STARMER

MP, LEADER OF THE OPPOSITION
15 November 2020

As has been discussed, most castaways tend to be either celebrities or else unknown people with extraordinary life stories. It's a relative rarity for a guest to be somebody who is both firmly in the public eye and yet, despite that status, something of an unknown quantity.

Sir Keir Starmer had been leader of the opposition for seven months when he visited the desert island in November 2020. His professional rectitude and intellectual rigour were beyond doubt yet, behind the formal demeanour, many commentators and voters were still unsure exactly *who he was*.

Lauren Laverne delved deep for the personality behind the politician, and discovered a man who rose from a humble background to become first Director of Public Prosecutions and then the potential next prime minister – without jettisoning his loves of football and northern soul.

• • •

Laverne opened by pointing out that her guest had been elected leader of the Labour Party at a very difficult time, in the wake of a landslide election defeat under his predecessor, Jeremy Corbyn. 'What has been the biggest challenge for you, personally?'

Without hesitation, Sir Keir Starmer identified trying to make his mark, and establish his identity, during the ongoing COVID-19 pandemic.

'I haven't yet made a speech to anyone other than a camera,' he said. 'My acceptance speech was made in my living room. You imagine a conference hall full of people. I had my armchair to aim my speech at!'

Asked by Laverne, Starmer confirmed that he felt it was his duty, in the national interest, to support Boris Johnson's Conservative government in their battle against coronavirus 'where they are getting it right – for example, on the lockdowns, we've supported them on that.

'But where they're getting it *wrong*, we've got to challenge them – and they've got it wrong in quite a number of places.'

Laverne: 'As a former barrister, you know about public speaking – but how different are the skills required of a politician?'

'They're completely different. If you're a lawyer, it's based on the facts – there's proper argument and a judge that makes the decision. Politics is the art of persuasion.'

'Some commentators have said that you're too lawyerly? That you lack charisma?' suggested Laverne.

'Oh, they've said a lot worse than that!'

'What do you make of it?'

'Look, it's water off a duck's back! I know who I am, I know what I am, I know what I believe in and what I've got to do. *That's* what I'm focused on.'

Starmer chose a northern soul single, Dobie Gray's 'Out on the Floor', for his first record. 'Can you dance?' wondered Laverne.

'Flips, spins and back drops are what you need for northern soul! A few years ago ... but I would not be foolish enough [*to try it*] now!'

As the song's strains faded away, Laverne turned to a difficult matter. An Equality and Human Rights Commission (EHRC) report had recently found evidence of antisemitism within Labour under Corbyn. 'It was a damning verdict,' admitted Starmer. 'A real day of shame.'

Subsequent events, continued Laverne, had seen Corbyn suspended from the Labour Party and Starmer accused of a '1980s-style purge of the left wing. How do you answer that?'

'No, there isn't. I have no intention of purging. I want the Labour Party to be a broad church. We are far better when we're united. But if we don't tackle antisemitism, we don't *deserve* to win.'

Laverne turned to Starmer's childhood. The second of four kids, and named after Labour Party founder Keir Hardie, he had grown up in Oxted, Surrey. His dad, Rodney, was a toolmaker. 'Tell me a little bit more about him.'

'I don't often talk about my dad. He was a difficult man. A complicated man. He kept himself to himself. He didn't particularly like to socialise so he wouldn't really go out very much.

'He was incredibly hard-working. He worked on a factory floor all his life and my enduring memory was he'd go to work at eight in the morning, come home at five for his tea, go back at six and work until ten at night. Five days a week.

'He also had utter devotion to my mum. My mum was very ill all of her life and my dad knew exactly the symptoms of everything that might go wrong with her. He knew exactly what drugs, or combination of drugs, or injection would be needed.

'He stopped drinking completely, just in case he ever needed to get to the hospital with her. On the many occasions that she *was* in hospital, he would stay with her the whole time. He wouldn't leave the hospital. He'd sleep on a chair or whatever was available.'

Laverne: 'It sounds like he was dealing with a lot, and also not home so much because of working all the time. Were you close?'

'I wouldn't say we were close. I understood who he was, and what he was, but we weren't close. And I regret that.'

The host turned to Starmer's mum, Josephine. 'She used to be a nurse?'

'Yes, a very *proud* nurse. She got Still's disease when she was eleven. It's an attack on the immune system. They told her she'd be in a wheelchair by the time she was twenty, and she wouldn't be able to have children.

'A drug was discovered while she was a teenager, and they put her on steroids. It gave her the ability to walk in her twenties and to have four children, which she didn't think would happen. But steroids have long-term effects and she paid a heavy price as she got iller and iller.

'She couldn't use her limbs and she was very prone to infections. As young children, we spent a lot of time in and out of high-dependency units with my mum, thinking we were going to lose her.

'I remember one occasion, when I was about thirteen or fourteen, my dad phoning me from the hospital and saying, "I don't think your mum's going to make it. Will you tell the others?" That was tough. That was *really* tough.'

Laverne: 'What do you think now, looking back?'

'My dad died a couple of years ago. My mum died just weeks before I got into Parliament. I look back with pride. I look back with regrets.'

Although his parents were 'Labour through and through', Starmer said, his family never discussed politics. 'So where did your politics come from, then?' asked Laverne. 'What sparked your interest?'

'I got interested in politics at a very early age and joined East Surrey Young Socialists – the youth section of the local Labour Party – when I was sixteen. There weren't many of us in East Surrey. About four.'

Laverne: 'How did the Home Counties react to your radical politics?'

'Pretty negatively, as we sort of marched around East Surrey, up long drives, telling people that we thought nationalisation was the answer!'

Starmer recalled intending to study politics at university until his parents suggested law could be a better option. He agreed, from a position of deep ignorance.

'I arrived at university: I had never met a lawyer. I didn't really know what lawyers *did*. I don't think I knew the difference between a solicitor and a barrister. But, for me, it was an incredible journey – a boy from Oxted goes to Leeds University.'

He soon specialised in human rights law. 'Why?' wondered Laverne.

'I became fascinated by the idea that, at the end of the atrocities of the Second World War, countries around the world came together and made commitments to each other to honour human rights.

'And I became really taken with the *idea* behind human rights. It's not so much the individual rights but the human *dignity* that sits behind rights. How we treat individuals. How we treat them fairly. Equally.'

Laverne: 'Were you driven? What kind of student were you?'

'I was, there's no getting away from it!' laughed her guest. 'I've always been pretty driven and hardworking. But once I'd discovered human rights, I so enjoyed it that it didn't feel like a burden.'

Indeed, Starmer was so diligent and conscientious a scholar that it almost cost his shared student house their television.

'I was busy working, deep in thought. One of the other people in the house came in and said, "Keir, what are you *doing*? Didn't you *notice*?" And my flatmate had intercepted two people walking out of our flat with the television. I was oblivious that we were being burgled!'

Laverne asked about a 'radical magazine' that Starmer had co-edited in his university days: *Socialist Alternative*. 'What did you cover?'

'Oh, we were out to change the world! But, sadly, more copies of that magazine ended up under my bed than distributed to the world at large.'

Laverne: 'You interviewed Tony Benn for one article. In another, you denounced centrism and argued that Labour's future lay with the grassroots left. You sound like the people who give you a hard time now!'

'Yes. I said a lot of things then. Tony Benn was an incredible person to interview. I went to his house in Holland Park. He let me sit in Keir Hardie's chair! There was a wooden chair which he'd got from Keir Hardie, which he let me sit in to interview him.

'Yes, I was very much of that view at the time. I said some things that were daft, of course, but that's part of it.'

Laverne: '*Daft*, do you think?'

'Well, I've learned that the important thing in life is to hold your ideas up to the light and see if they withstand scrutiny. But that takes time. As I've grown, I've learned the power of saying: "*I don't know. Let's have a look at that.*"'

'Are you prepared to say that as a leader?'

'I'm prepared to say it and I *do* say it. The best decisions that leaders make are fully challenged by other people.'

Laverne continued to recap Sir Keir's career. Called to the Bar in 1987, he co-founded Doughty Street Chambers, and was later a human rights adviser to the Northern Ireland Policing Board as it strove to implement the Good Friday Agreement. This was an eventful posting.

'I was on the ground outside the Ardoyne shopfronts in north Belfast on 12 July when the parades were happening. We were there with our clipboards, and suddenly golf balls were being thrown and there were petrol bombs. I was thrown in the back of a police van for safety.'

In 2008, Keir Starmer was appointed the UK's Director of Public Prosecutions. He was, reflected Laverne, a surprise choice.

'You'd never prosecuted a case in court. You were not known as a fan of state power. As a lawyer, you'd represented Poll Tax protestors and striking miners. How much soul-searching did you have to do before you accepted the job?'

'There was a lot of thinking about it, and talking,' admitted Starmer. 'But I had spent quite a lot of time challenging the state – the police prosecutors – for not doing their job properly. And I felt that actually stepping up, and taking responsibility, was important.'

After Starmer chose Baddiel, Skinner and the Lightning Seeds' Euro '96 anthem 'Three Lions', Laverne turned to his love of football – and the fact that, at the age of fifty-eight, he still played for an eight-a-side team.

'I've been playing football every week since I was ten, and I still do,' he confirmed. 'I still see myself as the, sort of, driving force of midfield, but that brings chuckles now from those that I play with!'

Returning to politics, Laverne wondered how hard it had been for Sir Keir Starmer – 'a passionate Remainer, who was devastated by the result of the referendum' – to serve as shadow Brexit secretary under Jeremy Corbyn, 'a leader who held a more neutral position on Brexit'.

'Jeremy and I actually worked very closely, very well, together on it,' claimed Starmer. 'Brexit wasn't easy for any opposition leader.'

'Last year, you fought to include a second referendum in the Labour manifesto,' recalled Laverne, adding that some commentators felt this decision had contributed to the party's poor performance in the 2019 election. 'Do you have any regrets about how you handled the issue?'

'I acknowledge this came up on the door in different ways across the country. In the north-west, north-east and parts of the Midlands, it came up in a very negative way. I've got to accept that.

'It was differently received in places like Scotland. There was never an easy position for our party in that election. I think the important thing now is to recognise we've left the EU, Leave/Remain is over, and we have to aim for the best deal we can have with the EU.'

As it neared its end, she wondered how his politics had changed from his days as a sixteen-year-old, handing out leaflets in the streets of Oxted.

'I think, like most people, I started off as the radical who knew everything. Now, I'm much more open to ideas; much more *questioning* of ideas. I think the fundamentals, in many respects, are still there.'

'Do you still consider yourself a socialist?'

'Yes,' replied Sir Keir Starmer. 'Yes, I do.'

• • •

After a further two years in the job, Sir Keir Starmer is, by now, at least able to address live speeches to wider audiences than his living-room armchair. Reviews of his performance as Labour leader remain mixed, but he looks to have guided the party from its 2019 landslide defeat to a position where, in the summer of 2022, its opinion-poll performances give it grounds for guarded optimism. It remains to be seen whether Sir Keir can reverse the trend of four consecutive general election defeats for Labour next time around – and, in the process, possibly revive the fortunes of the East Surrey Young Socialists.

DISCS CHOSEN

'Out on the Floor'
Dobie Gray
'It reminds me of my early days in London, with a group of friends in a really grotty flat above a sauna and massage parlour'

Beethoven's Symphony No. 6 in F major, 'Pastoral'
Berlin Philharmonic Orchestra
'It's one of my dad's favourite bits of music. It will remind me of him'

'Welcome to My World'
Jim Reeves
'It was my mum's favourite song'

'Falling and Laughing'
Orange Juice
'This absolutely captures those early years at university'

'Oh, Happy Day'
Edwin Hawkins Singers
'This is about Northern Ireland. There's an expression used a lot there: "Happy days!" It reminds me of the challenges we went through'

'Three Lions'
Baddiel, Skinner and the Lightning Seeds
'I was in the upper tier at Wembley for the semi-final of Euro '96 when we were playing Germany'

❤ **Second movement from Beethoven's Piano Concerto No. 5**
Ludwig von Beethoven
'The music that my wife walked in to at our wedding'

'Bridge Over Troubled Water'
Artists for Grenfell (featuring Stormzy)
'Grenfell brought a shudder to everyone. My children love Stormzy, so this beautiful song will remind me of my children'

BOOK
A detailed atlas with shipping lanes in it
'So I can get myself off this island'

LUXURY ITEM
A football
'It'll obviously be slightly different without anyone to play against'

73

SIR CLIFF RICHARD

SINGER, ACTOR, LIVING LEGEND
20 December 2020

Cliff Richard first appeared on *Desert Island Discs* back in the mists of time, aged twenty, in October 1960. A scream idol in those halcyon days, he was nevertheless respectful, well-spoken and scrupulously polite when grilled by Roy Plomley.

Sixty years on, it makes for amusing listening. Cliff told Plomley that 'I've just left my teens, and I don't like it!' and described one of his disc choices, Debbie Reynolds, as 'my first film-star crush'. He had jettisoned his birth name, Harry Webb, he explained, as it was 'too square'.

Asked by Plomley about his onstage 'frenzied movements', the young Cliff claimed that they were 'all spontaneous'. He offered a hostage to fortune – 'I couldn't live anywhere else but Britain!' – and declined his host's offer to take any of his own discs to the island: 'No thank you! I've had enough of *those*!'

A lifetime on, Sir Cliff Richard rocked up on the desert island for the second time, at Christmas 2020, at the age of eighty. He had by then spent six decades as an icon of the British pop world, originally fronting the Shadows then with his own chart-strafing, record-setting solo career.

Sir Cliff had sold 250 million records, embraced Christianity, endured decades of intrusive press interest in his personal life ... and, in 2014, suffered the devastating ordeal of being falsely accused of historic sex crimes, a nightmare that ended with him successfully suing both the South Yorkshire Police and the BBC.

They were all very good reasons why he made for an utterly captivating castaway. And, second time around, he *did* take some of his own discs to the island ...

• • •

Introducing Sir Cliff as 'at once familiar and enigmatic', Lauren Laverne marvelled that he was the only British artist to score number one hits in five consecutive decades – then, with her guest's permission, took him back sixty years with a crackly clip of his encounter with Roy Plomley.

Plomley: 'Is it a fact that you can't move about easily in the streets without the risk of being mobbed?'
Richard: 'In town they're slightly more blasé about it because I think they're used to bumping into people, but in the provinces, they don't hesitate. If

they see someone they know from the screen, they don't hesitate to gather around.'

Plomley: 'Yes, and that means that you can lose the buttons off your clothes?'

Richard: Oh, you can quite easily! They don't mean to do any harm, really!'

'How does it feel, listening back to your younger self?' asked Laverne.

'The thing I can't relate to is that I sounded quite confident back then, didn't I?' boggled Richard. 'I was only twenty!'

'How do you look back at that young man now?'

'Someone asked me, if I could advise that young Cliff Richard about anything, what would I say? And I'd say to him, "Whatever you're doing, keep doing it, because apparently it worked!"'

Laverne took Sir Cliff right back to the start of his story. He had been born Harry Rodger Webb in 1940, in what was then still called British India. 'What do you remember about your early years there?'

'Well, I left there when I was seven. I remember independence had come in 1947 and there was civil war kicking off. I remember being in bed and thinking, *Boy, there's a bang-bang!*

This armed conflict, accompanying the partition of the country into India and Pakistan, was to force Richard's family to leave for England. Initially, they stayed with family members in Carshalton in Surrey.

'You'd had a very comfortable life in India, but your dad struggled to find work at home, didn't he?' asked Laverne. 'And he had four kids to support.'

'We arrived with £5 sterling, which I have looked up and it's about £200 now. How can you have a wife, and four children, and survive on £200 and no work? Three of our main meals per week were two slices of toast with milky tea poured over them and sugar sprinkled on top.

'There was a period where ... my father had a sister in Waltham Cross, Hertfordshire, who had a spare room. There were six of us in there. We had bunkbeds on each side of the room and there was a narrow section in the middle that we lived in.'

Things looked up for the Webb family when, after two years in England, they were given a council house in Cheshunt. After Richard fell in love with rock and roll, his dad gave him a guitar for his sixteenth birthday. 'What did he teach you?' asked Laverne.

'The first song he taught me was called "The Prisoner Song". "*If I had the wings of an ...*" – fumble, fumble – "*... angel, over these prison walls I'd fly!*" I can remember not getting my fingers in the right positions!

'Mostly, I used to stand in front of the mirror, miming to an Elvis record with the guitar hanging around my neck. It made me feel the way that I thought rock and rollers *should* look and feel.'

Laverne took Richard back to forming a band, the Drifters, with friends in the late fifties. After they had a modicum of success, Harry Webb decided to change his name. 'How did you alight on Cliff Richard?'

'We went to play at the 2i's Coffee Bar [*in London*]. It's where Tommy Steele was discovered. And a guy from Ripley, in Derbyshire, said, "I'd like you to come and play in my ballroom. What's your name?"

'I said "Harry Webb" and he said, "OK, Harry Webb and the Drifters." I went, "No, no, no, that doesn't sound rock and roll to me! We're just the Drifters." And he said, "No, I need a [*singer's*] name, or we're not going to have you up there!"

'So [*the band*] went to a little pub around the corner. One combination of names was Cliff Russard. I said, "Cliff sounds good – a rockface, like rock and roll!" Somebody else suggested Cliff Richards, with an "s" on the end.

'A guy who had just joined the band at the 2i's, Ian Samwell, said, "Take the 's' off Richards!" So, I went into that pub as Harry Webb and came out as Cliff Richard.'

The conversation paused for music, and Richard chose the only disc to survive from his original 1960 list: 'Heartbreak Hotel' by Elvis Presley. 'That's what kicked me off,' he told Laverne, simply. 'I'm convinced now that's the reason why I've followed my dreams.'

By 1958, Cliff Richard and the Drifters had a record deal. Their debut single, 'Move It', went to number two in the chart. 'How quickly did life change for you after that?' asked Laverne.

'Oh, instantly! We were still at the Cheshunt council house and this cheque came through for £60. It seemed a small fortune to us! And I bought my mum a television set with it.'

Laverne: '"Move It" is credited as being the first British rock and roll song. John Lennon said, "Before Cliff Richard, there had been nothing worth listening to in British music." Quite an endorsement!'

'God bless him. Some journalists who think they're being cool – really, more *cruel* than cool – say to me, "You're not really cool." And I say, "*John Lennon* thought I was cool, so I'll go with John!"'

Laverne moved on to Richard's early sixties pop rivalry with the Beatles, including both artists vying to record in Abbey Road studio two. 'People think the Beatles owned studio two,' laughed Richard. 'They didn't. They were renting it. *We* owned it first!

'I've talked to Paul about it. He said, "You were always EMI's favourite boy. Every time we rang for studio two, you had it!" And I said, "Paul, *please*! Every time *we* rang, they told us, "No, the Beatles have got it ..."'

There was a pause for music from Sir Cliff's long-time friend, Olivia Newton-John, then Laverne moved on to an early tragedy in his life. In 1961, just after his band had been renamed the Shadows and his career had taken off, his dad, Rodger, died, aged just fifty-six. 'It must have knocked you side-ways?' the host said.

'It was a heart-breaking time for me. My dad missed the best. He was so behind me all the way through that I feel, sometimes, horribly angry that he died too early. He missed the first number one. He missed the knighthood. I miss my dad still.'

Laverne: 'After your dad's death, you began to develop an interest in Christianity. Then, in 1966, you were invited to speak at a rally held by the evangelist Billy Graham. Tell me about that decision to get up on stage in front of twenty-five thousand people and talk about your faith.'

'It was a terrifying moment for me. I was so scared, but it did lead to me beginning to be able to speak the name "Jesus" without feeling embarrassed. I don't know why people *are* embarrassed by that, but they sometimes are. But I don't feel that embarrassment any more.'

After a gospel duet, 'It Is Well', between Cliff and Sheila Walsh, Laverne turned to her guest's private life – a subject of feverish speculation in certain corners of Britain's tabloid media for the best part of sixty years.

'Although you've had some important relationships in your life, you've never married,' she said. 'You've said you were too committed to your career. How damaging do you think getting married would have been?'

'It would have no effect now at all. People being married and singing now doesn't have the effect it would have had when I was starting in the 1950s. It was just the way it was. People would say, "The girls are all squealing at you! You've got to be *available* for them!"

'I was dating a girl called Jean. We came out of Finsbury Park Empire and she sat on my lap in the front of the car. I waved at the fans, and they were throwing their programmes on the floor and stamping them in the gutter! And I thought, *Oh, no, no,* ...

'That focus was not going to be changed. I was never going to give up this career that I'd fought for. Now, it doesn't matter. Gary Barlow is married and has got children: no one minds. That's how it *should* have been then. But it wasn't.'

Laverne: 'You also have to be tough to survive press speculation about your private life, which you've always been subjected to?'

'Yes. I've lived with it for so long now that I don't care any more *what* they think or say. My private life is absolutely nobody's business but mine. And I tell them that.'

After a break for Bonnie Raitt, Laverne moved on to the catastrophic events for Sir Cliff Richard of 14 August 2014 – the terrible day that had, as he said, 'changed his life forever'.

'There was a raid on your home in Berkshire by the South Yorkshire Police, investigating historic sexual abuse allegations,' she said. 'The BBC filmed the raid from a helicopter and it was broadcast around the world. What do you remember about that day?'

'I remember the phone ringing in the kitchen of my house in Portugal. It was the guy who manages the apartment block [*in Berkshire*] and he said, "The police are here with a warrant to search your apartment."

'There was a TV in one of the rooms and we looked at it. That's when I saw the raid. I saw the helicopter outside the apartment block. It was a horrible, horrible time. I can't *begin* to tell you.

'[*The next day*] I was in the kitchen [*in Portugal*] and my legs gave way and I collapsed on the floor. I didn't faint, but I couldn't stand up. And I found myself weeping like a child.

'I was never suicidal but I thought a couple of times that I might die. I used to wake up with my pulse, my head, my heart, thumping like crazy and I was thinking, *I don't want to kill myself, but this could kill me.*

'But I survived it all. That's the main thing for me. I'm past it now. I don't think I'll ever get *over* it, though. It's not something that you can wipe from your memory.'

Laverne: 'You weren't charged: the case was dropped. In 2017, you settled with South Yorkshire Police. You won your privacy case against the BBC the following year. What did those outcomes mean to you?'

'I'd like to think that, when I won the court case against the BBC, it means that they would have to think really hard if ever they wanted to do something like that again.'

Sir Cliff Richard is on record as saying that only his Christian faith saw him through the scarcely survivable events of 2014–15. Asked by Lauren Laverne to choose just one disc to save from being washed away by an imaginary tidal wave on the island, his reply was instant and definite.

'Oh, I'd go for the gospel one. I'd go for "It Is Well". I would need to feel that God was with me. I would feel safe and I would feel well ...'

• • •

Sir Cliff Richard rolls on and on. Due to take his *The Great 80* tour on the road at the end of 2020, to mark his eightieth birthday, he was forced by the COVID-19 pandemic to postpone it but subsequently performed it, triumphantly, at the end of 2021 and start of 2022. Having famously sung live on Wimbledon's Centre Court when rain stopped play in 1996, he duly reprised the experience in July 2022 as part of that venerable old court's centenary celebrations. At the age of eighty-two, he is set to release his forty-sixth studio album, *Christmas with Cliff*, at the end of 2022. Don't rule out yet another Christmas number one ...

DISCS CHOSEN (2020)

'Rolling in the Deep'
Aretha Franklin
'That voice is, for me, the greatest voice ever'

'What's Love Got to Do with It'
Cliff Richard
'This was written for me by Terry Britten, who wrote "Devil Woman" for me. Somehow, the demo he sent to my office got sent back with a little message: "We don't think this is right for Sir Cliff!" So he gave it to Tina Turner instead ...'

'Heartbreak Hotel'
Elvis Presley
'It felt like something from outer space'

'I Honestly Love You'
Olivia Newton-John
'If I'm going to be on a desert island, I would still want to feel loved'

❤ **'It Is Well'**
Sheila Walsh (featuring Cliff Richard)
'Faith can get us through the most disastrous periods of our lives'

'I Can't Make You Love Me'
Bonnie Raitt

'Stayin' Alive'
The Bee Gees
'I went through that period in my life when I felt absolutely lost, but I kept telling myself: I WILL survive this'

'High Water Everywhere'
Joe Bonamassa
'A fantastic guitarist and outrageously wild singer'

BOOK

Wuthering Heights – Emily Brontë
'I did the show Heathcliff *– for the first time in my life on stage, I was not "Cliff Richard". I had become this horrible book character'*

LUXURY ITEM
His Gibson acoustic guitar
'I bought it in 1959 and it's got a very, very gentle sound'

'ISLE NEVER FORGET ...'
'I didn't hear *Desert Island Discs* in the very early years because I was in India as a boy and then, when we came to England, we didn't have a radio. When I *did* hear it, it was all very well-spoken *ac-tors* and huge stars. So, I was pleased to be asked on. I thought, *Oh my golly!*

'It was a bit nerve-wracking because I was so young. I sounded so much more confident than I was! Looking back at my list, I see that half of my records were black artists [*Pearl Bailey, Dakota Staton, Lena Horne and Ray Charles*]. I loved to listen to those great singers.

'I was surprised to be invited again because I thought people only got asked on once: *that's your lot!* But it was great to have that really long gap and then do it again. And it's still a really big show, just like it was back then.

'I enjoyed my first appearance, but I think I liked the second time more because I felt I had more stories to tell. When you're young and starting your career, everything is edgy and you don't really know what you're doing. You haven't grown into yourself.

'Talking about 2014, and the South Yorkshire Police, didn't bother me because it's no longer part of my life. I'll never forget it – of course not! But as I said on the show, I've got past it now. I'll never get over it, not fully, but I got past it.

'Only one record from my 1960 list survived to 2020 and it was always going to be "Heartbreak Hotel". Everyone knows that Elvis has been a major factor in my life. I always say it – if there hadn't been an Elvis, would there have even *been* a Cliff Richard?

'My last choice, "High Water Everywhere", may have surprised a few *Desert Island Discs* listeners! Well, I know that I'll be remembered for "Living Doll" and "Summer Holiday" but, deep down, I'd much rather be remembered for something *wild* like Joe Bonamassa!'

74

MALALA YOUSAFZAI

ACTIVIST, AUTHOR, NOBEL PRIZE WINNER
14 February 2021

Over the decades, *Desert Island Discs* has heard many inspiring tales of heroism, and of castaways overcoming unimaginable, catastrophic life events to become iconic world figures. Few such stories have been as spectacular as that of Malala Yousafzai.

A fervent campaigner for girls' education in her home area of the Swat Valley in Pakistan, Malala was just fifteen in October 2012 when a Taliban gunman boarded her school bus, asked, 'Who is Malala?' and shot her in the head. After Pakistani surgeons saved her life, she was airlifted to the Queen Elizabeth Hospital in Birmingham.

Settled in Britain, Malala overcame her injuries, graduated from Oxford University, continued to campaign for girls' education around the world – and, in 2014, was awarded the Nobel Peace Prize. Her journey made for a humbling yet ultimately life-affirming forty minutes of radio.

• • •

Lauren Laverne opened this February 2021 encounter by congratulating Malala on, the previous year, securing her Oxford Politics, Philosophy and Economics degree. 'And you enjoyed studying philosophy most of all. What did you love about it?'

'I like virtue ethics,' her guest replied. 'Virtues like kindness and generosity are taken for granted. Small deeds: just be kind! Smiling at someone can have a real impact and bring joy and happiness.'

Laverne asked if it were true that the pre-teen Malala had wanted to be a politician.

'When I was eleven years old, I said that I wanted to become prime minister of Pakistan, to fix the country. It was quite simple for me then! I was, like, *OK, when I become prime minister, I'll fix everything!*

'But what I have learned is that things are quite complicated. Right now, my focus is to work on girls' education. Then – I don't know – I could consider politics in twenty years, or something?'

Despite her guest's tender age of twenty-three, said Laverne, she had been an activist for more than ten years and was now world famous. How different was her public image from how she behaved at home?

'In the house, I am quite bossy, in a positive way,' claimed Malala, a smile in her voice. 'I lecture my brothers all the time: "Do *this*, don't do *that*!" Boys need a lot of lectures! It will help them in the future ...'

Laverne wondered, given the harrowing events of Malala's young life, how she had been able to cope. 'Do you find time to have fun?'

'I wasn't having much fun *before* university. But when I connected with people of my age, that was when I realised, *OK, I am actually not that old! I can still have the experiences of youth everyone else is having!*

'I started hanging out with friends: going to college balls, music events. When you are with your friends, you are having one of your best times ever. Childhood has sort of come back in me and I'm really happy for that.'

Laverne recapped that Malala Yousafzai had been born in north-west Pakistan, near the border with Afghanistan: an area sometimes described as the Switzerland of Asia. 'How would you describe it?'

'It is one of the most beautiful places that I have seen in my life. It is a valley surrounded by tall mountains and there is peace there. Peace that you are just in this beautiful part of nature.'

Malala's father, she explained, was a long way from typical of men in their patriarchal, often repressive region.

'I am lucky that I have an amazing feminist father – he was a feminist before he even knew the word "feminist". He was not just preaching the equality of women: he was actually doing it. He ensured that I got my education; got treated the same way as my brothers got treated.

'There were so many other young girls in Swat Valley who wanted to speak out and who *were* speaking out, initially. But their brothers and their fathers stopped them from speaking out. My father did not stop me. It's as simple as that.'

Laverne: 'What made him different, do you think?'

'My father had five sisters and there were two brothers. He noticed the discrimination with his own eyes. When his parents served food to all the children, the boys would get the bigger piece of meat than the girls.

'My grandfather, he educated the boys, but he did not send the girls to school. So, for my father, the question was why, just because he was a boy, he was getting all of these privileges?

'He decided that, when he will have his own daughter, he will make sure they are not discriminated against: that she gets equal amounts of food, is sent to school, and gets her education.

'When I was born, my father's cousin had been working on our family tree. It had the names of all the men who had been in our family, going back three hundred years, but there was no name of a woman in there. And my father took a pen, and he wrote in my name.'

Believing that boys and girls should be educated side by side, Malala's father co-founded a school in the Swat Valley, which his daughter attended. 'What kind of student were you?' enquired Laverne.

'I was a really good student. When I look back, I'm like, "Malala, you were doing great!" I was participating in every core curricular and extra-curricular activity, doing speeches, performing in any school event, going for anything!'

Laverne: 'You were keen for your father to do more to help children, especially those growing up from poorer backgrounds?'

'When I used to walk to school, I used to see many girls who were not in school. They would be going to other people's houses for domestic labour. Many of them would be on the garbage dumps, collecting metal pieces from the garbage. And I always had this question: *Why it is that I can go to school, but they can't?*'

Laverne moved forward to 2008. Driven out of Afghanistan by the US in the wake of the 9/11 terror attacks, the Taliban had relocated to the Swat Valley. 'You were eleven. What do you remember about that time?'

'Basically, life in fear. The Taliban would enter into people's houses just because they had spoken something, or they were just a bit suspicious that they were against them. And they would kill these people.

'In a square called Green Square, their bodies would be hanging there, with a note saying that nobody can remove this body until eleven am or twelve pm. It said, if anybody removes it – *your* body will be here, too.

'It's very difficult to understand the ideology. They literally misused the name of Islam.'

Laverne: 'When did you realise your father's school was under threat?'

'They were writing outside, on the walls of the school, that education is forbidden, and that if any girls go to the school, that you will see the consequences. My father closed the school on 15 January 2009 because that was the official deadline from the Taliban.

'It was very clear that if anybody kept their school open, their school would be bombed. I remember waking up on that day and just realising I could no longer go to school. *What does that mean for me? For my future?* It was a really sad day and I cried a lot.

'Around February, the Taliban agreed to allow girls until grade four. They said those girls are young and haven't yet reached puberty, when they should be married. They said they'd allow girls until grade four – and I was in grade five.

'We started going to school secretly. We did not go in school uniform. We used to wear our normal home clothes and hide our books under our scarves. And we kept going to school, even in that time.'

Malala was by now also writing an anonymous blog for the BBC, under a pseudonym, about life under the Taliban. 'Was it a case of you were more scared of what might happen if you *didn't* speak out than what might happen if you did?' asked Laverne.

'One hundred per cent. For me, the fear was living in that situation for my whole life. I don't know – you just feel this strength within you, even though you're tiny. And I'm still tiny. I'm five feet! I haven't grown an inch taller.'

After a song from *The Phantom of the Opera*, Laverne forwarded to 9 October 2012: 'the day that made headlines around the world. It was when what you call "the incident" happened. What do you remember about that afternoon?'

'I remember sitting in the school bus, talking to my friends. The bus driver was doing magic tricks with a pebble, hiding it – it was appearing and disappearing. I was fascinated, I love magic tricks.

'Then he started driving, and I just ... I don't remember anything. And then I wake up in hospital in Birmingham.'

'You have no memory of the incident itself? What did your friends tell you?'

'My best friend, Muniba, said a young man at the front had stopped the school bus. He was talking to the driver, then one guy came to the back of the bus and said, "Who's Malala?" Everybody was scared. Some of the girls were covering their faces. Some were not. I was not covering my face.

'I was like, "Muniba, what was I doing? Did I say anything?" She said, "No, you were not. You were just staring at the person. You squeezed my hand so tightly that I could feel the pain for days. Suddenly, bullets were fired, and you fell in my lap."'

After a few days of emergency treatment, Malala was airlifted in a medically induced coma to Queen Elizabeth Hospital in Birmingham, which specialises in treating injured military personnel. She came around after a week. 'What do you remember?' asked Laverne.

'I remember opening my eyes and I was trying to process whether I was alive, or if I was still in a dream – when you are not really dead but you are trying to get up, but you can't. I was grateful when I realised that I was alive. I cannot explain the thankfulness in my heart.

'I was worried about my father. That was literally the first question in my mind: *Where is my father?* Initially, I could not talk, because I had a tube in my neck for breathing. Whatever I wanted to say, I had to write it on a piece of paper.'

'What did you write?'

'I asked him to bring my physics books, because I was worried that I might be a bit behind in my physics revision for Pakistan! I did not know that the journey, and the time I would be spending in the UK, would be a lot longer than that ...'

Nine years on and fully recovered, Malala was now happily settled in Birmingham – at the host's request, she even performed an extremely creditable impersonation of a Brummie accent. 'You've said that you can have more than one home,' said Lauren Laverne. '*Do* you?'

'Birmingham has become home, but Swat Valley, Pakistan, that is always my first home,' declared Malala Yousafzai. 'That's still in our hearts and there is a sense of attachment to the land; to the soil.

'When you put your feet in this different piece of land, you just feel like you belong to it. I hope to go back to Pakistan soon, to see my home again ...'

• • •

Malala Yousafzai continues to campaign for girls' education around the world, including via the Malala Fund, the lobbying group and charity she co-founded with her father, Ziauddin. In August 2021, after the Taliban regained control of Afghanistan, she condemned their newly reintroduced ban on girls being educated beyond sixth grade, accusing them of wanting to 'erase girls and women from all public life in Afghanistan' and asking world leaders to 'take collective action to hold the Taliban accountable for violating the human rights of millions of women and girls'. This brave woman's struggle is far from over.

DISCS CHOSEN
'Rang'
Rahat Fateh Ali Khan and Amjad Sabri
'Sufi songs talk about the connection to God'

'Shinwara Lawangeena'
Zarsanga
'A well-known folk singer of Pakistan ... the Taliban would stop your car and search for cassettes to ensure you were not listening to music'

'Never Say Never'
Justin Bieber
'I used to listen to this song in Pakistan. I was very new to pop culture!'

❤ **'Hum Dekhen Ge'**
Iqbal Bano
'Whenever I feel hopelessness, I listen to this song'

'All I Ask of You' from *The Phantom of the Opera*
Sarah Brightman and Steve Barton
'I really like musicals – I watched The Phantom of the Opera *so many times!'*

'Kaari Kaari'
Quratulain Balouch
The song is in Urdu and from Pink, *a Bollywood movie that touches on the issue of women's rights*

'Love Always Comes as a Surprise' from the movie *Madagascar 3*
Peter Asher
'I am a big, big fan of animation!'

'Bibi Sherina'
Sardar Ali Takkar
'A song that talks to young Pashtun girls and says that education is your right'

BOOK
Complete works of Plato
'I studied Plato's Republic *at university and have become a big fan'*

LUXURY ITEM
Her lip balm
'I would be very happy with that forever!'

75

SOPHIA LOREN

ACTOR, CINEMATIC DEITY
21 February 2021

As that great philosopher Forrest Gump once observed about life itself: *Desert Island Discs* is like a box of chocolates. You never know what you're going to get. And that dictum was never truer than in February 2021, when Malala Yousafzai was followed on to the island, a week later, by Sophia Loren.

With a seventy-year film career behind her, Loren is a colossus of cinema and of the Golden Age of Hollywood. As Lauren Laverne noted, her movie co-stars had included Clark Gable, Gregory Peck, Cary Grant, Frank Sinatra, Paul Newman, Marlon Brando and Richard Burton ... not to mention being directed by Charlie Chaplin.

At the age of eighty-six, La Loren remained a sharp and amusing inter-viewee, particularly on the necessity of living your life driven by all-consuming passion, no matter how old you happen to be. When Lauren met Loren, a very diverting radio broadcast ensued.

• • •

Laverne began with that constant touchstone of Sophia Loren's life: living with passion. 'Where do you find that passion today?'

'You have it within you. If you have something in life that you really want to do because it's important for you, for your life or your children or your family, you do it. When it's worth it, I like to dare.'

Loren clearly felt that passion for her latest film, *The Life Ahead*, in which she played a Holocaust survivor. It was directed by her son, Edoardo Ponti. 'Did your relationship as mother and son help you to get to the heart of the issues in the film?' asked Laverne.

'Absolutely! Absolutely! We worked together in a very, very deep way. It was not a normal film.'

'It's an emotional film to watch. Was it emotional to make?'

'When you feel emotions in the right way, you don't even feel as if you are making an effort. You feel so much inside of yourself that you become the subject that you're doing. You don't see anything else but what you are doing.'

After a break for Ella Fitzgerald, after which Laverne reported that her guest had sung along with every word, the host turned to Loren's early life. She had been born Sophia Scicolone, in Rome in 1934, in a hospital ward for unmarried mothers.

'You describe your mother as a restless beauty with great dreams,' said Laverne. 'Tell me more about her.'

'My mother never knew who she was. She was a lost soul with a great, great way of wanting to do things, but not enough strength and flame inside to be able to overcome negative thinking and to join what she really wanted in her life.

'But she was a good person. A tender person. She was a good mother and she was a good pianist. But she never took care of it and had the kind of success that she could have had.'

Laverne: 'What about your father? How would you describe him?'

'Well, I cannot, because I don't know! I mean, I've seen him in my life maybe twice, three times. He was handsome, he was OK, but I don't think he was in love with her. If you love somebody, you are with the person – especially if you have children. My God, it's a miracle to have a child! It's wonderful to have a family!'

Laverne recapped that, finding raising a baby alone a struggle, Loren's mother had returned to her family home in Pozzuoli in Naples. 'You were very close to your grandmother?'

'Oh, *sì, ma nonna, nonna, nonna!* She was my mother, she was my father, she was my grandfather. She was everything for us. We were a family of nine, ten people – cousins, aunts – all together in one house.'

Laverne: 'Your mother was very beautiful?'

'She looked exactly like Greta Garbo! And when she started to know this, she would get the make-up like Greta Garbo, the blonde hair like Greta Garbo. Everything like Greta Garbo. And the people in the street would go around her. They wanted the autograph!

'Now, I know that it was all a joke, but then I thought my mother, her name was Greta Garbo! But it was not true.'

The likeness was so extreme that Loren's mother won a competition run by MGM film studios to find a Garbo lookalike. However, sighed Loren, the family matriarch had interceded.

'They wanted her in America but my *nonna*, my *nonna*, said: "What are you *doing*? You have two children! You cannot go!" People in a little town were scared of everything. They just wanted to stay in Pozzuoli, where they were born. *And what do you do in Pozzuoli?*'

Laverne: 'You were five when World War II broke out. You've said it was "the major theme of my childhood". What do you remember?'

'We were always in a battle with something. Bombing, and drama, and falling houses, and no food at all. It's incredible – I am talking to you about many, many years ago and I still think about these things like it was yesterday. It's very, very much alive. Very much terrible!'

'It was a fight for survival until the war was over?'

'Oh, yes, yes. When the Americans came in, my God, it was beautiful! Beautiful!'

The teenage Loren celebrated peace, and the reopening of cinemas, by immersing herself in films: 'Fred Astaire. Rita Hayworth. Ginger Rogers. We loved American movies, because they were in beautiful houses, and dancing!'

Laverne: 'When you were fifteen, your mother entered you in a local beauty pageant. You were one of the winners. How did you feel about your looks?'

'They called me "*sticetto*" – you know what that means? Little stick?'

'"Toothpick", I think we say here.'

'Yes, because I was so skinny! I was not at all the Italian beauty of today – nice and, you know, round! Not at all!'

In her late teens, this toothpick moved to Rome and began starring in photo-romance stories in magazines ('I was very well-known: *Bolero! Bolero!*'). Movies followed. In the early fifties, Loren had her first lead role in an adaptation of the Italian opera *Aida*. 'Did you feel you were on the cusp of something great?' wondered Laverne.

'I thought that it was very good for me to try, because I knew that I had a good ear for music.'

'What was it like on the set? Were you nervous, as the star?'

'No, not at all! I adored every moment of it! That's how I started really wanting to be in that place many times.'

Laverne: 'You were getting noticed but at the same time – this is hard to believe – some cameramen said you were difficult to photograph?'

'I didn't have the most normal face to be able to look good in any kind of lighting. My nose was too big. My mouth was too big. Everything was too big for them. Maybe the cameraman had another girl he wanted to put in my place. It was terrible! It was a war! A war!

'But I don't have a big face that you change. I liked my face. I liked the way I was. I liked to look at my face in the mirror when I was growing. I owned my face, and I wanted to keep it.'

Laverne: 'In 1951 you met the film producer, Carlo Ponti, the great love of your life. But you weren't able to marry until 1966. Why not?'

'He was married!' laughed Loren. '*Signora, signora*, what are you saying?'

'You were prepared to wait?'

'Absolutely! I think, when you love somebody, you have to wait all of your life!'

Loren chose Frank Sinatra's 'Fly Me to the Moon', which reminded her of 'my arrival in Hollywood in my twenties'. She had made a movie with Sinatra. 'What was he like to work with?' asked Laverne.

'He loved his – *Come si dice? Come si dice?* – trailer? He would stay in the trailer very often. He never sang on the set.'

Laverne: 'By 1953, you had a new name – Sophia Loren – and the following year, you were cast in Vittorio De Sica's *The Gold of Naples*. How much did that film change things for you?'

'Everything! Everything! The role was perfect for me. It was the role of a girl of sixteen years, Neapolitan, no money, no food. The street was her home. That was the character of the film.

'I didn't know what it was, acting. I didn't know what it was. *Nothing, nothing, nothing.* I really have De Sica in my heart, because I really owe to him a lot of what I got from lines. He did this like a teacher but with a lot of simplicity. Wonderful person!'

'You said he taught you to believe in yourself?'

'Working with him, I didn't have to believe in myself. I *was* myself.'

In 1957, said Laverne, Loren made her first English-language movie, *The Pride and the Passion*, with Cary Grant, who later proposed to her. 'But you turned him down. Why?'

'Because I was already engaged with Carlo, I think! No? And also, when *this kind of thing* happens on a set, I've always been careful about it. Because a set is something: the world is something else.'

Laverne: 'You were an incredible Scrabble player and would play on set with your co-stars. You beat everyone?'

'I was cheating. I like to cheat because I have fun!'

'Who gave you the most trouble?'

'Richard Burton.'

'You beat him?'

'I was cheating him a lot. And then, when he found out, he said, "I'm never going to play with you again!"'

Loren reminisced about being directed by Charlie Chaplin in 1967's *A Countess from Hong Kong*. 'You don't do a picture with this person every day! I mean, this was his last film! One of the greatest moments of my working life!'

Five years earlier than that, Laverne recapped, Loren had won an Oscar for best actress for De Sica's *Two Women*. It was the first time the prize had gone to a non-English-speaking performance. 'You beat Audrey Hepburn and Natalie Wood – but you didn't go to the ceremony?'

'No, because the Oscars for us, in Italy, were far away! It's an *Italian* film. You do not feel it is possible that you are going to win.'

Laverne: 'How did you spend that night?'

'I was with friends, doing a little party just to be together, pretending that we were not thinking that there was, in Hollywood, the Oscars. *Pretending.* De Sica was there with me.

'The phone rang: "Hi, hi! It's Cary!" I said, "Yeah?" "Yeah, you won!" I almost fainted. *I almost fainted.* I say, "Carlo, Carlo! *Telefono*! Cary Grant! Cary Grant!"

'Wonderful moments! I mean, really! This kind of prizes – you cannot say in words how you feel! It's impossible because it's unique. It's wonderful. It's great! It's great! It's great!'

As her interlocution with one of the truly defining figures in cinematic history came to an end, Lauren Laverne wondered where she would think of, fondly, as home, from her desert island – Rome, or Naples?

'I was born in Rome, by chance, but my heart, and myself, and my physique ... I am from Naples!' declared Sophia Loren. 'I am from these people. I've always been with them.

'Rome? Yes, beautiful, but my life, my childhood, was solely in Naples. And I think if you are in a place during your childhood, it's a place that you will remember forever. *Forever.*'

• • •

Still a formidable presence as she nears the end of her eighties, Sophia Loren is one of the last remaining links to the Golden Age of Hollywood and the sole surviving actor on the American Film Institute's *100 Years ... 100 Stars* list, which was compiled for that organisation's centenary celebrations in 1999. Her beauty, talent and passion are such that you can almost forgive her cheating at Scrabble. *Almost.*

DISCS CHOSEN
'I've Got You under My Skin'
Ella Fitzgerald
'Ella's voice represented America to me'

'Clair de lune' from Debussy's *Suite bergamasque*
Tamás Vásáry
'My mother was a concert pianist and would play this piece'

'Lara Says Goodbye to Yuri' from the soundtrack to *Doctor Zhivago*
Maurice Jarre
'This is the film that my husband, Carlo, was most proud of. He was a great artist. I miss him every day of my life'

'Fly Me to the Moon (In Other Words)'
Frank Sinatra

'Oggi Sono Io'
Mina
'Mina represents so many chapters of my life and connects me to my love of Italy'

'The Marketplace at Limoges' from Mussorgsky's *Pictures at an Exhibition*
Carlo Ponti with the Russian National Orchestra
'This is conducted by my son, Carlo'

'Io sì' from the soundtrack of *The Life Ahead*
Laura Pausini

❤ **'Caruso'**
Lucio Dalla
'This reminds me of what it means to be Neapolitan'

BOOK
Letters from a Young Father – Edoardo Ponti
'A poetry book that my son wrote for his daughter before she was born. It's beautiful when you see your son turn into a father'

LUXURY ITEM
A pizza oven
'I cannot live without a pizza. Neapolitans invented pizza!'

76

RICHARD OSMAN

WRITER, BROADCASTER
26 December 2021

F. Scott Fitzgerald famously said that there are no second acts in American lives. At Christmas 2021, Lauren Laverne welcomed to the desert island a Brit who had reinvented himself not once but twice, and thus was now firmly into the third act of his own life drama.

Obsessed with TV game shows as a kid, Richard Osman had been a producer on quizzes such as *Deal or No Deal* and *8 Out of 10 Cats* before moving in front of the camera to co-present a quiz show he also co-devised, *Pointless*. As if this was not enough, he then penned a book, 2020's *The Thursday Murder Club*, which was to become one of the fastest-selling novels in British publishing history.

His multiple successes appeared enviable yet Osman had had far from an easy life, as was evident as he opened up to Laverne about boyhood parental desertion, his debilitating lack of confidence about being 6 feet 7, and battling a crippling eating disorder. *Desert Island Discs* presented a Christmas story with dark undertones but a very happy ending.

• • •

Lauren Laverne began the show by explaining that Richard Osman had spent twenty years as a TV producer and executive before becoming a presenter on *Pointless* in his forties. She wondered if that show gained from the contestants always being in pairs.

'Exactly, because you can then have questions that people can chat about to each other,' he agreed. '*Pointless* is more fun because you always have an opinion of a pair of people. With a married couple, you have an opinion on who's married well.

'On *Pointless* – this is terrible, I shouldn't say it, but we always do it – there'll be a man and woman who say they're "friends". And you go ... *I don't know about that. Really? Are you friends, or do you think ... look, she's "friends". I think he wants to be more than friends ...*'

After a burst of Morecambe and Wise's theme tune, 'Bring Me Sunshine', Laverne turned the conversation to her guest's childhood in Haywards Heath, Sussex. Initially happy, it was then hit by a major trauma.

'Because I don't see very well, I've never been a child who is hugely engaged in the world. Just someone who's on the sidelines, I think. But I was very deeply content. I found it very easy to entertain myself, and I had the most wonderful mum in the world.

'My father left when I was young, about nine, and that was probably the end of that innocence, I suspect.'

Laverne: 'Your dad leaving was a sudden and seismic change?'

'Yeah. It couldn't have been more English. There was never a raised voice in our house until the day we were called into our front room. I had a glass of orange squash.

'He said that he was in love with someone else, and he was leaving, and he hoped that was OK. A complete shock. It was the 1970s, so no one really knew how to handle these things. It was handled very badly.

'He moved out instantly. I didn't see him for a very long time and no one really explained to me what had happened. So, I put up a front of: *It doesn't worry me, I'm not fussed, I didn't really need my dad anyway.*'

Laverne: 'You didn't maintain a relationship after he left?'

'He moved up to the Midlands and occasionally I had to go up to see him. I might have to get a coach from Gatwick to Rugby and he would meet me there. You'd think: *This doesn't seem right for a ten-year-old!*

'Eventually, I threw a little tantrum and I said, "I don't want to see you any more!" Which, of course, was looking for attention. But it was taken at face value, so I didn't see him any more.'

For his second record, Osman chose 'Metal Mickey' by Suede – a band whose bassist is his brother, Mat. He admitted that seeing the group on *Top of the Pops* for the first time had been a revelation for him.

'It was like someone had punched a hole in the sky for me! "You're on *Top of the Pops*, mate, with your friends!" I was so proud of him – and also, self-ishly, I thought, *Oh, we can do it! There are opportunities out there! You can make it, if you want ...*'

As the song ended, Laverne wondered how her guest's mother had coped with her husband deserting the family.

'She was extraordinary. We wouldn't have any money, but we'd go to Italy on a coach for forty-eight hours and stay in a tent. I look back and I think, *Oh my God! You, with two kids on a coach, for forty-eight hours!* It must have been miserable.

'She became a full-time primary-school teacher – a perfect job for her – and would do home work every night, stuffing envelopes for companies for 0.001p each. I would hear her crying sometimes, and I'd obviously try to blank it out. It wasn't allowed past my defensive wall.'

Given the love his mother had shown him, and the sacrifices she had made, Osman said the best part of his success was the things he was now able to give her. 'I bought her where she lives. She wouldn't have been able to afford it, and she absolutely adores it.'

Laverne broached a medical affliction suffered by Osman – nystagmus, a condition that causes uncontrolled eye movement. 'How much impact did it have on you when you were growing up?'

'It's a thing where the world is essentially in soft focus. It's like being in the fog all the time. You can't drive.

'When I was in school, I could never see the board. I couldn't see the text-books in front of me. I can't see the birds in the trees. If I'm watching cricket, or something, I can't see the ball.

'So TV was incredibly important to me, because they'll show me a slow motion of the ball in cricket. They'll show me a bird in a tree that I wouldn't see ...

'I'd rather be able to see well. I'd love that! But, listen, I see beautiful things sometimes that no one else would ever see. I see a haze in the distance. You know it's a building: I don't. I just see this beautiful experimental painting.'

Laverne: 'As a child, you started coming up with formats for games, quiz-zes, even TV shows. How did that start to happen?'

'All of my TV success really comes from sport,' Osman explained. 'In sport, you've got knockout cups; you've got things like the Ryder Cup, where you've got individuals playing against each other, then pairs playing against each other.

'Watching TV – *Family Fortunes*, and those kinds of shows – my brain was interested in how they put it together: *Oh, that's right. OK, why have you done that? Why have you made that decision?*'

At fifteen, Osman worked as a volunteer on Radio Sussex. 'The first band I interviewed was Pop Will Eat Itself. They were not impressed with me!' From school, he went on to Cambridge University – and, after graduating, into the world of television production.

Laverne: 'You joined production company Planet 24 then moved to Hat Trick Productions, writing for *Have I Got News for You?* and *Whose Line Is It Anyway?* Around this time, you were also dealing with personal issues that had started to come to the surface. What happened?'

'My career was going well, I had kids, I had all the things that I thought I needed, the things that were going to make everything OK. And none of them did.

'Getting older, I was working out that I was slightly directionless and I had various addictive behaviours as well. And as soon as you have an addictive behaviour, you know something's up ...'

Laverne: 'Like what?' Richard Osman took a deep breath.

'My addictive behaviour has always been food. It has been since I was incredibly young. It's not seen as ... it doesn't have the doomed glamour of drugs, or alcohol, or anything like that.

'But if an alcoholic came to my house, they'd be shocked to see there are bottles of gin and wine completely untouched, because an alcoholic couldn't *have* that in their house. And if I came to your house and there were crisps, or chocolate bars in the freezer, I'd be, like, *How? What? How are they untouched?* if I'm going through an episode.

'That's the thing. It's booze, but food. The addiction is identical. The secrecy of consuming these things: the shame behind it.

'And food is a tricky one. Booze, and drugs, you can just give up. It's incredibly difficult, but, you know, a zero-tolerance policy. Whereas if you're addicted to food, or to love, things that are quite sustaining, you still have to have them.'

Laverne: 'How bad did it get for you?'

'Listen! There hasn't been a day of my life, since the age of nine, where I haven't thought about problems with food and how it affects me. It will be with me the rest of my life. I know that. I'm either controlling it, or *not* controlling it, at any given time.

'These days, I control it more often than I don't. But again, because you *have* to eat, it's actually quite hard and sometimes you do slip. But I try my best and I certainly have no shame about it now.'

Moving on, Laverne asked Osman about going from being a producer to a presenter on *Pointless*. 'The only thing that's ever terrified me about TV is the studio audience,' he admitted. 'A camera, I'm fine with. People at home, having their tea, I'm fine with.

'When I'm in front of raked seating, and members of the public looking at me, I think, *What on earth am I doing here?* I feel *such* a fraud! But I'm so thrilled that I did it. What a weird side-project, you know ...'

Laverne: 'And, recently, a *third* act. In 2020, your debut novel, *The Thursday Murder Club*, came out. It's about friends in a retirement community who solve crimes. And your mum is the inspiration?'

'Yeah. Just where she lives – a beautiful retirement community down in Sussex, surrounded by fascinating people who've done extraordinary things. And, literally, just a thought – *Wow, this would be an amazing place for a murder!* – came into my mind.

'I thought, *My God, I'm surrounded by people with amazing skills! We've got ourselves a gang, and they can solve it!* And it's like *The A-Team*, but everyone's over seventy ...'

For his penultimate record, Osman chose 'Ran' by Future Islands, which he admitted gave him a very emotional moment when he listened to it, in the back of a car, after a signing session for *The Thursday Murder Club* at a bookshop near his childhood home.

'Sometimes, it's important to be proud of yourself, and that's difficult for people. It's difficult for me. I just thought, *You know what? I'm really, really proud of myself!* And I just burst into tears in the back of the car.

'I did it quietly, so the driver didn't notice. But I was in tears because I was proud of what I'd done, and I'd worked so hard.'

Richard Osman was now divorced from the mother of his two children but, he stressed, maintained strong relationships with them: 'I love them very much – I endlessly tell them!' His son, noted Laverne, had inherited his dad's height.

'You're six-foot-seven. He's six-foot-five. I think you gave him some advice about making his way in the world, and being proud of his height?'

'Yeah. You know, I grew up very awkward. I couldn't see, I was six-foot-seven – I would think, *My God!* I couldn't have been more physically ashamed. And I've had years of, sort of, coming to terms with it.

'All I said to him was: "Listen, when you walk in a room, you've only got two options, right? Everybody in the room is either going to say, 'Wow, who is that really tall guy?' or 'Who's that really tall guy who looks really awkward about being tall?'"

'I said, "You don't have another option, which is 'Who's that ordinary-sized guy?' It just doesn't exist. So, when you walk into a room, you've just got to *own* your height."'

As he introduced his final song, 'A Little Respect' by Erasure, Richard Osman reflected that his life's journey had been uneven at times, but he was very contented with the destination it had brought him to.

'I've been very lucky the last few years,' he reflected. 'I feel like I'm in a place that I want to be. I'm happy with myself. I've got these beautiful kids. I've met the woman that I'm going to be with for the rest of my life: Ingrid.

'I just think the motivations of being younger have gone: competition and ambition. You soon realise that that rocket fuel disappears and it's all about happiness. And my kids bring me happiness and Ingrid brings me happiness.'

• • •

Richard Osman's *The Thursday Murder Club* was to go on to sell more than a million copies in the UK alone. Its 2021 follow-up, *The Man Who Died Twice*, then became one of the fastest-selling novels in British publishing history. To concentrate on his literary career, Osman quit *Pointless*, after thirty series, in April 2022. However, he was never going to leave TV game shows *completely* behind: he continues to co-present its spin-off series, *Celebrity Pointless*.

DISCS CHOSEN
'Bring Me Sunshine'
Morecambe and Wise
'A song that, for anybody over a certain age, just screams "Television!"'

'Metal Mickey'
Suede

'Drag Racer' (theme tune for the BBC's snooker coverage)
The Douglas Wood Group
'Sport gives me such joy, and one sport which gives me a huge amount of joy is snooker'

❤ **'You Can't Stop the Beat'**
The Cast of *Hairspray*
'A song that's so full of joy'

'Extraordinary Machine'
Fiona Apple
'This is for my kids. When they were younger, I tried to make them listen to cool music, because all parents do'

'American Boy'
Estelle (featuring Kanye West)
'It reminds me of sitting in the make-up room at Pointless*'*

'Ran'
Future Islands

'A Little Respect'
Erasure
'Whenever we have a party, this is where the party changes gear'

BOOK
Hercule Poirot: The Complete Short Stories – Agatha Christie
'I can't help turning everything into a format. It was a Christie vs P.G. Wodehouse final – and Christie won! Well played, everyone!'

LUXURY ITEM
A pad of paper, a pen and a dice
'As a kid, I would lie on the floor with a pad, pen and dice and make all sorts of imaginary sports tournaments. I would spend hours and hours, so happy in that sort of reverie ...'

77
OTI MABUSE

DANCER EXTRAORDINAIRE
6 March 2022

In 2020, Oti Mabuse became the first professional dancer to win *Strictly Come Dancing* two years in a row. She did so by coaxing increasingly impressive performances out of her partner, comedian Bill Bailey, who had been nobody's idea of the favourite to win when the competition began.

Poetry in motion on the dance floor, the lithe Mabuse was clearly also a deeply driven and committed competitor. The sources and depth of her personal motivation became evident when she dropped in on Lauren Laverne's desert island in March 2022.

Mabuse told Laverne about growing up in post-apartheid South Africa, the huge role in her life played by her mother, Dudu, and her oldest sister (and *Strictly* judge) Motsi, the 'magic of *Strictly*' … and the culture shock that she experienced, at eleven years old, on first experiencing the delights of a grey day in Blackpool.

• • •

Greeting her guest, Lauren Laverne quoted her describing dance as 'two bodies creating one movement'. 'What are the most important qualities for a dance partner to have, for you?' she asked.

'For me, it's first the chemistry,' replied Mabuse. 'There has to be something that is unexplainable that the two have. That chemistry – whether it's friendship, love, passion – sparks so much, because the goals and the intentions are aligned.'

Laverne mentioned her guest's most recent, high-profile partner: the unlikely *Strictly* champion, Bill Bailey. 'Did you think that the pair of you would be winners when you took your first steps on the dance floor?'

'With Bill? Absolutely not! I remember just having deep conversations and I was, like, "The whole point of *Strictly*, and what we love so much, is that it is one place where everything is possible."

'Bill was the oldest winner of *Strictly* and, at first glance, you wouldn't think it's possible. And then he does it! It's the magic of *Strictly*.'

After a blast of Beyoncé, the conversation turned to Mabuse's celebrity status. She boggled that the *Daily Mail* had considered it newsworthy that she had picked up her dog's poop in a park at 7am. 'It would have been worse if you'd *not* picked it up!' noted Laverne, correctly.

Born in Pretoria in 1990, the year Nelson Mandela was released from jail, Mabuse grew up in 'a very different South Africa than your parents grew up in,' said Laverne. She asked about her teacher mother, Dudu.

'A force of nature, my mum! Growing up, it wasn't easy. She was in the 1976 riots when the youth of South Africa stormed and refused to learn in Afrikaans any more. They wanted to be taught in English.'

'When we grew up, she was very strict. Like, we were not allowed to do *anything*! The only thing we did was go to school and sports weekends. We didn't even have weekends off. We were dancing.'

- Laverne: 'Dance was a passion that she'd loved but not been able to pursue?'

'There were no dance schools. There were no dance teachers. It was very segregated. And she always loved it. She always wanted to do it. She always wanted to wear those big ballroom dresses and have her hair done. But in those years, black people weren't allowed to. They weren't even allowed to be in the same room, or on the same dance floor, as white people.

'Then one day, when she was old and working as a secretary, she saw a dance competition. And she was, like, "It's such a shame that I couldn't do it but I'll see if one of my daughters will." She took Motsi, and Motsi fell immediately in love with the dancing.'

Laverne clarified that Motsi is ten years older than Oti.

'Yes – I wasn't born when she started dancing. And there was no one teaching black kids to dance where we lived. So, my mum was: "Right! I'm going to turn the pre-school where I work into a dance school!"

'She took all the kids in the neighbourhood and put them into dancing. She realised that after rehearsals it was too late for them to walk home, so she started her own transport company to pick them up from their schools, take them to dance school, then take them home.'

Similarly hard-working, Mabuse's father, Peter, was a lawyer. Yet his passage through college had not been straightforward.

'I remember my grandma telling me the story that they couldn't afford university,' she said. 'So, my grandma opened a tavern. She used to sell alcohol to make money to send my dad to school.'

'Wow!' said an astonished Laverne.

'I know, right? My whole family is full of *women who just do things*. And then he set up a law firm in an area, Hammanskraal, where people couldn't afford to pay for law. If you were wrongly arrested – a lot of black people were being arrested, and didn't have representation – you would go to my dad and he was able to help.'

After a break for Luther Vandross, Mabuse described loving dance for as long as she could remember and throwing herself into childhood lessons. She soon began to compete – and, aged eleven, entered her first international competition, in glamorous Blackpool.

'What did you make of it, when you got there?' inquired Laverne.

'It's a big, big deal! Leaving the country is a big deal! Being able to compete overseas is a big deal! You have dancers from all over, and all ages, planning their lives around this one competition!

'I remember getting there. It was so windy and so grey and there was a beach. And the promenade – it's called the promenade, right? – lights were on and it was getting so dark! It was dark at three-thirty in the afternoon! I was like, "Oh, my gosh! The days are so short!"'

'Welcome to the north!' commented a wry Laverne.

'Yeah! But you spend most of your time in this beautiful ballroom with a shiny brown floor made out of wood, and the ceiling had paintings and art, and the balcony had sculptures on it. And it looked like nothing I'd ever seen in my life!

'No one spoke the same language, but somehow we were playing after we danced. We were in Europe! And you're not really sad if you don't win because you're going to go get a pick 'n' mix afterwards.

'I remember asking my mum for money to go on the rides and she said, "I'm saving money so that we can have food later on." We used to have half a burger, then save it and have half a burger later. Then she'd save money for us to go to the arcades with the other kids, as well.'

Back in South Africa, said Mabuse, she was good at school but did not apply to university as she was so set on becoming a dancer. Her mum did not approve of this plan at all.

'She was like, "No, you need to go to school, because if this dancing thing doesn't work out, you need a back-up!" So she took my school report without telling me, and applied to university without telling me.'

Mabuse thus found herself studying civil engineering in Tshwane, near Pretoria. She ended up enjoying elements of the course.

'I fell in love with engineering, and the maths and science side of it, and problem-solving. Building something from scratch. Going to a field with just one tree, and sand, and building a community there. Building houses for people who can't afford a living.'

Despite this, on graduating and taking an engineering job, Mabuse was still resolved to become a full-time dancer. This caused more familial tension.

'What did your parents say?' asked Laverne.

'They were *absolutely* against it! They were: "This is the worst decision ever!" But I really wasn't happy, because being an engineer full-time meant I couldn't dance.

'I was, like, "No! I can't do this! I can't live my life unhappy! I'm only twenty-one. *This can't be it.* This can't be the journey that I've chosen for my life. I want more out of life, and I'm not getting it right now."'

Defying parental outrage, Mabuse quit her job. Her sister, Motsi, was by now living in Germany, and she went to join her to try to kick-start a dance career. Once there, she met the man she was to marry: Marius.

Laverne: 'You were looking for a dance partner. Tell me about your first impressions of him.'

'Oh, gosh! My first impressions weren't great, because we had planned a date where we would meet in the studio. Not a *date* date, but a day we were going to meet, and you dress up, right?

'So, the day before that was the only day where I was left alone in the house to do nothing. And so my goal was to spend the whole day in pyjamas, with masks, and watch movies and eat ice cream.

'And Marius decided he would come the day before, when I looked atrocious! He was like: "I actually love seeing you like this, because this is who you *really* are, rather than what you were going to show me!" And it was just chemistry, you know? *That chemistry.*

'It's in the hand: it's in how it feels when he leads. *Could I follow that lead?* And, besides us getting along together, we danced really well together, so the whole thing was just like *de-de-de-de-de*. It just came together nicely.'

From Germany, Mabuse found her way to Britain and *Strictly Come Dancing*. Laverne reflected on how well the BBC's Saturday-night prime-time dancing competition was reflecting – and maybe even shaping – ever-changing modern societal attitudes. 'Strictly had its nineteenth series last year and it was so emotional when Rose Ayling-Ellis, who is deaf, lifted the winner's trophy,' she said. 'Same-sex couples are a regular part of the show: John and Johannes, last year. How important is the programme for changing people's perceptions?'

'No show has done it so well, so classy, so effortless, so beautifully impactful! I danced with [*Paralympian*] Jonnie Peacock, the first person with a disability on *Strictly*. Jonnie inspired – and still inspires – so many kids who thought they couldn't dance, they couldn't run.

'The same was true of [*fellow Paralympian*] Lauren [*Steadman*], who had arm amputation. The way *Strictly* does stuff is so beautiful and so pure!'

As the show neared its end, Mabuse selected her 'favourite song of all time' – 'It's My Life' by Bon Jovi. As it climaxed, Lauren Laverne praised her guest's exuberant reaction to all of her music choices.

'Oti, it's made me so happy that you've danced all the way through your *Desert Island Discs* today!' she laughed. 'Full air-guitar on that track! Will you dance on your island, do you think?'

'No, I will be looking for food!' replied Oti Mabuse. 'I would probably sing, because nobody can hear me! I will pretend that I'm Toni Braxton, or Beyoncé – or Bon Jovi ...'

• • •

Early in 2022, Oti Mabuse joined the judging panel of ITV dance show *Dancing on Ice* and also returned to her native land to film a one-off BBC documentary, *Oti's South African Odyssey*. In the same week as her *Desert Island Discs*, she announced that she was to leave *Strictly Come Dancing* after seven years on the show. Oti admitted that she 'cried for hours' when she told the show's producers she was quitting, but added: 'I lived my best life on that show but I didn't want to hold on and get to the point where I wasn't happy any more. I left when I was at the peak – but when you know it's time to go, you know.'

DISCS CHOSEN
'Lose My Breath'
Beyoncé (with Kelly Rowland and Michelle Williams)
Just before I go on [on Strictly], *every time, I get riddled with nerves, and this song pumps me up'*

'My Afrikan Dream'
Vicky Sampson
'It always reminds me of the journey South Africa went through'

'A Song for Mama'
Boyz II Men
'It reminds me about my mum and how amazing and determined she is'

'Dance with My Father'
Luther Vandross
'It was my wedding dance with my dad'

'Un-break My Heart'
Toni Braxton
'This was the first song I realised, OK, there's a thing called love, and I'm grow-ing up!'

'I'm Not a Girl, Not Yet a Woman'
Britney Spears
'It describes exactly how I was feeling in what moment when I knew it was time for me to move on [from engineering to dancing]'

❤ 'It's My Life'
Bon Jovi
'It represents taking control and living the best life ever that you can'

'Survivor'
Destiny's Child
'This represents me and my sisters – we used to sing it because we're three girls, and Destiny's Child was three'

BOOK
Will – Will Smith
'I just love Will Smith – I think he's amazing'

LUXURY ITEM
A photo with her grandma
'I take it with me everywhere. I love my grandma – she passed when I was nineteen, and I think she's my guardian angel'

78

BONO

SINGER, SONGWRITER, ACTIVIST
26 June 2022

Over the decades, *Desert Island Discs* has repeatedly demonstrated its ability to attract the world's biggest music stars to its shores. And in the twenty-first century, no rock star has a shorter name or a more prodigious, globe-straddling reputation and influence than Bono.

The achievements of Bono's band, U2, are mind-boggling. Since they played their first gig in Dublin in the punk rock year of 1977, they have sold more than 170 million albums, won an unequalled twenty-two Grammy Awards, and staged some of the most spectacular and inventive stadium tours in rock history.

But music is only part of Bono's story. His affiliation to, and passionate lobbying for, the Drop the Debt campaign in the nineties contributed massively to the cancellation of billions of dollars owed by thirty-five of the world's poorest countries, and launched him on a high-profile parallel career of global activism that continues to this day.

Yet even the world's most public figures have secrets, and Bono's June 2022 encounter with Lauren Laverne saw him make a revelation about his family history that was to make media headlines around the world. Here was a castaway that you missed at your peril ...

• • •

Lauren Laverne welcomed her guest by his birth name, Paul Hewson, then turned to his multi-faceted alter ego. 'You once said, "There are a lot of Bonos, and some annoy me more than others." I wonder who we're going to meet on the island today?'

'Well, if I'm going to be on the island for a very long time, I'll enjoy waking up each morning to see which one I am,' Bono replied.

'You don't know on the day?'

'No. I know there is an annoying gene in there. I'm a bit of a squeaky wheel. When my instinct tells me to follow through on something, I won't let go. *That* version of Bono, I could do without on an island!'

After Peter Frampton's 'Show Me the Way', which Bono explained was the first song that he'd ever sung *well* with the teenage U2 in their school-gym rehearsals, Laverne moved to his multi-faith background.

'You were born in 1960. Your mum, Iris, was Protestant and your dad, Bob, was Catholic. Sectarianism was a huge issue in Ireland at the time. Did your parents' different backgrounds cause problems for them?'

'I think my father's family didn't turn up at their wedding. There were some issues. But my father was very, very elegant about all this.

'He used to drive us to St Canice's Church of Ireland church, because he felt my mother should have the choice in which religion we grew up in. And then *he* would drive to the little Catholic church, a hundred yards away.'

Laverne: 'What about music when you were young? Were you musical as a little boy?'

'I had, in my head, melodies from an early age, and I just couldn't get them out ... I think I've been constructed in such a way that I don't really function without other people's help, and I find that sometimes quite frustrating. That's why I'm so blessed I'm in a band with The Edge – the most extraordinary musician of the age. One of them, frankly.

'If I hadn't [*been with him*], I don't know what would have happened. I'd have had to learn to do that myself. I don't know if I could have. So, yeah, there's a bit of anger at that. I've had some anger management discussions – I got really angry with the guy! I'm a work in progress!'

Bono's engaging levity receded when Laverne turned gently to the defining, devastating event of his adolescence: the death of his mother.

'When you were fourteen, your mother, Iris, died suddenly. She suffered a brain aneurysm at her father's funeral. You say you don't have many memories of her, but what comes to mind when you picture her?'

'Laughing a lot. The mischief was upon her. One of the neighbours told her: "That boy, he needs to be disciplined with the cane!" My mother was, like, "A cane?" And she was chasing me down the garden! I was terrified, but I looked back and saw her laughing. She just couldn't take that seriously.

'I wrote a song about Iris on [*U2's 2014 album*] *Songs of Innocence.* In some ways, I wrote songs *to get back to her.* Though she went away physically, in other ways, the absence made itself known and it was a great gift for me, because I filled it with music.'

Laverne: 'After she died, it became an all-male household. You, your dad, and your brother Norman, grieving this terrible loss. You said the house wasn't a home after that?'

'It's pocketbook psychology, but I immediately found *another* family when I formed U2. I found Ali. It happened very quickly.'

Bono had, indeed, started dating his wife of forty years, Ali, in the same fateful 1976 week that he formed U2. 'But what about life at home?' asked Laverne. 'What happened to your relationship with your father?'

'You know, it's a complicated relationship with Bob. I'm sure I was hard to deal with. The annoying gene would have been very present. And I subsequently understood he was coping with other stuff in his life, and I feel I wasn't there for him in a way I should have been.

'I apologised to my father in a little chapel in France, after he passed away.

There was nobody there. I lit a candle, I got on my knees and I said, "Look, I'm sorry I wasn't there for you. You went through a lot. Please forgive me." And I felt free.'

Laverne described Bono finding refuge, after his mother's death, in music and in his friendships. One schoolfriend, Guggi, bestowed on him his world-famous nickname: 'It came from a hearing-aid shop that was called Bono Vox?' checked Laverne.

'Guggi, to be fair to him, did *not* speak Latin, so he will not have known that "*bono vox*" means "good voice". I don't even know why you would call a hearing-aid shop that! But, yes, there *was* one, and I *did* get named that.'

Laverne: 'Take me back to September 1976. You auditioned for a band with your schoolfriends: drummer Larry Mullen Jr; The Edge, who played guitar; and a bassist, Adam Clayton.'

'Yeah. Larry posted a notice on Mount Temple Comprehensive School's board. Adam, he arrives – he's just been thrown out of a posh boarding school, and people are, like, "Who is ...? Wow!" He's going, "Where is the smoking room?" Like ... *What? Smoking room?!*

'Edge was following him around, because he was his friend. And Edge, therefore, couldn't tell us that Adam couldn't play, but Larry could!

'And even though we were really crap, it was just brilliant. The noise; the sound of a real drum kit; the silver and gold of the cymbals; the orchestral sound of those cymbals. Edge had an out of tune extraordinariness. It was still extraordinary.

'Even when we eventually got a record deal, we were still very, very erratic. But erratic is OK. The real enemy of great is "very good", and the one thing that U2 were *not* was very good.'

After a break for Noel Gallagher's High Flying Birds, Laverne marvelled that the original line-up of U2 were still together, more than forty-five years later. 'What do you put your longevity down to?'

'I mean, we break up all the time!' claimed Bono. 'It's the truth. After usually the good albums! We have broken up many times, and it's also a good thing to say to yourself, *You know what? We might be done!*

'The thing that has kept us there is *unfinished business*. A sense that we still haven't maybe got to that sound we hear in our head, and the song – *that song*. So, if you're going to serve the song, you might as well do it with the people who understand you and who can tell you where to go.

'We have all gone through moments when somebody has stepped on our toe and I've been in a huff and a puff. But in U2, presently, we're OK with that. But I don't know for how long.'

Laverne moved on to her guest's political activism, 'especially in Africa, and tackling poverty and HIV/AIDS there. But some of this work did bring you into conflict with your bandmates?'

'Yeah, it was very difficult for the band to see me *in certain company*,' admitted Bono. 'It was excruciating for them. But they gave me their blessing. They believed it was the right thing to do if we could get certain things across the line.

'I remember Edge saying to me, "But, please, *not* Senator Jesse Helms!" – who was a sort of right-wing firebrand, who was really helpful. Edge said, "You'd never invite him to a U2 show, would you?" And I said, "I have!"

'He came with his wife, Dot, this old-man giant who'd given me "the blessing", as he said. He'd repented for the way he'd spoken about AIDS, publicly, on the steps of the Senate. And there's a picture of Edge dodging him in the backstage area!

'But you don't have to agree with everyone on everything if the one thing you agree with them on is important enough. It's hard for an Irish singer with a big mouth to bite his tongue. But I've learned to do it, and it's been good for me, and it's been effective.'

Laverne turned to a vexed topic for U2 – the widespread condemnation they had received for moving their royalty income overseas, to avoid paying higher rates of tax in Ireland. 'How do you respond to your critics?' she asked. Bono did so by coming out swinging.

'I don't agree with them. I think at the root of this is a false idea, that if you're tough-minded in your activism, you somehow have to be soft-headed in your business.

'There's a lot of reasons to not like our band. This is not one of them. We pay a lot of tax and we're very proud to pay tax. So, it's just like, Really? Why would WE be the poster child for this? Is it to do with something else?'

This was a desert-island conversation that had ranged far and wide, but as it wended towards its home straight, it took a surprise turn. Laverne returned to the topic of the reaction of Bono's father, Bob, to the death of the singer's mother, Iris.

'You said that he had his own stuff going on that he was dealing with, alongside his grief. And, in 2000, you found out more about that – some surprising news about your family, that came out of the blue. You found that you had a half-brother. What happened?'

'Well, yeah. I *do* have another brother, whom I love and adore, that I didn't know I didn't have, or maybe I did,' answered Bono, sounding momentarily tongue-tied. 'My father was obviously going through a lot, but partly his head was elsewhere because his heart was elsewhere.

'I think that was a part of a problem I was probably picking up as a kid. It's a very close family, and I could tell that my father had a very deep friendship with this gorgeous woman, who was part of the family. And then they had a child, and this was all kept secret.'

Laverne: 'Did your mum know?'

'No. Nobody knew.'

'Did you get to talk to your dad about it, after you found out?

'Yes, I did.'

'Did it help?'

'I asked him, did he love my mother? And he said yes. I said, how could this happen? He said, it *can*, and he was trying to put it right. Trying to do the right thing. He wasn't apologising. He was just stating: *These are the facts, and I'm at peace with it.*'

After Bono chose Verdi's *La Traviata* for his dad, Laverne touched on a serious health scare which had seen him have major surgery in 2016. 'It's a big deal to have your chest cut open, and it was a long surgery!' he replied. 'I tend to – and I shouldn't – judge things by their effect on the music. And it certainly made me even *more* vulnerable to music.'

Laverne: 'U2 is not the only longstanding relationship in your life. You married Ali in 1982, and went on to have four children together. In your forthcoming memoir, you write very movingly about the walks you take together on Killiney Hill, where you live. Why is that time so important to you?'

'I write about how I wish, when I'm with her, that I would not be thinking sometimes about the call I was supposed to make,' reflected Paul Hewson, aka Bono Vox.

'Ali's such strong stuff that she distracts my mind. She's the only one who can really turn that off. I'm besotted by her, and she's always just out of reach, and so I have to struggle to be in the frame with her. And that's what turns the phone off ...'

• • •

Bono's *Desert Island Discs* revelation about his secret half-brother was to make newspaper headlines from Ireland to Indonesia. The singer was to open up far more about this, and all other facets of his life, when he published his autobiography, *Surrender*, in November 2022, a memoir which, he said, 'drew in detail what he had only previously sketched in songs'. Quixotically, it also contained forty original drawings by the singer. U2 are currently on hiatus and, after they have finished 'breaking up all the time', will be back with more albums and tours.

DISCS CHOSEN

'Show Me the Way'

Peter Frampton

'When I sang that song [at U2's first rehearsal], *something went off. A teenage boy turned a song into a prayer'*

❤ **'Every Grain of Sand'**

Bob Dylan

'It just connects me to the eternal'

'Abide with Me'
Emeli Sandé and the Fron Choir
'I love choral singing and she's a sacred talent'

'Dead in the Water'
Noel Gallagher's High Flying Birds
'He has this thing where the songs just take him wherever they want to take him'

'Ice Cream Sundae'
Inhaler
'They're very good. My son happens to be the singer'

'Agolo'
Angélique Kidjo
'Joy is one of the key elements of music, and here is a wellspring of it'

Prelude to Act 1 from Verdi's *La Traviata*
National Philharmonic Orchestra
'The one that used to bring my father to wherever he went ... this opera is about a son and a father'

'Someone Somewhere (in Summertime)'
Simple Minds
'You'll feel some early U2 in this song, and we learned from them'

BOOK
Ulysses – James Joyce
'It's one-hundredth anniversary is this year, and Ulysses *is a story of home. Here's to you, James Joyce!'*

LUXURY ITEM
His catgut Spanish guitar
'I could lie down on the island and maybe improve my guitar playing'

79

ADELE

SINGER, SONGWRITER
3 July 2022

When you reach the top, you just keep on climbing. In July 2022, a week after *Desert Island Discs* had hosted one of the world's biggest rock stars in Bono, it welcomed a true modern cultural phenomenon: one of the biggest-selling British female recording artists of all time.

Adele Adkins's sales statistics are staggering. Her first album, 2008's *19*, recorded when she was precisely that age, went eight-times platinum in the UK. Its follow-up, 2011's *21*, remains the biggest-selling album of the twenty-first century. Her two subsequent records, *25* and *30*, were the top-selling albums of 2015 and 2020 respectively.

It would have been understandable if such precipitous success had gone to a young diva's head, but when Adele swam ashore the island, her chatty charm and no-nonsense demeanour fully justified Lauren Laverne's description of her as 'the superstar next door'. Assuming, that is, that your neighbour had sold 120 million records ...

• • •

Laverne began by pointing out that her thirty-four-year-old guest had 'been through everything you sing about – heartbreak, marriage, becoming a parent, divorce, the loss of a parent. You say that you're feeling more peaceful now than you have in a long time. What is that down to?'

'A lot of therapy,' began Adele. 'But also, now I'm getting older, I ain't got time for drama. I ain't got time for arguing. I don't put myself any more in situations that drain me. I'll just be like: *I'm good. I'm chilled. I'm gonna walk away from it.*'

After a first-record choice of 'Roam' by the B-52's, Laverne rewound to Adele's earliest days. 'You were born Adele Laurie Blue Adkins, which is a particularly great name. Your mum, Penny, was just eighteen and an art student. You were a real tight little unit, the pair of you, growing up?'

'Thick as thieves! We were thick as thieves and really good friends, me and my mum.'

'She was a maker. What did she make?'

'She used to decorate the house, and stuff. My earliest claim to fame was, Mystic Meg on the Lottery – my mum made her big gothic chair.'

Laverne: 'You were surrounded by music. Your mum played the piano and guitar. She took you to gigs, as well?'

'Well, she wanted to go to the gigs and she was a young mum. She didn't have any childcare, so she used to take me with her. She'd sneak me in under her trench coat. My earliest memory of a show is the Beautiful South at Brixton Academy.

'There was a bodybuilder there, some random guy who became friends with my mum and her friends. He picked me up and put me on his shoulders, so I got to see the whole show. I was tiny: three or four.'

'Can you remember when you started to play music yourself?' asked Laverne.

'My mum had a piano in the house. Every day, when I got home from school, I would sit down and teach myself ... I wouldn't even call them chords! Just random things that sounded nice. Then I started writing them in a book. I was about thirteen.'

'And what were you writing about? Your life? Do you remember?'

'I remember one of the first songs was called "This is My Life". I'm a sad person, and I don't always know why ... it was deep. I was talking about being in pain. My Grandpy died when I was ten and I was traumatised by that. So maybe it was from that and I just hadn't figured it out.'

Adele fondly recalled family holidays staying with her grandparents in Wales. 'You and your Grandpy were incredibly close,' noted Laverne. 'I think you dedicated a song to him at Glastonbury?'

'My whole set! I just imagined him there. He would have been proud as punch. He would've hated all that mud and them people, though. He'd be like, "Oh, what the bloody hell's going on?"'

Laverne: 'Your parents separated when you were very little and your dad, Mark, moved back to Wales, where he was from. How do you look back on your relationship with him?'

'I remember being very excited to see him, whenever I did, but it was always a bit of a let down. I didn't really have his attention. He'd say he'd come and then he didn't. If he *did* come, we'd go out for half an hour and then he'd drop me home.

'He had a disease. He was an alcoholic. He was a really *big* alcoholic and he had loads of demons. But I didn't really understand that when I was younger. I decided to stop seeing him when I was twelve, because I'd gone to surprise him for Father's Day and he didn't come.

'I saw him very briefly when I was about fifteen, when my great-grandma died, and he did apologise then, but *I was fifteen*. I didn't want to hear it. I was a teenager, you know!

'Then, when I found out he was ill a few years ago, I got the call and I drove straight there. It was hard, but it was definitely one of the biggest moments of my life, in a good way, when I went to see him.'

Laverne: 'He had cancer, and sadly died last year. Were you able to make your peace with him?'

'Yeah, when I found out he was sick. And we really got on, which was amazing, but also sad, because ...'

'The missed time?'

'Yeah, and also he was bloody funny! I don't remember that when I was little. But it was really nice. We laughed, and we gossiped, and we cried, and it was great for both of us.'

Moving on, Laverne noted that Adele has always been 'known for your very raw and heartfelt writing. Is it a case that you put in songs what you're feeling, perhaps even if you can't say it?'

'Oh, one hundred per cent! I'm very articulate but my communication skills aren't always great. I'm still working on that today, because I get so defensive. I explode rather than have an adult conversation. Looking back on *19* and *21* and *25* – I get so many answers out of songs for myself.'

Laverne rewound to 2002, when the fourteen-year-old Adele auditioned for the BRIT School in Croydon. 'How much was riding on you getting a place there?' The reply was quintessential Adele Adkins.

'I really wanted to go. A lot of my friends started getting pregnant, and I wasn't worried that *I* would, but we weren't so close any more because they couldn't come to school all the time. My mum was more worried about that side of it and she wanted to give me real focus.

'And I had the time of my life there. It was such a melting pot of every type of teenager. People doing amazing nu-soul, people doing rock, people writing amazing pop songs. I was like, *I'm just going to play my guitar, just rap my feelings.* It was absolute heaven!'

Laverne: 'Do you think your potential was recognised early at the BRIT School?'

'I was always chosen third by the teachers!' Adele recalled. 'There were two other singers that were chosen for everything. I don't feel like I put myself forward all the time like I could have.'

'What was that about?'

'You'd have to audition ... one time, we did *Dark Side of the Moon* and I remember my mum being, like, "You should go and audition for 'Great Gig in the Sky' ..."'

Laverne: 'Because it's got a huge vocal line in it!'

'... but there were three *massive* vocalists in my year. I didn't want that pressure that comes with, *OK, I'm going to put myself forward – what if I don't get it?* I could do without it, and being so anxious that I can't enjoy it.'

Laverne recapped that in Adele's final year at the BRIT School, a friend put her demo online. A record executive, Nick Huggett from XL Recordings, got in touch. 'How quickly did everything happen for you?'

'I'd never *heard* of XL. A friend, Ben, who is my guitarist now, used to play guitar when I sang at the school. I was like, "Will you come with me? I'm scared. What if he's a weirdo?"

'We got on the tube from Brixton to Notting Hill and we saw a little mews house – it's not a big corporate building. So, you can imagine, I weren't that impressed. I was like, *What is this?* But I got inside, and ... it's magical! Prodigy, M.I.A., Dizzee Rascal, White Stripes. And I met Nick, and he was like, "All right, mate?" and we got on.

'He was, like, "Who's your manager?" And I was, like, "Oh, Pat at the Gap!" because I was working at the Gap on High Street Ken at the time. And he was like, "I don't know them ... what's their surname?"'

Adele admitted that, as she used to regularly tip new music artists on her MySpace page, she had assumed Huggett wanted to employ her as a talent scout. 'When did the penny drop that they wanted to sign you as an *artist*?' asked Laverne.

'When he said how much he loved my songs. *And that's it.* That's how it happened.'

Newly signed to XL, Adele's breakthrough single was 2008's 'Chasing Pavements', which hit number twenty-one in America after she performed it on *Saturday Night Live*. 'It had a typically gutsy Adele backstory,' noted Laverne, asking her guest for the inspiration behind the lyric.

'Well, I was seeing this guy. I went to an indie club night called Frog and he was in there, kissing this girl. I got so angry, and fed up, and slapped him around the face! And then I ran out because security came after me, because they saw me do it.

'I was running down Tottenham Court Road, down into Regent Street and Oxford Street. *Just chasing the pavements.* And I was, like, *Bing!* I went to the studio the next day to pick up my guitar and we wrote "Chasing Pavements" that day.'

Laverne: 'You won your first two Grammys for that album. That must have been quite a night for you?' Adele's answer certainly confirmed this supposition.

'I had no shoes on! I had gum in my mouth! I thought Duffy was going to win it. U2 were there, Coldplay were there, Kanye was there, and they called my name!

'I had bright blue gum in my mouth. I had a blue plaster on my finger, because I'd pulled off my acrylic the night before, having a tickling fight with my boyfriend. And no shoes ... it was just crazy!'

Laverne moved on to Adele's second album, *21*. 'By that point, you'd won two Grammys and achieved stratospheric record sales. It must have seemed exhilarating but a bit scary too?'

'It was really intense,' agreed her guest. 'At times it was really hard to enjoy, because I couldn't keep up with the pace. It got to the point where sometimes I didn't even know where I was and what day it was.'

Talking about the pressure of media scrutiny, Adele admitted to mixed feelings about the recent press and social media coverage of her weight loss.

'I *understand* why the press are fascinated by it,' she began, 'because I didn't share my journey like everyone does. Other people would have a DVD out by now, and I just did it on the quiet, for myself. But I felt terrible for some people that felt other people's comments meant *they* weren't looking good.'

Laverne: 'You felt that people congratulating you would be interpreted negatively by people who were bigger?'

'For some people, it was, and I felt terrible. They were, like, fifteen. There was some other people who felt very betrayed by me: "Oh, she's given in to the pressure of it!" But, like, *you* ain't holding my hand at night, at four am, when I'm crying my heart out with anxiety, needing a distraction!'

Adele had recently been caught up in a media storm after postponing a high-profile Las Vegas residency twenty-four hours before it was due to begin. 'How did you balance the fans' disappointment with your own creative decision that the concerts couldn't go ahead?' asked Laverne.

Adele sighed. 'I don't know. I definitely felt everyone's disappointment. I was devastated, and frightened about letting them down. I thought I could pull it together and make it work and I couldn't.

'And I stand by that decision. I don't think any other artists would have done what I did and that's why I think it was such a massive, massive story.

'I was, like, *I don't care. You can't buy me. You can't buy me for nothing.* I'm not going to do a show because I *have* to, or because people are going to be let down, or we're going to lose loads of money. I'm like: *The show's not good enough.*

'And it was horrible. The reaction was brutal – *brutal*. I was a shell of a person for a couple of months.'

Laverne: 'How did you get through it?'

'I just had to wait it out. I had to wait it out and just grieve it, I guess. Just grieve the shows and get over the guilt. Because it was brutal.'

The host moved on to happier conversational terrain. 'Adele, your son, Angelo, was born in 2012. Did being a mother affect you in ways you weren't expecting?'

'Every single way! Every single way. Good, bad, strange. I *love* being a mum. Like, Angelo has just fallen in love with music, and we sit down and have the most intense conversations ... it's heavenly.'

Adele was now divorced from Angelo's father, Simon, but the pair were still close and co-parenting. Laverne suggested that the break-up 'must have been a tough period for all of you?'

'It was, but it was never *really* tricky, because we're such good friends. And over my dead body is my kid having a messy divorce in his life! There are no issues, and there *were* no issues.'

Laverne: 'Looking beyond thirty to forty, maybe even fifty, how do you imagine life looking?'

'I definitely would like a couple more kids. It'd be wonderful if we can. But, if not, I've got Angelo. I just want to be happy.'

Asked how she felt she would fare, cast ashore on the desert island, the upbeat and ever-resilient Adele had a distinctly sunny prognosis: 'Listening to all these songs, I think I'd have a *right* laugh!'

'I'm glad to hear that!' chuckled Lauren Laverne. 'Adele, thank you very much for letting us hear your *Desert Island Discs*.'

'Oh, thank *you*!' said Adele Adkins. 'I've *always* wanted to do it! Thank you so much! I loved it ...'

• • •

From her alcoholic absent father to feeling guilt about her weight loss, Adele's visit to the desert island was unmissable for the same reason as her raw, powerhouse albums are so successful: because this most candid, confessional of artists and human beings never holds anything back. Her postponed Las Vegas concerts are now due at the end of 2022. There was no need for fans to worry. They were *always* going to happen.

DISCS CHOSEN

'Roam'
The B-52's
'Me and my mum used to sing it and dance around the living room in Tottenham ...'

❤ **'Dreams'**
Gabrielle
'It's the very, very first song I remember in my life ... I was mesmerised by her'

'You Might Need Somebody'
Shola Ama
'She has this insane vibrato in her voice, like a hummingbird'

'He Needs Me'
Nina Simone
'This song made me stop in my tracks ... I cried my eyes out'

'Bills, Bills, Bills'
Destiny's Child
'Beyoncé is the artist of my life'

'I'd Rather Go Blind'
Etta James

'Maps'
Yeah Yeah Yeahs
'She's a bloody superstar'

'For All We Know'
Donny Hathaway

BOOK
The Sun and Her Flowers – Rupi Kaur
'Every little poem is its own massive story that blows your mind and takes your brain to other places'

LUXURY ITEM
A self-inflatable mattress
'Because I love my sleep'

80

KATE MOSS

SUPERMODEL, BUSINESSWOMAN
24 July 2022

Supermodel Kate Moss has long been the enigma of British fashion. She lives her life by the famous aphorism of her former boyfriend, Johnny Depp: 'Never complain, never explain.' One of the most photographed female celebrities in the world is also one of the most rarely interviewed.

It was thus a major coup for *Desert Island Discs* when Moss agreed to set a pedicured foot on the island in July 2022. Millions of people had spent decades poring over photos of this megastar model, but it was very likely the first time that most of them had ever heard her speak.

It was worth the wait. When Moss sat down with Lauren Laverne, she was chatty and outgoing about everything from sexual exploitation in the fashion world to being made a scapegoat for heroin chic and drug abuse to why she had spoken up for Johnny Depp in his recent libel trial against Amber Heard. A rollicking forty minutes positively flew by.

You know what they say: *it's always the quiet ones.*

• • •

Welcoming her illustrious castaway to the island, Lauren Laverne began by asking what constituted a dream photo shoot for Kate Moss.

'The dream team, the dream hair and make-up, photographer, stylist, set design,' her guest replied. 'It's like a puzzle that gets put together with pieces of everybody, and that puzzle comes to life on set.

'When I step on set, I always feel like it's my first shoot. I always find myself on set, in front of the camera, thinking, *What am I going to do? I've forgotten! I really don't know what I'm doing!*

'As soon as the camera starts clicking, I find myself in character. Once the first picture's done, I feel I know who I am in that story, in that puzzle, because I'm actually really shy in front of the camera. I don't like having my picture taken when it's not at work.'

'Really?' asked a surprised-sounding Laverne.

'I don't like having selfies or snapshots. I find it difficult to be myself in front of the camera. It's much easier to be somebody else.'

Laverne: 'And you love music?'

'In my next life, I want to be in a band! I love singing. Chrissie Hynde is always, like, "Let's do a record together!" But I'm just too shy. I'm not confident enough to think of myself as a singer.'

After a Kanye West gospel choir version of Soul II Soul's 'Back to Life', which Moss had arranged to be specially mixed for *Desert Island Discs*, Laverne turned to her guest's childhood. 'Did you think you'd be in Croydon forever?'

'No. My dad worked for Pan American so we used to go to America every summer. We went to LA and drove from San Francisco. We went to Hawaii. We travelled a lot when I was a kid so I knew there was a big world out there.

'I remember coming home from a holiday once and it was raining and grey. We got in my dad's Beetle and it was cold. And I remember thinking, *I like American cars*. I liked the way they had those big seats at the front you can sit across. So, I already had the motivation to get out of Croydon.'

Laverne asked about her guest's mum, Linda, a homemaker who also worked as a barmaid. 'What are your memories of her?'

'She was always quite glamorous. She was fun.'

'What about when you grew up? You got interested in sneaking out to nightclubs as a teenager. Was she strict with you?'

'She *tried* to be! I used to go to a Wednesday-night student night down Cinderella Rockerfella's. She would say, "Be home by midnight!" One night I wasn't, and she came in her dressing gown and dragged me out. Shame! Traumatising!'

Despite this intervention, Moss continued, her mother and her travel agent father, Peter, were reasonably relaxed as parents. 'On my thirteenth birthday, I had a party. He was upstairs, doing the ironing, and it was *carnage* downstairs. And they just let me get on with it.'

Laverne: 'Did they trust you, then?'

'No. I don't think they trusted me, but they couldn't really control me. I did what I wanted. I was very headstrong.'

'Your parents split when you were thirteen. How did you deal with that?'

'I started smoking spliff and hanging out with boys a lot older than me, who kind of took me under their wing and protected me. They would take me to London on the train. I would get changed from my school uniform and go to [*Soho bar*] Fred's.

'I didn't even like the taste of alcohol! I would drink Long Island iced tea because it didn't taste of alcohol. But it's quite a strong drink ...'

Laverne: 'Do you think there was a sadness there?'

'Yeah, definitely.'

'About your parents?'

'Yeah, I was heartbroken.'

'Who were you living with?'

'I was living with my mum. My brother went to live with my dad. So that was difficult, as well. We would see each other at school but it was all a bit dark.'

After a break for Neil Young, Laverne switched the conversation to the pivotal moment in Kate Moss's young life. 'In 1988, when you were fourteen, you went on holiday to the Bahamas with your brother and your dad. On your way home, life completely changed for you. What happened?'

'I was sitting in economy and Simon, Sarah Doukas's [*Moss's agent*] brother, came up to me on the plane and said, "My sister owns a model agency. She'd like to meet you."

'I went to meet her in her seat. I recognised her from *The Clothes Show Live* so I knew she was a real model agent. And they gave me their card and said, "When you get home, come and see us."'

Laverne: 'What did you think? That something would come of it?'

'Ah, no! I would *never* have said to anybody, "I want to be a model." I thought that was just vain: somebody who says that thinks that they're beautiful! And I never did. I just thought, *Oh my God, I'm going to take a chance.*'

The model agency began sending the fourteen-year-old Moss on castings. 'Did anybody come with you?' wondered Laverne.

'My mum came with me one day, and then said, "You're on your own!" It was a hard slog. You were given an *A–Z* and a list of addresses, and there were eight a day, from nine to six.

'I was just in awe of everything in the office. It was so busy, and models everywhere, and beautiful people, and shouting – a lot of atmosphere! I was like, *Wow, this is so cool!* So, Mum said, "You're on your own!" and I was, like, "Fine! I'll do it on my own, then!"'

Laverne wondered if the young, unaccompanied Moss had found herself in 'difficult situations' at castings. 'What kind of things did you have to deal with?'

'I had a horrible experience for a bra catalogue. I was only fifteen and he said, "Take your top off." I took my top off, and I was really shy then about my body. He said, "Take your bra off!" I could feel there was something wrong, so I got my stuff and I ran away.'

Laverne: 'How did that experience affect you?'

'I think it sharpened my instincts. I can tell a wrong 'un a mile away.'

A pause for David Bowie's 'Life on Mars?' and then Laverne moved on to the 1990 commission that had put Moss firmly on the map at sixteen.

'The photographer, Corinne Day, shot you on the beach at Camber Sands for *The Face*. Those images defined the early part of the decade. What do you remember about the shoot?'

'That scrunched-up nose on the cover [of *The Face*] – she would say, "Snort like a pig!" to get that picture. I'd be, like, "I don't *want* to snort like a pig!" She would be: "Snort like a pig! *That's* when it looks good!"'

Laverne: 'She was happy to push your buttons?'

'I cried a lot.'

'Did you?'

'Yeah.'

'What did you cry about?'

'Being naked. I didn't want to take my top off, and she would say, "If you *don't* take your top off, I won't book you for *Elle.*" And I would cry.'

Laverne: 'I'm watching you talking about that, and it seems like in some ways it's difficult to take yourself back there?'

'Yeah, it *is* quite difficult. It's painful. She was my best friend and I really loved her but she was a very tricky person to work with. But, you know, the pictures are amazing. She got what she wanted, and I suffered for them but they did me a world of good, really. They changed my career.'

On the strength of those photos, recapped Laverne, US designer Calvin Klein was to book Moss for an underwear campaign, shot in New York with actor Mark Wahlberg. 'How do you remember that shoot?'

'Not very good memories.'

'Why not?'

'[*Wahlberg*] was very macho and it was all about him. He had a big entourage and I was just this, kind of, model.'

'You felt objectified?'

'Completely. And vulnerable, and scared. I think they played on my vulnerability. I was quite young and innocent, so Calvin loved that.

'Luckily, I was living with Mario's [*photographer and former boyfriend Mario Sorrenti*] mum, Francesca, and she insisted that she come with me, because I didn't feel well at all before the shoot. For a week or two, I couldn't get out of bed, and I had severe anxiety. The doctor gave me Valium.

'And she said, "You're not having those pills!" If I felt nauseous, she would give me a quarter of a Valium or half a Valium. But she never gave me the actual bottle. Then, after the shoot, it was fine.'

By this point, said Laverne, Moss was a huge success, and with this success came controversy. In 1993, Corinne Day took more photos of her, this time in the model's own flat, in her underwear.

'Some of these photos are now in the V&A archive. But at the time, some commentators accused you of glorifying thinness and drug use. The style was dubbed "heroin chic". What were your thoughts about what they were saying about you?'

'I think I was a scapegoat for a lot of people's problems,' ventured Moss. 'I was never anorexic. I never have been. I had never taken heroin. I was thin because I didn't get fed at fashion shoots or in shows, and I'd *always* been thin. And ... it was a fashion shoot!

'It was shot at my flat, and that's how I could afford to live at the time. I think it was a shock because I wasn't voluptuous; I was just a normal girl. I wasn't a glamazon model.'

Laverne reminded Moss of the most famous saying attributed to her: 'Nothing tastes as good as skinny feels.' The laughing model revealed that she had never actually coined the phrase: it had been written and stuck to her home fridge by a flatmate who was trying to diet.

'I was doing an interview and [*I said it because*] it was funny. But they were, like, *soundbite!* And that was that!'

After a break for the Rolling Stones' 'Sympathy for the Devil', Laverne turned to Moss's hedonistic reputation. 'You've always been an incredibly hard worker, hugely successful, but you've *played* hard, too. Where does that fun-loving streak in you come from?'

'Well, my mum used to say, "You can't have fun all the time!" And I used to say, "Why not? *Why* can't I?" I wanted to go to work and do my job, and I wanted to have fun as well.'

Laverne: 'In 2005, a newspaper published photographs that appeared to show you taking cocaine. How did you react when you saw those photos?'

'I felt sick,' admitted Moss. 'And was quite angry, because everybody that I knew took drugs. So for them to focus on me, and to try to take my daughter away, I thought was really hypocritical.'

Laverne: 'No charges were brought. You issued a statement apologising to the people you'd let down by your behaviour. Why did you want to make that statement?'

'I mean, I kind of ... *had* to apologise, really. If people were looking up to me ... I had to apologise.'

Laverne commented that Moss's friends in fashion had supported her through the scandal and she had reciprocated in kind. She had backed John Galliano after the designer was found guilty of racist abuse in Paris in 2011.

Moss had also, mere weeks ago, testified on behalf of Johnny Depp in his US libel trial against Amber Heard, refuting the claim that her former boyfriend had once pushed her downstairs. 'Those gestures could have backfired on you,' noted Laverne. 'What made you come out on their behalf?'

The answer was simple. 'I believe in the truth, and I believe in fairness and justice. I know that John Galliano is not a bad person. He had an alcohol problem and people aren't themselves when they drink. They say things that they would *never* say if they were sober.

'And I know the truth about Johnny. I know he never kicked me down the stairs. I had to say that truth.'

Having learned many dos and don'ts over her thirty-year fashion career, Moss had in 2016 set up her own talent agency. Her nineteen-year-old daughter, Lila, was on its books. 'What advice have you given her about the industry?' asked Laverne.

'I've said to her, "You don't have to do anything you don't want to do. If you don't want to do the shoot, if you don't feel comfortable, if you don't want to model – don't do it."

'I take care of my models. I make sure they are with agents at shoots so, when they are being taken advantage of, there's somebody there to say: "I don't think that's appropriate."'

Having been a fixture on London's fashion, music and social scenes for three decades, Moss had, earlier in 2022, sold her home in the capital and uprooted to the Cotswolds. 'How much has life changed for you since you moved?' asked Laverne.

'Oh my God, I'm obsessed with gardening! I have got a membership to the garden centre. I go with my mum and we have the best time!'

'And what about your wild times and your partying days?' wondered Lauren Laverne. 'Have you put those behind you?'

'Yeah,' confirmed Kate Moss. 'It's boring to me now. I mean, I love a dance, but I'm definitely not into being out of control any more. I like to get to bed. I like to get up early and do my meditation, before anyone's up. I like to be in control ...'

• • •

The moral of the tale? For somebody so reluctant to give interviews, Kate Moss really is very good at them. Maybe she was just waiting for a suitable platform. And that is the eternal appeal of *Desert Island Discs* – this iconic, timeless, unique radio entity, perennially able to welcome the great and the good to its sandy shores to rifle through their record collections and open their hearts. This beloved British broadcasting institution remains always familiar, yet always surprising ... And the best thing of all? More than eighty years since a young Roy Plomley had that idea that was so simple that it bordered on genius, *Desert Island Discs* still sounds like it's just getting going. It probably is.

DISCS CHOSEN
'Back to Life'
Soul II Soul (Kanye West's Sunday Service Choir remix)
'We would blast it down Croydon High Street and think we were the coolest people ...'

'A Whiter Shade of Pale'
King Curtis
'My mum and dad walked down the aisle to this on the organ'

'Harvest Moon'
Neil Young
'I used to think, Oh God, this whiny old man! *Then I was with Johnny Depp, I met Neil Young and I fell in love with this music'*

'Life on Mars?'
David Bowie
'I would dance around and think, in my fantasy, the song was about me'

'Oh! Sweet Nuthin''
The Velvet Underground
'I played it every day during the pandemic. It uplifted me'

'Sympathy for the Devil'
Rolling Stones
'My thread with the Rolling Stones is quite multilayered'

❤ **'My Sweet Lord'**
George Harrison
'It was released the week he died and I couldn't stop crying. I thought, What's wrong with me? *Then I found out I was pregnant with Lila ...'*

'Madame George'
Van Morrison
'It reminds me of every happy moment – holidays, summer days, driving my car through country lanes and the sun shining'

BOOK

The Little Prince – Antoine de Saint-Exupéry
'I read it to my god-daughter and to my daughter and I just think it's the most beautiful book'

LUXURY ITEM

A cashmere blanket in duck egg blue or pink

ACKNOWLEDGEMENTS

I would like to thank all of the castaways who gave permission for their visits to the island to be reproduced in this book, particularly those who kindly granted me a follow-up interview: Dame Judi Dench, Dame Joan Collins, Dame Joanna Lumley, Marianne Faithfull, Kathleen Turner, Paul Abbott, Dame Eliza Manningham-Buller, Ahdaf Soueif, Lemn Sissay, Levi Roots, Davina McCall, Caitlin Moran, Dr Sabrina Cohen-Hatton, Russell T Davies, Professor Dame Elizabeth Anionwu, Sharon Horgan and Sir Cliff Richard. Thank you to my editors, Yvonne Jacob and Nell Warner, for their skilled and sensitive management of author tantrums, and for being sympathetic and flexible on deadlines when a serious close-family illness unexpectedly disrupted my writing schedule. At *Desert Island Discs* HQ, many thanks to John Goudie for feeding through to me yellowing transcripts of Roy Plomley interviews when no audio existed, and to Ruth Gardiner for keeping an eye on the text. Finally, I'd like to thank my wife, Helen, a *Desert Island Discs* devotee, for pointing me towards less-well-known but classic castaways, and my son, Spike, for occasionally allowing me to use my laptop to write this book when he didn't require it for printing out pictures of dinosaurs.

Ian Gittins